Signature Edition

Answer Key
Grade 3

Siegfried Engelmann
Susan Hanner

Columbus, Ohio

SRAonline.com

Printed in the United States of America.

Send all inquiries to this address:
SRA/McGraw-Hill
4400 Easton Commons
Columbus, OH 43219

ISBN: 978-0-07-612587-6
MHID: 0-07-612587-4

3 4 5 6 7 8 9 10 MAZ 13 12 11 10 09 08

The McGraw·Hill Companies

WORKBOOK

1

Name ____________________

A

1. What's the name of geese that are all white? snow geese
2. What's the name of geese that are gray and black and white? Canada geese
3. Both geese and ducks are water birds, but geese are a lot bigger.
4. You can tell male geese from female geese because ▬.
   - male geese have brighter colors
   - male geese are larger
   - male geese have longer feathers
5. What color are all geese when they are born? yellow
6. How old are geese when they mate for the first time? 3 (years old)
7. After male and female geese mate, they stay together ▬.
   - for the summer
   - for a full year
   - until one goose dies

B Story Items

8. Most geese live for about 30 years.
9. How old was Old Henry? 35 (years old)
10. What was the name of the lake the flock stayed at during the summer? Big Trout Lake
11. In which season did the flock leave the lake? fall
12. In which direction did the flock fly? south
13. How far was the flock going? two thousand miles

WORKBOOK

14. Who didn't want to make the trip? (Old) Henry
15. He said that he was too Ideas: old, tired to fly so far.
16. What will happen to Big Trout Lake during the winter? Idea: It will freeze.

WORKBOOK

2

Name ____________________

A

1. Make an **R** on Big Trout Lake.
2. What country is the **R** in? Canada
3. Make an **F** on Crooked Lake.
4. Which lake is farther north? Big Trout Lake
5. Make a **Y** next to the lake that freezes in the winter.

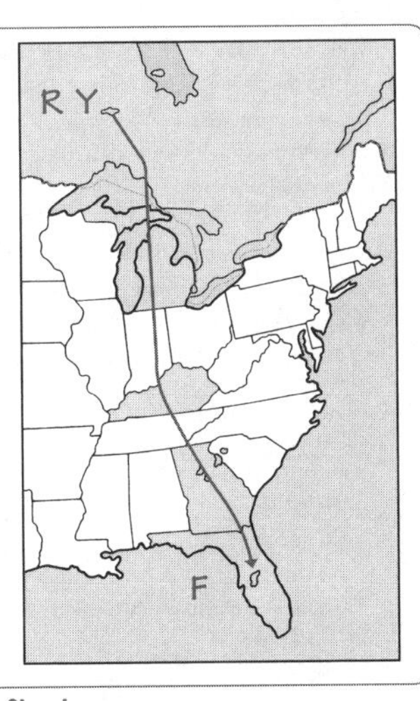

6. Geese live in large groups called flocks
7. In what country are most wild geese born? Canada
8. Where do these geese spend every summer? Canada
9. In which direction do the geese fly in the fall? south
10. What is this trip called?
    - mating
    - migration
    - hibernation

WORKBOOK

11. Why do the geese leave Canada in the fall?
    - There is no snow.
    - The lakes freeze.
    - The flock needs to fly.
12. Every fall, Old Henry's flock went to the state of Florida.

B Story Items

13. Henry first mated with his wife when they were both three (3) years old.
14. Henry's wife had died five (5) years ago.
15. How had Henry felt ever since she had died?
    - free
    - tired
    - lonely
16. After the flock had been gone for nine (9) days, Henry saw another goose.
17. Was that goose **old** or **young?** young
18. The goose told Henry, "I couldn't learn to fly because ▬."
    - my leg was hurt
    - my wing was hurt
    - I was too small
19. When geese learn to fly, do they start **in the water** or **on the land?** on the land
20. They run with their wings out to the side.

GO TO PART D IN YOUR TEXTBOOK.

TEXTBOOK

supposed to be on your way to Florida."

The young goose said, "Oh, I couldn't learn to fly because my leg was hurt."

Old Henry knew about that problem. When young geese learn to fly, they start out by running faster and faster. They hold their wings out to the side as they run. Then they flap their wings and fly. But if they can't run fast, they can't fly. Later, geese learn to take off from the water, but that's not the first thing they learn about flying.

"Well," Henry said. "If you don't have anything better to do, swim out here and join me. I would be glad to have your company."

D Number your paper from 1 through 11.

Review Items

1. What's the name of geese that are gray and black and white?
2. What's the name of geese that are all white? snow geese
3. What color are all geese when they are born? yellow
4. You can tell male geese from female geese because ___.
   - male geese have brighter colors
   - male geese have longer feathers
   - male geese are larger
5. How old are geese when they mate for the first time? 3 (years old)
6. After male and female geese mate, they stay together ___.
   - for the summer
   - for a full year
   - until one goose dies
7. Most geese live for about ___ years. 30
8. What was the name of the lake where Henry's flock stayed during the summer? Big Trout Lake
9. In which season did the flock leave the lake? fall
10. In which direction did the flock fly? south
11. How far was the flock going? 2 thousand miles

1. Canada geese

WORKBOOK

3

Name ____________________

A

1. Write the directions **north, south, east** and **west** in the boxes on map 1.
2. In which direction do geese migrate in the fall? south
3. In which direction do geese migrate in the spring? north
4. Make a line that starts at the circle on the map and goes north.
5. If you start at the circle and move to the number **4,** in which direction do you go? south

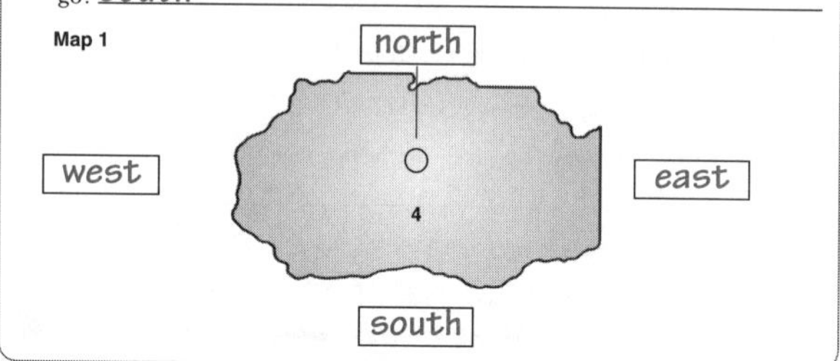

Look at map 2 on the next page.

6. What country is the **A** in? Canada
7. What country is the **B** in? United States
8. What **state** is the **B** in? Florida
9. If you started at the **B** and went to the **A,** in which direction would you go? north

WORKBOOK

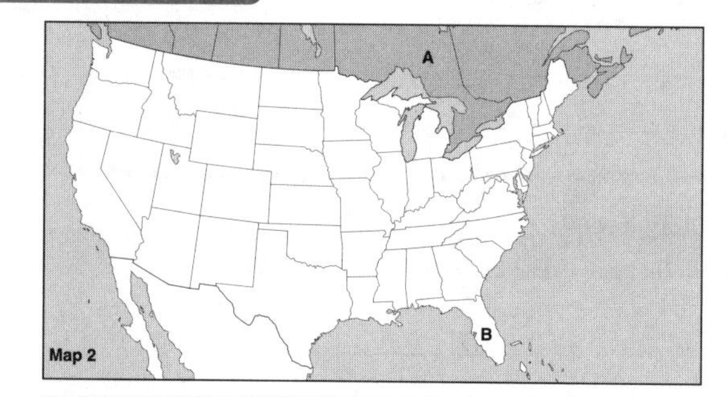

B Story Items

10. What was the name of the young goose? Tim
11. When was that goose born? Ideas: In June; several months earlier
12. How old was he?
    - more than a year
    - less than half a year
    - more than half a year
13. When young geese learn to fly, they hold their wings out as they ___.
    - walk
    - run
    - swim
14. Tim couldn't learn to fly because he couldn't run
15. Was his leg still hurt? no
16. **Underline** the 2 things that Henry said he would do for Tim.
    - show him how to stay warm
    - fly with him to Florida
    - teach him how to fly
    - build a warm house for him
    - tell him how to get to Florida

GO TO PART D IN YOUR TEXTBOOK.

TEXTBOOK

D Number your paper from I through 13.

Review Items

1. What's the name of geese that are all white? snow geese
2. What's the name of geese that are gray and black and white?
3. What color are all geese when they are born? yellow
4. How old are geese when they mate for the first time?
5. After male and female geese mate, how long do they stay together? Idea: until one goose dies
6. Most geese live for about ___ years. 30
7. Geese live in large groups called ___. flocks
8. Where are most wild geese born? Canada
9. In which direction do geese fly in the fall? south
10. What is this trip called?
    - migration
    - mating
    - hibernation
11. How had Henry felt ever since his wife had died? lonely
12. When geese learn to fly, do they start in the water or on the land? on the land
13. They run with their ___ out to the side. wings

2. Canada geese
4. 3 (years old)

WORKBOOK

4

Name ______________________

A

Look at the map below.

1. What's the name of the place shown by the letter **A?** equator
2. Which letter shows the coldest place? M
3. Which letter shows the hottest place? A
4. Which letter is farthest from the equator? M

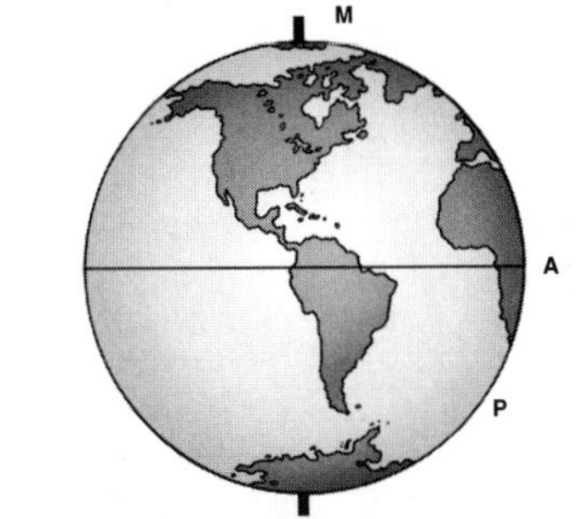

5. The earth is shaped like a ball.
6. The hottest part of the earth is called the ▬.
   - pole
   - desert
   - equator
7. What's the name of the line that goes around the fattest part of the earth?
   equator
8. What's the name of the spot that's at the top of the earth?
   North Pole

WORKBOOK

9. What's the name of the spot that's at the bottom of the earth?
   South Pole
10. The pole s are the coldest places on the earth and the equator is the hottest place on the earth.
11. How many poles are there? 2
12. Are the equator and the poles **real marks** on the earth or **pretend marks?**
    pretend marks
13. The farther you go from the equator, the ▬ it gets.
    - colder
    - fatter
    - hotter

B Story Items

14. Henry taught Tim to fly. Tim was supposed to run down the hill and hold his wings out to the side.
15. What was Tim supposed to do when Henry honked?
    Idea: start flapping his wings
16. Did Tim take off the first time he tried? yes
17. Did he keep on flying? no
18. Why? Ideas: He got scared; he stopped flapping.
19. Did Tim do better the second time he tried? yes
20. How high did the geese fly? Idea: More than a mile high
21. Where did they land? Ideas: In the water; on Big Trout Lake
22. Who was going too fast when they landed? Tim

GO TO PART D IN YOUR TEXTBOOK.

TEXTBOOK

also made a landing, but it was not perfect. He was going too fast, and he landed with a great splash. Both geese laughed. Tim shouted, "I can fly."

"You sure can," Henry said.

D Number your paper from 1 through 11.

Review Items

1. You can tell male geese from female geese because ▬.
   - male geese are larger
   - male geese have brighter colors
   - male geese have longer feathers
2. What was the name of the lake where Henry's flock stayed during the summer? Big Trout Lake
3. In which season did the flock leave the lake? fall
4. In which direction did the flock fly? south
5. How far was the flock going? 2 thousand miles
6. Geese live in large groups called ▬. flocks
7. Where are most wild geese born? Canada

Look at the map.

8. What country is the red dot in?
9. What country is the blue dot in?
10. What **state** is the blue dot in?
11. If you started at the red dot and went to the blue dot, in which direction would you go?

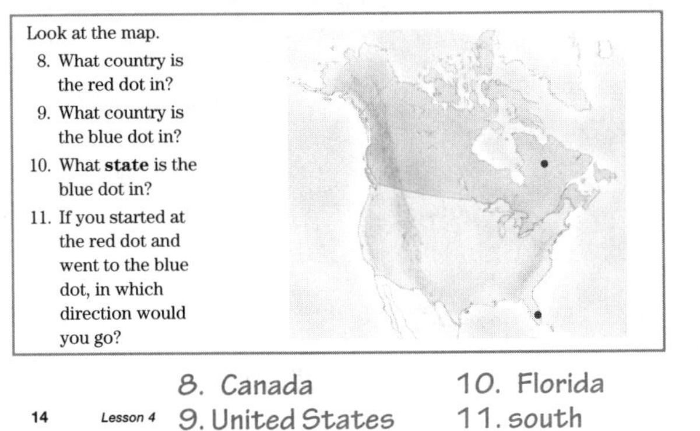

8. Canada
9. United States
10. Florida
11. south

WORKBOOK

5

Name ______________________

A

Choose from these words to answer each item:

- moon
- Florida
- equator
- geese
- pole
- Canada
- migration
- sun

1. The heat that the earth receives comes from the sun.
2. The part of the earth that receives more heat than any other part is the
   equator
3. The parts of the earth that receive less heat than any other part are called the
   poles

B Story Items

4. How many days did Tim practice flying? three (3)
5. When Tim flew in the direction that felt best, in which direction did he fly?
   south
6. How much of the lake was frozen by the end of the third day that Tim practiced?
   - almost all
   - half
   - all
7. How much of the lake did Henry think would be frozen by the next morning? all
8. Was Tim able to understand what Henry explained about the landing places? no
9. How many landing places are there on the trip to Florida? five (5)
10. The first landing place is a field next to a pond.
11. That landing place has two (2) barns on it.

WORKBOOK

Skill Items

The horses became restless on the dangerous route.

12. What word tells about how you get to a place? route
13. What word tells how you feel when you want to do something different? restless

Review Items

14. In which direction do geese fly in the fall? south
15. What is this trip called? migration
16. In which direction do geese fly in the spring? north

17. Write the directions **north, south, east** and **west** in the boxes.
18. Make a line that starts at the circle on the map and goes east.
19. If you start at the circle and move to the number **3,** in which direction do you go? west

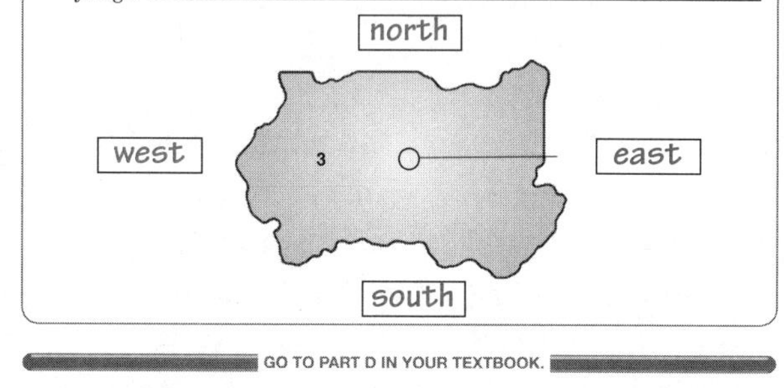

GO TO PART D IN YOUR TEXTBOOK.

TEXTBOOK

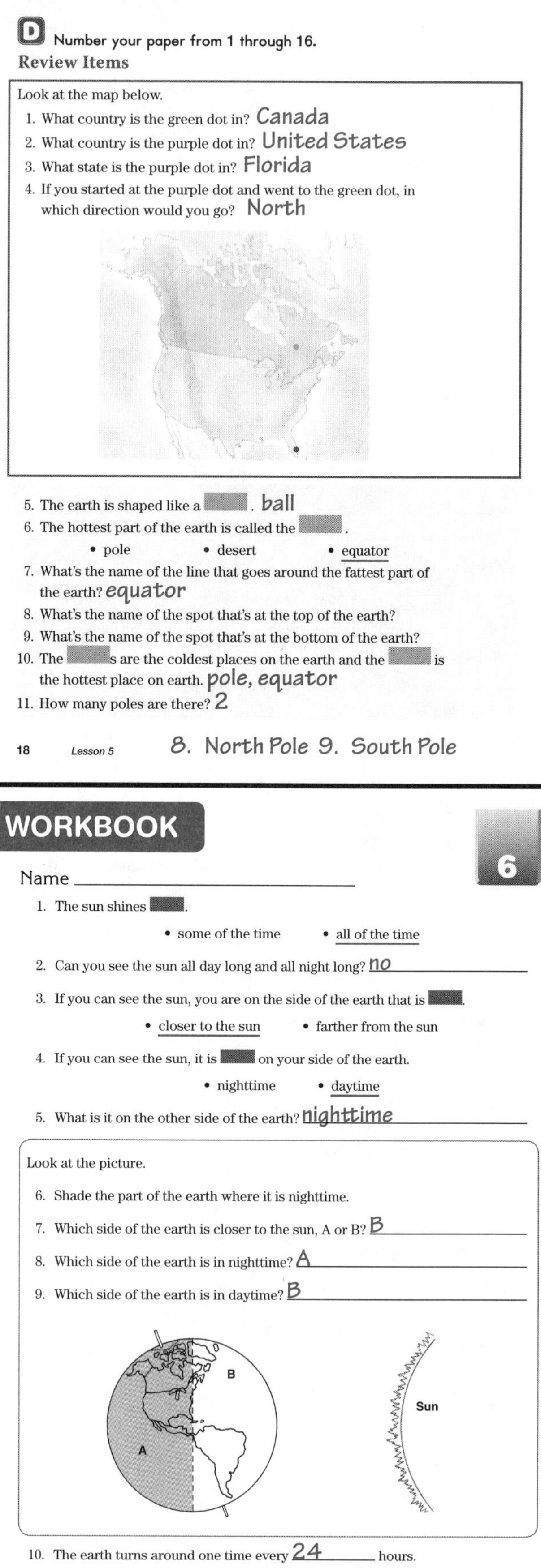

D Number your paper from 1 through 16.

Review Items

Look at the map below.

1. What country is the green dot in? Canada
2. What country is the purple dot in? United States
3. What state is the purple dot in? Florida
4. If you started at the purple dot and went to the green dot, in which direction would you go? North

5. The earth is shaped like a ▬. ball
6. The hottest part of the earth is called the ▬.
   - pole
   - desert
   - equator
7. What's the name of the line that goes around the fattest part of the earth? equator
8. What's the name of the spot that's at the top of the earth?
9. What's the name of the spot that's at the bottom of the earth?
10. The ▬s are the coldest places on the earth and the ▬ is the hottest place on earth. pole, equator
11. How many poles are there? 2

 8. North Pole 9. South Pole

TEXTBOOK

12. The farther you go from the equator, the ▬ it gets.
    - hotter
    - fatter
    - colder

Look at the map below.

13. What's the name of the place shown by the letter **C**? North Pole
14. Which letter shows the coldest place? C
15. Which letter shows the hottest place? F
16. Which letter is farthest from the equator? C

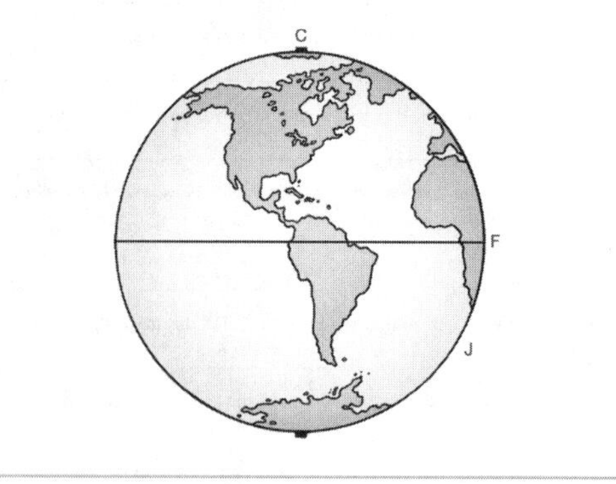

WORKBOOK

6

Name ____________________

1. The sun shines ▬.
   - some of the time
   - all of the time
2. Can you see the sun all day long and all night long? no
3. If you can see the sun, you are on the side of the earth that is ▬.
   - closer to the sun
   - farther from the sun
4. If you can see the sun, it is ▬ on your side of the earth.
   - nighttime
   - daytime
5. What is it on the other side of the earth? nighttime

Look at the picture.

6. Shade the part of the earth where it is nighttime.
7. Which side of the earth is closer to the sun, A or B? B
8. Which side of the earth is in nighttime? A
9. Which side of the earth is in daytime? B

10. The earth turns around one time every 24 hours.

WORKBOOK

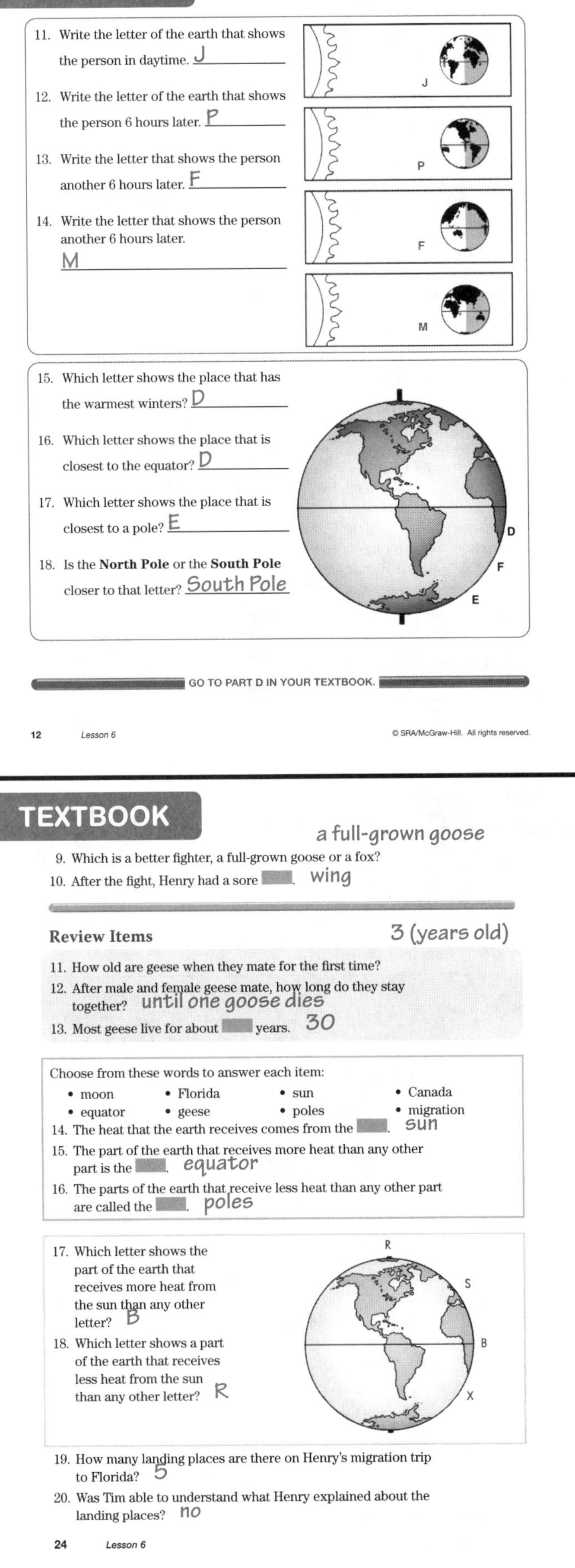

11. Write the letter of the earth that shows the person in daytime. J
12. Write the letter of the earth that shows the person 6 hours later. P
13. Write the letter that shows the person another 6 hours later. F
14. Write the letter that shows the person another 6 hours later. M

15. Which letter shows the place that has the warmest winters? D
16. Which letter shows the place that is closest to the equator? D
17. Which letter shows the place that is closest to a pole? E
18. Is the **North Pole** or the **South Pole** closer to that letter? South Pole

GO TO PART D IN YOUR TEXTBOOK.

TEXTBOOK

D Number your paper from 1 through 20.

Story Items

1. Where did Henry and Tim spend their last night at Big Trout Lake?
   - on the water
   - in a barn
   - <u>in the woods</u>
2. In the morning, Henry told Tim that he would ▬.
   - tell Tim more about the trip
   - <u>fly part of the way with him</u>
3. Henry told Tim, "Don't land where you see ▬ geese."
   - many
   - <u>a few</u>
   - no
4. Write the letters of the **2** kinds of places that are safe for geese.
   a. <u>places with many geese</u>
   b. <u>places with no geese or ducks</u>
   c. places with a few geese
   d. places with a few ducks
5. When the two geese flew over the landing place, did Tim recognize it? no
6. After they landed, which goose was attacked? Tim
7. What attacked that goose? a fox
8. What did Henry do? Ideas: bit the fox on the neck and ears; attacked the fox

TEXTBOOK

9. Which is a better fighter, a full-grown goose or a fox? a full-grown goose
10. After the fight, Henry had a sore ▬. wing

Review Items

11. How old are geese when they mate for the first time? 3 (years old)
12. After male and female geese mate, how long do they stay together? until one goose dies
13. Most geese live for about ▬ years. 30

Choose from these words to answer each item:

- moon
- Florida
- sun
- Canada
- equator
- geese
- poles
- migration

14. The heat that the earth receives comes from the ▬. sun
15. The part of the earth that receives more heat than any other part is the ▬. equator
16. The parts of the earth that receive less heat than any other part are called the ▬. poles
17. Which letter shows the part of the earth that receives more heat from the sun than any other letter? B
18. Which letter shows a part of the earth that receives less heat from the sun than any other letter? R

R
S
B
X

19. How many landing places are there on Henry's migration trip to Florida? 5
20. Was Tim able to understand what Henry explained about the landing places? no

WORKBOOK

7

Name ____________________

A

1. Which letter on the map shows Big Trout Lake? C
2. Which letter shows the landing place in Kentucky? A
3. Which letter shows the landing place in Michigan? B
4. Which letter shows the landing place in Florida? D
5. Which letter shows the landing place in Canada? E

C
E
B
A
D

6. Which letter shows Crooked Lake? D
7. Which letter shows the first landing place? E
8. Which letter shows the second landing place? B
9. Draw the path the geese take on their migration south.

B Story Items

10. Did Henry tell Tim about his sore wing? no
11. He got a sore wing when he fought with the/a fox
12. Henry told Tim about the next landing place. He also made a ▬.
    - mess
    - <u>map</u>
    - story
13. Did Tim recognize the next landing spot? no
14. So what did Henry do?
    - <u>led Tim to the landing place</u>
    - told Tim how to get to the landing place

WORKBOOK

15. **Circle** the picture that shows the correct landing spot.

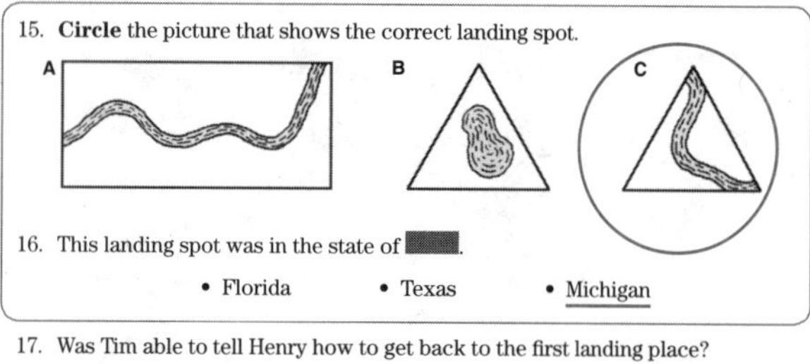

16. This landing spot was in the state of ▬▬.
   - Florida
   - Texas
   - Michigan

17. Was Tim able to tell Henry how to get back to the first landing place?
yes

18. What did the two geese see on the second day they were at the triangle-shaped field?
Idea: another flock of geese

19. Was that flock going to **Florida** or **Mexico**? Mexico

20. When Tim and Henry left Big Trout Lake, Henry had planned to take Tim to the first 3 landing places.

21. Now Henry realized that somebody would have to fly farther with Tim. How far? Idea: all the way to Florida

22. Was Henry sure that he would be able to fly that far with Tim?
no

GO TO PART D IN YOUR TEXTBOOK.

TEXTBOOK

went to that place. So somebody would have to lead him all the way to Florida. Henry's problem was that his wing felt worse than ever. Henry didn't know how much more of the trip he would be able to make.

Tim and Henry rested a second day. That day was the first time they saw another flock of geese. The flock formed a great V in the sky. Both Henry and Tim had eyes far sharper than human eyes. So they were able to see all the geese in that flock. Henry said, "There must be more than 60 geese in that flock."

"Are they going to the same place we're going?" Tim asked.

"No," Henry said. "They are heading a little bit to the west, so they are probably going to Mexico."

Tim asked, "Have you ever been to Mexico?"

Henry said, "No. The only place I've ever gone in the winter is to Crooked Lake in Florida. And that's what you'll do. Every year, you'll fly to Crooked Lake. Then in the spring you'll go back to Canada."

D Number your paper from 1 through 13.

Review Items

3. nighttime

1. The sun shines ▬▬.
   - all of the time
   - some of the time
2. Can you see the sun all day long and all night long? No
3. If you cannot see the sun, it is ▬▬ on your side of the earth.
4. What is it on the other side of the earth? daytime
5. The earth turns around one time every ▬▬ hours. 24

Look at the picture.

6. Which side of the earth is closer to the sun, A or B? A
7. Which side of the earth is in nighttime? B
8. Which side of the earth is in daytime? A

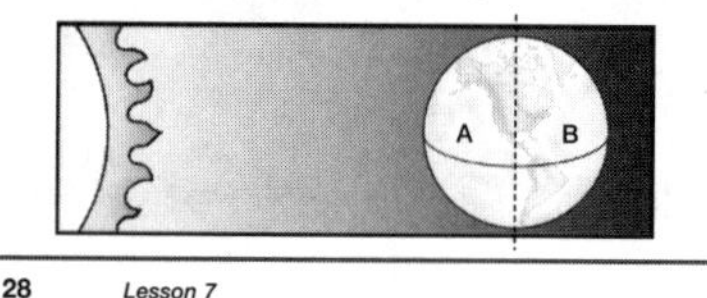

TEXTBOOK

9. Which letter shows the place that has the warmest winters? T
10. Which letter shows the place that is closest to the equator? T
11. Which letter shows the place that is closest to a pole? N
12. Is the **North Pole** or the **South Pole** closer to that letter?
South Pole

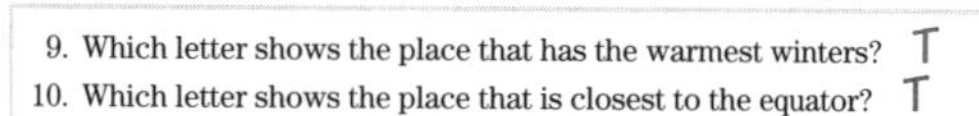

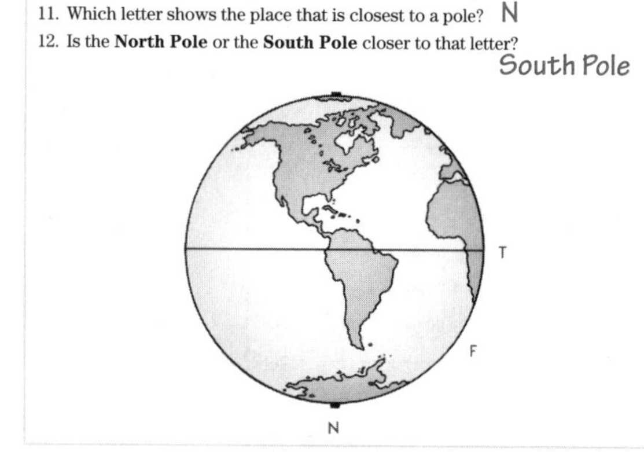

13. Write the letters of the **2** kinds of places that are safe for geese. a, c
   a. places with many geese
   b. places with a few geese
   c. places with no geese or ducks
   d. places with a few ducks

WORKBOOK

8

Name ____________________

A Story Items

1. How many Great Lakes are there? 5 (five)

2. Color the Great Lakes on the map.

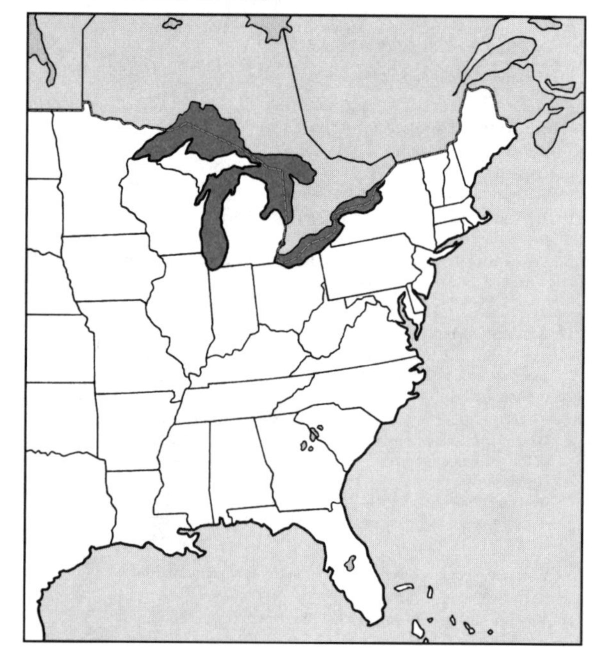

WORKBOOK

B **Review Items**

3. Which letter on the map below shows the landing place in Kentucky? M
4. Which letter shows Big Trout Lake? L
5. Which letter shows the landing place in Michigan? Z
6. Which letter shows the landing place in Canada? X
7. Which letter shows the landing place in Florida? K
8. Which letter shows Crooked Lake? K
9. Which letter shows the first landing place? X
10. Draw the path that the geese in Henry's flock take on their migration south.

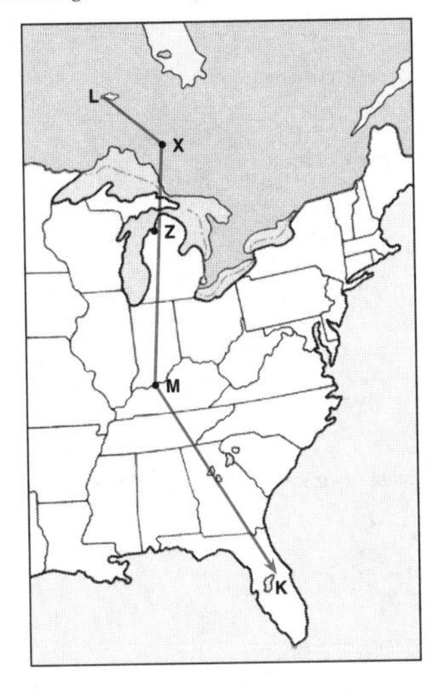

GO TO PART D IN YOUR TEXTBOOK.

TEXTBOOK

D Number your paper from 1 through 28.

1. How many heat lines are hitting place A on the map? 10
2. How many heat lines are hitting place B? 8
3. How many heat lines are hitting place C? 4
4. Write the letter of the place that's the hottest. A
5. Write the letter of the place that's the coldest. C
6. Write the letter of the place that has the warmest winters. A
7. Write the letter of the place that's the farthest from the equator. C
8. You know that place A is hotter than place C because place A ▬.

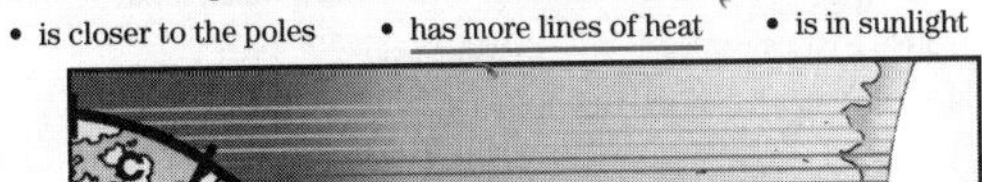

- is closer to the poles
- has more lines of heat
- is in sunlight

Story Items

9. About how far was it from the landing place in Michigan to the one in Kentucky? a little more than 300 miles
10. How did Henry feel by the end of that trip?
11. Which goose wanted to land at the regular landing place in Kentucky? Henry
12. What kept them from landing there?
    - The lake was frozen.
    - Hunters were at that landing place.
    - Too many geese were at that landing place.
13. Henry and Tim landed at a place that was about ▬ miles away. 5

10. Ideas: His wing was very sore; tired

TEXTBOOK

14. Did Henry plan to stay at this landing place **one day** or **two days**? two days
15. Another ▬ landed at the landing place the next day. flock
16. How many geese were in that flock?
17. Where was that flock going? Florida; Reedy Lake
18. That flock spent summers on one of the ▬ ▬.
19. Henry asked if ▬ could fly with that flock. Tim
20. Did the leader of that flock think this plan was okay? yes

Review Items

21. In which direction do geese fly in the fall? south
22. What is this trip called? migration

23. At which letter would the winters be very, very cold? A
24. At which letter would the winters be very, very hot? P

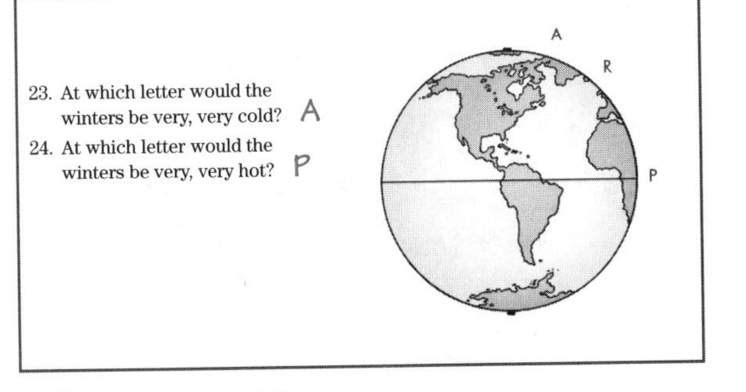

16. more than eighty geese
18. big lakes

TEXTBOOK

25. Write the letter of the earth that shows the person in daytime. A
26. Write the letter of the earth that shows the person 6 hours later. B
27. Write the letter that shows the person another 6 hours later. C
28. Write the letter that shows the person another 6 hours later. D

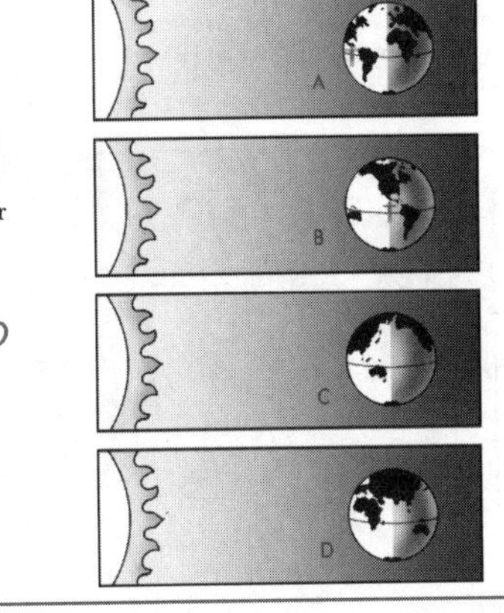

WORKBOOK

Name ____________

A

1. The earth makes a circle around the sun one time every ▬.
   - hour
   - day
   - year
2. How many days does it take the earth to make one full circle around the sun? 365
3. **Fill in the blanks to show the four seasons.** winter, spring, summer, fall, winter, spring, summer, fall
4. Write the missing seasons on the picture below.
5. Shade half of earth A and half of earth C.

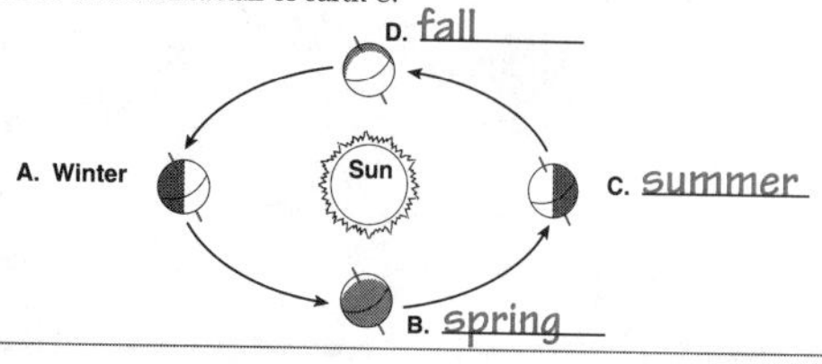

A. Winter
B. spring
C. summer
D. fall
Sun

B Story Items

6. When Tim and Henry were in Kentucky, did Henry want to fly farther south? no
7. Tim said he'd fly with the flock if Henry would fly with them.
8. Was it **easier** or **harder** to fly with a large flock? easier
9. Were Tim and Henry **near** or **far** from the point of the V? far
10. Flying near the back of a large flock is like riding your bike ▬.
    - with the wind
    - against the wind

WORKBOOK

11. Look at the picture. Write **H** on the goose that has to work the hardest. H
12. Color the air that is moving in the same direction the flock is moving.

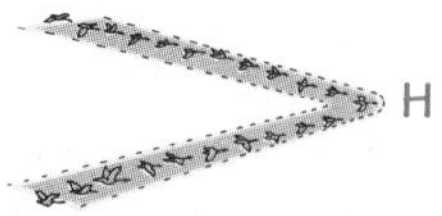

Review Items

Look at the picture.

13. Shade the part of the earth where it is nighttime.
14. Which side of the earth is closer to the sun, A or B? B
15. Which side of the earth is in nighttime? A
16. Which side of the earth is in daytime? B

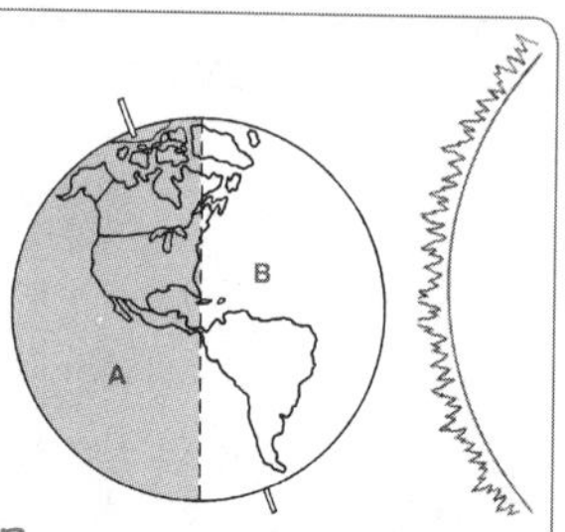

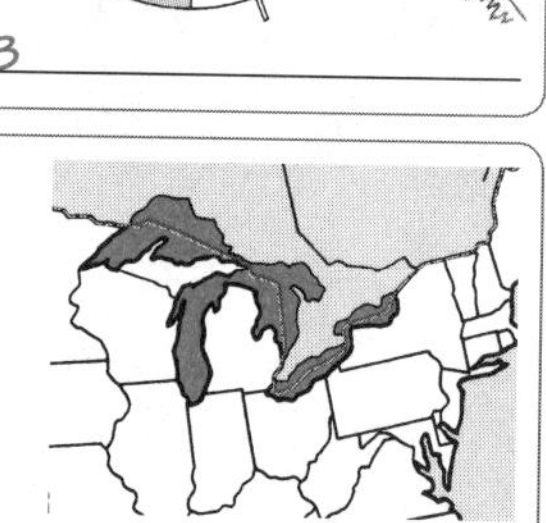

17. How many Great Lakes are there? five (5)
18. Color the Great Lakes on the map.

GO TO PART D IN YOUR TEXTBOOK.

TEXTBOOK

Henry said, "I don't know. This is not on the route I've taken. We always land at Clarks Hill Lake. It's much bigger than this lake and it's farther east."

Then Henry asked the old goose behind him, "What's the name of that lake?"

"Jackson Lake."

About ten minutes later the flock landed on Jackson Lake.

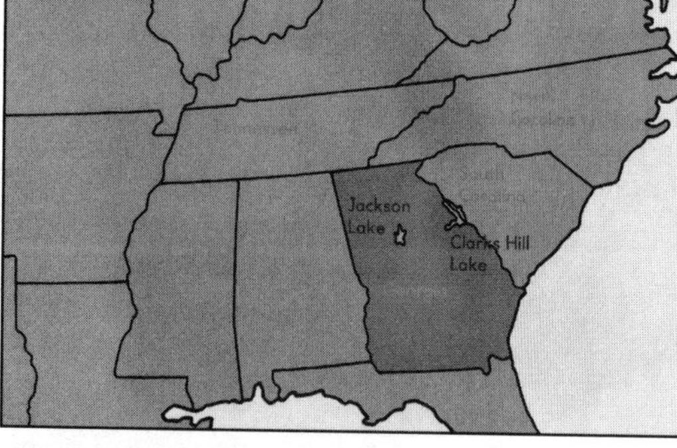

D Number your paper from 1 through 19.

Story Items

1. Henry noticed that his wing felt ▬ because it didn't have to work very ▬. better, hard
2. What's the name of the lake where the flock landed? Jackson Lake
3. In what state is that lake? Georgia
4. Had Henry landed there before? No
5. At what lake did Henry's flock usually land? Clarks Hill Lake
6. Which lake is farther east? Clarks Hill Lake
7. Do you think Henry will be able to continue flying south with the flock? yes

TEXTBOOK

Review Items

8. What's the name of the line that goes around the fattest part of the earth? equator
9. What's the name of the spot that's at the top of the earth?
10. What's the name of the spot that's at the bottom of the earth?
11. Write the letters of the 2 kinds of places that are safe for geese. a, c
    a. places with many geese
    b. places with a few geese
    c. places with no geese or ducks
    d. places with a few ducks

12. How many heat lines are hitting place A on the map? 10
13. How many heat lines are hitting place B? 8
14. How many heat lines are hitting place C? 4
15. Write the letter of the place that's the hottest. A
16. Write the letter of the place that's the coldest. C
17. Write the letter of the place that has the warmest winters. A
18. Write the letter of the place that's farthest from the equator. C
19. Why is place A hotter than place C?

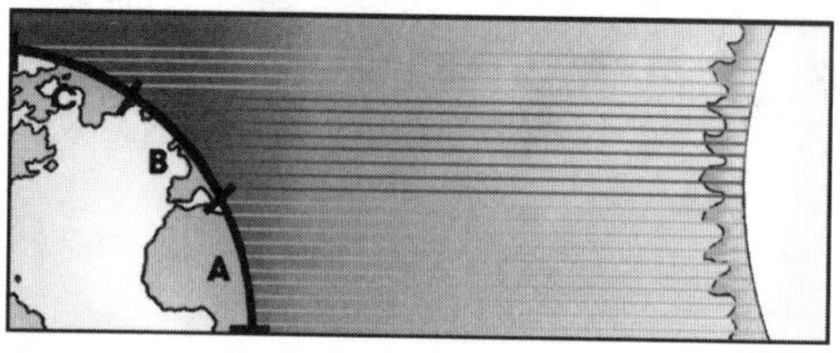

A
B

9. North pole
10. South Pole
19. Idea: It has more lines of heat.

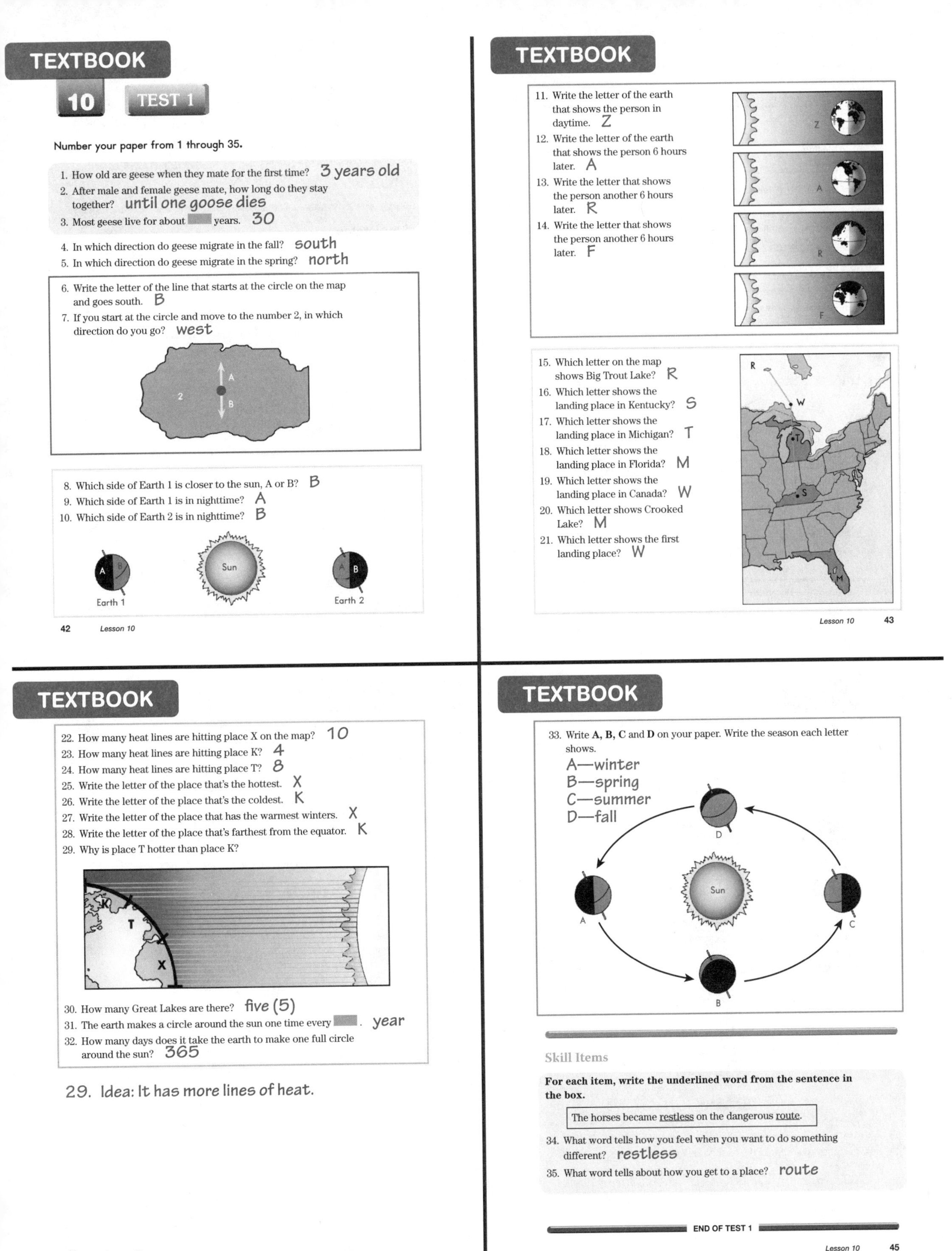

TEXTBOOK

10 TEST 1

Number your paper from 1 through 35.

1. How old are geese when they mate for the first time? 3 years old
2. After male and female geese mate, how long do they stay together? until one goose dies
3. Most geese live for about ▬ years. 30
4. In which direction do geese migrate in the fall? south
5. In which direction do geese migrate in the spring? north
6. Write the letter of the line that starts at the circle on the map and goes south. B
7. If you start at the circle and move to the number 2, in which direction do you go? west

8. Which side of Earth 1 is closer to the sun, A or B? B
9. Which side of Earth 1 is in nighttime? A
10. Which side of Earth 2 is in nighttime? B

TEXTBOOK

11. Write the letter of the earth that shows the person in daytime. Z
12. Write the letter of the earth that shows the person 6 hours later. A
13. Write the letter that shows the person another 6 hours later. R
14. Write the letter that shows the person another 6 hours later. F

15. Which letter on the map shows Big Trout Lake? R
16. Which letter shows the landing place in Kentucky? S
17. Which letter shows the landing place in Michigan? T
18. Which letter shows the landing place in Florida? M
19. Which letter shows the landing place in Canada? W
20. Which letter shows Crooked Lake? M
21. Which letter shows the first landing place? W

TEXTBOOK

22. How many heat lines are hitting place X on the map? 10
23. How many heat lines are hitting place K? 4
24. How many heat lines are hitting place T? 8
25. Write the letter of the place that's the hottest. X
26. Write the letter of the place that's the coldest. K
27. Write the letter of the place that has the warmest winters. X
28. Write the letter of the place that's farthest from the equator. K
29. Why is place T hotter than place K?

30. How many Great Lakes are there? five (5)
31. The earth makes a circle around the sun one time every ▬. year
32. How many days does it take the earth to make one full circle around the sun? 365

29. Idea: It has more lines of heat.

TEXTBOOK

33. Write **A, B, C** and **D** on your paper. Write the season each letter shows.

A—winter
B—spring
C—summer
D—fall

Skill Items

For each item, write the underlined word from the sentence in the box.

The horses became restless on the dangerous route.

34. What word tells how you feel when you want to do something different? restless
35. What word tells about how you get to a place? route

END OF TEST 1

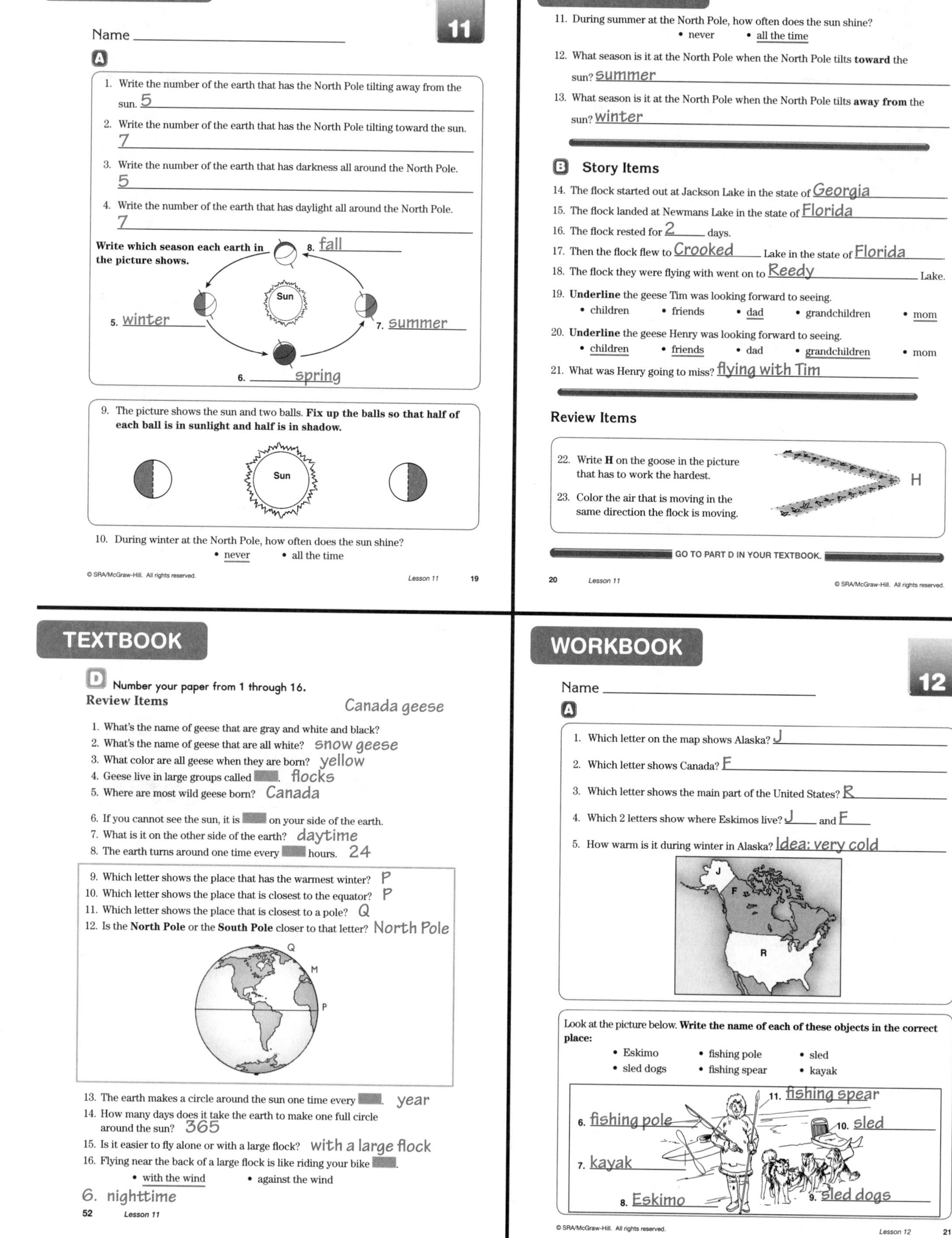

WORKBOOK

Name ______________

A

1. Write the number of the earth that has the North Pole tilting away from the sun. 5
2. Write the number of the earth that has the North Pole tilting toward the sun. 7
3. Write the number of the earth that has darkness all around the North Pole. 5
4. Write the number of the earth that has daylight all around the North Pole. 7

Write which season each earth in the picture shows.

9. The picture shows the sun and two balls. **Fix up the balls so that half of each ball is in sunlight and half is in shadow.**

10. During winter at the North Pole, how often does the sun shine?
   - never
   - all the time

WORKBOOK

11. During summer at the North Pole, how often does the sun shine?
   - never
   - all the time
12. What season is it at the North Pole when the North Pole tilts **toward** the sun? summer
13. What season is it at the North Pole when the North Pole tilts **away from** the sun? winter

B Story Items

14. The flock started out at Jackson Lake in the state of Georgia.
15. The flock landed at Newmans Lake in the state of Florida.
16. The flock rested for 2 days.
17. Then the flock flew to Crooked Lake in the state of Florida.
18. The flock they were flying with went on to Reedy Lake.
19. **Underline** the geese Tim was looking forward to seeing.
   - children • friends • dad • grandchildren • mom
20. **Underline** the geese Henry was looking forward to seeing.
   - children • friends • dad • grandchildren • mom
21. What was Henry going to miss? flying with Tim

Review Items

22. Write **H** on the goose in the picture that has to work the hardest.
23. Color the air that is moving in the same direction the flock is moving.

GO TO PART D IN YOUR TEXTBOOK.

TEXTBOOK

D Number your paper from 1 through 16.

Review Items

1. What's the name of geese that are gray and white and black? Canada geese
2. What's the name of geese that are all white? snow geese
3. What color are all geese when they are born? yellow
4. Geese live in large groups called ███. flocks
5. Where are most wild geese born? Canada
6. If you cannot see the sun, it is ███ on your side of the earth.
7. What is it on the other side of the earth? daytime
8. The earth turns around one time every ███ hours. 24
9. Which letter shows the place that has the warmest winter? P
10. Which letter shows the place that is closest to the equator? P
11. Which letter shows the place that is closest to a pole? Q
12. Is the **North Pole** or the **South Pole** closer to that letter? North Pole

13. The earth makes a circle around the sun one time every ███. year
14. How many days does it take the earth to make one full circle around the sun? 365
15. Is it easier to fly alone or with a large flock? with a large flock
16. Flying near the back of a large flock is like riding your bike ███.
   - with the wind
   - against the wind

6. nighttime

WORKBOOK

12

Name ______________

A

1. Which letter on the map shows Alaska? J
2. Which letter shows Canada? F
3. Which letter shows the main part of the United States? R
4. Which 2 letters show where Eskimos live? J and F
5. How warm is it during winter in Alaska? Idea: very cold

Look at the picture below. **Write the name of each of these objects in the correct place:**

- Eskimo
- fishing pole
- sled
- sled dogs
- fishing spear
- kayak

WORKBOOK

12. What kind of boat do Eskimos use in the summer? kayak
13. Why don't they use those boats in the winter? Ideas: because the water is frozen; because of ice floes; because the winds are too strong

B Story Items

14. Who met Tim at Crooked Lake? his mom and dad
15. Why were they surprised to see Tim? Idea: They didn't think they would see him again.
16. The first geese to greet Henry were his friends.
17. Were Henry's children, grandchildren and great grandchildren in the same flock as Henry? yes
18. In the winter, Henry gave the young geese practice in flying in a V.
19. The flocks started to fly north again in the month of January.
20. They did not arrive at Big Trout Lake until the month of April.
21. So it took them 4 months to make the trip north.
22. After the flocks arrived at Big Trout Lake, Tim and the other young geese left the flock.
23. How old were all these geese? Idea: almost a year old
24. Where did those geese move to? Sandy Lake
25. What lake would this flock go to in the fall? Crooked Lake

Review Item

26. The picture shows the sun and two balls. **Fix up the balls** so that half of each ball is in sunlight and half is in shadow.

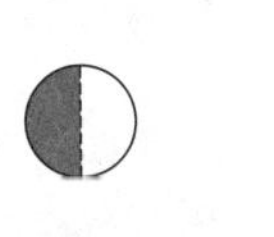

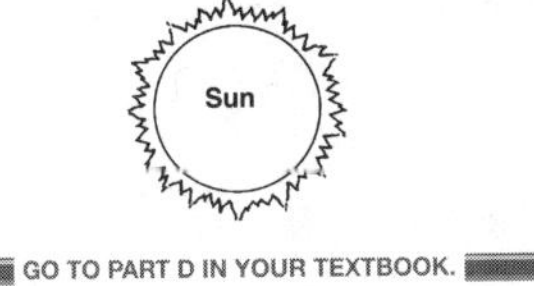

GO TO PART D IN YOUR TEXTBOOK.

TEXTBOOK

D Number your paper from 1 through 11.

Review Items

1. When geese learn to fly, do they start in the water or on the land? on the land
2. They run with their ▬ out to the side. wings

3. Which letter shows the part of the earth that receives more heat from the sun than any other letter? P
4. Which letter shows a part of the earth that receives less heat from the sun than any other letter? F

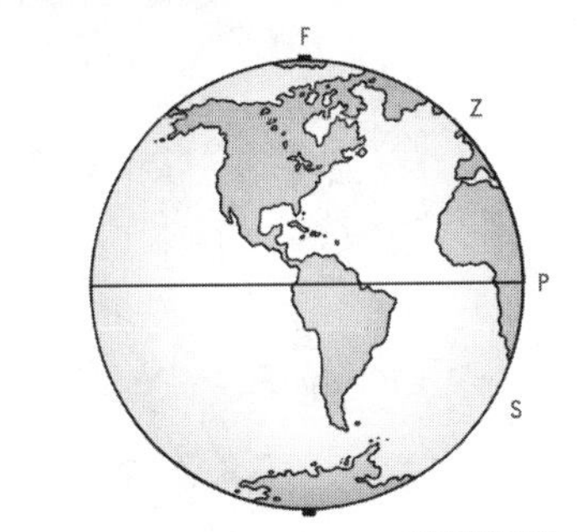

5. The sun shines ▬.
   - some of the time
   - all of the time
6. Can you see the sun all day long and all night long? no
7. Write the letters of the 2 kinds of places that are safe for geese. a, c
   a. places with many geese
   b. places with a few ducks
   c. places with no geese or ducks
   d. places with a few geese

TEXTBOOK

8. During winter at the North Pole, how much does the sun shine?
   - never
   - all the time
9. During summer at the North Pole, how much does the sun shine?
   - never
   - all the time
10. What season is it at the North Pole when the North Pole tilts toward the sun? summer
11. What season is it at the North Pole when the North Pole tilts away from the sun? winter

WORKBOOK

13

Name ____________________

A

Label each animal in the picture below.

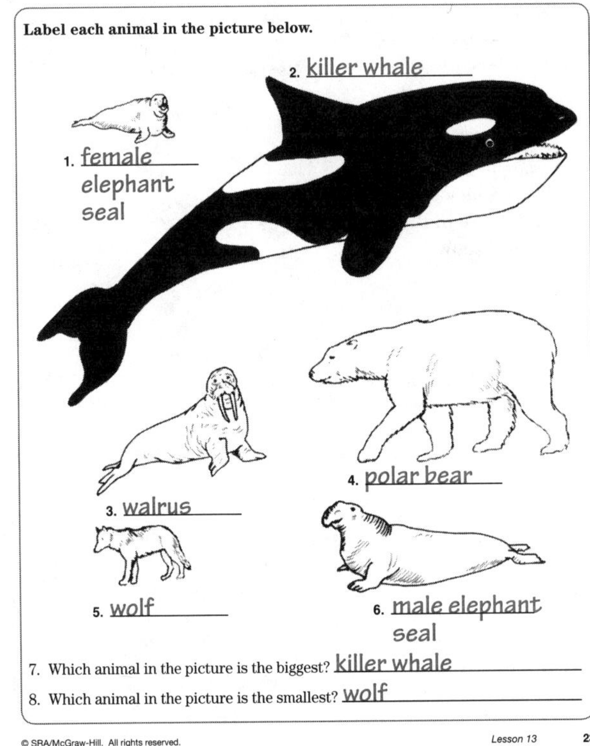

7. Which animal in the picture is the biggest? killer whale
8. Which animal in the picture is the smallest? wolf

WORKBOOK

B

Write these words in the correct places on the map.

9. pebbled beach
10. killer whales
11. summer home
12. path
13. ice floe
14. seals
15. walruses

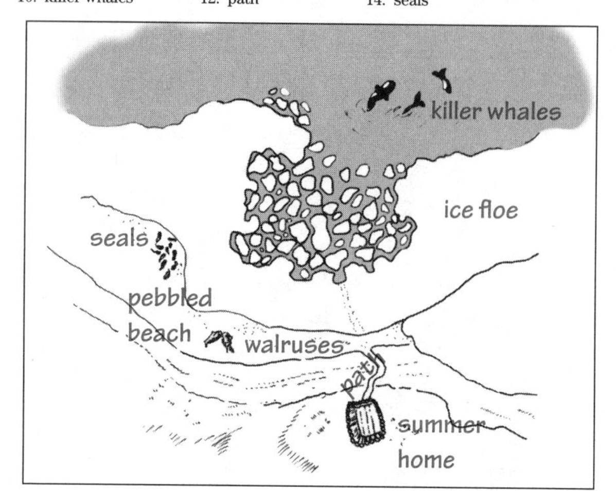

16. At the end of summer, the beach where Oomoo lived was different from the picture in 3 ways. What was different about the ice floe? Idea: The ice floe melted.
17. What was missing from the water? killer whales
18. What was missing from the beach? seals and walruses

GO TO PART E IN YOUR TEXTBOOK.

TEXTBOOK

E Number your paper from 1 through 22.

Story Items

1. When days get longer, is the North Pole tilting **toward the sun** or **away from the sun**? toward the sun
2. When days get shorter, is the North Pole tilting **toward the sun** or **away from the sun**? away from the sun
3. Oomoo and Oolak might have a hard time going to sleep at night in the summertime. Tell why.
4. In April, the sun shines for more than ▬ hours each day in Alaska. 12
5. What kind of animal did Oomoo see at the end of the story? polar bear
6. How far was Oomoo from that animal? Idea: no more than three meters
7. During Oomoo's winter, there is no ▬.
   - daytime
   - nighttime
8. Write the letter of the globe that shows how the earth looks on the first day of winter. A
9. Write the letter of the globe that shows how the earth looks on the first day of summer. B

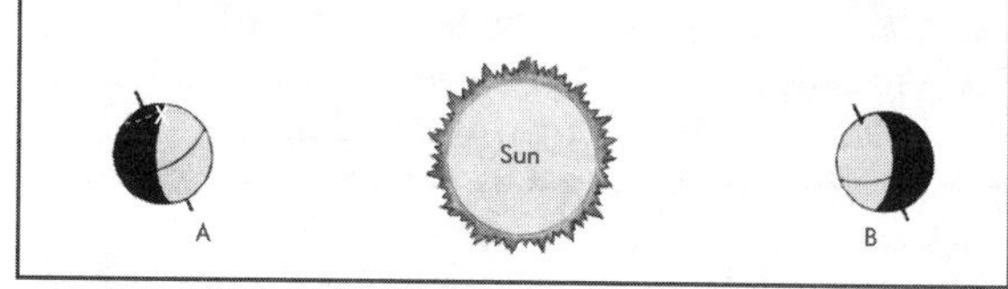

3. Idea: because the sun shines all the time

TEXTBOOK

Review Items

10. Write the number of the earth that has the North Pole tilting away from the sun. 14
11. Write the number of the earth that has the North Pole tilting toward the sun. 16
12. Write the number of the earth that has darkness all around the North Pole. 14
13. Write the number of the earth that has daylight all around the North Pole. 16

Write which season each earth in the picture shows.

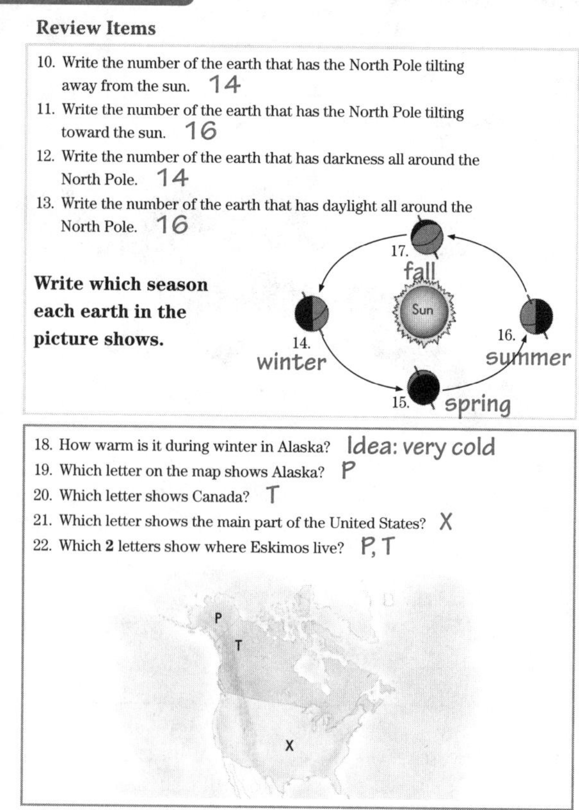

18. How warm is it during winter in Alaska? Idea: very cold
19. Which letter on the map shows Alaska? P
20. Which letter shows Canada? T
21. Which letter shows the main part of the United States? X
22. Which **2** letters show where Eskimos live? P, T

WORKBOOK

14

Name ____________________

A

1. In what season are animals most dangerous in Alaska? spring
2. During what season do female animals in Alaska have babies? spring
3. Female animals fight in the spring to protect their babies.
4. Name 2 kinds of Alaskan animals that are dangerous in the spring. Ideas: polar bears, wolves, walruses

B Story Items

5. What had happened to Usk's mother? Idea: Hunters shot her (three years ago).
6. When Oomoo first saw Usk, Usk was no bigger than a puppy.
7. About how tall was Usk when he stood up now? three meters
8. Oomoo's father said, "Full-grown bears are not ▬."
   - cubs
   - pets
   - dogs
9. Usk had become less playful last fall.
10. Oomoo didn't run up and hug Usk because she remembered what her father had told her.
11. What did Oolak throw at Usk? a snowball
12. Why did Oolak do that? Idea: He wanted to play with Usk.

Skill Items

Scientists do not ignore ordinary things.

13. What word means that you don't pay attention to something? ignore
14. What word tells about things that you see all the time? ordinary
15. What do we call highly-trained people who study different things about the world? scientists

WORKBOOK

Review Items

Write these words in the correct places on the map.

16. ice floe
17. summer home
18. killer whales
19. walruses
20. pebbled beach
21. path
22. seals

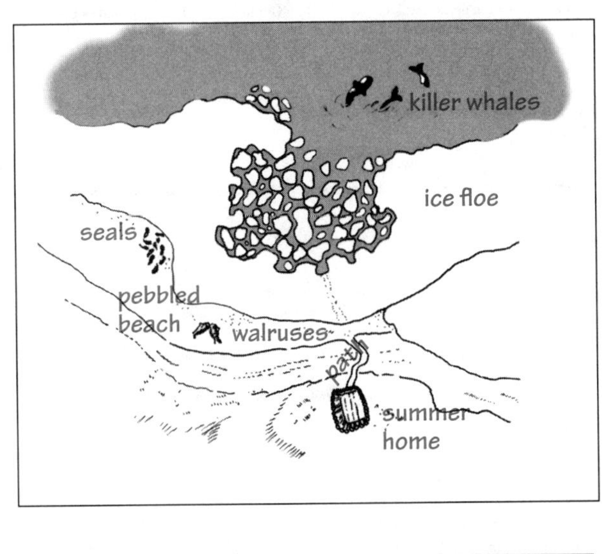

GO TO PART D IN YOUR TEXTBOOK.

TEXTBOOK

D Number your paper from 1 through 16.

Review Items

Choose from these words to answer each item:

- Canada
- equator
- moon
- Florida
- migration
- geese
- sun
- poles

1. The heat that the earth receives comes from the ▬. sun
2. The part of the earth that receives more heat than any other part is the ▬. equator
3. The parts of the earth that receive less heat than any other part are called the ▬. poles

Write the name of each numbered object in the picture. Choose from these names:

- fishing pole
- sled dogs
- spear
- sled
- Eskimo
- kayak

TEXTBOOK

10. When days get longer, is the North Pole tilting **toward the sun** or **away from the sun**? toward the sun
11. When days get shorter, is the North Pole tilting **toward the sun** or **away from the sun**? away from the sun
12. In April, the sun shines for more than ▬ hours each day in Alaska. 12

13. Which globe shows how the earth looks on the first day of winter? Q
14. Which globe shows how the earth looks on the first day of summer? F

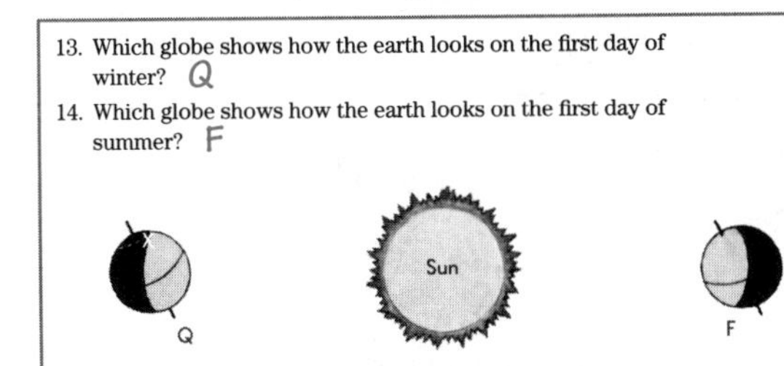

15. What kind of boat do Eskimos use in the summer? kayak
16. Why don't they use those boats in the winter?
    Ideas: because the water is frozen; because of the ice floes; because the winds are too strong

WORKBOOK

15

Name ____________________

A

1. What state is at the north end of the route on the map?
   Alaska
2. What country is at the south end of the route? Canada
3. About how many miles is the route? 2,500
4. Write **OO** where Oomoo and Oolak lived.
5. Write **OH** where Old Henry lived in the summertime.

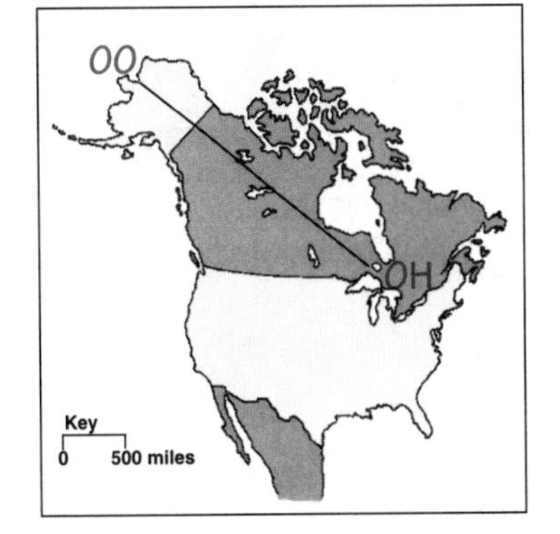

B Story Items

6. What happened when Usk nudged Oolak with his nose?
   Idea: Oolak fell down.

WORKBOOK

7. Usk started chasing Oomoo after Idea: Oomoo hit him with a snowball.
8. When Usk caught up to Oomoo, what did he grab?
   - boot
   - collar
9. Then what did Usk do to Oomoo? Idea: He pushed her over.
10. Who made the children stop playing? their father
11. When Oomoo reached her father, she didn't look at him. Why? Idea: because she knew he was upset with her.
12. Will the father let the children play with Usk? no

Review Items

13. Write the missing seasons on the picture below.
14. Shade half of earth A and half of earth C.

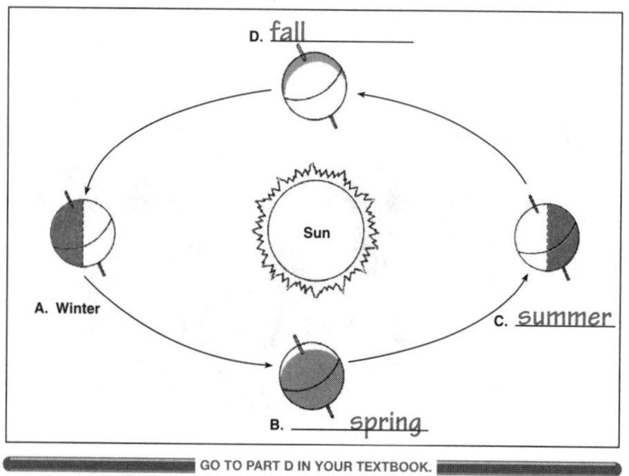

GO TO PART D IN YOUR TEXTBOOK.

TEXTBOOK

slide in a great circle and then turn over, tossing Oomoo and Oolak into the snow. Sometimes Usk would . . .

"Oomoo," her father shouted.

Oomoo stopped thinking of sledding with Usk and looked up on the top of the hill, where her father was standing. "Oomoo," he shouted again. "Oolak, come here now." Oomoo and Oolak scrambled up the slope through the wet snow.

The top of the hill was free of snow. Oomoo stamped the snow from her feet and looked down. She did not want to look at her father. She could feel that he was looking at her.

"Oomoo, I am ashamed of you," he said. "What season of the year is it?" Oomoo answered quietly.

Her father said, "And in what season are bears the most dangerous?"

"Spring," she said.

"And what did I tell you about playing with Usk?"

Oomoo replied, "We should not go near him."

Her father said, "If you cannot stay away from that bear, you will have to stay where he will not go."

D Number your paper from 1 through 20.

Skill Items

Here are three events that happened in the story:

a. Her father said, "And in what season are bears the most dangerous?"

b. Oolak got to his feet and started to stumble through the pebbles.

c. With his big pink tongue hanging out, he looked like a great big white dog.

1. Write the letter of the event that happened near the beginning of the story. b
2. Write the letter of the event that happened near the middle of the story. c
3. Write the letter of the event that happened near the end of the story. a

TEXTBOOK

Use the words in the box to write complete sentences.

ignore	splat	route	Eskimos	ordinary
playful	scientists	restless	constant	

4. The horses became ___ on the dangerous ___. restless, route
5. ___ do not ___ ___ things. scientists, ignore, ordinary

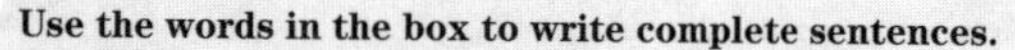

Review Items

6. In which direction do geese fly in the fall? south
7. What is this trip called? migration
8. The earth is shaped like a ___. ball
9. The hottest part of the earth is called the ___.
   - pole
   - desert
   - equator
10. The ___s are the coldest places on the earth and the ___ is the hottest place on the earth. pole, equator
11. How many poles are there? 2
12. The farther you go from the equator, the ___ it gets.
    - colder
    - fatter
    - hotter

13. At which letter would the winters be very, very cold? F
14. At which letter would the winters be very, very hot? R

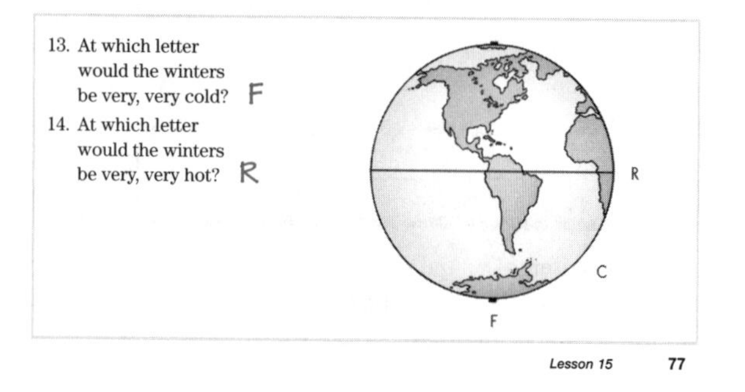

TEXTBOOK

15. Is it easier to fly alone or with a large flock? with a large flock
16. Flying near the back of a large flock is like riding your bike ___.
    - with the wind
    - against the wind
17. What season is it at the North Pole when the North Pole tilts toward the sun? summer
18. What season is it at the North Pole when the North Pole tilts away from the sun? winter
19. In what season are animals most dangerous in Alaska? spring
20. During what season do female animals in Alaska have babies? spring

WORKBOOK

Name ______________________ **16**

A

1. About how long are killer whales? 12 meters
2. Compare the size of killer whales with the size of other whales. **Killer whales** Idea: are shorter than other whales.
3. Are killer whales fish? no
4. Are killer whales **warm-blooded** or **cold-blooded?** warm-blooded
5. Name 3 animals that are warm-blooded. Ideas: bears, humans, dogs
6. Name 3 animals that are cold-blooded. Ideas: fish, sharks, reptiles

B Story Items

7. How long did Oomoo and Oolak have to stay near the summer house? 2 days
8. What kind of house was the summer house? a tent
9. What kind of house was the winter house? a cave
10. Which house was bigger? the summer house
11. What was the only problem with the summer house? bugs
12. Name 3 kinds of biting insects that Alaska has in the spring. mosquitoes, biting flies, no-see-ums
13. Why was Oomoo's summer home in a place where the wind blew hard? Idea: When the wind blew, the bugs stayed away.
14. What were the male seals on the beach fighting for? the best place on the beach

WORKBOOK

15. What were the killer whales waiting for? Idea: the seals to enter the water
16. What were Oomoo and her father in when the killer whales came close to them? a kayak
17. How many whales were there? 3

Skill Items

Here are three events that happened in the story:

a. They were swarming by the thousands on the beach about half a mile from Oomoo's summer home.
b. Then Oomoo's father ordered Oomoo to stay near their summer house for two full days.
c. "I never want to be that close to killer whales again," she said to herself.

18. Write the letter of the event that happened near the beginning of the story. b
19. Write the letter of the event that happened near the middle of the story. a
20. Write the letter of the event that happened near the end of the story. c

Review Items

21. How many Great Lakes are there? five (5)
22. Color the Great Lakes on the map.

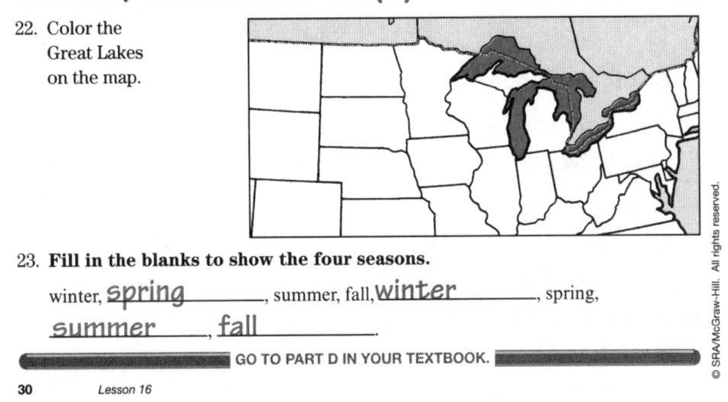

23. **Fill in the blanks to show the four seasons.**

winter, spring, summer, fall, winter, spring, summer, fall.

GO TO PART D IN YOUR TEXTBOOK.

TEXTBOOK

D Number your paper from 1 through 13.

Review Items

Write the name of each animal in the picture.

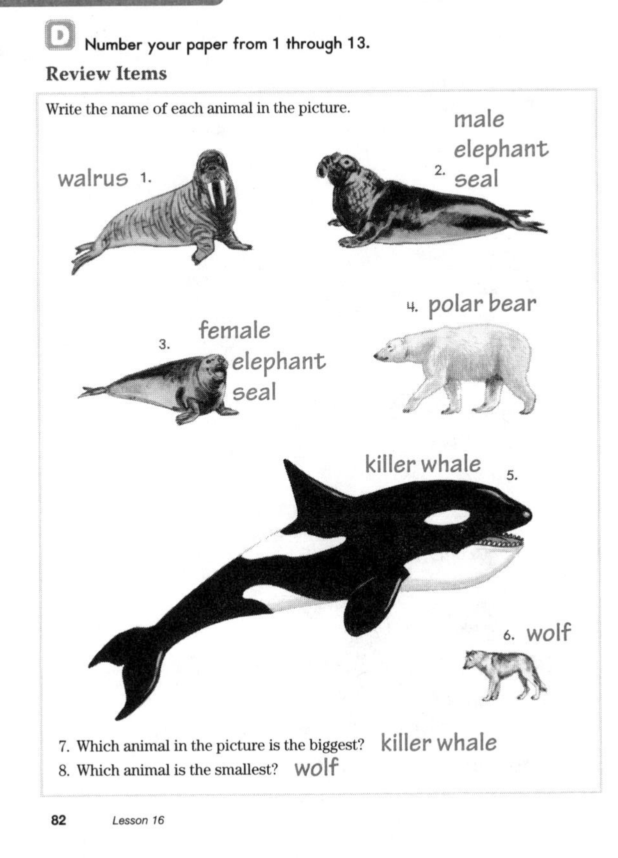

7. Which animal in the picture is the biggest? killer whale
8. Which animal is the smallest? wolf

TEXTBOOK

9. Female animals fight in the spring to protect ▬. their babies
10. Name 2 kinds of Alaskan animals that are dangerous in the spring. Ideas: polar bears, wolves, walruses

11. The map shows a route. What state is at the north end of the route? Alaska
12. What country is at the south end of the route? Canada
13. About how many miles is the route? 2,500

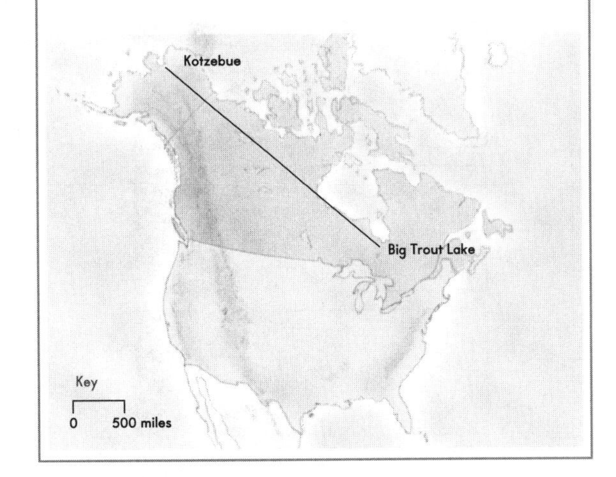

WORKBOOK

Name ______________________ **17**

A

Here are three events that happened in the story:

a. During the winter, you can walk far out on the frozen ocean.
b. But even if the killer whales didn't attack you, you would die within a few minutes after you went into the water.
c. For a moment, Oomoo was going to say, "That's a pretty long way to drift."

1. Write the letter of the event that happened near the beginning of the story. a
2. Write the letter of the event that happened near the middle of the story. b
3. Write the letter of the event that happened near the end of the story. c

B Story Items

4. During which season do ice floes start? spring
5. During the winter in Alaska, you can walk far out on the ocean. Tell why. Idea: The ocean is frozen.
6. Do ice floes make noise in the winter? yes
7. Why do ice floes make noise in the spring? Idea: because they are breaking up
8. When Oomoo played on the ice floe in the spring, she could never go out to the end of the ice floe. What was at the end of the ice floe? killer whales
9. You are out in the ocean on an ice chunk that melts. Name 2 ways you could die. Idea: get attacked by killer whales; the cold water
10. Oomoo and Oolak were drifting on something. What was it? an ice chunk

WORKBOOK

11. Write **north, south, east** and **west** in the boxes.
12. Make an **X** where the killer whales stay.
13. Make a **Y** on an ice chunk where Oomoo is not supposed to go.
14. Make a **Z** on the ice chunk Oomoo and Oolak are on.
15. **Make an arrow** from the **Z** to where they would go if the wind blows from the east. Show the path the ice chunk should follow.

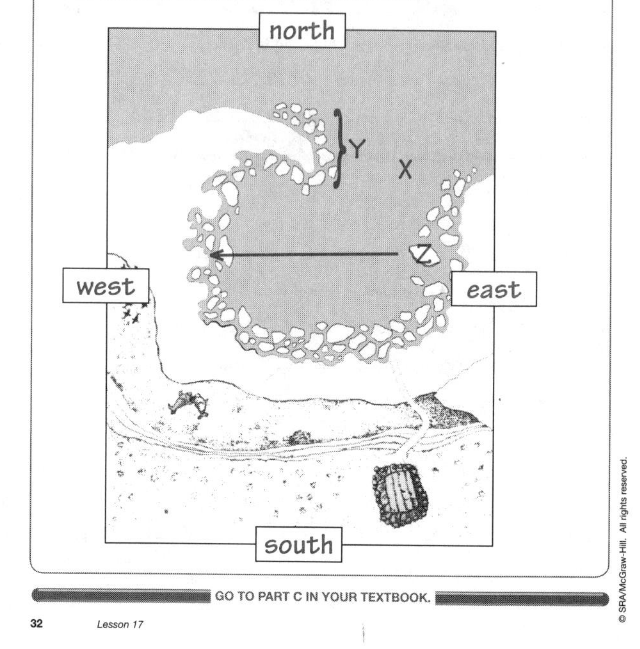

GO TO PART C IN YOUR TEXTBOOK.

TEXTBOOK

C Number your paper from 1 through 17.

Review Items

1. Write the letter of the earth that shows the person in daytime. P
2. Write the letter of the earth that shows the person 6 hours later. F
3. Write the letter that shows the person another 6 hours later. J
4. Write the letter that shows the person another 6 hours later. B

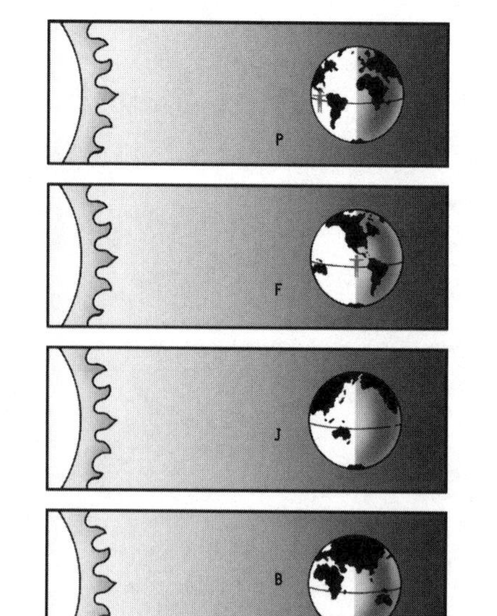

TEXTBOOK

5. Which letter on the map shows Alaska? J
6. Which letter shows Canada? F
7. Which letter shows the main part of the United States? R
8. Which 2 letters show where Eskimos live? J, F
9. How warm is it during winter in Alaska? Idea: very cold

J
F
R

10. About how long are killer whales? 12 meters
11. Compare the size of killer whales with the size of other whales.
12. Are killer whales fish? no
13. Tell if killer whales are **warm-blooded** or **cold-blooded**.
14. Name 3 animals that are warm-blooded.
15. Name 3 animals that are cold-blooded.

11. Idea: Killer whales are smaller than other whales.
13. warm-blooded
14. Ideas: bears, humans, dogs
15. Ideas: fish, sharks, reptiles

TEXTBOOK

16. Which globe shows how the earth looks on the first day of winter? Z
17. Which globe shows how the earth looks on the first day of summer? B

B

WORKBOOK

18

Name ____________

A

1. Name 2 things that can make an ice chunk drift. wind and currents
2. In which direction will you drift when you're in an ocean current?
   Idea: in the same direction the current moves
3. In which direction will you drift when you're in a strong wind?
   Idea: in the direction of the wind

4. Write **north, south, east** and **west** in the correct boxes.
5. In which direction is ocean current **A** moving? north
6. In which direction is ocean current **B** moving? west
7. Which direction is the wind coming from? south
8. Make an arrow **above** ice chunk **C** to show the direction the current will move the ice chunk.
9. Make an arrow **above** ice chunk **D** to show the direction the current will move the ice chunk.

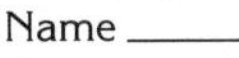

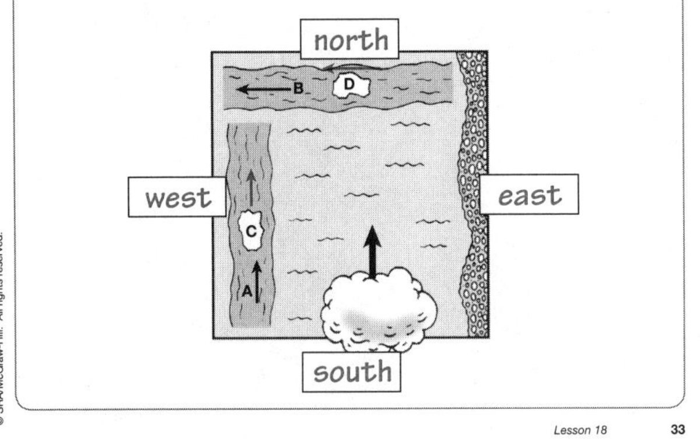

WORKBOOK

B Story Items

10. If you're out on the ocean and you spot a green cloud, what should you do?
    Idea: get to shore immediately
11. What 2 things do those clouds bring? strong winds and rain
12. Did Oomoo and Oolak follow the rule about watching the sky? no
13. Was the water **smooth** or **rough** where the wind hit the water? rough
14. How fast was the wind moving? 40 miles per hour
15. In which direction was the ice chunk headed? Ideas: straight north; into the ocean
16. Name the direction the ice chunk was drifting **before** the big wind came up.
    west
17. Name the direction the ice chunk was drifting **after** the big wind hit it.
    north
18. Where were the flies and mosquitoes thick?
    - near the shore
    - near the tent
    - over the ocean
19. Where were the flies and mosquitoes not as thick?
    - near the shore
    - near the tent
    - over the ocean
20. What did Oomoo and Oolak do to make the ice chunk rock?
    Idea: jumped on it
21. Name 2 things that tell about the cloud that Oomoo saw. (Any 2:) fat; green; low; storm cloud; it covered the sun

Review Item

22. The picture shows the sun and two balls. Fix up the balls so that half of each ball is in sunlight and half is in shadow.

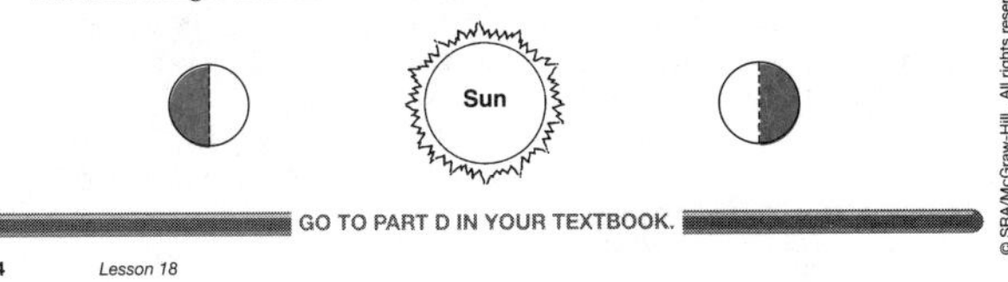

GO TO PART D IN YOUR TEXTBOOK.

TEXTBOOK

D Number your paper from 1 through 19.

Skill Items

She actually repeated that careless mistake.

1. What word means **to do something again**? repeated
2. What word means the opposite of **careful**? careless
3. What word means **really**? actually

Here are three events that happened in the story:

a. The wind tore across the ocean like a great rake.
b. And the cloud was not the kind of cloud you see when the weather is nice.
c. Soon there were very few insects bothering Oomoo and her brother.

4. Write the letter of the event that happened near the beginning of the story. c
5. Write the letter of the event that happened near the middle of the story. b
6. Write the letter of the event that happened near the end of the story. a

Review Items

7. Which letter shows the place that has the warmest winters? P
8. Which letter shows the place that is closest to the equator? P
9. Which letter shows the place that is closest to a pole? Y
10. Is the North Pole or the South Pole closer to that letter? North Pole

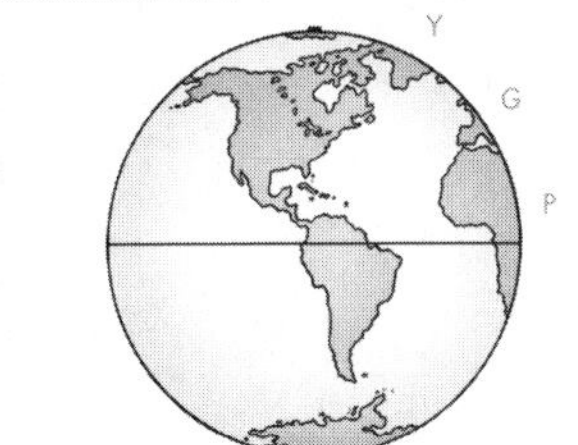

TEXTBOOK

11. The earth makes a circle around the sun one time every ▬. year
12. How many days does it take the earth to make one full circle around the sun? 365
13. When days get longer, is the North Pole tilting toward the sun or away from the sun? toward the sun
14. When days get shorter, is the North Pole tilting toward the sun or away from the sun? away from the sun
15. In April, the sun shines for more than ▬ hours each day in Alaska. 12

16. During which season do ice floes start? spring
17. During winter in Alaska, you can walk far out on the ocean. Tell why. Idea: because it is frozen
18. Do ice floes make noise in the winter? yes
19. Why do ice floes make noise in the spring? Idea: because the ice is breaking up

WORKBOOK

Name 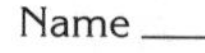

Story Items

1. The wind blew Oomoo and Oolak off course. In which direction were they drifting before the big wind blew? west
2. In which direction did the big wind blow them? north
3. When Oomoo heard Oolak's voice, she turned to look at him. Where was Oolak? in the water
4. What did Oomoo put in the water to help Oolak? her legs
5. Just as Oomoo was sliding off the ice chunk, a huge wave hit it. Where did Oomoo and Oolak end up? on the middle of the ice chunk
6. When Oolak asked Oomoo, "Are we going to die?" did Oomoo say what she really thought? no
7. When the wind died down, rain and hail began to fall. Which made more noise, the **wind** or the **rain and hail**? rain and hail
8. Which was colder, the **ocean water** or the **rain**? ocean water
9. How long did the rain come down hard?
   - 10 minutes
   - an hour
   - half an hour (underlined)
10. At the end of the story, what did Oomoo see beyond the ice floe? killer whales
11. Did she tell Oolak what she saw? no
12. Tell why. Idea: She didn't want to worry/scare him.
13. After the big wind died down, Oomoo and Oolak shouted for help. Why couldn't anyone hear them? Ideas: The heavy rain and hail made too much noise; they were too far from shore.

WORKBOOK

14. Make an arrow from the **X** to the C-shaped ice floe. Show the path the ice chunk was supposed to follow.
15. Which letter shows where the ice chunk was at the end of today's story? B
16. Which letter shows where the killer whales were? C
17. Make an arrow from the **Q** to show which way the big wind blew.

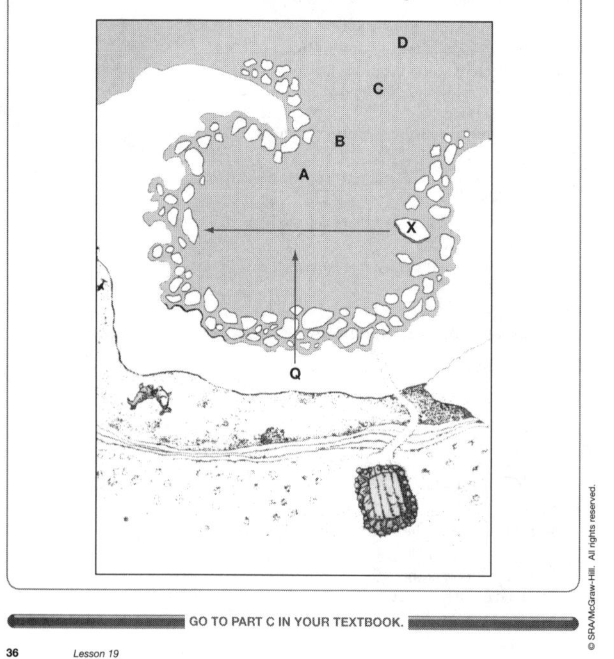

GO TO PART C IN YOUR TEXTBOOK.

TEXTBOOK

C Number your paper from 1 through 20.

Skill Items

1. Scientists do not ignore ordinary things.

Use the words in the box to write complete sentences.

ordinary	repeated	enter	scientists	ignore
careless	rootless	actually	hitch	

1. ▬ do not ▬ ▬ things.
2. She ▬ ▬ that ▬ mistake.

2. She actually repeated that careless mistake.

Here are three events that happened in the story:

a. Oomoo noticed that the ice chunk was very close to the end of the ice floe.
b. Sometimes they would roll out of the water so that she could see the black-and-white markings around their heads.
c. Just as Oomoo was sliding off, a huge wave hit the shore side of the ice chunk.

3. Write the letter of the event that happened near the beginning of the story. a
4. Write the letter of the event that happened near the middle of the story. c
5. Write the letter of the event that happened near the end of the story. b

Review Items

6. Name 2 things that can make an ice chunk drift. wind and current
7. In which direction will you drift when you're in an ocean current? Idea: in the same direction the current moves
8. In which direction will you drift when you're in a strong wind? Idea: in the direction of the wind
9. What kind of boat do Eskimos use in the summer? kayak
10. Why don't they use those boats in the winter? Ideas: because the water is frozen; because of the ice floes; because the winds are too strong

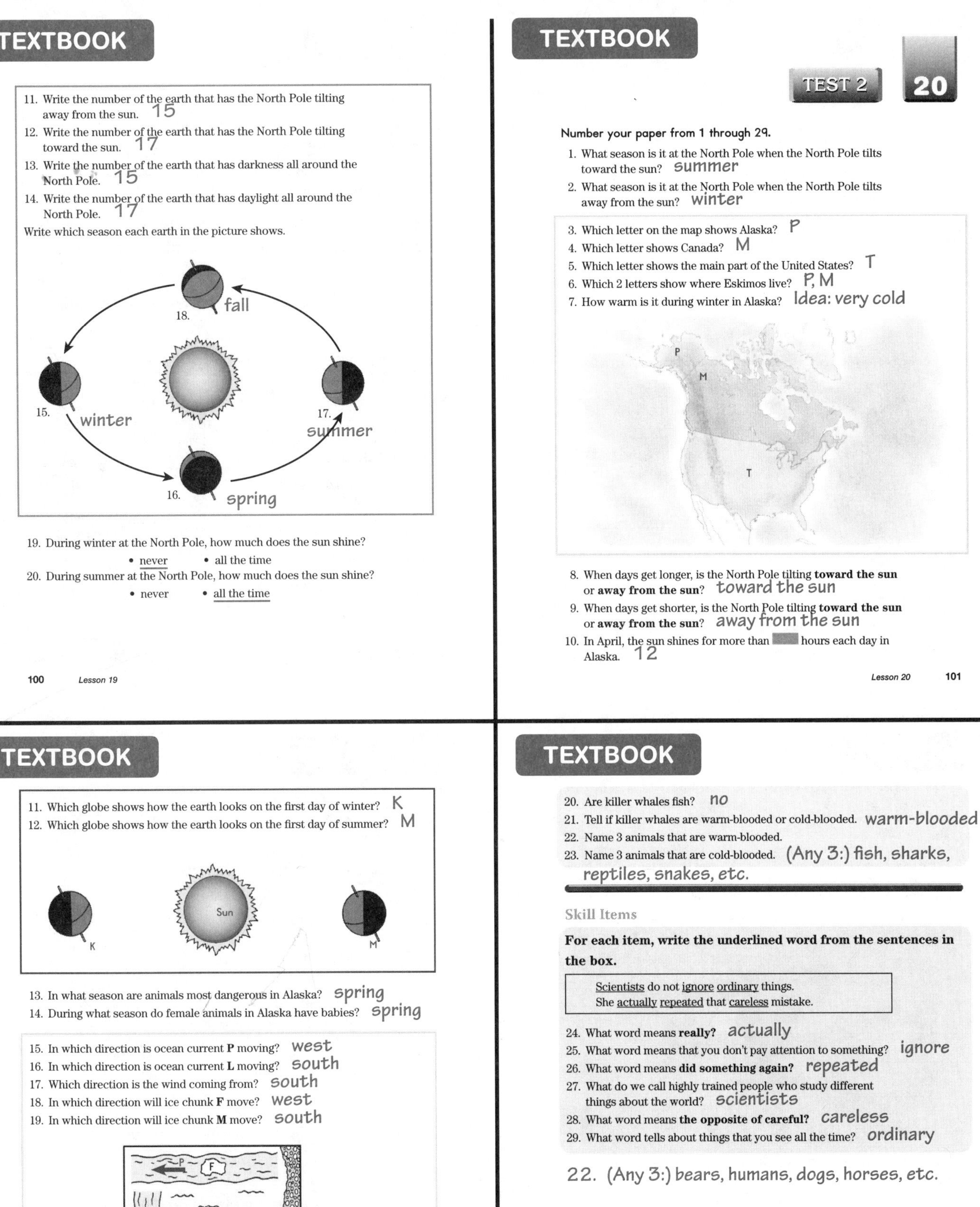

TEXTBOOK

11. Write the number of the earth that has the North Pole tilting away from the sun. 15
12. Write the number of the earth that has the North Pole tilting toward the sun. 17
13. Write the number of the earth that has darkness all around the North Pole. 15
14. Write the number of the earth that has daylight all around the North Pole. 17

Write which season each earth in the picture shows.

18. fall
15. winter
17. summer
16. spring

19. During winter at the North Pole, how much does the sun shine?
 • <u>never</u> • all the time
20. During summer at the North Pole, how much does the sun shine?
 • never • <u>all the time</u>

100 *Lesson 19*

TEXTBOOK

TEST 2 **20**

Number your paper from 1 through 29.

1. What season is it at the North Pole when the North Pole tilts toward the sun? summer
2. What season is it at the North Pole when the North Pole tilts away from the sun? winter
3. Which letter on the map shows Alaska? P
4. Which letter shows Canada? M
5. Which letter shows the main part of the United States? T
6. Which 2 letters show where Eskimos live? P, M
7. How warm is it during winter in Alaska? Idea: very cold

8. When days get longer, is the North Pole tilting **toward the sun** or **away from the sun**? toward the sun
9. When days get shorter, is the North Pole tilting **toward the sun** or **away from the sun**? away from the sun
10. In April, the sun shines for more than ▬ hours each day in Alaska. 12

Lesson 20 101

TEXTBOOK

11. Which globe shows how the earth looks on the first day of winter? K
12. Which globe shows how the earth looks on the first day of summer? M

13. In what season are animals most dangerous in Alaska? spring
14. During what season do female animals in Alaska have babies? spring

15. In which direction is ocean current **P** moving? west
16. In which direction is ocean current **L** moving? south
17. Which direction is the wind coming from? south
18. In which direction will ice chunk **F** move? west
19. In which direction will ice chunk **M** move? south

102 *Lesson 20*

TEXTBOOK

20. Are killer whales fish? no
21. Tell if killer whales are warm-blooded or cold-blooded. warm-blooded
22. Name 3 animals that are warm-blooded.
23. Name 3 animals that are cold-blooded. (Any 3:) fish, sharks, reptiles, snakes, etc.

Skill Items

For each item, write the underlined word from the sentences in the box.

<u>Scientists</u> do not <u>ignore</u> <u>ordinary</u> things.
She <u>actually</u> <u>repeated</u> that <u>careless</u> mistake.

24. What word means **really?** actually
25. What word means that you don't pay attention to something? ignore
26. What word means **did something again?** repeated
27. What do we call highly trained people who study different things about the world? scientists
28. What word means **the opposite of careful?** careless
29. What word tells about things that you see all the time? ordinary

22. (Any 3:) bears, humans, dogs, horses, etc.

END OF TEST 2

Lesson 20 103

WORKBOOK

Name ______________________ 21

A

1. What are clouds made of? Idea: tiny drops of water
2. What kind of cloud does picture **A** show? storm cloud
3. Write the letter of the clouds that may stay in the sky for days at a time. C
4. Write the letter of the storm clouds. A
5. Write the letter of the clouds that have frozen drops of water. B
6. Write the letter of the clouds that may be five miles high. A
7. Look at cloud A. At which number does a drop of water start? 1
8. What happens to the drop at the number **2**? Idea: It freezes.
9. Draw 2 arrows on cloud **A** to show how a hailstone forms and returns to 1.

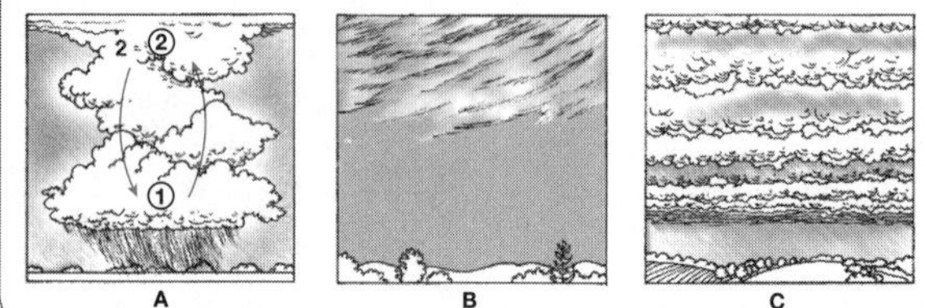

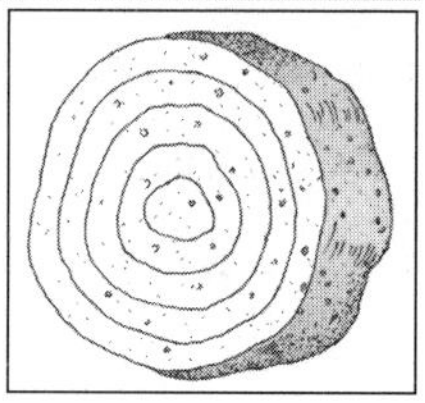

10. If you break a hailstone in half, what will you see inside the hailstone? rings
11. The picture shows half of a hailstone. How many times did the stone go through a cloud? 5

WORKBOOK

B Story Items

12. Oomoo slapped her boot on the ice to make noise. Why did she want the people on shore to hear the noise? Idea: so she and Oolak would be rescued
13. Why did she want the killer whales to hear the noise? Idea: She hoped that the sound would scare them away.
14. Was Oomoo sure that someone would hear her? no
15. About how far was the ice chunk from the tent? more than a mile
16. About how far was the ice chunk from the killer whales? 100 meters

Review Items

17. Write **north, south, east** and **west** in the correct boxes.
18. In which direction is ocean current **J** moving? east
19. In which direction is ocean current **K** moving? north
20. Which direction is the wind coming from? north
21. Make an arrow above ice chunk **L** to show the direction the current will move the ice chunk.
22. Make an arrow above ice chunk **M** to show the direction the current will move the ice chunk.

north / west / east / south
M K L J

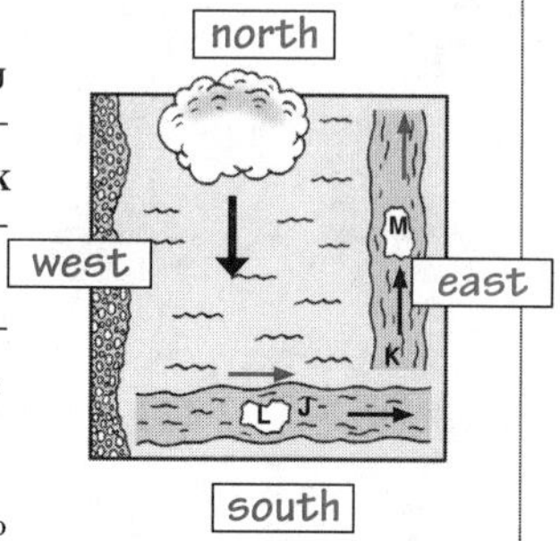

GO TO PART D IN YOUR TEXTBOOK.

TEXTBOOK

their heels into dents in the surface of the ice.

"Play sled," she told Usk. "Play sled. Go home."

At first, Usk just rolled over and almost got the laces tangled in his front paws. "Home," Oomoo repeated. "Play sled and go home."

Usk stayed next to the ice chunk, making a playful sound. "Home," Oomoo shouted again.

Then Usk seemed to figure out what he was supposed to do. Perhaps he saw the fins of the killer whales. He got low in the water and started to swim toward shore.

D Number your paper from 1 through 12.

Story Items

1. What were Oomoo's boot laces made of? (long, thick) strips of animal skin
2. What did Oomoo do with the laces after she tied them together?
3. What did she want Usk to do? Idea: pull them to safety
4. Did Usk immediately understand what he was supposed to do? No
5. What did Usk start doing at the end of the story? Idea: swimming toward shore

2. Idea: Put them around Usk's neck

TEXTBOOK

Review Items

6. The map shows a route. What state is at the north end of the route? Alaska
7. What country is at the south end of the route? Canada
8. About how many miles is the route? 2500

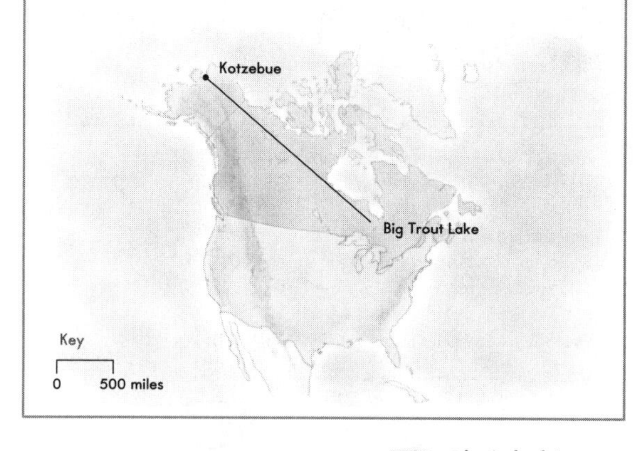

9. Female animals fight in the spring to protect ▬. their babies
10. Name 2 kinds of Alaskan animals that are dangerous in the spring.
11. Is it easier to fly alone or with a large flock? with a large flock
12. Flying near the back of a large flock is like riding your bike ▬.
    - with the wind
    - against the wind

10. Ideas: Polar bears, wolves, walruses

WORKBOOK

Name ______________________ **22**

A

Look at the pile in the picture.

1. Things closer to the bottom of the pile went into the pile earlier.
2. Which object went into the pile **first?** shoe
3. Which object went into the pile **last?** rock
4. Which object went into the pile **earlier**—the knife or the book? book
5. Which object went into the pile **earlier**—the pencil or the cup? cup
6. Which object went into the pile **just after** the bone? cup
7. Which object went into the pile **just after** the pencil? knife

WORKBOOK

B **Story Items**

8. Oomoo and Oolak dug their heels into dents in the ice so that Usk could not Idea: pull them into the water.
9. What did Oomoo see that scared her? a killer whale
10. Why did Oomoo slap the ice with her hand? Idea: to scare off the killer whale
11. While Oomoo and Oolak sat by the tent, they had to study the sky and the ocean.
12. They had to do that so they would remember to look at the sky.
13. Did Oomoo find out why the killer whale didn't attack Usk? No
14. The people of the village formed a big ring. Who stood in the middle of the ring? Usk
15. What did the women give Usk? Idea: a large smoked fish
16. What did Oomoo's father paint on each side of Usk? Idea: outline of a killer whale
17. Why were Oomoo and Oolak so proud of Usk? Idea: because he saved their lives

Review Items

18. **Fill in the blanks to show the four seasons.**
winter, spring, summer, fall, winter,
spring, summer, fall

GO TO PART D IN YOUR TEXTBOOK.

TEXTBOOK

The day was peaceful, with the wind blowing gently from the ocean. Oomoo watched the sky and the ocean. From time to time, she looked at the killer whales. She wondered what that whale had thought, and why it hadn't attacked Usk. "You will never understand the whale," an old man of the village had told her.

That afternoon, everyone in the village gathered at Oomoo's tent. The people formed a great ring. They sang. Then Oomoo's father led Usk into the middle of the ring. Women brought him a large smoked fish—his favorite food. He gulped it down and wagged his head from side to side. Then Oomoo's father took blue paint and painted the outline of a whale on each side of Usk.

"Let this bear live under the sign of the whale," her father said. "Let no hunter shoot this bear or bother this bear. If this bear needs food, feed this bear. We owe much to this bear. Let us thank him."

The people from the village cheered and danced. Oomoo and Oolak danced with the others. They were very, very proud of their bear. They knew that they should not play with him because he was a bear, not a playmate. But they also knew that they owed their lives to that huge, white, playful bear.

D Number your paper from 1 through 17.

1. Things closer to the bottom of the pile went into the pile ▬. earlier

Look at the pile in the picture.

2. Which object went into the pile **first?** shoe
3. Which object went into the pile **last?** rock

TEXTBOOK

Review Items

Write the name of each animal in the picture.

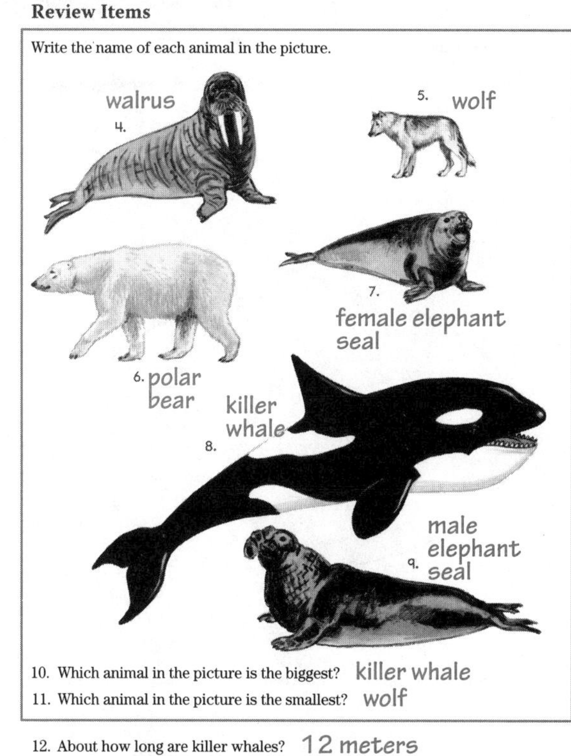

10. Which animal in the picture is the biggest? killer whale
11. Which animal in the picture is the smallest? wolf

12. About how long are killer whales? 12 meters
13. Compare the size of killer whales with the size of other whales. Idea: Killer whales are smaller than other whales.

TEXTBOOK

14. tiny drops of water

14. What are clouds made of?
15. What kind of cloud does the picture show? storm cloud
16. What happens to a drop of water at **B**? Idea: It freezes.

17. The picture shows half a hailstone. How many times did the stone go through a cloud? 6

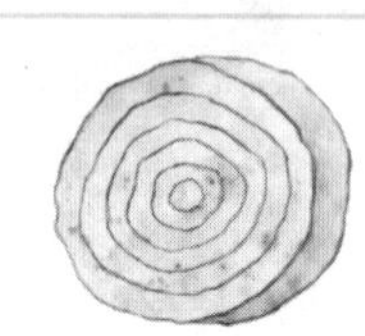

WORKBOOK

23

Name

Story Items

1. Write the letter of the layer that went into the pile **first.** A
2. Write the letter of the layer that went into the pile **next.** B
3. Write the letter of the layer that went into the pile **last.** D
4. Which layer went into the pile **earlier**—B or C? B
5. Which layer went into the pile **earlier**—A or C? A
6. Write the letter of the layer where we would find the skeletons of humans. D
7. Write the letter of the layer that has dinosaur skeletons. C
8. Write the letter of the layer where we find the skeletons of horses. D

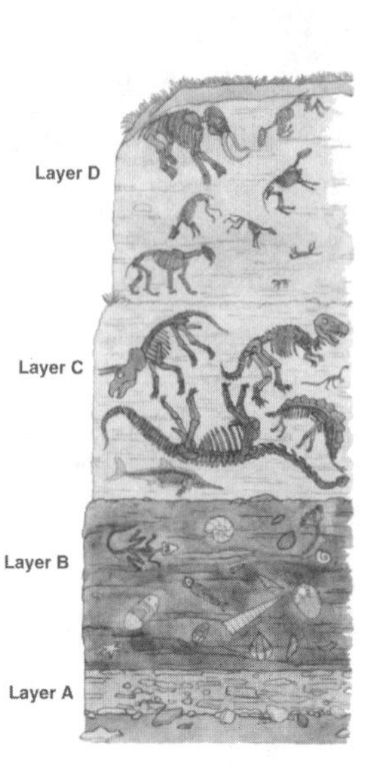

9. What's the name of layer C? Mesozoic
10. Write the letter of the layer we live in. D
11. Are there any dinosaur skeletons in layer D? no
12. Which came earlier on Earth, dinosaurs or horses? dinosaurs

WORKBOOK

13. Which came earlier on Earth, strange sea animals or dinosaurs? sea animals
14. What kind of animals lived in the Mesozoic? dinosaurs

Review Items

15. Write the missing seasons on the picture below.
16. Shade half of Earth **A** and half of Earth **C**.

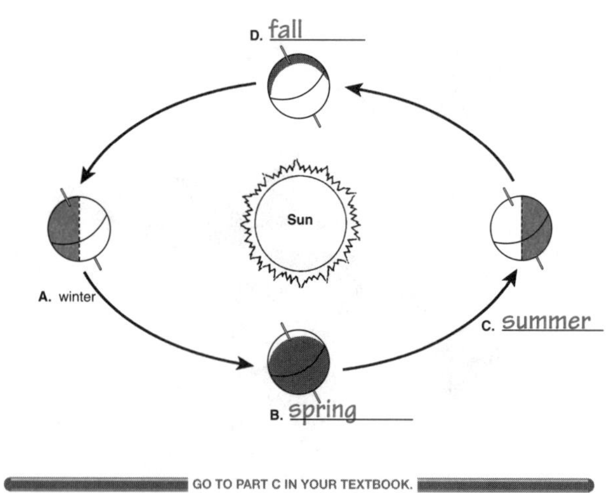

GO TO PART C IN YOUR TEXTBOOK.

TEXTBOOK

C Number your paper from 1 through 20.

Skill Items

The smell attracted flies immediately.

1. What word means **right now**? immediately
2. What word means **really interested** the flies? attracted

Review Items

3. The sun shines ▬.
   - some of the time
   - all of the time
4. Can you see the sun all day long and all night long? no
5. If you can see the sun, is it **daytime** or **nighttime** on your side of the earth? daytime
6. What is it on the other side of the earth? nighttime
7. The earth turns around one time every ▬ hours. 24
8. How many heat lines are hitting place X on the map? 4
9. Write the letter of the place that's the coldest. X
10. Why is place T hotter than place X? Idea: It has more lines of heat.

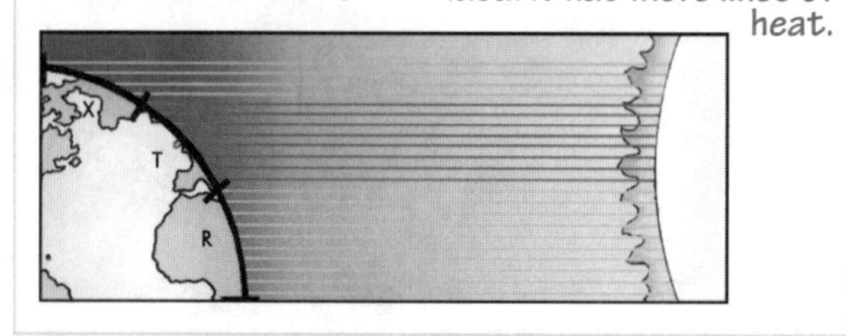

TEXTBOOK

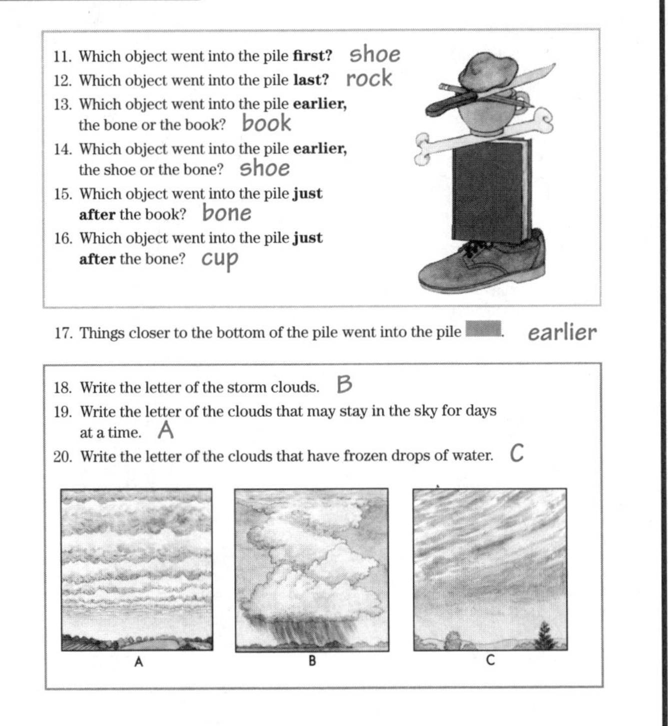

11. Which object went into the pile **first?** shoe
12. Which object went into the pile **last?** rock
13. Which object went into the pile **earlier,** the bone or the book? book
14. Which object went into the pile **earlier,** the shoe or the bone? shoe
15. Which object went into the pile **just after** the book? bone
16. Which object went into the pile **just after** the bone? cup

17. Things closer to the bottom of the pile went into the pile ▬. earlier

18. Write the letter of the storm clouds. B
19. Write the letter of the clouds that may stay in the sky for days at a time. A
20. Write the letter of the clouds that have frozen drops of water. C

A B C

WORKBOOK

Name ____________________ 24

A Story Items

1. How old was Edna Parker? 13
2. How did Edna usually feel on the ship?
   - happy
   - bored
   - nervous

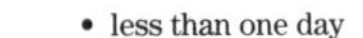

3. Why wouldn't Edna be bored on this trip? Idea: Her friend Carla was along.
4. Where was the ship starting from? Florida
5. Where was it going? Andros Island
6. How far was the trip? 120 miles
7. How long would it take?
   - more than one day
   - one day
   - less than one day
8. Draw an **arrow** on the map below to show the trip.

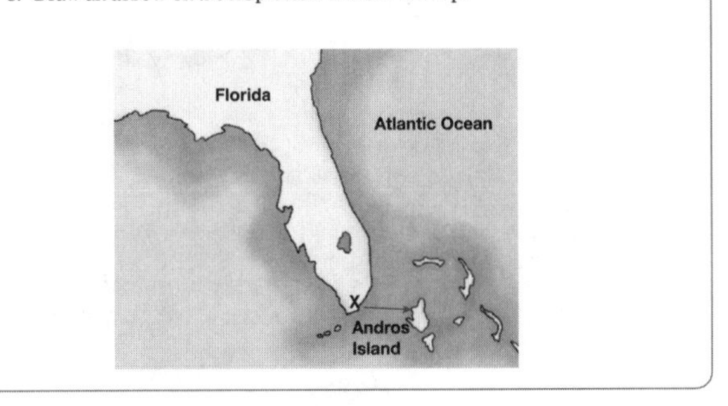

WORKBOOK

9. The ship would pass through a place where hundreds of ships have sunk or been lost. Name that place. Bermuda Triangle
10. **Underline** the 3 things you find in the Bermuda Triangle.
    - huge waves
    - mountains
    - streams
    - whirlpools
    - sudden storms
    - icebergs
11. As the girls left the map room, Captain Parker told them to stay away from the sides of the ship and the lifeboats.

Review Items

Look at the picture below.

12. Shade the part of the earth where it is nighttime.
13. Which side of the earth is closer to the sun, **A** or **B**? B
14. Which side of the earth is in nighttime? A
15. Which side of the earth is in daytime? B

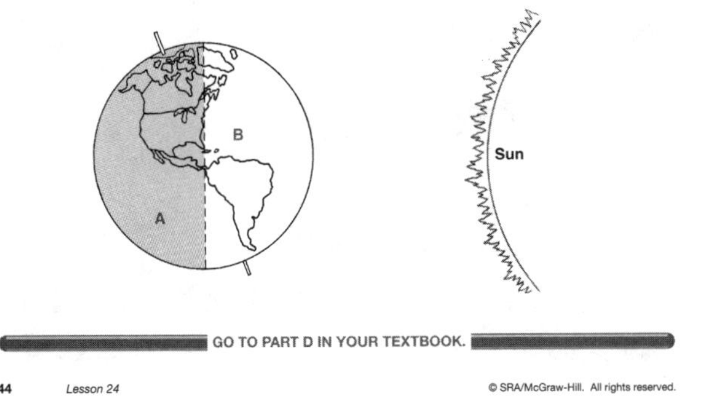

GO TO PART D IN YOUR TEXTBOOK.

TEXTBOOK

"Yes," Captain Parker said. "Those are tiny whirlpools. The kind of whirlpools that you find in the Bermuda Triangle are just like those, except they are big enough to suck a ship down."

"Wow," Carla said.

Edna was trying to imagine a huge whirlpool.

Captain Parker said, "Well, girls, Andros Island is only 120 miles from here, so we should arrive there in less than a day. We should have a smooth trip. The weather looks good. I am going to look over some maps now. You girls may play on deck, but stay away from the sides of the ship. And stay away from the lifeboats."

"All right, Dad," Edna said, and the girls rushed onto the deck.

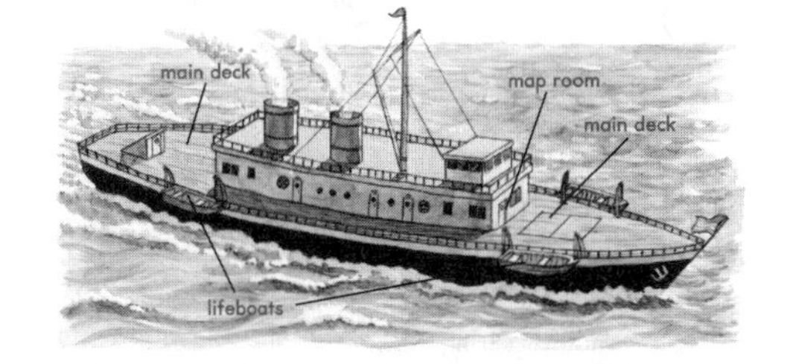

D Number your paper from 1 through 27.

Use these names to answer the questions:
Tyrannosaurus, Triceratops.

1. What is animal A? Triceratops
2. What is animal B? Tyrannosauraus

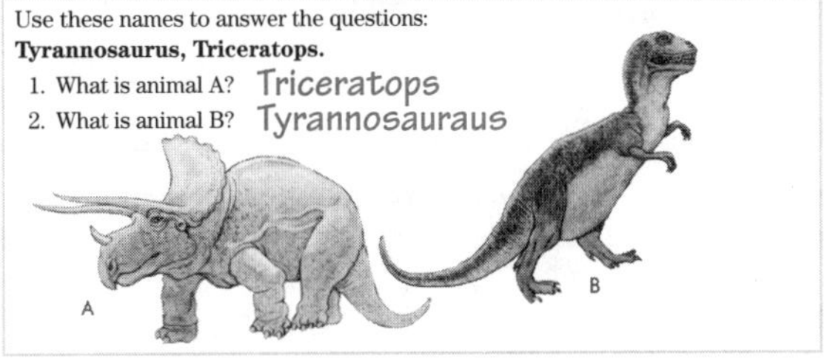

TEXTBOOK

Skill Items 3. She actually repeated that careless mistake.

Use the words in the box to write a complete sentence.

immediately	restless	repeated	actually	moaned
attracted	careless	ordinary	gently	

3. She ▬ ▬ that ▬ mistake.
4. The smell ▬ flies ▬.

4. The smell attracted flies immediately.

Review Items

Look at the map.

5. What's the name of the place shown by the letter C? North Pole
6. Which letter shows the coldest place? C
7. Which letter shows the hottest place? F
8. Which letter is farthest from the equator? C

9. During which season do ice floes start? spring
10. During winter in Alaska, you can walk far out on the ocean. Tell why. Idea: The ocean is frozen solid.
11. What kind of boats do Eskimos use in the summer? kayak
12. Why don't they use those boats in the winter? Ideas: because the water is frozen; because of the ice floes; because the winds are too strong

TEXTBOOK

13. Which letter shows the part of the earth that receives more heat from the sun than any other part? M
14. Which letter shows the part of the earth that receives less heat from the sun than any other part? P

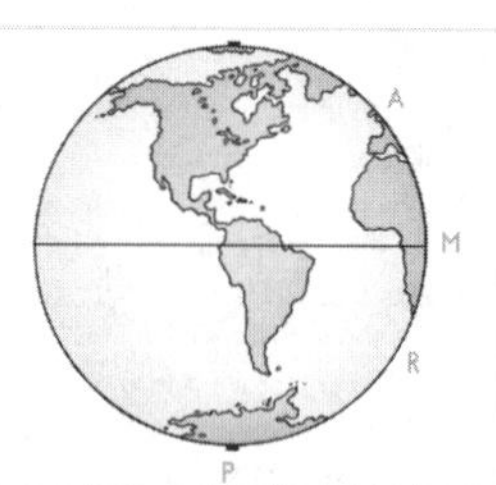

15. Which came **earlier** on Earth, dinosaurs or horses? dinosaurs
16. Which came **earlier** on Earth, strange sea animals or dinosaurs?

17. Write the letter of the layer that went into the pile **first.** A
18. Write the letter of the layer that went into the pile **next.** B
19. Write the letter of the layer that went into the pile **last.** D
20. Which layer went into the pile **earlier,** B or D? B
21. Which layer went into the pile **earlier,** A or D? A
22. Write the letter of the layer where we would find the skeletons of humans. D
23. Write the letter of the layer that has dinosaur skeletons. C
24. Write the letter of the layer where we would find the skeletons of horses. D
25. Write the letter of the layer we live on. D
26. What's the name of layer C? Mesozoic

Layer D
Layer C
Layer B
Layer A

27. What kind of animals lived in the Mesozoic? dinosaurs

 16. strange sea animals

WORKBOOK

25

Name ____________

A Story Items

1. How old was Edna Parker? 13
2. How did Edna usually feel on the ship?
   - happy
   - bored
   - nervous
3. As the girls left the map room, Captain Parker told them to stay away from the sides of the ship and the lifeboats.
4. Why didn't the girls stay in the galley?
   - The cook complained about his tooth.
   - It was dirty.
   - It smelled bad.
5. The girls didn't stay in the engine room because the engineer told them that they would have to ▬.
   - go to the galley
   - work
   - sing
6. The girls decided not to climb the ▬.
   - stairs
   - mast
   - flag pole
7. Did any of the crew members play with Edna and Carla? no
8. Carla wanted to pretend that they were ▬.
   - on an island
   - on their own ship
   - on top of a mountain
9. Which girl wanted to play in the lifeboat? Carla
10. How many crew members were watching while Edna and Carla talked about playing in the lifeboat? none

WORKBOOK

Story Items

After Edna and Carla left the map room, they went to different places on the ship.

11. Write the letter that shows where they went just after they left the map room. A
12. Write the letter that shows where they went next. C
13. Write the letter that shows where they sat down in the sun. D

Review Items

14. How many Great Lakes are there? five (5)
15. Color the Great Lakes on the map.

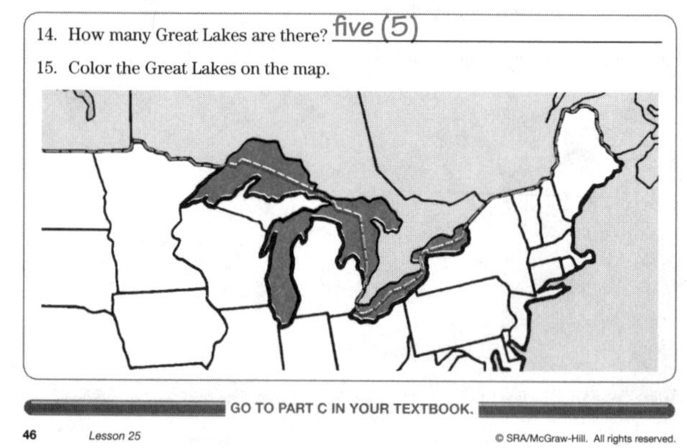

GO TO PART C IN YOUR TEXTBOOK.

TEXTBOOK

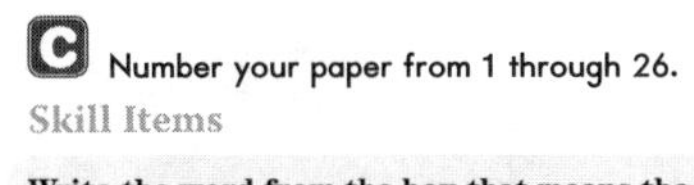

C Number your paper from 1 through 26.

Skill Items

Write the word from the box that means the same thing as the underlined part of each sentence.

they'd	spices	center	leaning
we'd	discovered	throne	hay

1. They put the table in the <u>middle</u> of the room. center
2. The horses came running to get some <u>dried grass</u>. hay
3. <u>We would</u> rather play a game. we'd

Review Items

Use these names to answer the questions: **Tyrannosaurus, Triceratops.**

4. What is animal K?
5. What is animal L?

4. Tyrannosauraus
5. Triceratops

6. Captain Parker's ship passed through a place where hundreds of ships have sunk or been lost. Name that place. Bermuda Triangle
7. Write the letters of the 3 things you find in the Bermuda Triangle. b, c, d
   - a. streams
   - b. sudden storms
   - c. huge waves
   - d. whirlpools
   - e. ice floes
   - f. mountains
8. When geese learn to fly, do they start in the water or on the land? on land
9. They run with their ▬ out to the side. wings

TEXTBOOK

10. What's the name of the line that goes around the fattest part of the earth? equator
11. What's the name of the spot that's at the top of the earth? North Pole
12. What's the name of the spot that's at the bottom of the earth? South Pole

Choose from these words to answer each item:
- moon
- Florida
- sun
- equator
- geese
- poles
- Canada
- migration

13. The heat that the earth receives comes from the ▬. sun
14. The part of the earth that receives more heat than any other part is the ▬. equator
15. The parts of the earth that receive less heat than any other part are called the ▬. poles
16. Write the letters of the 2 kinds of places that are safe for geese. c, d
   - a. places with a few geese
   - b. places with a few ducks
   - c. places with many geese
   - d. places with no geese or ducks

Write the name of each numbered object in the picture. Choose from these names:
- kayak
- spear
- Eskimo
- fishing pole
- sled
- sled dogs

17. sled dogs
18. sled
19. fishing pole
20. spear
21. Eskimo
22. kayak

23. Do ice floes make noise in the winter? yes
24. Why do ice floes make noise in the spring?
25. In which direction will you drift when you're in an ocean current?
26. In which direction will you drift when you're in a strong wind? Idea: with the wind

24. Idea: because the ice is breaking up
25. Idea: in the same direction as the current

WORKBOOK

26

Name ______________________

A **Story Items**

1. When today's story began, Edna and Carla were pretending they had their own ship. Who was the captain? Carla
2. **Underline** 3 things the first mate did to look more like a sailor.
   - <u>took off her shoes</u>
   - wore short pants
   - wore a sailor suit
   - <u>rolled up her pants</u>
   - <u>wrapped a handkerchief around her head</u>
3. What happened to the lifeboat when the girls were in it?
   - <u>It dropped into the water.</u>
   - It turned over.
   - It rang a bell.
4. What part of the lifeboat hit the water first, the bow or the stern? bow
5. What happened to Edna when the boat hit the water?
   - She fell out of the boat.
   - <u>She bumped into Carla.</u>
   - She hit her head.
6. What 2 things did the girls do to make the people on the large ship notice them? Ideas: waved (their arms) and yelled
7. Did anyone notice them? no
8. When Edna and Carla turned around, they saw one of these clouds. Write the letter of that cloud. B

WORKBOOK

9. When the girls started bailing, there was about 5 inches of water in the boat.
10. What made the girls stop bailing?
    - a whirlpool
    - <u>a wind</u>
    - an airplane
11. At the end of the story, how high were the waves? 20 feet high
12. How fast were the winds moving? 40 miles per hour

Review Items

13. In which direction do geese migrate in the fall? south
14. In which direction do geese migrate in the spring? north
15. Write the directions **north, south, east** and **west** in the boxes.
16. Make a line that starts at the circle on the map and goes north.
17. If you start at the circle and move to the number **2,** in which direction do you go? east

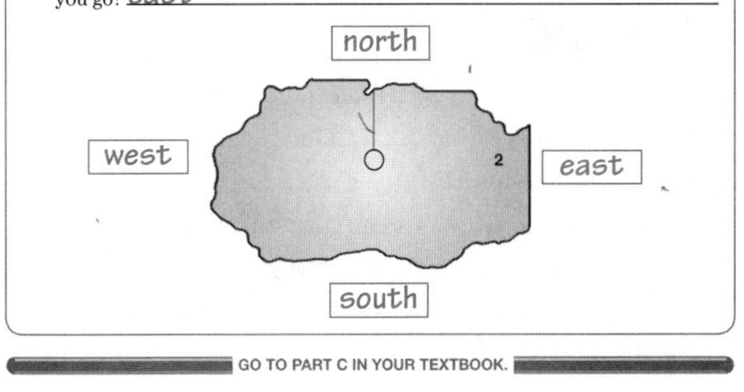

GO TO PART C IN YOUR TEXTBOOK.

TEXTBOOK

waved their arms. They continued to wave as the large ship became smaller, smaller, smaller. Then the girls stopped waving and continued to watch the large ship. Now it was only a dot on the glassy water.

Suddenly, as the girls watched the dot, a very cool breeze hit them from behind. The air suddenly had a different smell. The wind roughed up the surface of the water.

Edna turned around and looked up. Behind the lifeboat was a great storm cloud. It rose up and up. "Oh no," Edna said. Then her mind started to work fast. "Let's start bailing water out of this boat. We're in for a storm."

When the girls started bailing, there was about 5 inches of water in the bottom of the boat. The girls bailed and bailed. The waves got bigger and bigger. Now there was only about 3 inches of water in the boat, but the waves hitting the boat were very big and they were starting to splash over the side. The girls bailed and bailed and the waves splashed and splashed. Now there was about 4 inches of water in the boat.

The girls had to stop bailing when a terrible wind hit the boat. The waves were so large that Edna had to hang on to the side of the boat. She just kept hanging on and hoping that the storm would stop. But the waves were now over 20 feet high and the winds were moving forty miles per hour. The boat was going up and down the waves.

C Number your paper from 1 through 19.

Here are three events that happened in the story.
Write **beginning, middle** or **end** for each event.

1. The girls had to stop bailing when a terrible wind hit the boat. end
2. The ropes were making a howling sound as they ran through the wheels that had been holding the lifeboat. middle
3. Carla pretended to take out her spyglass and look around. beginning

Review Items

4. In which direction do geese fly in the fall? south
5. What is this trip called? migration
6. Geese live in large groups called ■. flocks

TEXTBOOK

7. Where are most wild geese born? Canada

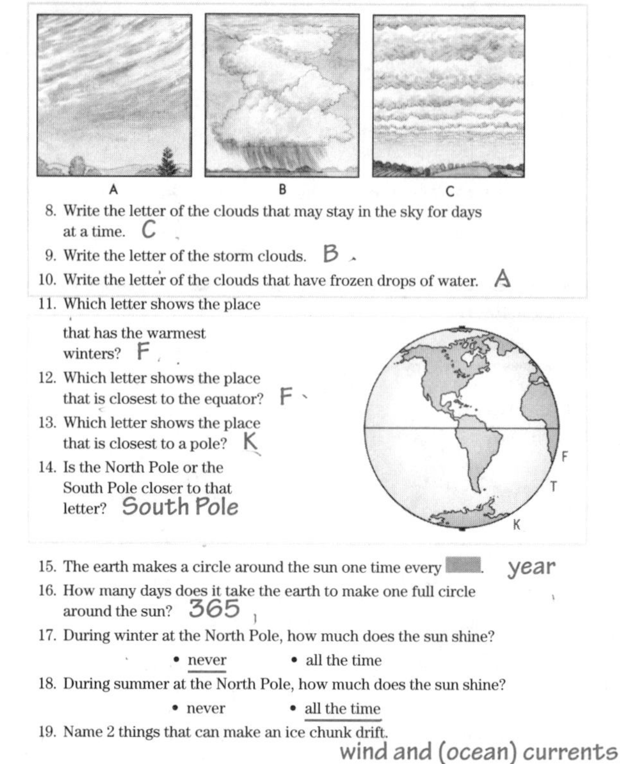

8. Write the letter of the clouds that may stay in the sky for days at a time. C
9. Write the letter of the storm clouds. B
10. Write the letter of the clouds that have frozen drops of water. A
11. Which letter shows the place that has the warmest winters? F
12. Which letter shows the place that is closest to the equator? F
13. Which letter shows the place that is closest to a pole? K
14. Is the North Pole or the South Pole closer to that letter? South Pole
15. The earth makes a circle around the sun one time every ■. year
16. How many days does it take the earth to make one full circle around the sun? 365
17. During winter at the North Pole, how much does the sun shine?
    - never
    - all the time
18. During summer at the North Pole, how much does the sun shine?
    - never
    - all the time
19. Name 2 things that can make an ice chunk drift. wind and (ocean) currents

WORKBOOK

Name ____________________

A

1. Whirlpools are made up of moving water.
2. A whirlpool is shaped like a funnel.
3. What happens to something that gets caught in a whirlpool? Idea: It goes around and around as it moves down.
4. What happened to the lifeboat when the girls got in it? Idea: It dropped into the water.
5. When today's story began, Carla shouted that she saw land. What did she really see? a (huge) wave
6. When could Edna see in the distance?
    - at the top of a wave
    - at the bottom of a wave
7. After the giant wave hit, the boat was being sucked into a (giant) whirlpool.
8. Some things happened so fast that Carla and Edna had to try to figure out what they were. What two things did Edna remember? the flash and the splash
9. What made the blinding flash? lightning
10. What fell from the sky? hailstones; hail
11. Did the boat land near the whirlpool? ~~no~~ yes
12. How did Edna feel when the sea was calm again? Ideas: sick; dizzy
13. About how deep was the water when Edna stepped out of the lifeboat? 1 meter
14. About how far was it from the lifeboat to the beach? half a mile

WORKBOOK

Review Items

15. Write **north, south, east** and **west** in the correct boxes.
16. In which direction is ocean current **P** moving? north
17. In which direction is ocean current **Q** moving? west
18. Which direction is the wind coming from? west
19. Make an arrow next to ice chunk **R** to show the direction the current will move the ice chunk.
20. Make an arrow above ice chunk **S** to show the direction the current will move the ice chunk.

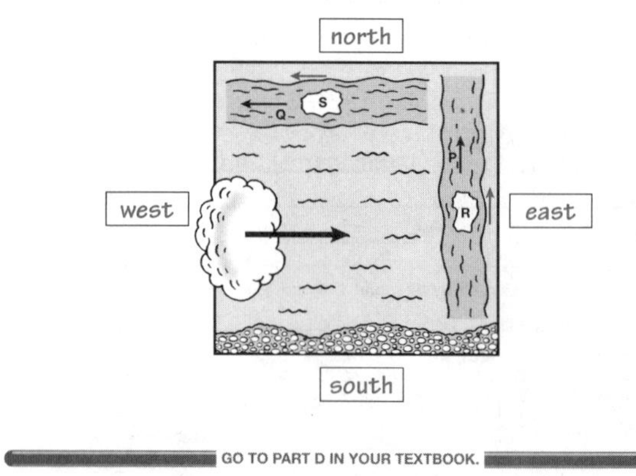

GO TO PART D IN YOUR TEXTBOOK.

TEXTBOOK

D Number your paper from 1 through 18.

Skill Items

Write the word from the box that means the same thing as the underlined part of each sentence.

hooves	tame	modern	tusks
charging	English	ancient	

1. We visited the very, very old city. ancient
2. My pet goat is not wild. tame
3. The hunters wanted the elephant's large, curved teeth. tusks
4. We visited a very new city. modern

Review Items

The rim of the volcano exploded.

5. What word means **made a bang and flew apart?** exploded
6. What word means **a mountain formed from hot flowing rock?** volcano
7. What word means **the top edge** of the volcano? rim

8. The earth is shaped like a ▬. ball
9. The ▬s are the coldest places on the earth and the ▬ is the hottest place on the earth. pole, equator

10. At which letter would the winters be very, very cold? C
11. At which letter would the winters be very, very hot? F

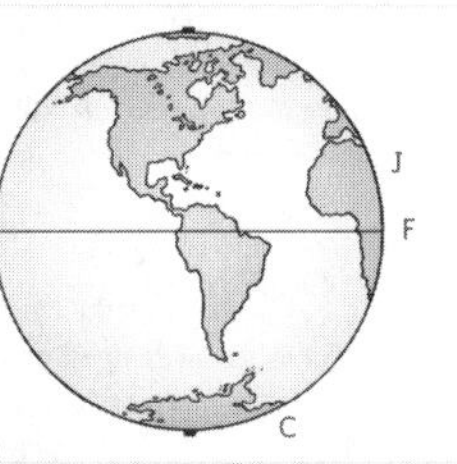

TEXTBOOK

12. Write the letter of the earth that has the North Pole tilting away from the sun. A
13. Write the letter of the earth that has the North Pole tilting toward the sun. C
14. Write the letter of the earth that has darkness all around the North Pole. A
15. Write the letter of the earth that has daylight all around the North Pole. C
16. Write **A, B, C** and **D.** Then write the season each earth in the picture shows.

A: winter
B: spring
C: summer
D: fall

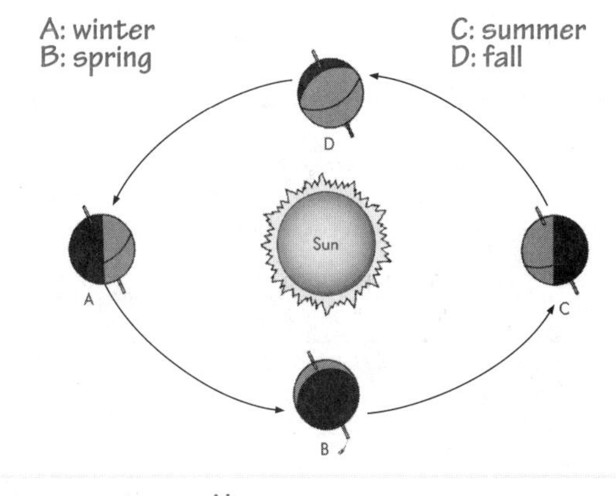

17. Are killer whales fish? No
18. Tell if killer whales are **warm-blooded** or **cold-blooded.** warm-blooded

WORKBOOK

28

Name ____________________

A

Story Items

1. After the giant wave hit the boat in the last story, what was the boat being sucked into? a whirlpool
2. Some things happened so fast that Carla and Edna had to try to figure out what they were. What made the blinding flash? lightning
3. What fell from the sky? hailstones; hail
4. About how far was it from the lifeboat to the beach? half a mile
5. What was right behind the beach? jungle
6. What was strange about the sand on the beach? Idea: It was red.
7. Edna and Carla woke up when it was dark. What woke them up? Idea: noise
8. The animal Edna saw was as big as some of the trees
9. Did the animal walk on **4 legs** or **2 legs?** 2 legs
10. Where did the girls go to spend the last part of the night? Idea: under the lifeboat
11. Did the girls get much sleep? no
12. What was the first thing the girls discovered in the red sand? footprints
13. The footprints were ▬ long.
    - a foot
    - a yard
    - half a meter

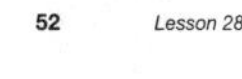

WORKBOOK

Review Items

14. Write the letter of the earth that shows the person in daytime. A
15. Write the letter of the earth that shows the person 6 hours later. B
16. Write the letter that shows the person another 6 hours later. C
17. Write the letter that shows the person another 6 hours later. D

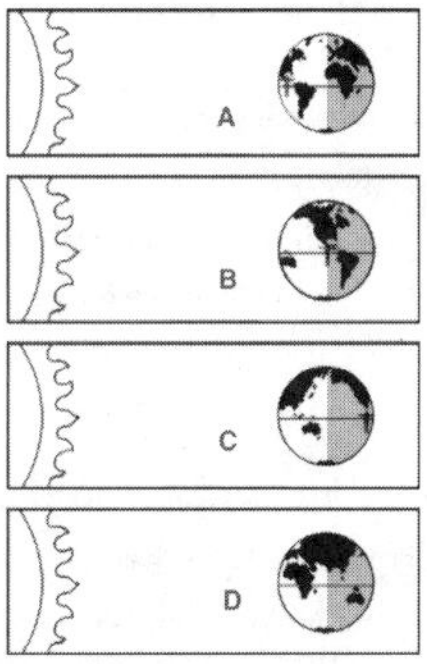

18. Which letter on the map shows Alaska? J
19. Which letter shows Canada? F
20. Which letter shows the main part of the United States? R
21. Which 2 letters show where Eskimos live? J and F
22. How warm is it during winter in Alaska? very cold

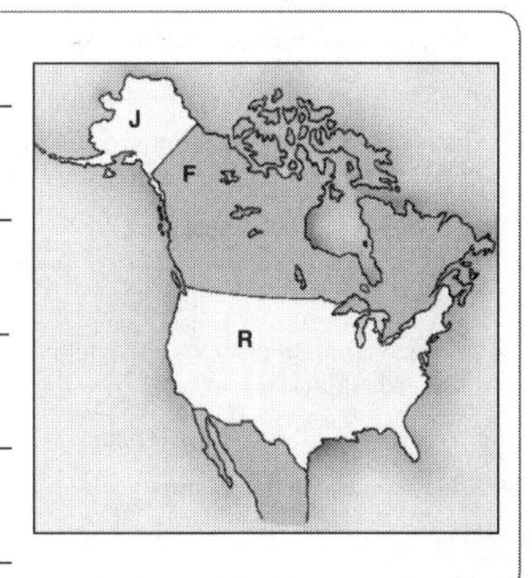

GO TO PART C IN YOUR TEXTBOOK.

TEXTBOOK

her foot and made a noise. Edna sat up so suddenly that she hit her head on the inside of the lifeboat.

That was the longest night that Edna remembered. She kept waiting for the sky to become light. She wasn't sure which part would become light first, because she didn't know where east was. The first part to get light was over the jungle. Then it seemed that a year passed before it was light enough to see the ocean clearly. The sun was not up yet, but the birds were squawking and screaming in the jungle.

At last, Edna and Carla crawled out from under the lifeboat. The first thing they did was walk to where they had seen the outline of the huge animal. As soon as they got close to the spot, they saw the animal's huge footprints in the red sand.

When Edna looked at the footprints, she knew that there was an animal on this island that looked like no other living animal anyone had ever seen. It left footprints that were a yard long!

C Number your paper from 1 through 22.

Skill Items

Write the word from the box that means the same thing as the underlined part of each sentence.

speech	excited	screech	box
certain	armor	pouch	surface

1. She put her keys in the small bag. pouch
2. The sharp sound of the peacock startled me. screech
3. I am sure about the answer to the question. certain

Use the words in the box to write complete sentences.

volcano	practiced	attracted	exploded
sense	immediately	strangely	

4. The smell ▬ flies ▬. attracted, immediately
5. The rim of the ▬ ▬. volcano, exploded

TEXTBOOK

11. (Any 3): fish, sharks, reptiles, snakes, etc.

Review Items

6. What season is it at the North Pole when the North Pole tilts toward the sun? summer
7. What season is it at the North Pole when the North Pole tilts away from the sun? winter
8. Female animals fight in the spring to protect ▬. their babies
9. Name 2 kinds of Alaskan animals that are dangerous in the spring. Ideas: polar bears, wolves, walruses
10. Name 3 animals that are warm-blooded. (Any 3): bears, humans, dogs, cats, etc.
11. Name 3 animals that are cold-blooded.

12. What are clouds made of?
13. What kind of cloud does the picture show? storm cloud
14. What happens to a drop of water at **B**? Idea: It freezes.

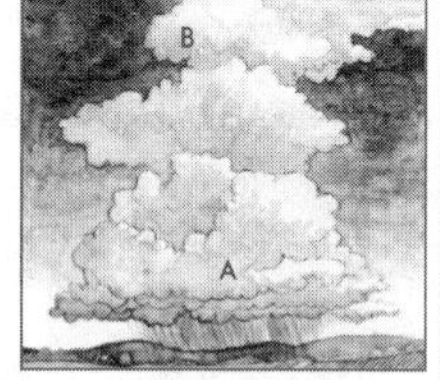

15. Which object went into the pile **first?** shoe
16. Which object went into the pile **last?** rock
17. Which object went into the pile **earlier,** the cup or the book? book
18. Which object went into the pile **earlier,** the bone or the book? book
19. Which object went into the pile **just after** the pencil? knife
20. Which object went into the pile **just after** the bone? cup
21. Whirlpools are made up of moving ▬. water
22. A whirlpool is shaped like a ▬. funnel

12. tiny drops of water

WORKBOOK

29

Name ____________

A Story Items

1. What was strange about the sand on the beach where Edna and Carla landed? Ideas: It was red; it had big footprints.
2. The footprints of the animal were a yard long.
3. How many toes did each footprint have? 3
4. What did the size of the footprints tell about the size of the animal?
   - It was bigger than a bear.
   - It was a bear.
   - It was smaller than a bear.
5. How did Edna know that the animal was very heavy?
   - The footprints were long.
   - The footprints made deep dents.
   - The footprints had 3 toes.
6. What part of the animal made the deep groove between the footprints? tail
7. Edna wasn't sure if she wanted to follow the animal. **Underline** 2 things that tell what the parts of her mind wanted to do.
   - read about dinosaurs
   - run
   - think
   - learn more about the animal
   - find something to eat
8. Edna saw something next to the path that she recognized from a picture in a book. What did she see?
   - a stream
   - a tree
   - a bug
9. What else was in that picture?
   - dinosaurs
   - ships
   - rocks
10. How did that make her feel? Idea: afraid

WORKBOOK

11. Write the letter of the footprint made by the heaviest animal. B
12. Write the letter of the footprint made by the lightest animal. C

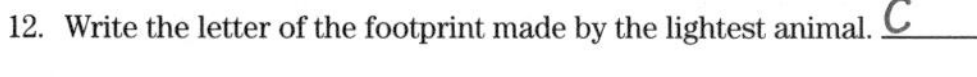

The picture shows marks left by an animal.

13. Make an arrow from dot **A** to show the direction the animal is moving.
14. Write the letter of the part that shows a footprint. T
15. Write the letter of the part that shows the mark left by the animal's tail. J

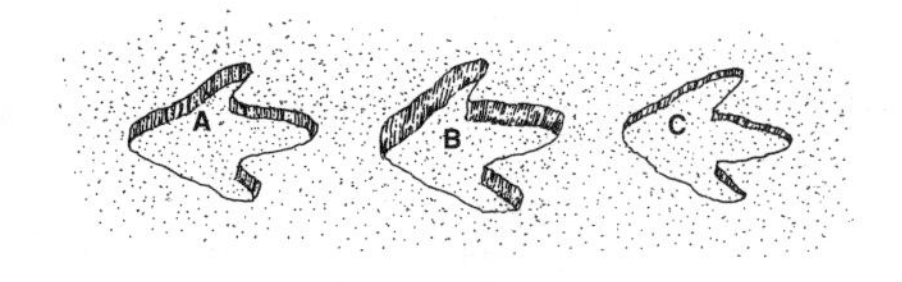
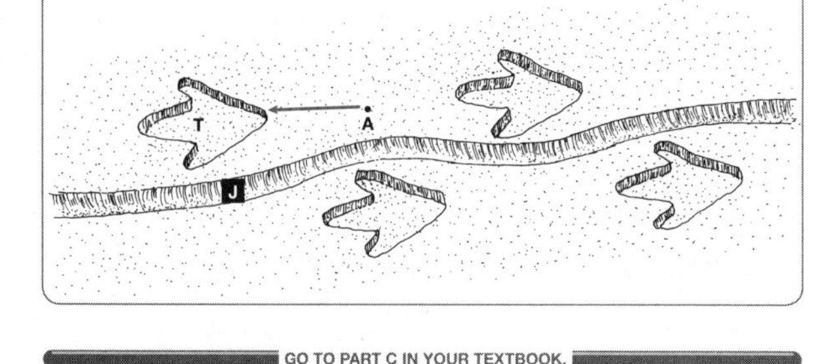

GO TO PART C IN YOUR TEXTBOOK.

TEXTBOOK

C Number your paper from 1 through 23.

Review Items

1. When days get longer, is the North Pole tilting toward the sun or away from the sun? toward the sun
2. When days get shorter, is the North Pole tilting toward the sun or away from the sun? away from the sun
3. In April, the sun shines for more than ▬ hours each day in Alaska. 12

4. Which globe shows how the earth looks on the first day of winter? R
5. Which globe shows how the earth looks on the first day of summer? K

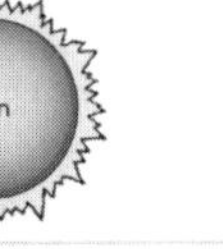

Use these names to answer the questions:
Tyrannosaurus, Triceratops.

6. What is animal X? Triceratops
7. What is animal Y? Tyrannosaurus

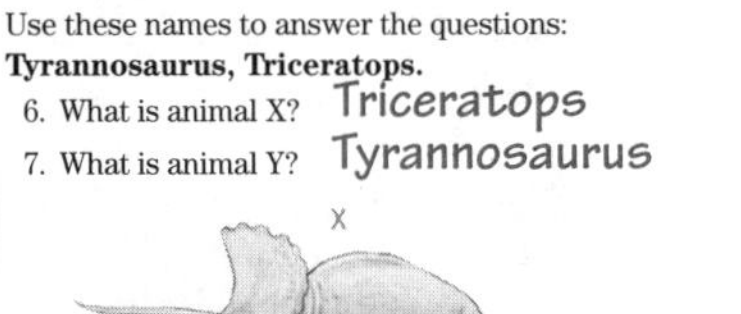

TEXTBOOK

8. Which came **earlier** on Earth, dinosaurs or horses? dinosaurs
9. Which came **earlier** on Earth, strange sea animals or dinosaurs? strange sea animals

10. Write the letter of the layer that went into the pile **first.** A
11. Write the letter of the layer that went into the pile **next.** B
12. Write the letter of the layer that went into the pile **last.** D
13. Which layer went into the pile **earlier,** B or C? B
14. Which layer went into the pile **earlier,** A or C? A
15. Write the letter of the layer where we would find the skeletons of humans. D
16. Write the letter of the layer that has dinosaur skeletons. C
17. Write the letter of the layer where we would find the skeletons of horses. D
18. Write the letter of the layer we live on. D
19. What's the name of layer C? Mesozoic

20. What kind of animals lived in the Mesozoic? dinosaurs
21. Captain Parker's ship passed through a place where hundreds of ships have sunk or been lost. Name that place.
22. Write the letters of the 3 things you find in the Bermuda Triangle. c, d, f

a. streams	d. sudden storms
b. ice floes	e. mountains
c. huge waves	f. whirlpools

23. What happens to something that gets caught in a whirlpool? Idea: It goes around and around as it moves down.

21. Bermuda Triangle

TEXTBOOK

30 TEST 30

1. tiny drops of water

Number your paper from 1 through 36.

1. What are clouds made of?
2. What kind of cloud does the picture show? storm cloud
3. What happens to a drop of water at **B**? Idea: It freezes.

4. The picture shows half a hailstone. How many times did the stone go through a cloud? 6

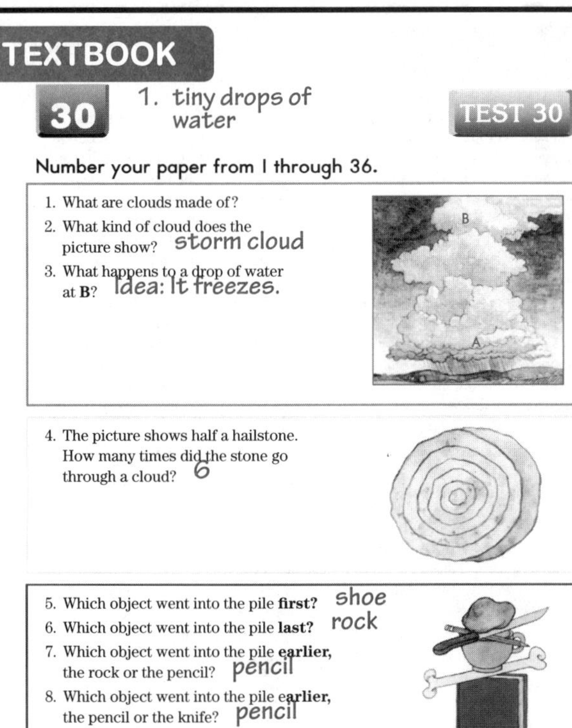

5. Which object went into the pile **first?** shoe
6. Which object went into the pile **last?** rock
7. Which object went into the pile **earlier,** the rock or the pencil? pencil
8. Which object went into the pile **earlier,** the pencil or the knife? pencil
9. Which object went into the pile **just after** the knife? rock
10. Which object went into the pile **just after** the rock? nothing

11. Things closer to the bottom of the pile went into the pile ▬. earlier
12. Which came **earlier** on Earth, dinosaurs or horses? dinosaurs

TEXTBOOK

13. Which came **earlier** on Earth, strange sea animals or dinosaurs? strange sea animals

14. Write the letter of the layer that went into the pile **first.** A
15. Write the letter of the layer that went into the pile **next.** B
16. Write the letter of the layer that went into the pile **last.** D
17. Which layer went into the pile **earlier,** B or A? A
18. Which layer went into the pile **earlier,** A or C? A
19. Write the letter of the layer where we would find the skeletons of humans. D
20. Write the letter of the layer that has dinosaur skeletons. C
21. Write the letter of the layer where we would find the skeletons of horses. D
22. Write the letter of the layer we live on. D
23. What's the name of layer C? Mesozoic

24. What kind of animals lived in the Mesozoic? dinosaurs

Use these names to answer the questions:
Tyrannosaurus, Triceratops.

25. What is animal F? Tyrannosaurus
26. What is animal G? Triceratops

TEXTBOOK

27. Write the letters of the things you find in the Bermuda Triangle. c, e, f
    - a. ice floes
    - b. mountains
    - c. whirlpools
    - d. streams
    - e. huge waves
    - f. sudden storms
28. Whirlpools are made up of moving ▬. water
29. A whirlpool is shaped like a ▬. funnel
30. What happens to something that gets caught in a whirlpool?

31. Write the letter of the footprint made by the heaviest animal. K
32. Write the letter of the footprint made by the lightest animal. J

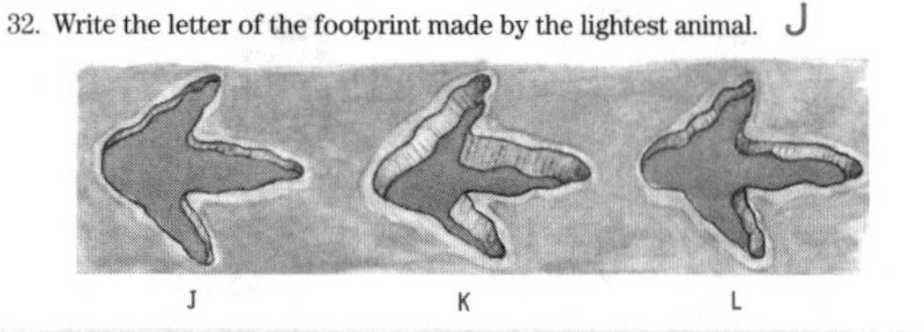

Skill Items

For each item, write the underlined word or words from the sentences in the box.

The smell attracted flies immediately.
The rim of the volcano exploded.

33. Which underlined word refers to a mountain formed from hot flowing rock? volcano
34. Which underlined word means **right now?** immediately
35. Which underlined word means the **top edge?** rim
36. Which underlined word means **made a bang and flew apart?** exploded

END OF TEST 3

30. Idea: It goes around and around as it moves down.

WORKBOOK

Name 9. Ideas: the bird-like animal; the flying dinosaur

31

A Story Items

1. Edna and Carla saw a winged animal. Was that animal a bird? no
2. How do you know?
   - It had teeth.
   - It didn't have a beak.
   - It didn't have feathers.
3. Its wings were covered with something that looked like ▬.
   - feathers
   - leather
   - hair
4. How long ago did those winged animals live on Earth?
   - a thousand years ago
   - a million years ago
   - a hundred million years ago
5. **Underline** the name of the dinosaur the girls saw.
   - Triceratops
   - Mammoth
   - Tyrannosaurus
6. What cracked the tree that Edna was hiding behind?
   - Tyrannosaurus's head
   - Tyrannosaurus's foot
   - Tyrannosaurus's tail
7. What happened to Edna when the tree cracked? Idea: She went flying.
8. Before Edna started to run, she heard noises from the clearing. What made the leathery flapping sound?
   - Tyrannosaurus
   - the flying dinosaur
   - Carla
9. Whose bones were making the crunching sound?
10. Tyrannosaurus didn't hear Edna running because it was ▬.
    - sleeping
    - eating
    - scratching
11. As Edna ran through the jungle toward the beach, what did she see on the path? a snake
12. Did Edna slow down when she saw it? no
13. When Edna got to the beach, she realized that something was wrong. What was wrong? Ideas: Carla was not with her; she forgot (about) Carla.

WORKBOOK

Review Items

14. Write **north, south, east** and **west** in the correct boxes.
15. In which direction is ocean current **F** moving? west
16. In which direction is ocean current **G** moving? north
17. Which direction is the wind coming from? west
18. Make an arrow above ice chunk **H** to show the direction the current will move the ice chunk.
19. Make an arrow above ice chunk **I** to show the direction the current will move the ice chunk.

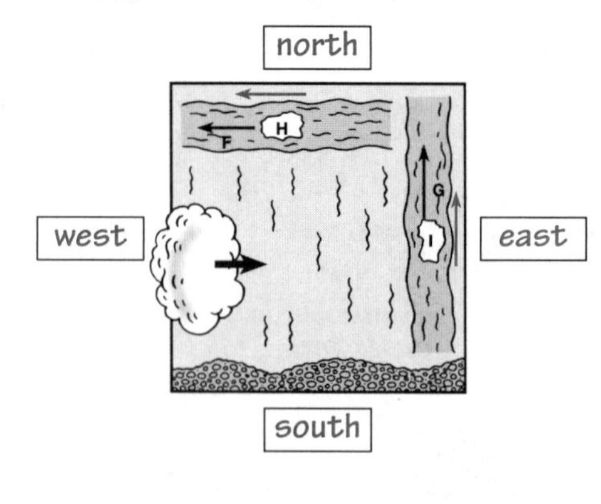

GO TO PART C IN YOUR TEXTBOOK.

TEXTBOOK

great leap she jumped over the snake and kept on running. When the girls had gone into the jungle, the path had seemed long. Now it seemed longer. It seemed as if it would never end. "Run," she said out loud between her breaths. "Run. Run."

Edna ran until she could see the beach ahead of her. Then her mind slowly began to work again. She stopped and turned around. There was nothing on the path behind her. Good. Good. Tyrannosaurus was making so much noise eating that flying animal that it couldn't hear Edna. Besides, Tyrannosaurus already had a meal. What would it want with a tiny animal like Edna? Edna wouldn't be much more than a mouthful for the monster. Edna was thinking now. She walked out onto the red sand of the beach.

She was out of breath. Now she began to realize how frightened she had been. She had been so frightened that she forgot about everything. She forgot about being careful. Suddenly, Edna turned all the way around. She had forgotten about Carla. Where was Carla?

Edna looked in all directions, but she couldn't see Carla.

C Number your paper from 1 through 20.

Skill Items

Here are three events that happened in the story.
Write **beginning, middle** or **end** for each event.

1. Edna went flying into the soft plants that covered the floor of the jungle. middle
2. A huge bird-like animal sailed down from above the jungle. beginning
3. She had been so frightened that she forgot about everything. end

Story Items

4. Write the letter of the footprint made by the lightest animal. E
5. Write the letter of the footprint made by the heaviest animal. D

C D E

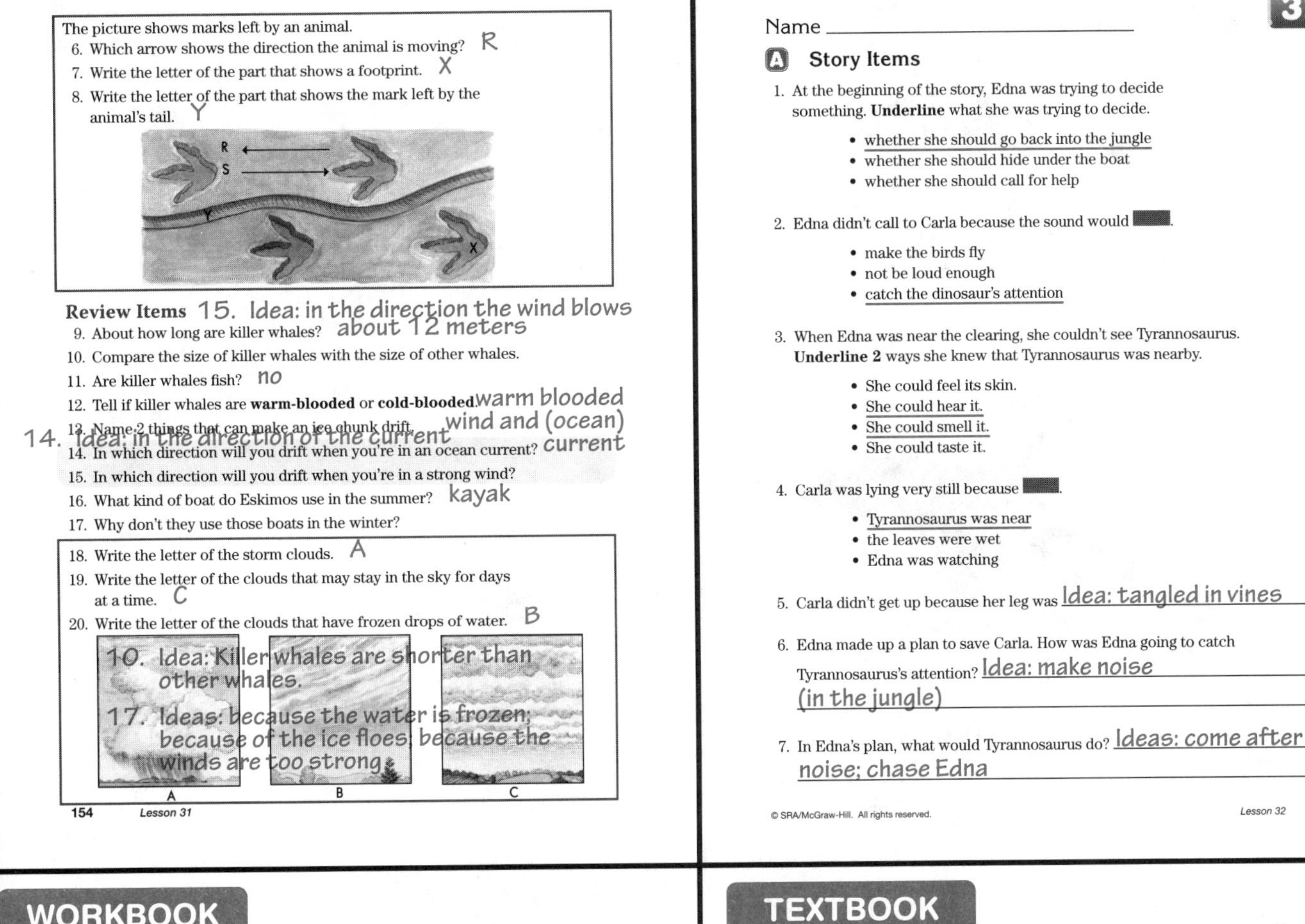

TEXTBOOK

The picture shows marks left by an animal.

6. Which arrow shows the direction the animal is moving? R
7. Write the letter of the part that shows a footprint. X
8. Write the letter of the part that shows the mark left by the animal's tail. Y

Review Items 15. Idea: in the direction the wind blows

9. About how long are killer whales? about 12 meters
10. Compare the size of killer whales with the size of other whales.
11. Are killer whales fish? no
12. Tell if killer whales are **warm-blooded** or **cold-blooded**. warm blooded
13. Name 2 things that can make an ice chunk drift. wind and (ocean) current
14. In which direction will you drift when you're in an ocean current? 14. Idea: in the direction of the current
15. In which direction will you drift when you're in a strong wind?
16. What kind of boat do Eskimos use in the summer? kayak
17. Why don't they use those boats in the winter?
18. Write the letter of the storm clouds. A
19. Write the letter of the clouds that may stay in the sky for days at a time. C
20. Write the letter of the clouds that have frozen drops of water. B

10. Idea: Killer whales are shorter than other whales.

17. Ideas: because the water is frozen; because of the ice floes; because the winds are too strong

WORKBOOK

Name ____________

A Story Items

1. At the beginning of the story, Edna was trying to decide something. **Underline** what she was trying to decide.
   - whether she should go back into the jungle
   - whether she should hide under the boat
   - whether she should call for help
2. Edna didn't call to Carla because the sound would ____.
   - make the birds fly
   - not be loud enough
   - catch the dinosaur's attention
3. When Edna was near the clearing, she couldn't see Tyrannosaurus. **Underline 2** ways she knew that Tyrannosaurus was nearby.
   - She could feel its skin.
   - She could hear it.
   - She could smell it.
   - She could taste it.
4. Carla was lying very still because ____.
   - Tyrannosaurus was near
   - the leaves were wet
   - Edna was watching
5. Carla didn't get up because her leg was Idea: tangled in vines.
6. Edna made up a plan to save Carla. How was Edna going to catch Tyrannosaurus's attention? Idea: make noise (in the jungle)
7. In Edna's plan, what would Tyrannosaurus do? Ideas: come after noise; chase Edna

WORKBOOK

8. What would Carla do? Ideas: free her leg; run to safety
9. Did Edna get to try her plan? no
10. What came into the clearing when Tyrannosaurus was moving back and forth? (3) Triceratops
11. What were Edna and Carla trying to do at the end of the story? Idea: get Carla's leg free

Review Items

12. What kind of boat do Eskimos use in the summer? kayak
13. Why don't they use those boats in the winter? Ideas: because the water is frozen; because of the ice floes; because the winds are too strong
14. During which season do ice floes start? spring
15. During winter in Alaska, you can walk far out on the ocean. Tell why. Idea: because the ocean is frozen solid
16. Do ice floes make noise in the winter? yes
17. Why do ice floes make noise in the spring? Idea: because the ice floes are breaking apart

GO TO PART C IN YOUR TEXTBOOK.

TEXTBOOK

C Number your paper from 1 through 22.

Skill Items

Write the word from the box that means the same thing as the underlined part of each sentence.

armor	gulped	shabby	docked
graph	mast	bailed	boots

1. He quickly swallowed the milk. gulped
2. She got some new mukluks. boots
3. The animal's hard covering protects it from enemies. armor

The new exhibit displayed mysterious fish.

4. What word describes things we don't understand? mysterious
5. What word means **an arrangement of things for people to look at?** exhibit
6. What word means **showed?** displayed

Review Items

7. How long ago did dinosaurs live on Earth?
   - 30 thousand years ago
   - 1 million years ago
   - 100 million years ago
8. In what season are animals most dangerous in Alaska? spring
9. During what season do female animals in Alaska have babies? spring
10. About how long are killer whales? 12 meters
11. Compare the size of killer whales with the size of other whales. Idea: Killer whales are shorter than other whales.

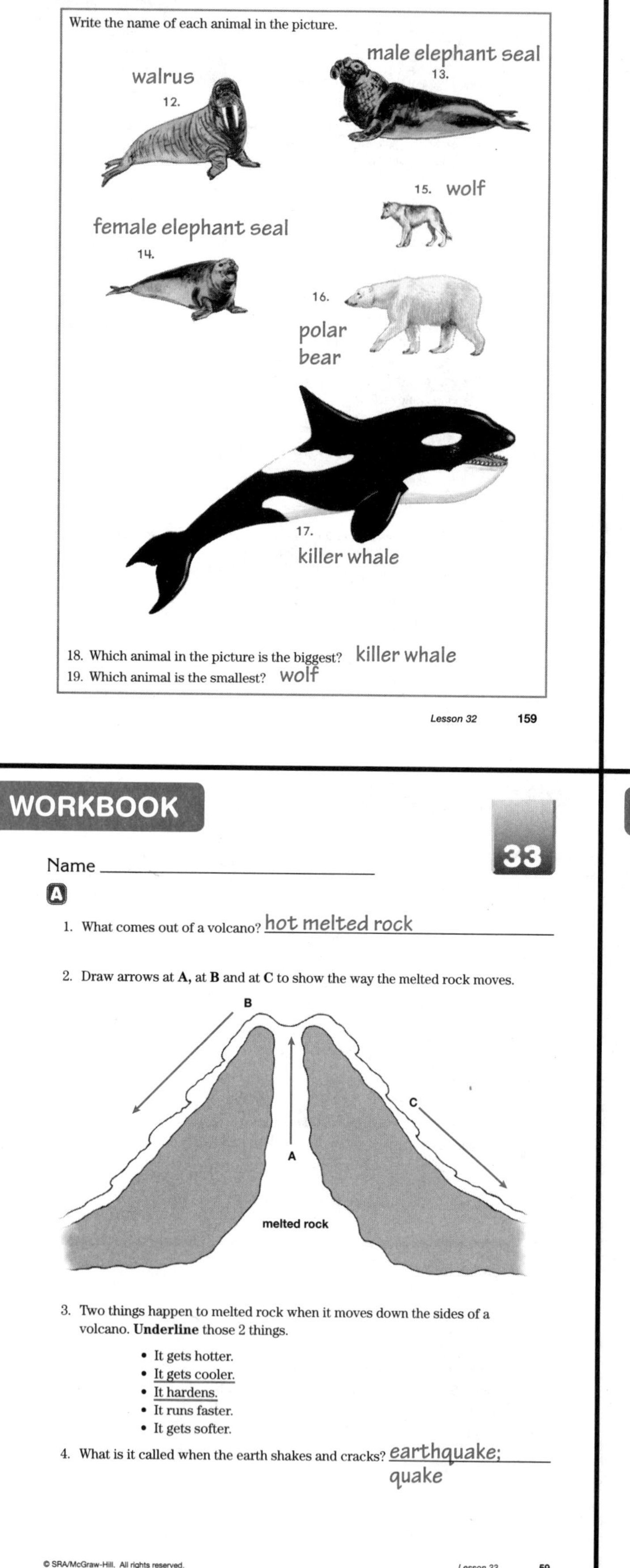

TEXTBOOK

Write the name of each animal in the picture.

18. Which animal in the picture is the biggest? killer whale
19. Which animal is the smallest? wolf

WORKBOOK

33

Name ____________

A

1. What comes out of a volcano? hot melted rock

2. Draw arrows at **A,** at **B** and at **C** to show the way the melted rock moves.

3. Two things happen to melted rock when it moves down the sides of a volcano. **Underline** those 2 things.
   - It gets hotter.
   - It gets cooler.
   - It hardens.
   - It runs faster.
   - It gets softer.

4. What is it called when the earth shakes and cracks? earthquake; quake

TEXTBOOK

20. The map shows a route. What state is at the north end of the route? Alaska
21. What country is at the south end of the route? Canada
22. About how many miles is the route? 2500 (miles)

Kotzebue

Big Trout Lake

Key

0 500 miles

WORKBOOK

B Story Items

5. When Edna was near the clearing in the last story, she couldn't see Tyrannosaurus. **Underline** 2 ways she knew that Tyrannosaurus was nearby.
   - She could taste it.
   - She could hear it.
   - She could feel its skin.
   - She could smell it.

6. What came into the clearing when Tyrannosaurus was moving back and forth? (3) Triceratops

7. At the beginning of today's story, Tyrannosaurus was fighting ____.
   - Triceratops
   - a mammoth
   - a flying dinosaur

8. Who won the fight? (the 3) Triceratops

9. What kept making the earth rock from side to side?
   - earthquakes
   - the volcano
   - the storm

10. What made the boiling cloud of smoke? volcano

11. Why did Edna fall down on the beach? Idea: because the earth kept moving

12. When the girls were in shallow water, what formed underwater? a crack

13. Who fell into the crack? Edna

14. What did the volcano do just after Edna got into the boat? It exploded.

15. Did the girls know where they were going to go at the end of the story? no

GO TO PART D IN YOUR TEXTBOOK.

TEXTBOOK

Edna rubbed her eyes with one hand and looked in the direction of the voice. Carla was sitting in the boat. She helped Edna get into the boat. The sky was so dark now that it was almost like night.

Suddenly, there was a terrible explosion. The explosion had so much force that it seemed to press the air against Edna's face. This pressing feeling came before the sound of the explosion. The sound was like nothing that Edna had ever heard. It was so loud that her ears rang for hours. That explosion had so much force that it knocked down all the trees on the island.

The girls began to row away from the island. "Where are we going to go?" Carla asked.

"I don't know," Edna replied. "I don't know." She did know one thing, however. She knew that she didn't want to be near that island.

D Number your paper from 1 through 25.

Skill Items 1. The rim of the volcano exploded.

Use the words in the box to write complete sentences.

displayed	adventure	exploded	reason
rim	glanced	mysterious	directed

1. The ___ of the volcano ___.
2. The new exhibit ___ ___ fish.

2. The new exhibit displayed mysterious fish.

Review Items

3. What season is it at the North Pole when the North Pole tilts toward the sun? summer
4. What season is it at the North Pole when the North Pole tilts away from the sun? winter
5. In what season are animals most dangerous in Alaska? spring
6. During what season do female animals in Alaska have babies? spring
7. Things closer to the bottom of the pile went into the pile ___. earlier

TEXTBOOK

8. Write the letter of the layer that went into the pile first. A
9. Write the letter of the layer that we live on. D
10. Which layer went into the pile later, A or B? B
11. Write the letter of the layer where we would find the skeletons of humans. D
12. Write the letter of the layer where we find the skeletons of dinosaurs. C
13. Write the letter of the layer where we find the skeletons of horses. D
14. What's the name of layer C? Mesozoic

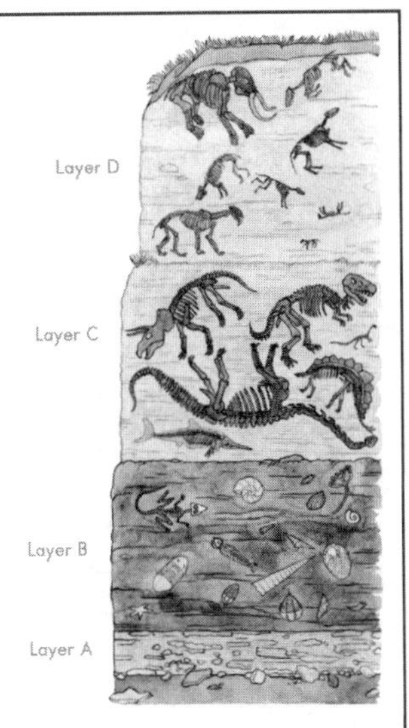

TEXTBOOK

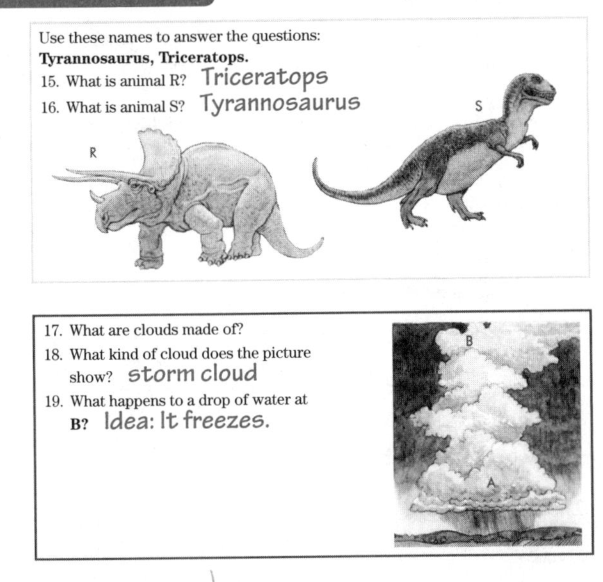

Use these names to answer the questions:
Tyrannosaurus, Triceratops.

15. What is animal R? Triceratops
16. What is animal S? Tyrannosaurus

17. What are clouds made of?
18. What kind of cloud does the picture show? storm cloud
19. What happens to a drop of water at **B**? Idea: It freezes.

20. The picture shows half a hailstone. How many times did the stone go through a cloud? 6

17. tiny drops of water

TEXTBOOK

21. Which letter on the map shows Alaska? E
22. Which letter shows Canada? N
23. Which letter shows the main part of the United States? T
24. Which 2 letters show where Eskimos live? E, N
25. How warm is it during winter in Alaska? Idea: very cold

WORKBOOK

Name ____________________

A Story Items

1. What color was the water where it was shallow? green
2. What color was the water where it was deepest? dark (or deep) blue
3. Edna had blisters on her hands from rowing; the oars.
4. As the girls sat in the lifeboat, they could see a billowing cloud in the distance. What was making that cloud? volcano
5. Name 2 kinds of supplies you'd need to stay on the ocean for a long time. Ideas (any 2): fresh water; food; sun protection
6. In which direction were the girls drifting? west
7. Edna was thirsty. Why didn't she drink some ocean water?
   - It was warm.
   - It was salty
   - It was dirty.
8. What made the boat move faster and faster? whirlpool; currents
9. While the lifeboat was in the whirlpool, why did the clouds seem to be spinning?
   - because of the wind
   - because the boat was spinning
   - because she was sick
10. Did the girls know how they got out of the whirlpool? no
11. The water in the bottom of the boat was very warm, so that water had been in the boat for ▇▇.
    - a few seconds
    - a few minutes
    - a long time
12. After Edna woke up, she saw fish. What color was the water? dark blue
13. Why was Edna thinking about chewing on raw fish?
    - because she needed toothpaste
    - because she needed food
    - because she needed water

WORKBOOK

Review Items

14. Draw arrows at **X**, at **Y** and at **Z** to show the way the melted rock moves.

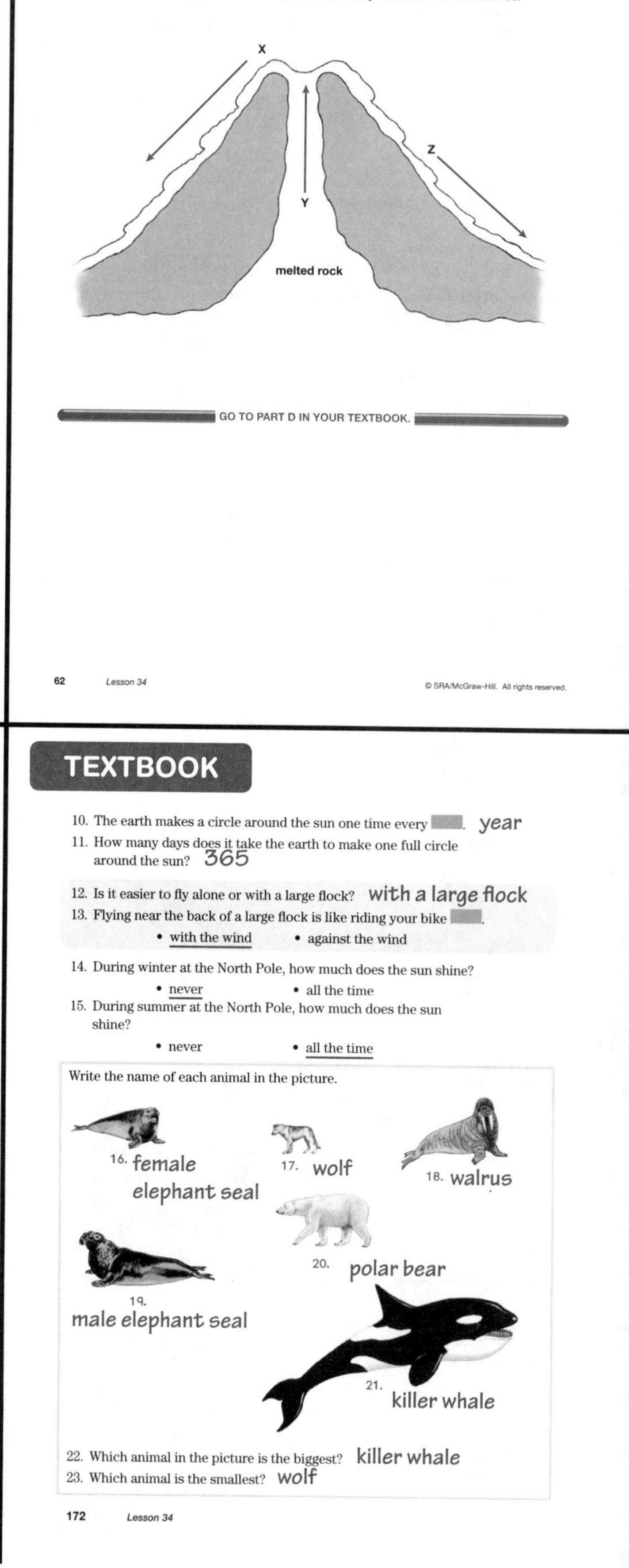

GO TO PART D IN YOUR TEXTBOOK.

TEXTBOOK

D Number your paper from 1 through 23.

Skill Items

Write the word or words from the box that mean the same thing as the underlined part of each sentence.

shriek	breath	swift	armor
skeletons	an instant	a sense	tangle

1. The animal bones were near the big old tree. skeletons
2. He was afraid for a moment. an instant
3. The runner was very fast. swift

Review Items

4. Write the letters of the 3 things you find in the Bermuda Triangle. a, b, f
   - a. sudden storms
   - b. whirlpools
   - c. ice floes
   - d. mountains
   - e. streams
   - f. huge waves
5. Write the letter of the footprint made by the heaviest animal. R
6. Write the letter of the footprint made by the lightest animal. S

R S T

7. How long ago did dinosaurs live on Earth?
   - 10 million years ago
   - 100 million years ago
   - 100 thousand years ago
8. Two things happen to melted rock when it moves down the sides of a volcano. Name those 2 things. Idea: cools and hardens
9. What is it called when the earth shakes and cracks? earthquake

TEXTBOOK

10. The earth makes a circle around the sun one time every ▇▇. year
11. How many days does it take the earth to make one full circle around the sun? 365
12. Is it easier to fly alone or with a large flock? with a large flock
13. Flying near the back of a large flock is like riding your bike ▇▇.
    - with the wind
    - against the wind
14. During winter at the North Pole, how much does the sun shine?
    - never
    - all the time
15. During summer at the North Pole, how much does the sun shine?
    - never
    - all the time

Write the name of each animal in the picture.

16. female elephant seal
17. wolf
18. walrus
19. male elephant seal
20. polar bear
21. killer whale

22. Which animal in the picture is the biggest? killer whale
23. Which animal is the smallest? wolf

WORKBOOK

35

Name ____________________

A Story Items

1. What did Edna see that told her a ship was in the distance? (slim line of) smoke
2. How did she know it wasn't from the island?
   - It billowed.
   - It didn't billow.
   - It was black.
3. Whose ship was it? Captain Parker's; Edna's dad's
4. Why did Edna feel ashamed when she saw her father? Ideas: because she had played in the lifeboat; she had done something he'd told her not to do.
5. The girls needed some care when they got back on the ship. Name 3 things they needed. Ideas (any 3): water, food, medicine for blisters, sunburn cream, bandages
6. Did Captain Parker believe the girls' story? no
7. On what day of the week did the girls go overboard? Monday
8. On what day of the week did the girls think it was when they got back on the ship? Tuesday
9. What day was it really when they got back on the ship? Monday
10. What did Edna find to make her think the adventure really happened? red sand (in her pocket)
11. The sand in Edna's pocket must have come from the island.

Review Items

12. How long ago did dinosaurs live on Earth? ____________
13. What is it called when the earth shakes and cracks? earthquake

12. a hundred million years ago (Accept "millions of years ago.")

WORKBOOK

14. Write the missing seasons on the picture below.
15. Shade half of earth A and half of earth C.

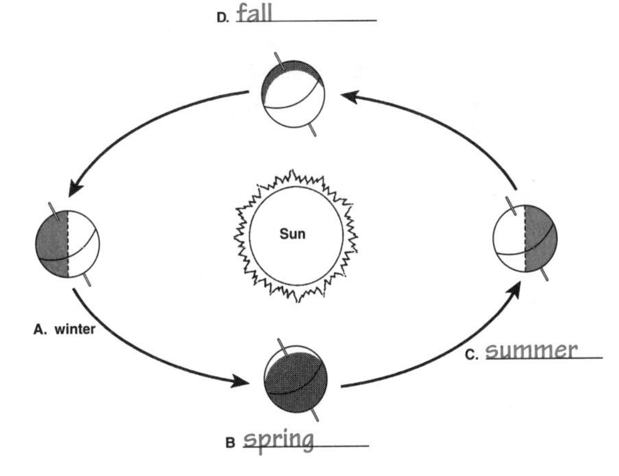

GO TO PART C IN YOUR TEXTBOOK.

TEXTBOOK

C Number your paper from 1 through 22.

Skill Items

Here are three events that happened in the story.
Write **beginning, middle** or **end** for each event.

1. In the distance was a slim line of smoke. beginning
2. Captain Parker opened a door and talked to one of the crew members. middle
3. Later that afternoon, Edna was taking her wet clothes to the laundry room. end

She automatically arranged the flowers.

4. What word means **without thinking?** automatically
5. What word means that she put things where she wanted them? arranged

Review Items

6. Captain Parker's ship passed through a place where hundreds of ships have sunk or been lost. Name that place. Bermuda Triangle
7. Two things happen to melted rock when it moves down the sides of a volcano. Name those 2 things. Idea: It cools and hardens.
8. The picture shows marks left by an animal. Which arrow shows the direction the animal is moving? M
9. Write the letter of the part that shows the mark left by the animal's tail. G
10. Write the letter of the part that shows a footprint. F

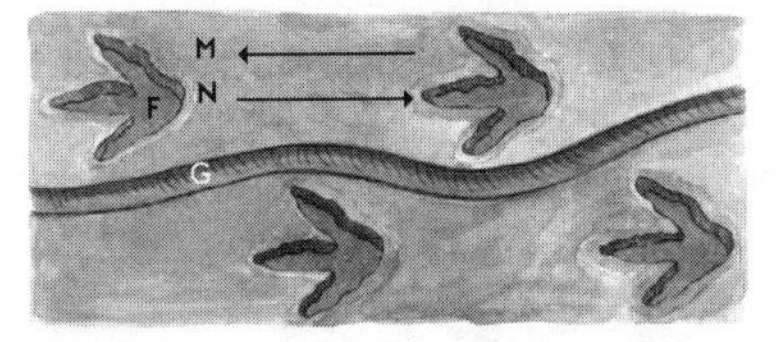

TEXTBOOK

11. The earth makes a circle around the sun one time every ▬. year
12. How many days does it take the earth to make one full circle around the sun? 365
13. How many heat lines are hitting place R on the map? 4
14. How many heat lines are hitting place A? 10
15. How many heat lines are hitting place M? 8
16. Write the letter of the place that's the hottest. A
17. Write the letter of the place that's the coldest. R
18. Write the letter of the place that has the warmest winters. A
19. Write the letter of the place that's farthest from the equator. R
20. Why is place M hotter than place R?

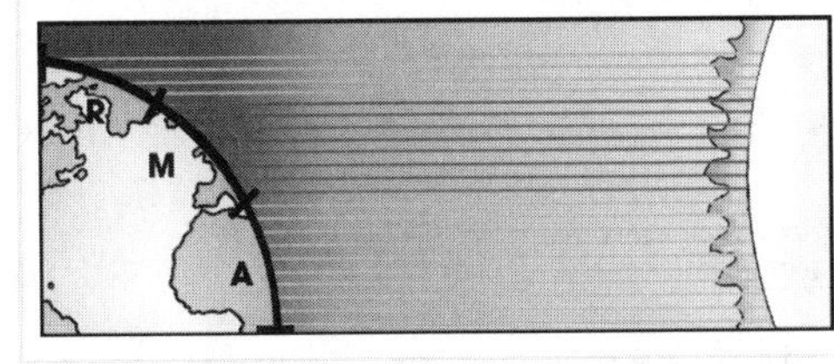

21. During winter at the North Pole, how much does the sun shine?
    - never
    - all the time
22. During summer at the North Pole, how much does the sun shine?
    - never
    - all the time

20. Ideas: It is closer to the equator; it has more heat lines hitting it.

WORKBOOK

Name ____________

A

1. Name 3 things that are made by humans. Ideas (any 3): planes, radios, cars, windows, etc.
2. What is a person doing when the person makes an object for the first time? inventing
3. The person who makes an object for the first time is called an inventor.
4. The object the person makes is called an invention.
5. Most of the things that we use every day were invented after the year ▬.
   - 1800
   - 1900
   - 2200
6. **Underline** the 5 things that were not invented by anybody.
   - chairs
   - horses
   - flowers
   - grass
   - planes
   - bottles
   - snakes
   - spiders
   - rugs

B **Story Items**

7. **Underline** 2 reasons it was embarrassing to go places with Grandmother Esther.
   - She walked fast.
   - She chewed gum.
   - She talked loudly.
   - She talked a lot.
   - She mumbled to herself.
8. What did Grandmother Esther like to talk about? Idea: inventing
9. Did she look at the displays of dinosaurs for a long time? no
10. **Underline** 3 displays that Grandmother Esther wanted to see.
    - radios
    - airplanes
    - cave people
    - horses
    - clothing
    - automobiles

WORKBOOK

11. Grandmother Esther made a speech in the exhibit hall about the people who invented the airplane. How did Leonard feel? Idea: embarrassed
12. What did the other people in the exhibit hall do after the speech? Idea: clapped

Review Items

13. Write the missing seasons on the picture below.
14. Shade half of earth **A** and half of earth **C.**

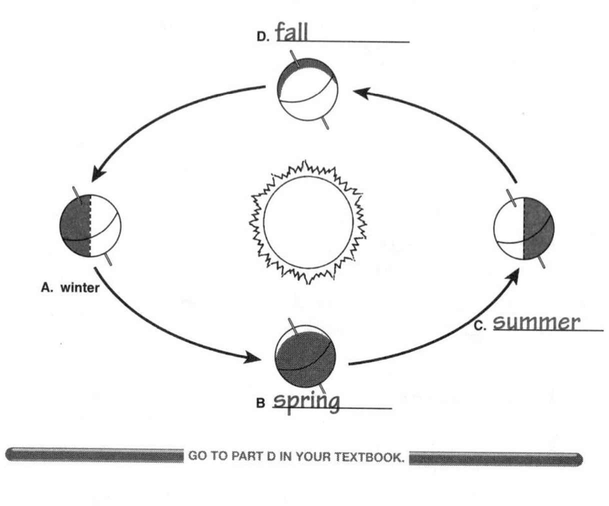

GO TO PART D IN YOUR TEXTBOOK.

TEXTBOOK

that it was possible for machines to fly, they began inventing better flying machines. They invented faster machines and bigger machines. Look at them!" She waved her arm in the direction of the other airplanes on display. Nearly everyone in the hall looked at the rows of planes.

Grandmother Esther marched down the center aisle of the display. In a great voice, she said, "But none of these later planes would be possible without the first one. And the first one would not have been possible without the inventors—those brave men who didn't listen to other people but who knew that we don't have to stand with our feet stuck in the mud. We can fly with the birds!"

The sound of her voice echoed through the hall. Then, one of the people who had been listening to her began to clap. Then others clapped. Soon there was a loud sound of clapping. Even the guard was clapping. Leonard was very embarrassed, but he didn't want to be the only one not clapping. So he clapped, too. He said to himself, "My grandmother is a real character."

D Number your paper from 1 through 18.

Skill Items

Write the word from the box that means the same thing as the underlined part of each sentence.

adventure	enormous	however	hardened
approached	displayed	mysterious	glanced

1. The ice cream became hard in the freezer. hardened
2. He went to school, but he was sick. however
3. She looked quickly at the sign. glanced

Use the words in the box to write complete sentences.

actually	exhibit	directed	automatically
character	displayed	divided	arranged

4. The new ▬ ▬ mysterious fish. exhibit, displayed
5. She ▬ ▬ the flowers. automatically, arranged

TEXTBOOK

Review Items

6. Which letter shows the place that has the warmest winters? X
7. Which letter shows the place that is closest to the equator? X
8. Which letter shows the place that is closest to a pole? P
9. Is the North Pole or the South Pole closer to that letter? South Pole

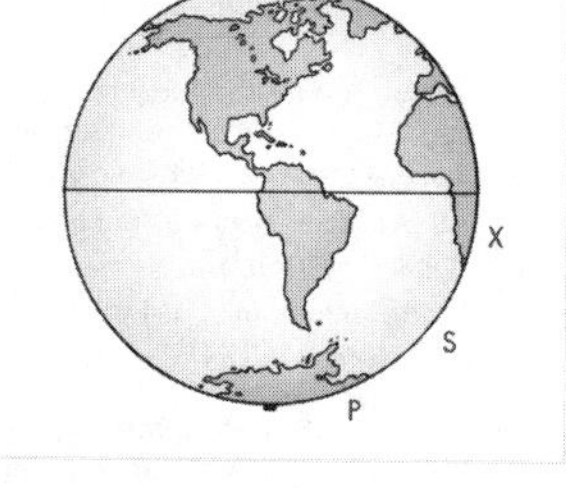

10. Write the letter of the earth that has the North Pole tilting away from the sun. A
11. Write the letter of the earth that has the North Pole tilting toward the sun. C
12. Write the letter of the earth that has darkness all around the North Pole. A
13. Write the letter of the earth that has daylight all around the North Pole. C
14. Write **A, B, C,** and **D.** Then write the season each earth in the picture shows.

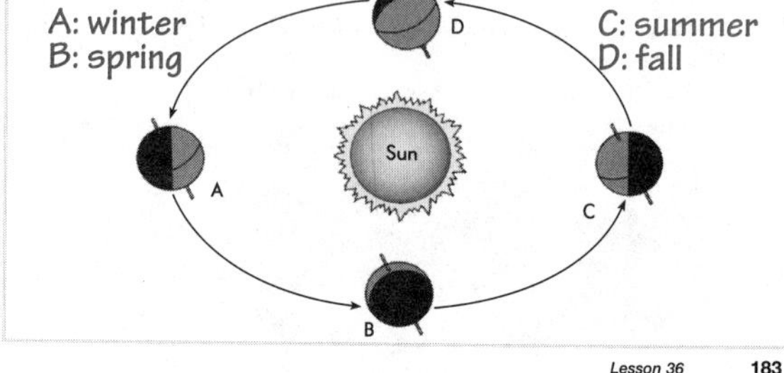

TEXTBOOK

15. Two things happen to melted rock when it moves down the sides of a volcano. Name those 2 things. Idea: cools and hardens
16. What is it called when the earth shakes and cracks? earthquake
17. Most of the things that we use everyday were invented after the year ____.
    - 1900
    - 2000
    - 1800
18. Write the letters of the 5 things that were not invented by anybody. a, c, d, f, h
    a. horses
    b. buildings
    c. flowers
    d. snakes
    e. shoes
    f. bushes
    g. doors
    h. cows
    i. wagons
    j. hats

WORKBOOK

Name ____________

A Story Items

1. What was wrong with the waterbed that Grandmother Esther invented?
   Idea: It leaked.
2. What did Grandmother Esther's folding bike sometimes do when a person was riding it? Idea: folded up
3. **Underline** 2 things that Grandmother Esther ate for lunch.
   - apple
   - cake
   - egg
   - cookie
   - donut
   - sandwich
4. Did Leonard know what he wanted to invent? no
5. At first Leonard thought that he couldn't be an inventor because
   Idea: Everything was already invented
6. Did Grandmother Esther agree? no
7. The men who invented the first airplane saw a need. What need?
   Idea: to get places faster
8. There was a need for the first automobile because people had problems with horses. **Underline** 2 problems.
   - Horses need care.
   - Horses are slow.
   - Horses are strong.
   - Horses like to run.
9. The first thing you do when you think like an inventor is find a need.
10. What's the next thing you do?
    - Ask questions.
    - Meet the need.
    - Go to a museum.

WORKBOOK

Review Items

11. Draw arrows at **J**, at **K** and at **L** to show the way the melted rock moves.

K
L
J
melted rock

12. What is a person doing when the person makes an object for the first time? inventing
13. The person who makes an object for the first time is called an inventor.
14. The object the person makes is called an invention.

GO TO PART C IN YOUR TEXTBOOK.

TEXTBOOK

Grandmother Esther was still talking as she ate her sandwich. "The inventor sees things that are not there yet. The inventor thinks about how things could be. Everybody else just sees things as they are now."

Leonard nodded his head. For a moment he thought about what she said. Then he asked, "But how do you think about things that haven't been invented? What do you do, just think of make-believe things?"

She coughed and then she shouted, "Make-believe? Inventors don't deal in make-believe. They deal in what people need. That's where the invention starts. The inventor looks around and notices that people have trouble doing some things. The inventor sees a need that people have." Grandmother Esther stuffed the rest of her sandwich in her mouth. In an instant, she continued talking. "After the inventor sees a need, the inventor figures out how to meet that need."

"I don't understand," Leonard said.

She pointed back toward the exhibit hall and said, "The two men who invented the airplane saw a need. They saw that people could get places faster if they could fly in a straight line rather than going around on roads. They said to themselves, 'Let's make something that will let people go places faster.' So they invented a flying machine."

She continued, "The person who invented the car saw a need. That person saw that horses were a lot of work. People spent a lot of time feeding them and taking care of them. With a car, people would save a lot of time. With a car they could also go faster from place to place."

She pointed her finger at Leonard. "Remember, if you want to be an inventor, start with a need. Then figure out how to meet that need."

C Number your paper from 1 through 21.

Review Items

1. Write the letters of the 3 things you find in the Bermuda Triangle. a, d, f
   a. huge waves
   b. mountains
   c. streams
   d. whirlpools
   e. ice floes
   f. sudden storms

TEXTBOOK

2. The picture shows half a hailstone. How many times did the stone go through a cloud? 6

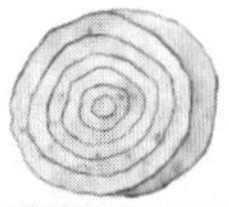

3. What is a person doing when the person makes an object for the first time? inventing
4. The person who makes an object for the first time is called an ▬. inventor
5. The object the person makes is called an ▬. invention

6. Write the letters of the 2 kinds of places that are safe for geese. b, d
   a. places with a few ducks
   b. places with no geese or ducks
   c. places with a few geese
   d. places with many geese

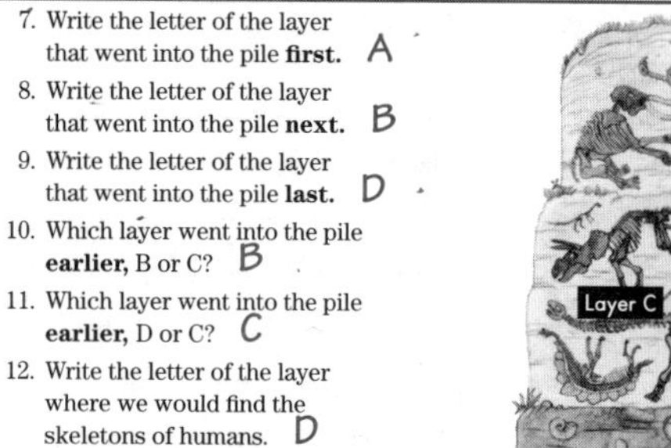

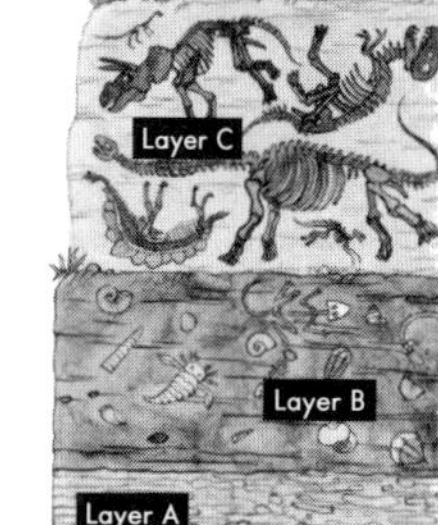

7. Write the letter of the layer that went into the pile **first.** A
8. Write the letter of the layer that went into the pile **next.** B
9. Write the letter of the layer that went into the pile **last.** D
10. Which layer went into the pile **earlier,** B or C? B
11. Which layer went into the pile **earlier,** D or C? C
12. Write the letter of the layer where we would find the skeletons of humans. D
13. Write the letter of the layer that has dinosaur skeletons. C
14. Write the letter of the layer where we would find the skeletons of horses. D

TEXTBOOK

15. When days get longer, is the North Pole tilting **toward the sun** or **away from the sun?** toward the sun
16. When days get shorter, is the North Pole tilting **toward the sun** or **away from the sun?** away from the sun
17. In April, the sun shines for more than ▬ hours each day in Alaska. 12

18. Which globe shows how the earth looks on the first day of winter? Q
19. Which globe shows how the earth looks on the first day of summer? P

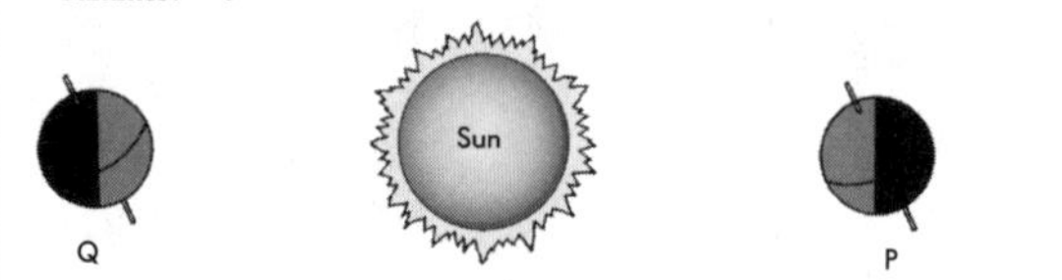

20. How long ago did dinosaurs live on the earth?
   - a hundred years ago
   - a hundred million years ago
   - a million years ago

Study Item

21. Today's story mentions the two men who invented the first airplane. Look in a book on airplanes, in an encyclopedia or on a computer and see if you can find out the names of these two men. Orville and Wilbur Wright

WORKBOOK

38

Name ______________________

A Story Items

1. What was wrong with the waterbed that Grandmother Esther invented?
   Idea: It leaked.
2. At first Leonard thought that he couldn't be an inventor because
   Idea: Everything was already invented
3. The first thing you do when you think like an inventor is find a
   need/problem
4. What's the next thing you do?
   - Ask questions.
   - Meet the need.
   - Go to a museum.
5. Leonard's father had two ideas for inventions. One was something that cut down on traffic. What was his other idea?
   Idea: a money tree
6. Did Leonard's father think like an inventor? no
7. Leonard's mother had an idea for an invention. What was it?
   Idea: an automatic list writer
8. Had Grandmother Esther heard that idea before? yes
9. Did Grandmother Esther like that idea? no
10. Did Leonard get any good ideas for inventions by talking to people?
   no
11. What did Leonard think the hardest part of being an inventor was?
   Idea: figuring out what to invent

WORKBOOK

Review Items

12. How many Great Lakes are there? five (5)
13. Color the Great Lakes on the map.

14. The picture below shows the sun and two balls. Fix up the balls so that half of each ball is in sunlight and half is in shadow.

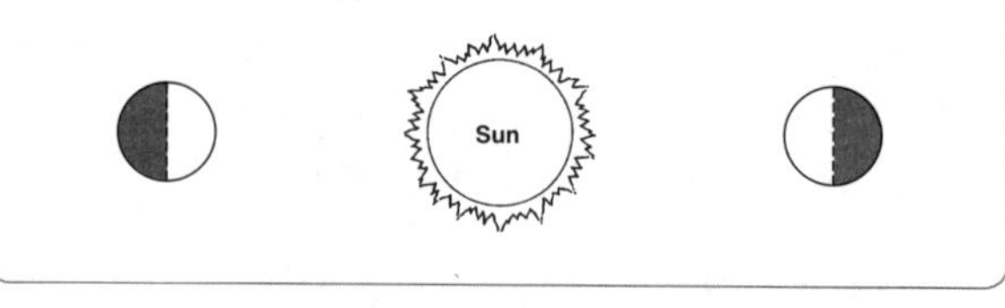

GO TO PART C IN YOUR TEXTBOOK.

TEXTBOOK

writes down things when you get low on them. But every time I turn around, here she is again, talking about that same invention. I think your mother's problem is that she hates to go grocery shopping and she doesn't like to make up grocery lists. Now I'm not saying that it's impossible to invent something that would make up lists. I'm just saying that you're looking at one inventor who doesn't know how to do it."

"Okay," Leonard said. "Thanks anyhow." As he left the room, Grandmother Esther was looking at her magazine, talking to herself. She was saying, "Again and again and again I kept telling her, I don't know how to do it. But she kept coming back with the same idea, that silly list writer."

During the week that followed, Leonard talked to nearly everybody about things they thought should be invented. At the end of the week, he didn't have any good ideas for inventions. But he had discovered something. People just don't seem to be very good at telling about things that they need. Leonard said to himself, "Maybe the hardest part of being an inventor is finding something to invent."

C Number your paper from 1 through 24.

Skill Items

They were impressed by her large vocabulary.

1. What word means they thought her vocabulary was very good? impressed
2. What word refers to all the words a person knows? vocabulary

Review Items

3. The men who invented the first airplane saw a need. What need? 3. Idea: to get to places faster
4. Write the letter of the footprint made by the heaviest animal. Q
5. Write the letter of the footprint made by the lightest animal. P

P Q R

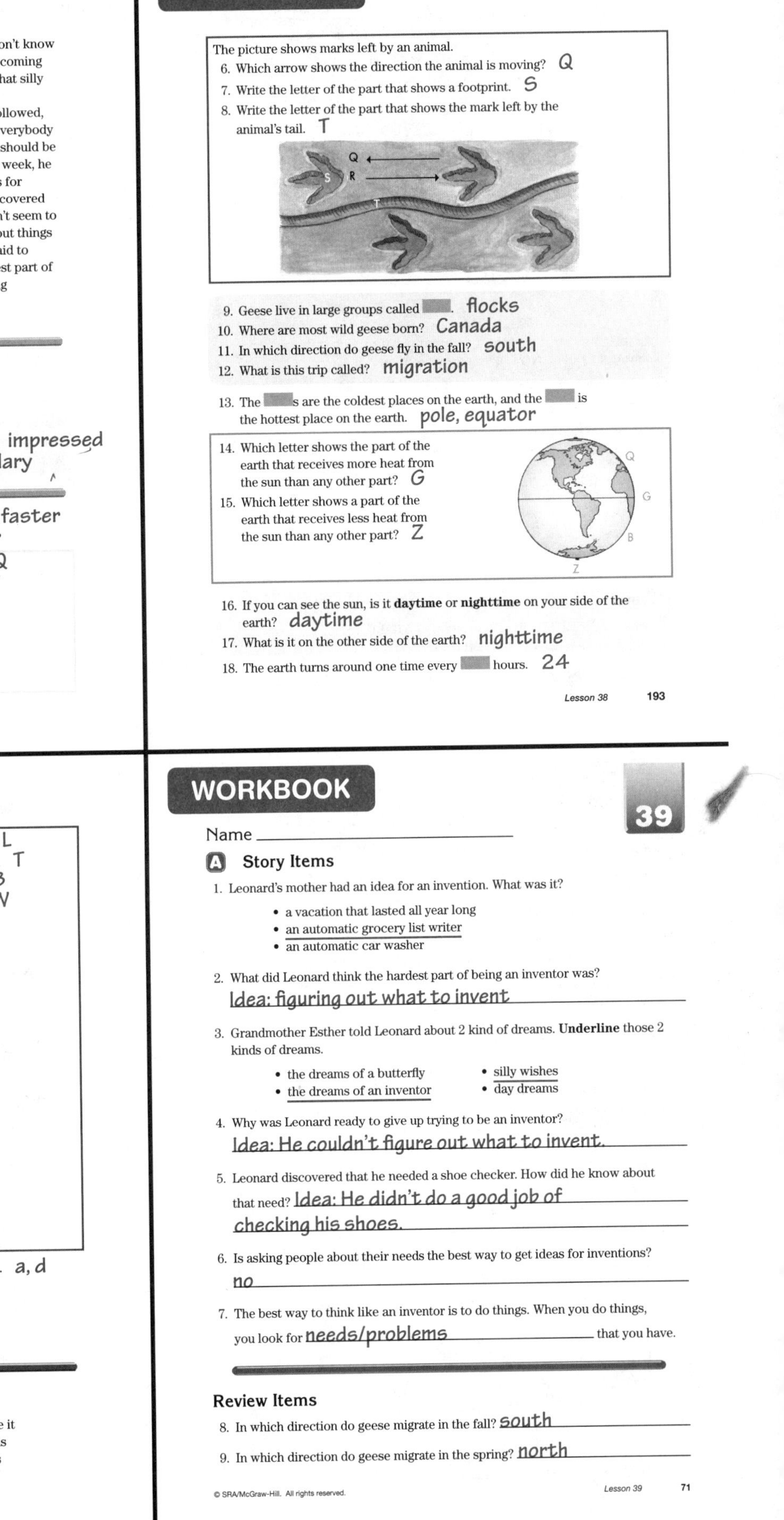

TEXTBOOK

The picture shows marks left by an animal.

6. Which arrow shows the direction the animal is moving? Q
7. Write the letter of the part that shows a footprint. S
8. Write the letter of the part that shows the mark left by the animal's tail. T

9. Geese live in large groups called ▇▇. flocks
10. Where are most wild geese born? Canada
11. In which direction do geese fly in the fall? south
12. What is this trip called? migration
13. The ▇▇s are the coldest places on the earth, and the ▇▇ is the hottest place on the earth. pole, equator
14. Which letter shows the part of the earth that receives more heat from the sun than any other part? G
15. Which letter shows a part of the earth that receives less heat from the sun than any other part? Z

16. If you can see the sun, is it **daytime** or **nighttime** on your side of the earth? daytime
17. What is it on the other side of the earth? nighttime
18. The earth turns around one time every ▇▇ hours. 24

TEXTBOOK

19. Write the letter of the earth that shows the person in daytime. L
20. Write the letter of the earth that shows the person 6 hours later. T
21. Write the letter that shows the person another 6 hours later. B
22. Write the letter that shows the person another 6 hours later. W

23. Write the letters of the 2 kinds of places that are safe for geese. a, d
    a. places with many geese
    b. places with a few geese
    c. places with a few ducks
    d. places with no geese or ducks

Study Item

24. The two-wheeled bicycle is not very old. It was probably hard for somebody to get the idea of a two-wheeled bicycle because it seemed impossible for somebody to move along on two wheels without falling over. Find out when James Starley invented his two-wheeled *Ariel* bicycle. 1871

WORKBOOK

39

Name ____________________

A Story Items

1. Leonard's mother had an idea for an invention. What was it?
   - a vacation that lasted all year long
   - an automatic grocery list writer
   - an automatic car washer
2. What did Leonard think the hardest part of being an inventor was?
   Idea: figuring out what to invent
3. Grandmother Esther told Leonard about 2 kind of dreams. **Underline** those 2 kinds of dreams.
   - the dreams of a butterfly
   - the dreams of an inventor
   - silly wishes
   - day dreams
4. Why was Leonard ready to give up trying to be an inventor?
   Idea: He couldn't figure out what to invent.
5. Leonard discovered that he needed a shoe checker. How did he know about that need? Idea: He didn't do a good job of checking his shoes.
6. Is asking people about their needs the best way to get ideas for inventions?
   no
7. The best way to think like an inventor is to do things. When you do things, you look for needs/problems that you have.

Review Items

8. In which direction do geese migrate in the fall? south
9. In which direction do geese migrate in the spring? north

WORKBOOK

10. Write the directions **north, south, east** and **west** in the boxes.
11. Make a line that starts at the circle on the map and goes north.
12. If you start at the circle and move to the number **4**, in which direction do you go? west

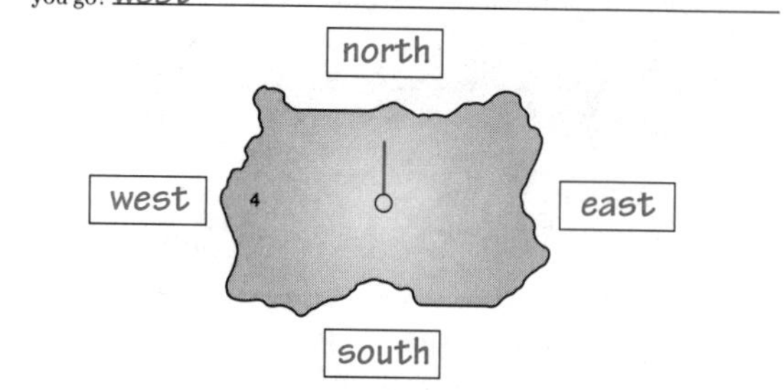

13. Shade the part of the earth where it is nighttime.
14. Which side of the earth is closer to the sun, **A** or **B?** B
15. Which side of the earth is in nighttime? A
16. Which side of the earth is in daytime? B

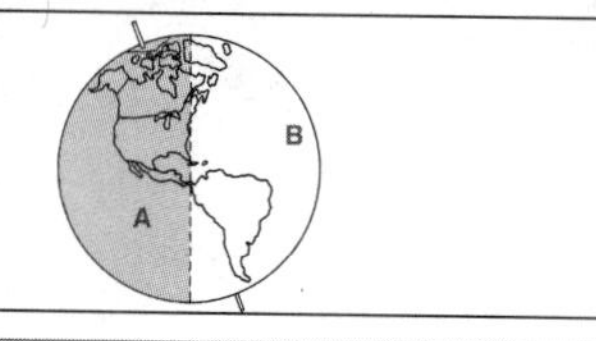

17. **Fill in the blanks to show the four seasons.**
winter, spring, summer, fall, winter, spring, summer, fall

GO TO PART C IN YOUR TEXTBOOK.

TEXTBOOK

when he had almost cleaned the last footprint on the kitchen floor, an idea hit him. It hit him so hard that it put a smile on his face. Just like that, he knew how to think like an inventor. He said out loud, "I need a shoe checker. I know I need it because when I don't have one, I don't do a good job of checking my shoes."

A shoe checker wasn't a bad idea for an invention. But the idea wasn't the most important thing to Leonard. The way he got the idea was the important thing. He didn't do something well. Then he figured out that he needed something to help him do it well.

That's how to figure out things to invent. You don't ask people. You do things. And when you do them, you pay attention to problems that you have. Each of the problems that you have tells you about something that you could invent to solve the problem.

Leonard's mother walked into the kitchen and saw Leonard smiling. "This is the first time I've seen you have a good time while you clean up a mess," she said.

"That's because I like this mess," Leonard said.

His mother shook her head. "He must take after his grandmother," she said to herself.

C Number your paper from 1 through 20.

Skill Items

Here are three events that happened in the story.
Write **beginning, middle** or **end** for each event.

1. Leonard's mother walked into the kitchen and saw Leonard smiling. end
2. Grandmother Esther was talking to herself about dreams. middle
3. One of Leonard's friends, Frank, suggested inventing a vacation that lasted all year long. beginning

Use the words in the box to write complete sentences.

impressed	arranged	honestly	stuffed
repeated	automatically	stomach	vocabulary

4. She ▬ ▬ the flowers. automatically, arranged
5. They were ▬ by her large ▬. impressed, vocabulary

TEXTBOOK

Review Items

6. The first thing you do when you think like an inventor is find a ▬. need/problem
7. What's the next thing you do? 7. Idea: figure out how to meet the need/solve the problem
8. Geese live in large groups called ▬. flocks
9. Where are most wild geese born? Canada
10. In which direction do geese fly in the fall? south
11. What is this trip called? migration

Choose from these words to answer items 12—14:
- moon
- Florida
- sun
- equator
- geese
- poles
- Canada
- migration

12. The heat that the earth receives comes from the ▬. sun
13. The part of the earth that receives more heat than any other part is the ▬. equator
14. The parts of the earth that receive less heat than any other part are called the ▬. poles
15. The sun shines ▬.
    - some of the time
    - all of the time
16. Can you see the sun all day long and all night long? no
17. Things closer to the bottom of the pile went into the pile ▬. earlier
18. Write the letter of the storm clouds. B
19. Write the letter of the clouds that may stay in the sky for days at a time. A
20. Write the letter of the clouds that have frozen drops of water. C

A B C

TEXTBOOK

TEST 4 40

Number your paper from 1 through 18.

1. How long ago did dinosaurs live on Earth? one hundred million years ago
2. Each picture has 2 arrows that show how the melted rock moves. Write the letter of the picture that shows 2 correct arrows. C

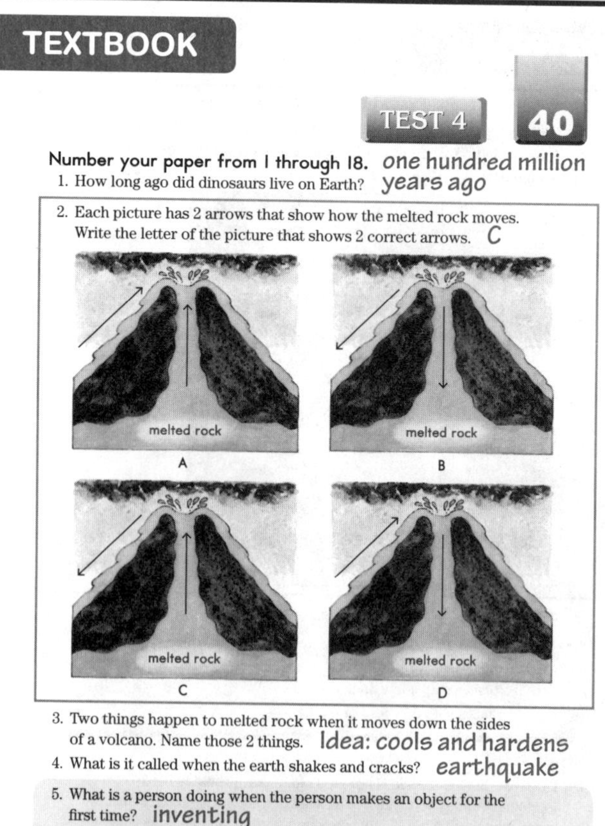

3. Two things happen to melted rock when it moves down the sides of a volcano. Name those 2 things. Idea: cools and hardens
4. What is it called when the earth shakes and cracks? earthquake
5. What is a person doing when the person makes an object for the first time? inventing
6. The person who makes an object for the first time is called an ▬. inventor
7. The object the person makes is called an ▬. invention

TEXTBOOK

8. Most of the things that we use every day were invented after the year ████.
   • 2200 • 1800 • 1600
9. Write the letters of the 5 things that were invented by somebody. a, d, f, g, j
   a. radios f. trains
   b. trees g. shoes
   c. killer whales h. birds
   d. desks i. dirt
   e. ice j. computers
10. The men who invented the first airplane saw a need. What need? Idea: to get to places faster
11. The first thing you do when you think like an inventor is find a ████. need/problem
12. What's the next thing you do? Idea: figure out how to meet the need/solve the problem

Skill Items

For each item, write the underlined word or words from the sentences in the box.

> She automatically arranged the flowers.
> They were impressed by her large vocabulary.
> The new exhibit displayed mysterious fish.

13. What underlining means **showed**? displayed
14. What underlining describes things we don't understand? mysterious
15. What underlining refers to all the words a person knows? vocabulary
16. What underlining means that she put things where she wanted them? arranged
17. What underlining means **an arrangement of things for people to look at?** exhibit
18. What underlining means they thought her vocabulary was very good? impressed

END OF TEST 4

WORKBOOK

Name 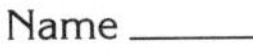

A Story Items

1. When Leonard did things like washing the car, what did he pay attention to? Idea: problems he had
2. Each problem told Leonard about something he could invent to solve the problem.
3. How long did Leonard try to find different problems? 3 weeks
4. What invention did he think would solve the problem he had with eggs? Idea: something to crack eggs
5. What problem did Leonard have with his clothes at bedtime? Idea: He forgot to hang up his clothes.
6. What invention did he think could solve that problem? Idea: a tape to remind him to hang up his clothes
7. What invention did Leonard think could solve the problem he had when it rained? Idea: a coat with an umbrella
8. What problem did Leonard have when he washed his dog? Idea: He got soaked.
9. Which invention did Leonard's mother think he should make? Idea: a grocery list writer
10. Did Grandmother Esther name an invention that Leonard should make? no

WORKBOOK

Review Items

Use these names to answer the questions: **Tyrannosaurus, Triceratops.**

11. What is animal A? Tyrannosaurus
12. What is animal B? Triceratops

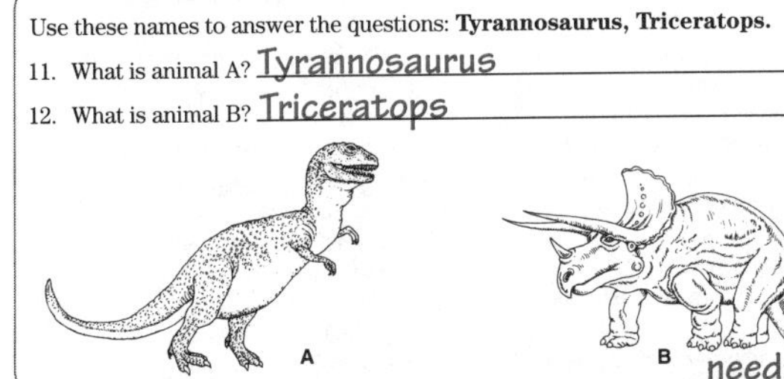

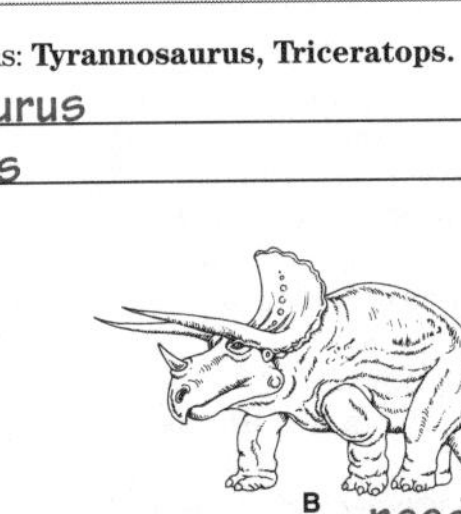

13. The first thing you do when you think like an inventor is find a need; problem.
14. What's the next thing you do? Idea: figure out how to meet the need/solve the problem
15. Write **north, south, east** and **west** in the correct boxes.
16. In which direction is ocean current **W** moving? east
17. In which direction is ocean current **X** moving? south
18. Which direction is the wind coming from? north
19. Make an arrow above ice chunk **Y** to show the direction the current will move the ice chunk.
20. Make an arrow next to ice chunk **Z** to show the direction the current will move the ice chunk.

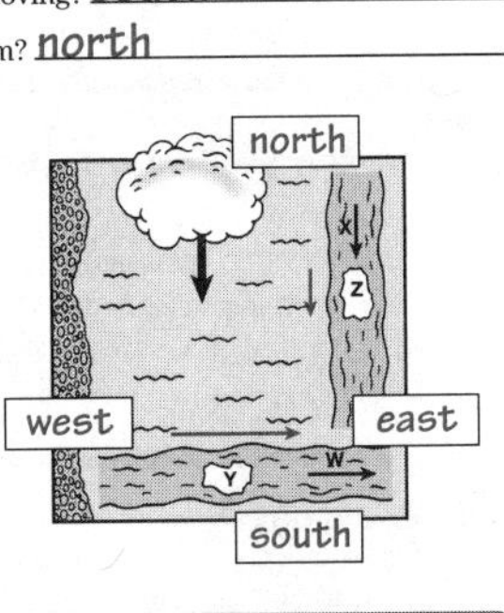

GO TO PART C IN YOUR TEXTBOOK.

TEXTBOOK

Then you'd put the dog in the tub. Next, you'd put the plastic box over the tub. The dog would stick its head out through one of the holes. You could reach through the other holes and wash the dog and you wouldn't get wet while you were washing the dog. "Not bad," Leonard said to himself when he got this idea. "Not bad at all."

Leonard made pictures of some of his ideas. He showed them to the members of his family and he explained how they worked. His father said, "Leonard, I'm impressed."

Leonard's mother said, "Leonard, those are very good ideas. But did you ever think of inventing a machine that would automatically write out the things that you need at the grocery store?"

When Leonard's mother mentioned the list-making machine, Grandmother Esther said, "Stop talking about that crazy invention. Leonard seems to have some good ideas here. They show that the boy has been thinking like an inventor. Now he needs to stop thinking and start inventing." She looked sternly at Leonard.

Leonard smiled and said, "But I still don't know which thing I should invent."

"They're all pretty good," his father said.

His mother said, "I like the machine that makes up a list of things to buy."

Leonard said, "I'm not sure I've found the right idea yet."

Leonard shook his head. He was becoming very tired of trying to be an inventor.

C Number your paper from 1 through 13.

Review Items 1. tiny drops of water

1. What are clouds made of?
2. What kind of cloud does the picture show? storm cloud
3. What happens to a drop of water at **B**? Idea: It freezes.

TEXTBOOK

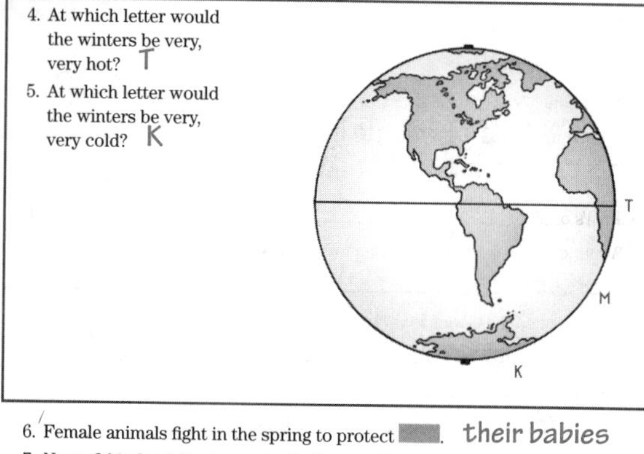

4. At which letter would the winters be very, very hot? T
5. At which letter would the winters be very, very cold? K

6. Female animals fight in the spring to protect ▬. their babies
7. Name 2 kinds of Alaskan animals that are dangerous in the spring. (Any 2:) polar bears, wolves, killer whales, walruses, etc.
8. Name 3 animals that are cold-blooded.
9. Name 3 animals that are warm-blooded.

10. Which object went into the pile **first?** shoe
11. Which object went into the pile **earlier,** the book or the pencil? book
12. Which object went into the pile **just after** the knife? rock

8. (Any 3:) fish, sharks, reptiles, etc.

13. What kind of animals lived in the Mesozoic? dinosaurs

9. (Any 3:) humans, bears, dogs, cows, etc.

WORKBOOK

Name ______________________

42

A Story Items

1. Underline the reasons that people on the street thought Grandmother Esther was mad at Leonard.
   - She made faces.
   - She pointed her finger.
   - She talked softly.
   - She talked loudly.
   - She kicked cats.
2. What invention did Leonard think could make his grandmother talk in a softer voice? Idea: a buzzer
3. What would the invention do when Grandmother Esther talked louder? Idea: buzz louder

Grandmother Esther explained how the electric eye works.

4. When somebody walks in the door, the body stops the beam of light from reaching the target
5. When the body stops the beam, what happens? Idea: The buzzer sounds.
6. What does that tell the shopkeeper? Idea: that someone is in the store
7. Why couldn't the people get into the bakery while Grandmother Esther talked? Idea: She was blocking the doorway.

WORKBOOK

8. What did those people say about Grandmother Esther's talk? Idea: It was interesting.
9. How did Leonard feel? Idea: embarrassed

10. Will the buzzer in the bakery make noise for picture A or picture B? B
11. What's the name of the invention shown in the pictures? electric eye

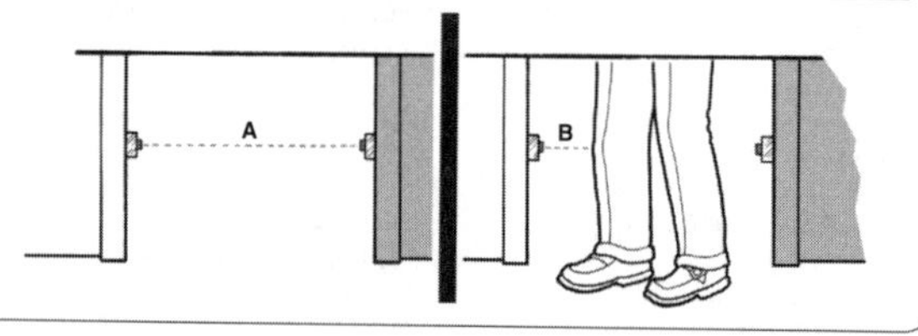

Review Items

12. What color are all geese when they are born? yellow
13. What's the name of geese that are all white? snow geese
14. What's the name of geese that are gray and white and black? Canada geese

GO TO PART C IN YOUR TEXTBOOK.

TEXTBOOK

beam of light and kept it from reaching the target, the buzzer sounded. She explained that the buzzer kept sounding as long as the beam was broken. So when somebody walked in the door, the body would stop the beam of light from reaching the target. When the body stopped the beam, the buzzer sounded. That buzzer told the shopkeeper that somebody was going through the door.

Grandmother Esther was kneeling in front of the doorway as she explained how the beam worked. Several people were trying to get into the bakery. They waited as she explained the electric eye. The shopkeeper was standing behind the counter, looking at her. When she finished her explanation of the electric eye, she said, "This is a good example of a clever invention. The electric eye is a simple invention, but it has many, many uses."

One of the people who was trying to get into the store said, "Very interesting."

The other person said, "Yes, very interesting."

The shopkeeper said, "Excuse me, could you stand aside and let these people come in?"

Leonard said, "Come on, Grandma, you're blocking the doorway."

And Grandmother Esther said, "Of course, the electric eye is not as great an invention as the airplane or the electric light. But the electric eye serves many needs."

The shopkeeper said, "Yes, it does."

Leonard said, "Come on, Grandma, I've got to go to school."

A Number your paper from 1 through 24.

Skill Items

He responded to her clever solution.

1. What word means **reacted?** responded
2. What word means very **smart?** clever
3. What word refers to solving a problem? solution

Review Items

4. When geese learn to fly, do they start in the water or on the land? on land
5. They run with their ▬ out to the side. wings

TEXTBOOK

6. The earth is shaped like a ▬. ball
7. The hottest part of the earth is called the ▬.
   - desert
   - equator
   - pole
8. What's the name of the spot that's at the bottom of the earth? South Pole
9. What's the name of the spot that's at the top of the earth? North Pole
10. What's the name of the line that goes around the fattest part of the earth? equator
11. What season is it at the North Pole when the North Pole tilts **away from** the sun? winter
12. What season is it at the North Pole when the North Pole tilts **toward** the sun? summer

Write the name of each numbered object in the picture. Choose from these names:

- kayak
- fishing pole
- spear
- sled
- Eskimo
- sled dogs

19. In what season are animals most dangerous in Alaska? spring
20. During what season do female animals in Alaska have babies? spring
21. About how long are killer whales? about 12 meters
22. Compare the size of killer whales with the size of other whales.
23. Are killer whales fish? no
24. Tell whether killer whales are **warm-blooded** or **cold-blooded**. warm-blooded

22. Idea: Other whales are longer than killer whales.

WORKBOOK

Name ____________________

A Story Items

1. Leonard got his idea for a great invention when Grandmother Esther told him to do something. What did she tell him to do?
   Idea: Turn off the lights.

Leonard's original invention had problems.

2. What does the light in a dark room do when you walk into the room?
   turn on
3. What does the light do when you leave the room?
   turn off
4. Let's say two people walk into a dark room. What happens to the light in the room when the first person enters?
   It turns on.
5. What happens to the light when the second person enters?
   It turns off.
6. What will Leonard use to make the lights work automatically?
   electric eye
7. Did Leonard's mother understand how his invention would work?
   no
8. Grandmother Esther told Leonard that every invention has
   problems
9. So what does the inventor have to do?
   - quit
   - solve the problems
   - hide the problems

WORKBOOK

Here's the rule about an electric eye: **Each time the beam of light is broken, the light changes.** Shade the bulbs that are off for each problem. The first problem is already done for you.

10. The light is off. The beam is broken 4 times.

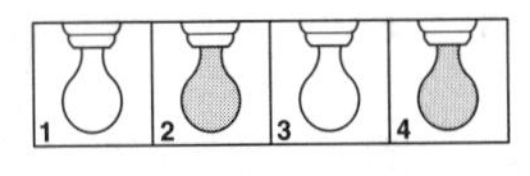

Is the light **on** or **off** at the end? off

11. Here's another problem. The light is off. The beam is broken 8 times.
    a. Shade the bulbs that are off.

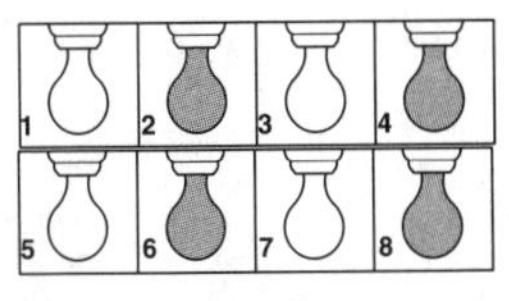

    b. Is the light **on** or **off** at the end? off

12. Here's another problem. The light is off. The beam is broken 3 times.
    a. Shade the bulbs that are off.

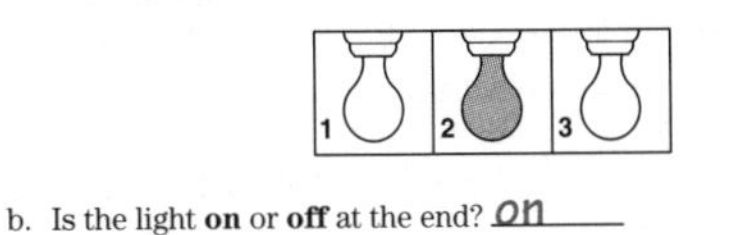

    b. Is the light **on** or **off** at the end? on

GO TO PART C IN YOUR TEXTBOOK.

TEXTBOOK

C Number your paper from 1 through 24.

Skill Items

Use the words in the box to write complete sentences.

device	outfit	solution	entered
impressed	mentioned	responded	vocabulary

1. They were ▬ by her large ▬. impressed, vocabulary
2. He ▬ to her clever ▬. responded, solution

Review Items

Here's how an electric eye at a store works.

3. When somebody walks in the door, the body stops the beam of light from reaching the ▬. target
4. When the body stops the beam, what does the device do next?
5. What does that tell the shopkeeper? Idea: that someone has come in the store

6. Write the letter of the layer that went into the pile first. A
7. Write the letter of the layer that went into the pile next. B
8. Write the letter of the layer that went into the pile last. D
9. Write the letter of the layer that we live on. D
10. What's the name of layer C? Mesozoic

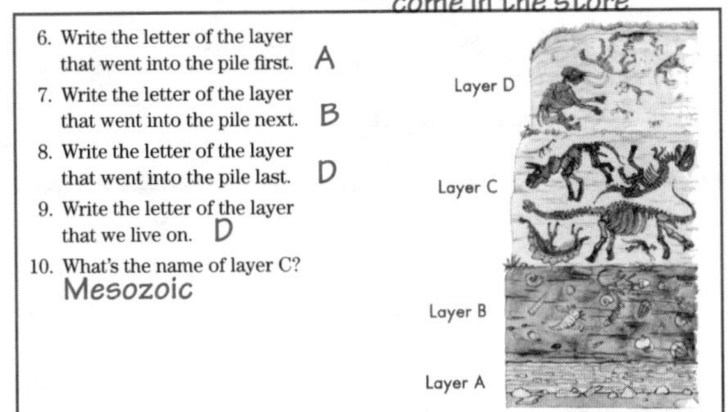

4. Idea: it sounds the buzzer

TEXTBOOK

11. Name the country that is just north of the United States. Canada
12. Which letter shows where the United States is? I
13. Which letter shows where Canada is? H

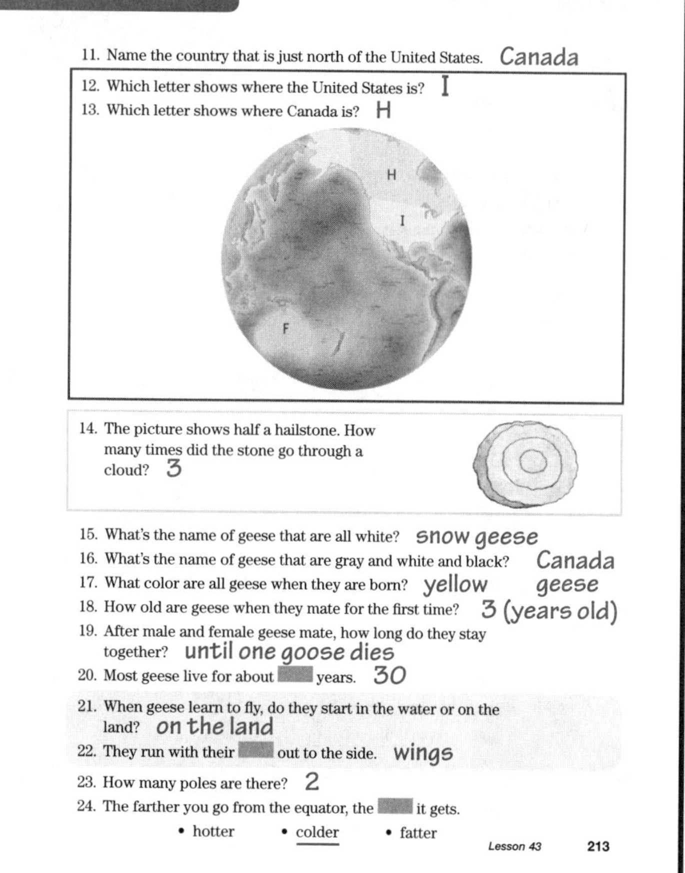

14. The picture shows half a hailstone. How many times did the stone go through a cloud? 3

15. What's the name of geese that are all white? snow geese
16. What's the name of geese that are gray and white and black? Canada geese
17. What color are all geese when they are born? yellow
18. How old are geese when they mate for the first time? 3 (years old)
19. After male and female geese mate, how long do they stay together? until one goose dies
20. Most geese live for about ▬ years. 30
21. When geese learn to fly, do they start in the water or on the land? on the land
22. They run with their ▬ out to the side. wings
23. How many poles are there? 2
24. The farther you go from the equator, the ▬ it gets.
    - hotter
    - colder
    - fatter

WORKBOOK

Name ______________________ **44**

A Story Items

1. At the beginning of today's story, Leonard was trying to solve this problem: When a second person goes into the room, ▬.
   - the lights go on
   - the lights stay on
   - the lights go off
2. Leonard saw a sign that gave him a clue about solving his problem. What kind of sign did he see?
   one-way
3. His invention had to know whether a person was moving ▬.
   - in or out
   - fast or slow
   - now or later
4. So how many beams does a doorway need? 2
5. If a person moves **into** the room, which beam will be broken first—the **inside beam** or the **outside beam?** outside beam
6. Which beam will be broken next? inside beam
7. Will the lights turn **on** or **off?** on
8. The picture shows two electric eye beams on the side of each door. The number **1** shows the beam that is broken first. The number **2** shows the beam that is broken next. On each picture, draw an arrow to show which way the person is moving. The first arrow is already drawn.

A B C

WORKBOOK

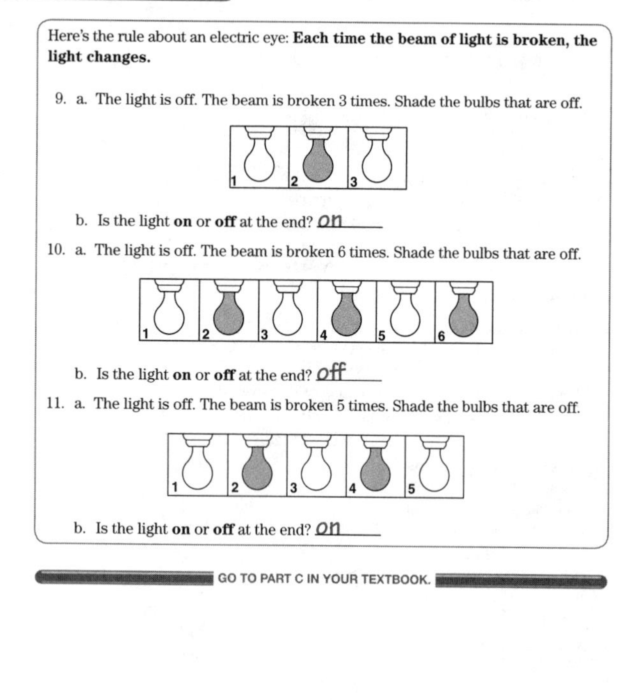

Here's the rule about an electric eye: **Each time the beam of light is broken, the light changes.**

9. a. The light is off. The beam is broken 3 times. Shade the bulbs that are off.
   b. Is the light **on** or **off** at the end? on
10. a. The light is off. The beam is broken 6 times. Shade the bulbs that are off.
    b. Is the light **on** or **off** at the end? off
11. a. The light is off. The beam is broken 5 times. Shade the bulbs that are off.
    b. Is the light **on** or **off** at the end? on

GO TO PART C IN YOUR TEXTBOOK.

TEXTBOOK

2. Ideas: almost jumped out of his seat; yelled "I've got it!"; got goose bumps

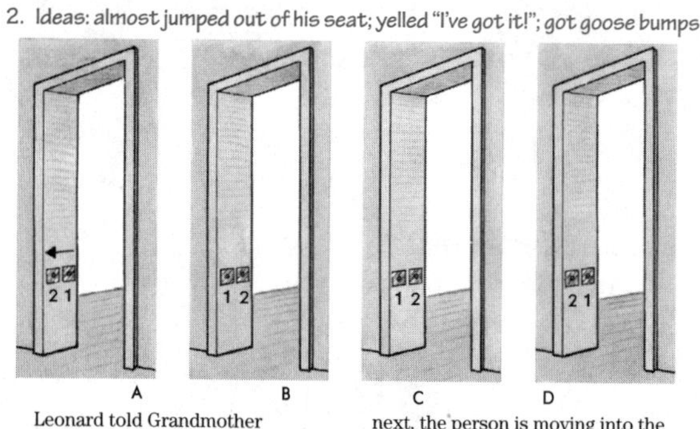

Leonard told Grandmother Esther how to solve the problem. "On the side of the door we put two electric eyes, not one." Leonard continued, "The electric eyes are side by side. When somebody goes through the door, they will break one beam first, then the second beam. If the outside beam is broken first and the inside beam is broken next, the person is moving into the room."

Leonard continued to explain, "If the inside beam is broken first and the outside beam is broken next, the person is moving out of the room. We make the electric eye device turn on the light if somebody goes into the room and turn off the light if somebody goes out of the room."

C Number your paper from 1 through 26.

4. Idea: because Grandmother Esther was playing drums

Story Items

1. In today's story, what was Leonard doing that made two boys on the street giggle and point at him? Idea: talking to himself
2. What did Leonard do when he figured out the solution?
3. Where was he? (arithmetic) class; in school
4. When Leonard got home, his mother was wearing earmuffs. Why?
5. How many electric eyes will Leonard need on each doorway? 2
6. How many beams will go across the doorway? 2

TEXTBOOK

7. Leonard's first invention had problems. Let's say two people walk into a dark room. What happens to the light in the room when the first person enters? It turns on.
8. What happens to the light when the second person enters? It turns off.

Review Items

9. Which came earlier on Earth, dinosaurs or horses? dinosaurs
10. Which came earlier on Earth, strange sea animals or dinosaurs? strange sea animals

11. What's the name of the place shown by the letter C? North Pole
12. Which letter shows the hottest place? F
13. Which letter shows the coldest place? C
14. Which letter is farthest from the equator? C

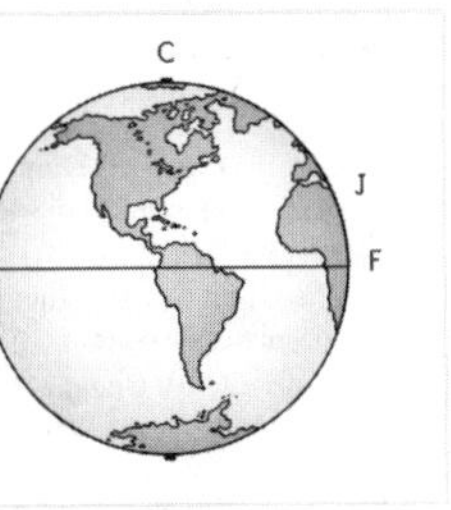

15. What are clouds made of?
16. What kind of cloud does the picture show? storm clouds
17. What happens to a drop of water at **B**? Idea: It freezes.

15. tiny drops of water

TEXTBOOK

18. Most geese live for about ▬ years. 30
19. How old are geese when they mate for the first time? 3 years old
20. After male and female geese mate, how long do they stay together? Idea: until one goose dies

21. Which letter shows the place that is closest to the equator? B
22. Which letter shows the place that is closest to a pole? F
23. Is the **North Pole** or the **South Pole** closer to that letter? South Pole

B
Q
F

24. Name 2 things that can make an ice chunk drift. wind and current

Study Items

Grandmother Esther talked about what a great invention the electric light bulb is. The man who invented it was named Thomas Alva Edison.

25. Find out when he invented the electric light bulb. 1879
26. Find out 2 other things that he invented. (Any 2:) phonograph; automatic telegraph system; stock quotation printer; kinetoscope; etc.

WORKBOOK

45

Name ____________________

A Story Items

1. In the last story, Leonard saw a sign that gave him a clue about solving his problem. What kind of sign did he see?
   one-way
2. Would a person be moving into the room or out of the room if the **inside** beam is broken first? out of the room
3. Which way would a person be moving if the **outside** beam was broken first?
   into the room
4. Leonard's original idea had a problem. What would happen if three people were in a room and one person left?
   Idea: The lights would go out.
5. Grandmother Esther told Leonard that his device could not
   count
6. Letting water out of the sink gave Leonard an idea about his counter. What number did his counter have to count to? zero: (0)
7. Every time somebody goes into the room, what does the counter do?
   • <u>+1</u> • –1 • –0
8. Every time somebody goes out of the room, what does the counter do?
   • +1 • <u>–1</u> • –0
9. What number does the counter end up at when the last person leaves the room? zero: (0)
10. What happens to the lights when the counter is at zero?
    They turn off.

WORKBOOK

The solid arrows show people going into the room. The dotted arrows show people leaving the room. For each picture, **underline** the word that tells about the lights in the room.

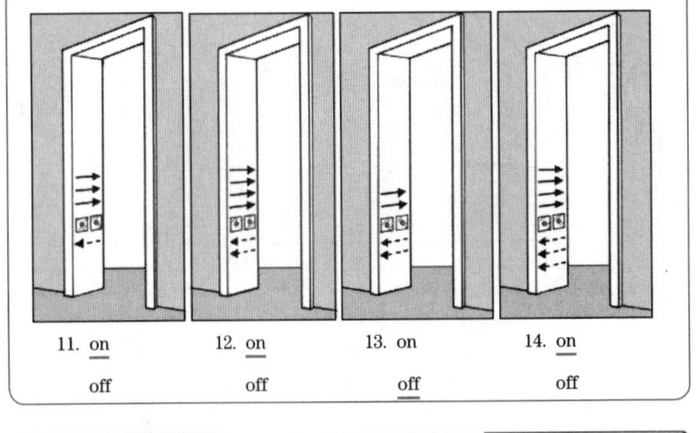

11. <u>on</u>	12. <u>on</u>	13. on	14. <u>on</u>
off	off	<u>off</u>	off

GO TO PART C IN YOUR TEXTBOOK.

TEXTBOOK

Leonard ran into the kitchen. Grandmother Esther was starting to eat her salad. He showed her the drawing and explained. "The device can tell each time somebody goes into the room and each time somebody goes out. So we make a counter that counts forward each time somebody goes into the room. If four people go into the room, the counter counts one, two, three, four. Each time somebody leaves the room, the counter counts backward. So if three people leave, the counter counts backward: three, two, one. But the lights don't go off until the counter counts back to zero."

Leonard continued to explain, "When the last person leaves the room, the counter counts back to zero. Now the lights go off."

Grandmother Esther jumped out of her chair, threw her arms around Leonard, and gave him a kiss.

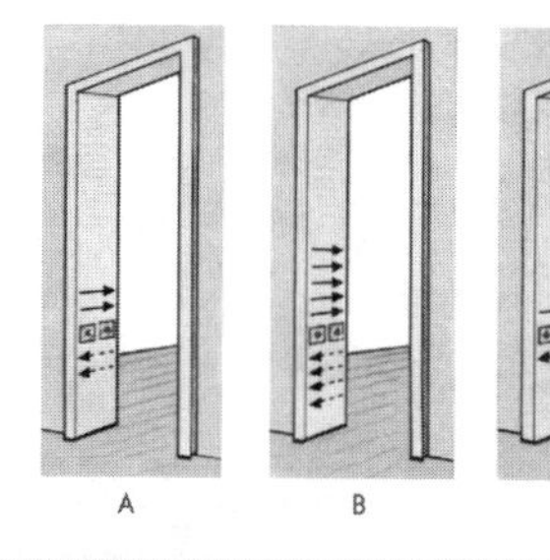

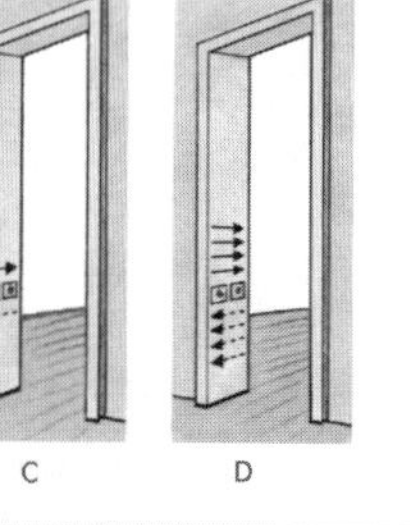

C Number your paper from 1 through 25.

Story Items

1. How many electric eyes did Leonard use for his invention? 2
2. How many beams went across the doorway? 2
3. If a person moves into a room, which beam will be broken first—the inside beam or the outside beam? outside beam
4. Which beam will be broken next? inside beam

TEXTBOOK

5. The solid arrows show how many times people went into the room. How many people went into the room? 3
6. The dotted arrows show how many people left the room. How many people left the room? 1
7. Are the lights on in the room? yes
8. How many more people would have to leave the room before the lights go off? 2

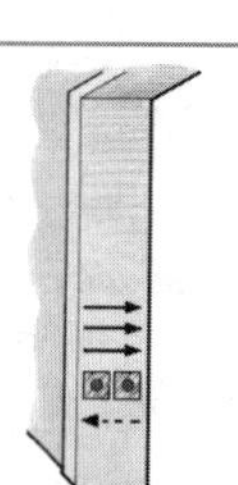

Skill Items

Here are three events that happened in the story.
Write **beginning, middle** or **end** for each event.

9. The water kept going out until there was zero water in the sink. middle
10. Leonard told Grandmother Esther that the one-way sign helped him figure out a solution. beginning
11. Leonard told his Grandmother Esther how the counter on his device would work. end

The patent attorney wrote an agreement.

12. What do we call a lawyer whose special job is getting patents for new inventions? patent attorney
13. What word means **lawyer?** attorney
14. What word means a **promise made by people?** agreement
15. What word names a license for somebody to be the only person who can make a product? patent

Review Items

16. How many days does it take the earth to make one full circle around the sun? 365
17. The earth makes a circle around the sun one time every ▬. year

TEXTBOOK

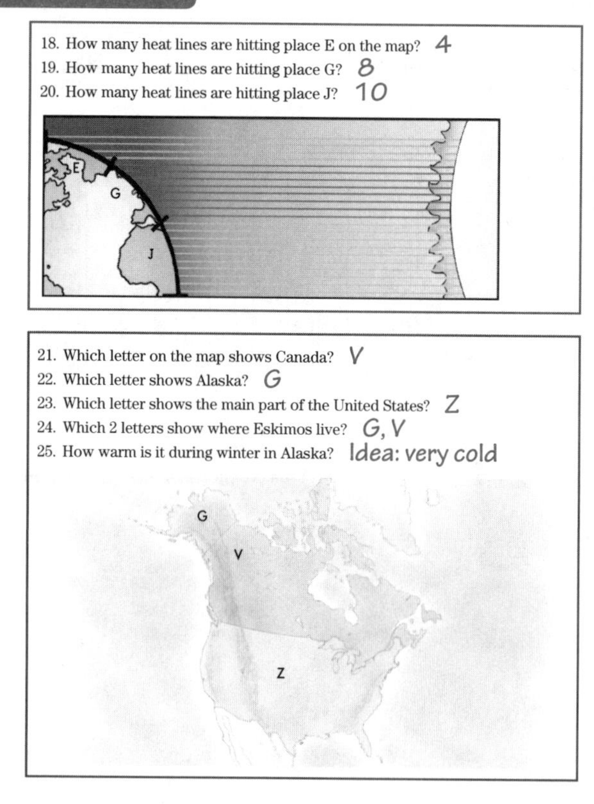

18. How many heat lines are hitting place E on the map? 4
19. How many heat lines are hitting place G? 8
20. How many heat lines are hitting place J? 10

21. Which letter on the map shows Canada? V
22. Which letter shows Alaska? G
23. Which letter shows the main part of the United States? Z
24. Which 2 letters show where Eskimos live? G, V
25. How warm is it during winter in Alaska? Idea: very cold

WORKBOOK

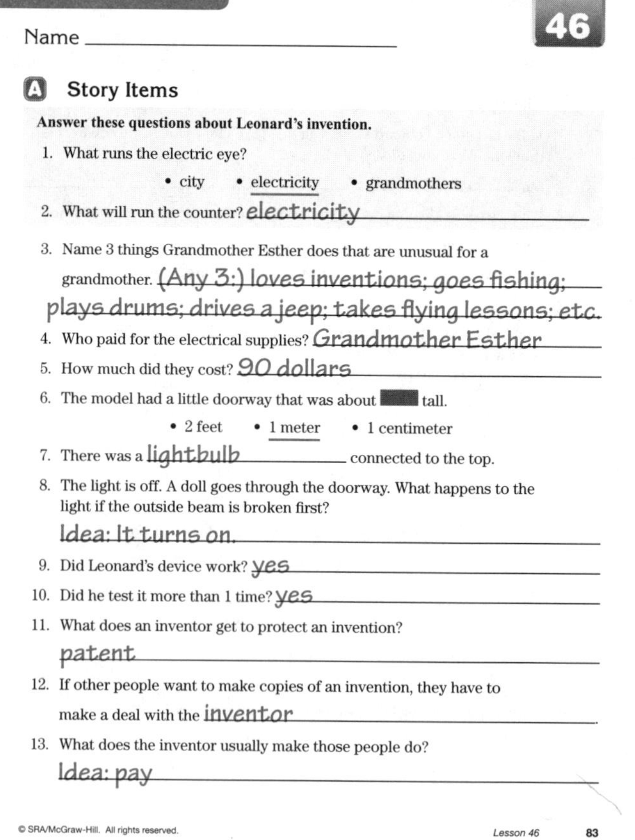

46

Name ____________________

A Story Items

Answer these questions about Leonard's invention.

1. What runs the electric eye?
   • city • electricity • grandmothers
2. What will run the counter? electricity
3. Name 3 things Grandmother Esther does that are unusual for a grandmother. (Any 3:) loves inventions; goes fishing; plays drums; drives a jeep; takes flying lessons; etc.
4. Who paid for the electrical supplies? Grandmother Esther
5. How much did they cost? 90 dollars
6. The model had a little doorway that was about ▬ tall.
   • 2 feet • 1 meter • 1 centimeter
7. There was a lightbulb connected to the top.
8. The light is off. A doll goes through the doorway. What happens to the light if the outside beam is broken first?
   Idea: It turns on.
9. Did Leonard's device work? yes
10. Did he test it more than 1 time? yes
11. What does an inventor get to protect an invention?
    patent
12. If other people want to make copies of an invention, they have to make a deal with the inventor.
13. What does the inventor usually make those people do?
    Idea: pay

WORKBOOK

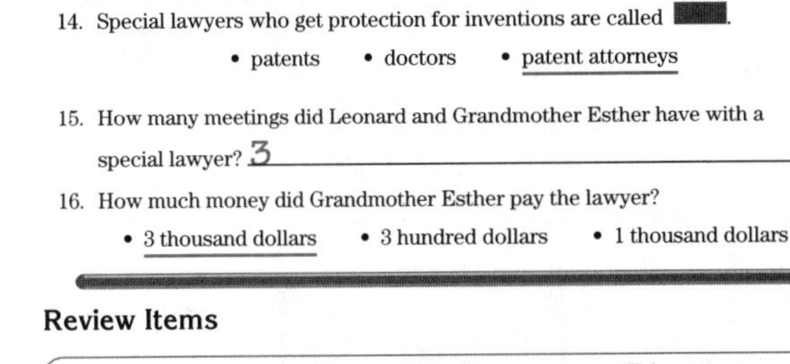

14. Special lawyers who get protection for inventions are called ___.
    - patents
    - doctors
    - patent attorneys
15. How many meetings did Leonard and Grandmother Esther have with a special lawyer? 3
16. How much money did Grandmother Esther pay the lawyer?
    - 3 thousand dollars
    - 3 hundred dollars
    - 1 thousand dollars

Review Items

Use these names to answer the questions: **Tyrannosaurus, Triceratops.**

17. What is animal P? Tyrannosaurus
18. What is animal J? Triceratops

P J

GO TO PART C IN YOUR TEXTBOOK.

TEXTBOOK

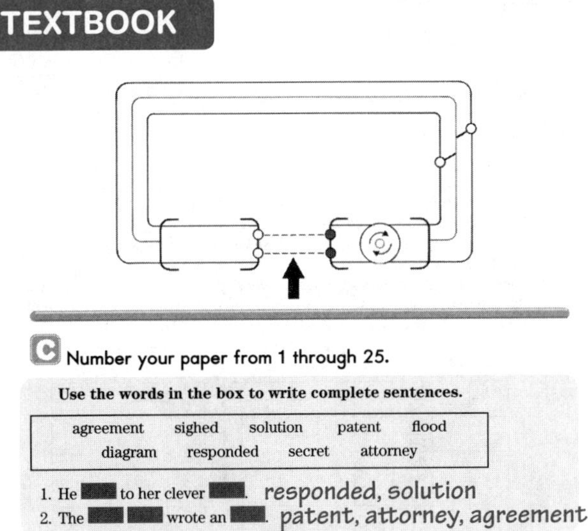

C Number your paper from 1 through 25.

Use the words in the box to write complete sentences.

agreement	sighed	solution	patent	flood
diagram	responded	secret	attorney	

1. He ___ to her clever ___. responded, solution
2. The ___ ___ wrote an ___. patent, attorney, agreement

Review Items

3. The solid arrows show how many times people went into the room. How many people went into the room? 4
4. The dotted arrows show how many times people left the room. How many people left the room? 3
5. Are the lights on in the room? yes
6. How many more people would have to leave the room before the lights go off? 1

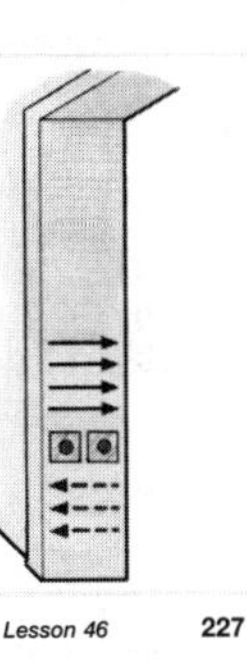

TEXTBOOK

Answer these questions about the counter on Leonard's device:

7. Every time somebody goes into the room, what does the counter do?
    - +1
    - -1
    - -0
8. Every time somebody goes out of the room, what does the counter do?
    - +1
    - -1
    - -0
9. What number does the counter end up at when the last person leaves the room? 0
10. What happens to the lights when the counter gets to that number? They turn off

For each picture, tell if the lights in the room are **on** or **off.** The solid arrows show people going into the room. The dotted arrows show people leaving the room.

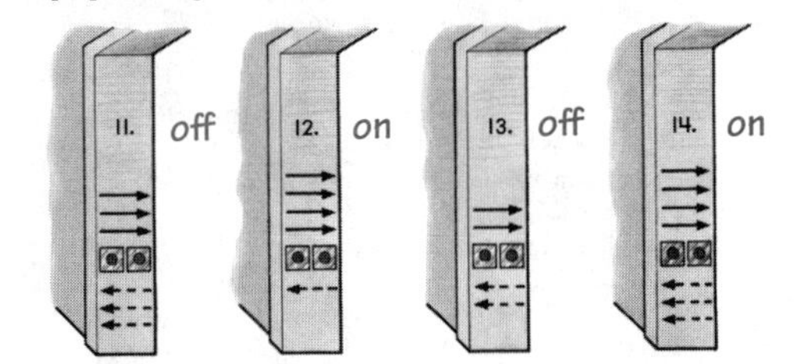

15. Two things happen to melted rock when it moves down the sides of a volcano. Name those 2 things. Ideas: cools and hardens
16. What is it called when the earth shakes and cracks? earthquake
17. The earth makes a circle around the sun one time every ___. year
18. How many days does it take the earth to make one full circle around the sun? 365

TEXTBOOK

19. Is it easier to fly alone or with a large flock? with a large flock
20. Flying near the back of a large flock is like riding your bike ___.
    - against the wind
    - with the wind
21. During winter at the North Pole, how much does the sun shine?
    - all the time
    - never
22. During summer at the North Pole, how much does the sun shine?
    - all the time
    - never
23. When days get shorter, is the North Pole tilting **toward** the sun or **away from** the sun? away from the sun
24. When days get longer, is the North Pole tilting **toward** the sun or **away from** the sun? toward the sun
25. In April, the sun shines for more than ___ hours each day in Alaska. 12

WORKBOOK

Name ______________________

47

A Story Items

1. On which table would Leonard set up his display? F16

Look at the picture below. Not all the spaces have numbers and letters.

2. **Fill in the letters** that go at the top of each aisle.
3. **Number** all the tables in the aisle where Leonard's display was.
4. **Circle** Leonard's table.
5. Leonard and his grandmother started where the **X** is. They first went across the hall to the correct aisle. Then they walked down that aisle to their table. **Draw a path** that shows how they went from the **X** to their table.

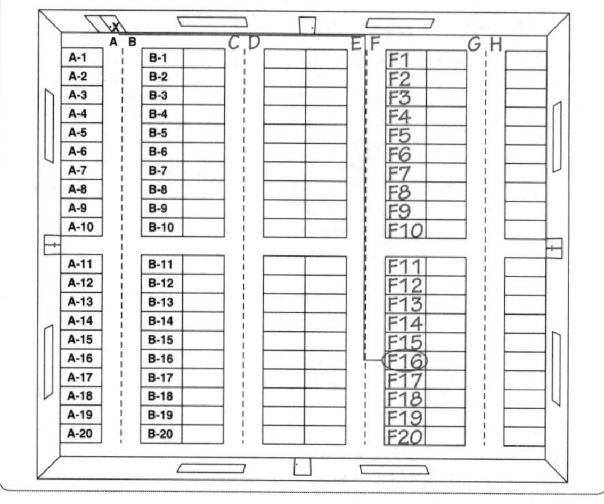

WORKBOOK

6. **Circle** Leonard's table.
7. What space is just north of Leonard's space? F15
8. What space is just west of Leonard's space? E16
9. What space is just south of Leonard's space? F17
10. What space is just east of Leonard's space? G16

North

West / East

A	B	C	D	E	F	G	H
A-1	B-1	C-1	D-1	E-1	F-1	G-1	H-1
A-2	B-2	C-2	D-2	E-2	F-2	G-2	H-2
A-3	B-3	C-3	D-3	E-3	F-3	G-3	H-3
A-4	B-4	C-4	D-4	E-4	F-4	G-4	H-4
A-5	B-5	C-5	D-5	E-5	F-5	G-5	H-5
A-6	B-6	C-6	D-6	E-6	F-6	G-6	H-6
A-7	B-7	C-7	D-7	E-7	F-7	G-7	H-7
A-8	B-8	C-8	D-8	E-8	F-8	G-8	H-8
A-9	B-9	C-9	D-9	E-9	F-9	G-9	H-9
A-10	B-10	C-10	D-10	E-10	F-10	G-10	H-10
A-11	B-11	C-11	D-11	E-11	F-11	G-11	H-11
A-12	B-12	C-12	D-12	E-12	F-12	G-12	H-12
A-13	B-13	C-13	D-13	E-13	F-13	G-13	H-13
A-14	B-14	C-14	D-14	E-14	F-14	G-14	H-14
A-15	B-15	C-15	D-15	E-15	F-15	G-15	H-15
A-16	B-16	C-16	D-16	E-16	F-16	G-16	H-16
A-17	B-17	C-17	D-17	E-17	F-17	G-17	H-17
A-18	B-18	C-18	D-18	E-18	F-18	G-18	H-18
A-19	B-19	C-19	D-19	E-19	F-19	G-19	H-19
A-20	B-20	C-20	D-20	E-20	F-20	G-20	H-20

South

GO TO PART C IN YOUR TEXTBOOK.

TEXTBOOK

announcements. One announcement was, "No smoking in the hall." Another announcement told the inventors where their tables were. Each inventor had a blue piece of paper that had a letter and a number on it. The announcer explained to the inventors that all slips that had the letter A would be in the first aisle, that the Bs would be in the next aisle, that the Cs would be in the next aisle, and so forth. Here's what it said at the top of Leonard's slip: F16.

As Leonard and his grandmother walked to the aisle, Leonard said, "This is the biggest hall I've ever seen in my life."

A	B	C	D	E	F	G	H
A-1	B-1	C-1	D-1	E-1	F-1	G-1	H-1
A-2	B-2	C-2	D-2	E-2	F-2	G-2	H-2
A-3	B-3	C-3	D-3	E-3	F-3	G-3	H-3
A-4	B-4	C-4	D-4	E-4	F-4	G-4	H-4
A-5	B-5	C-5	D-5	E-5	F-5	G-5	H-5
A-6	B-6	C-6	D-6	E-6	F-6	G-6	H-6
A-7	B-7	C-7	D-7	E-7	F-7	G-7	H-7
A-8	B-8	C-8	D-8	E-8	F-8	G-8	H-8
A-9	B-9	C-9	D-9	E-9	F-9	G-9	H-9
A-10	B-10	C-10	D-10	E-10	F-10	G-10	H-10
A-11	B-11	C-11	D-11	E-11	F-11	G-11	H-11
A-12	B-12	C-12	D-12	E-12	F-12	G-12	H-12
A-13	B-13	C-13	D-13	E-13	F-13	G-13	H-13
A-14	B-14	C-14	D-14	E-14	F-14	G-14	H-14
A-15	B-15	C-15	D-15	E-15	F-15	G-15	H-15
A-16	B-16	C-16	D-16	E-16	F-16	G-16	H-16
A-17	B-17	C-17	D-17	E-17	F-17	G-17	H-17
A-18	B-18	C-18	D-18	E-18	F-18	G-18	H-18
A-19	B-19	C-19	D-19	E-19	F-19	G-19	H-19
A-20	B-20	C-20	D-20	E-20	F-20	G-20	H-20

C Number your paper from 1 through 26.

Story Items

Write the words that go in the blanks to tell about the steps Leonard took to invent the electric eye device.

1. He started with a ▬.
   - solution
   - need
   - light

   Then he got an idea for an invention.
2. Then he built a ▬ of the invention to show it worked. model; display
3. Then he got a ▬ to protect his invention. patent

TEXTBOOK

4. What are businesses that make things called? manufacturers
5. What plan did Grandmother Esther have for getting in touch with these businesses?
   - an invention fair
   - a magazine
   - a lawyer
6. What was first prize at the invention fair? 20 thousand dollars
7. What was second prize? 10 thousand dollars
8. What did Grandmother Esther think they would win? first prize; 20 thousand dollars
9. On what day did the fair start? Friday
10. At what time did the fair start? noon
11. The invention fair was held in a great ▬. hall
12. Why couldn't the inventors set up their displays the night before the fair? Idea: There had been a basketball game.

Review Items

13. Things closer to the bottom of the pile went into the pile ▬. first; earlier; earliest
14. What does an inventor get to protect an invention? patent
15. Special lawyers who get protection for inventions are called ▬.
    - doctors
    - patents
    - patent attorneys
16. If other people want to make copies of an invention, they have to make a deal with the ▬. inventor
17. What does the inventor usually make those people do? Idea: pay
18. The solid arrows show how many times people went into the room. How many people went into the room? 3
19. The dotted arrows show how many times people left the room. How many people left the room? 1
20. Are the lights on in the room? yes
21. How many more people would have to leave the room before the lights go off? 2

TEXTBOOK

22. Write the letter of the earth that has the North Pole tilting away from the sun. A
23. Write the letter of the earth that has the North Pole tilting toward the sun. C
24. Write the letter of the earth that has darkness all around the North Pole. A
25. Write the letter of the earth that has daylight all around the North Pole. C
26. Write **A, B, C** and **D**. Then write the season each earth in the picture shows. A: winter; B: spring; C: summer; D: fall

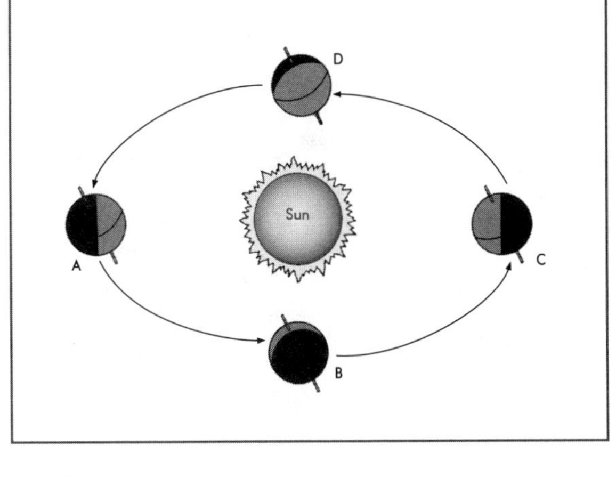

WORKBOOK

Name ______________________

A Story Items

1. Leonard was very disappointed when the fair opened. Tell why.
   - Lots of manufacturers showed up.
   - Not many people showed up.
   - Grandmother Esther talked too much.
2. How many people stopped at Leonard's display the first afternoon? 3
3. How many of them seemed very interested? Idea: none
4. Why don't smart manufacturers act interested in the inventions that they want?
   - so they don't have to pay as much for the invention
   - because they are at the fair all day long
   - because they want to pay more for the invention
5. After supper, there were great crowds of people at the fair. Were these people manufacturers? no
6. Did these people act interested in Leonard's invention? yes
7. Name 2 things that make you think the slim woman in the gray coat was a manufacturer. (Any 2:) She'd been at the fair since it opened; she didn't seem interested in Leonard's invention; she wrote in a little book.
8. Why would manufacturers want to make their deals before the prizes are announced?
   - so they could go home earlier
   - so they wouldn't have to pay as much
   - so they had something to do

WORKBOOK

9. Grandmother Esther gave 2 reasons that the manufacturers did not wait until the afternoon to make their deals. What are those 2 reasons? 2 ideas:
   1. The inventors would be busy (in the afternoon).
   2. It would take time to work out deals.

Look at the picture below.

10. Make an **I** by each inventor.
11. Make an **M** by each manufacturer.

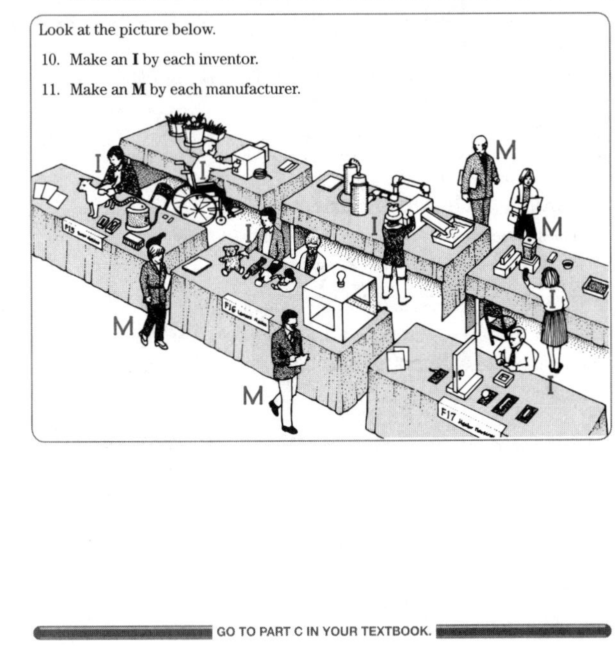

GO TO PART C IN YOUR TEXTBOOK.

TEXTBOOK

C Number your paper from 1 through 25.

Skill Items

The applause interrupted his speech.

1. What word means **broke into?** interrupted
2. What word means **the clapping?** applause

Review Items

3. Write the letters of the 3 things you find in the Bermuda Triangle. b, c, e
   a. ice floes c. whirlpools e. huge waves
   b. sudden storms d. streams f. mountains
4. Write the letter of the footprint made by the heaviest animal. G
5. Write the letter of the footprint made by the lightest animal. H

F G H

6. The picture shows marks left by an animal. Which arrow shows the direction the animal is moving? K
7. Write the letter of the part that shows a footprint. Y
8. Write the letter of the part that shows the mark left by the animal's tail. X

J K X Y

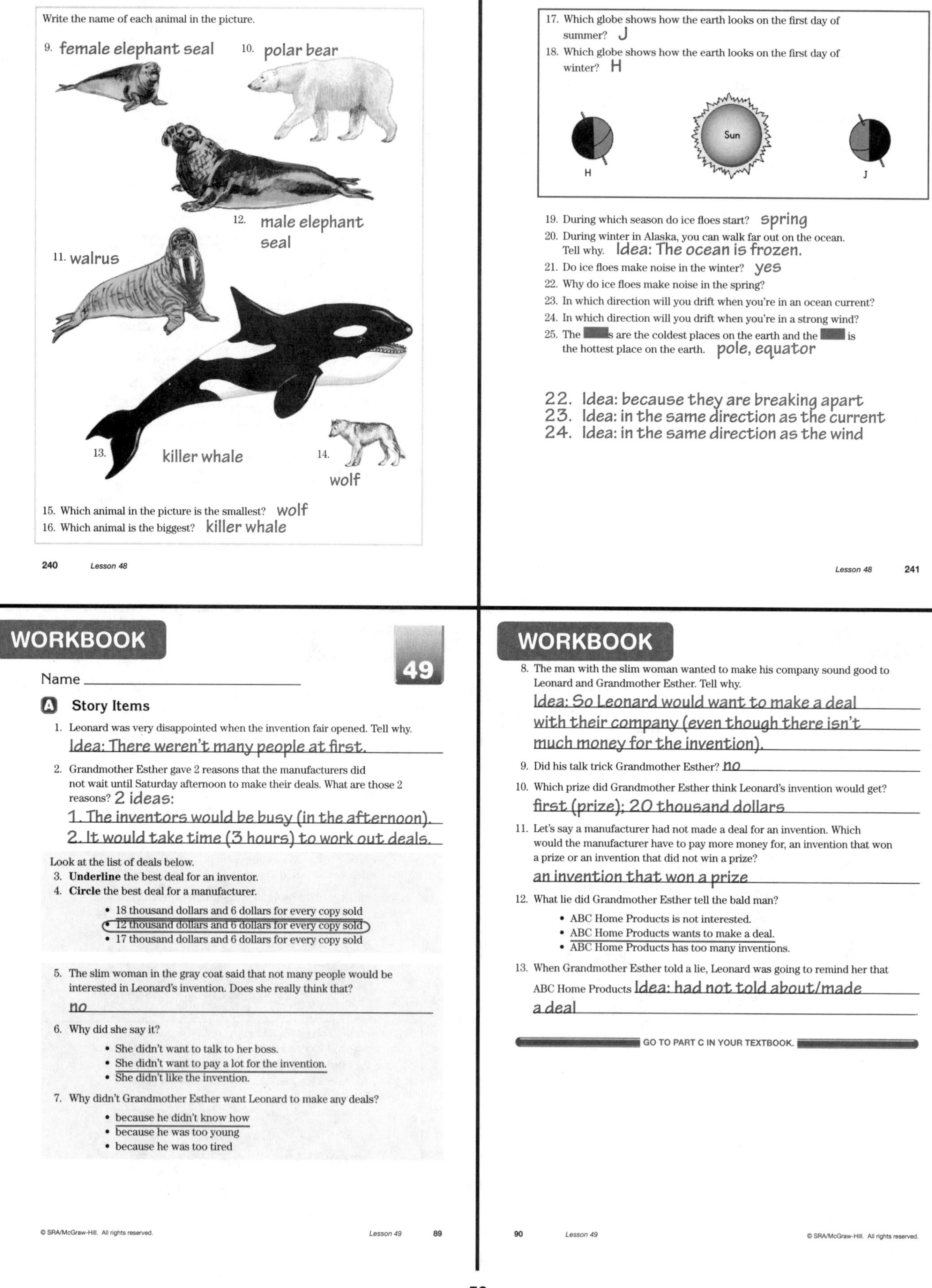

TEXTBOOK

Write the name of each animal in the picture.

9. female elephant seal
10. polar bear
11. walrus
12. male elephant seal
13. killer whale
14. wolf

15. Which animal in the picture is the smallest? wolf
16. Which animal is the biggest? killer whale

TEXTBOOK

17. Which globe shows how the earth looks on the first day of summer? J
18. Which globe shows how the earth looks on the first day of winter? H

19. During which season do ice floes start? spring
20. During winter in Alaska, you can walk far out on the ocean. Tell why. Idea: The ocean is frozen.
21. Do ice floes make noise in the winter? yes
22. Why do ice floes make noise in the spring?
23. In which direction will you drift when you're in an ocean current?
24. In which direction will you drift when you're in a strong wind?
25. The ___s are the coldest places on the earth and the ___ is the hottest place on the earth. pole, equator

22. Idea: because they are breaking apart
23. Idea: in the same direction as the current
24. Idea: in the same direction as the wind

WORKBOOK

49

Name ______________________

A Story Items

1. Leonard was very disappointed when the invention fair opened. Tell why.
   Idea: There weren't many people at first.
2. Grandmother Esther gave 2 reasons that the manufacturers did not wait until Saturday afternoon to make their deals. What are those 2 reasons? 2 ideas:
   1. The inventors would be busy (in the afternoon).
   2. It would take time (3 hours) to work out deals.

Look at the list of deals below.

3. **Underline** the best deal for an inventor.
4. **Circle** the best deal for a manufacturer.
   - 18 thousand dollars and 6 dollars for every copy sold
   - 12 thousand dollars and 6 dollars for every copy sold
   - 17 thousand dollars and 6 dollars for every copy sold

5. The slim woman in the gray coat said that not many people would be interested in Leonard's invention. Does she really think that?
   no
6. Why did she say it?
   - She didn't want to talk to her boss.
   - She didn't want to pay a lot for the invention.
   - She didn't like the invention.
7. Why didn't Grandmother Esther want Leonard to make any deals?
   - because he didn't know how
   - because he was too young
   - because he was too tired

WORKBOOK

8. The man with the slim woman wanted to make his company sound good to Leonard and Grandmother Esther. Tell why.
   Idea: So Leonard would want to make a deal with their company (even though there isn't much money for the invention).
9. Did his talk trick Grandmother Esther? no
10. Which prize did Grandmother Esther think Leonard's invention would get?
    first (prize); 20 thousand dollars
11. Let's say a manufacturer had not made a deal for an invention. Which would the manufacturer have to pay more money for, an invention that won a prize or an invention that did not win a prize?
    an invention that won a prize
12. What lie did Grandmother Esther tell the bald man?
    - ABC Home Products is not interested.
    - ABC Home Products wants to make a deal.
    - ABC Home Products has too many inventions.
13. When Grandmother Esther told a lie, Leonard was going to remind her that ABC Home Products Idea: had not told about/made a deal

GO TO PART C IN YOUR TEXTBOOK.

TEXTBOOK

give us your business card. You're going to tell us your best deal. And then we're going to see if that deal is better than the deal ABC Home Products wants to make."

"But Grandma," Leonard said. He was going to remind her that ABC Home Products had not told about the deal they wanted to make.

She interrupted Leonard and said, "I know what you're thinking, Leonard. You want to go with ABC Home Products. But we have to give these other manufacturers a chance, too."

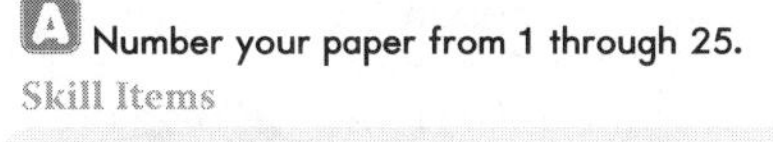

A Number your paper from 1 through 25.

Skill Items

Use the words in the box to write complete sentences.

company	applause	owed	patent	connected
attorney	prize	agreement	interrupted	

1. The ▬ ▬ wrote an ▬.
2. The ▬ ▬ his speech.

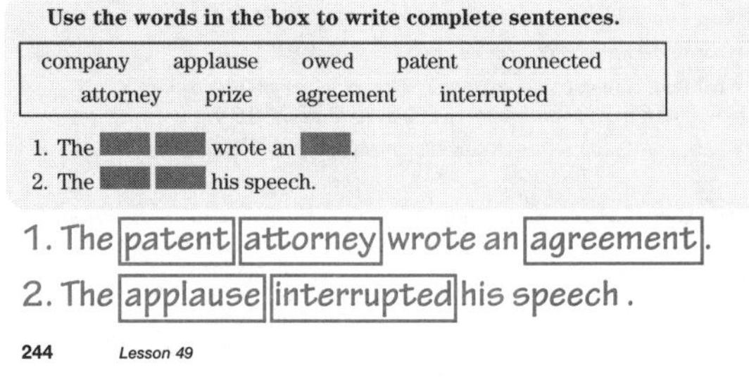

1. The patent attorney wrote an agreement.
2. The applause interrupted his speech.

TEXTBOOK

Review Items 3. tiny drops of water; 4. storm cloud

3. What are clouds made of?
4. What kind of cloud does the picture show?
5. What happens to a drop of water at **B**? Idea: It freezes.

6. What is a person doing when the person makes an object for the first time? inventing
7. The person who makes an object for the first time is called an ▬. inventor
8. The object the person makes is called an ▬. invention
9. What are businesses that make things called? manufacturers
10. Geese live in large groups called ▬. flocks
11. Where are most wild geese born? Canada
12. In which direction do geese fly in the fall? south
13. What is this trip called? migration

Choose from these words to answer each item:

- moon
- Florida
- sun
- Canada
- equator
- geese
- poles
- migration

14. The heat that the earth receives comes from the ▬. sun
15. The part of the earth that receives more heat than any other part is the ▬. equator
16. The parts of the earth that receive less heat than any other part are called the ▬. poles

TEXTBOOK

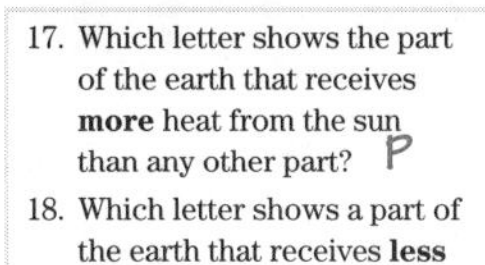

17. Which letter shows the part of the earth that receives **more** heat from the sun than any other part? P
18. Which letter shows a part of the earth that receives **less** heat from the sun than any other part? R

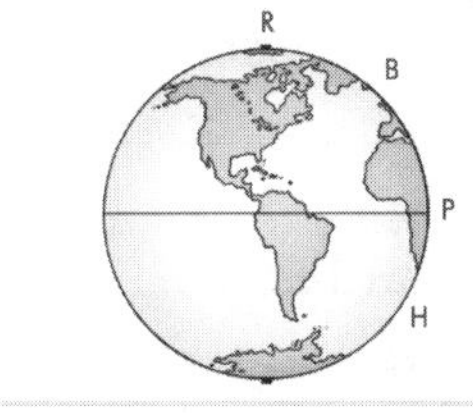

19. If you cannot see the sun, is it **daytime** or **nighttime** on your side of the earth? nighttime
20. What is it on the other side of the earth? daytime
21. The earth turns around one time every ▬ hours. 24

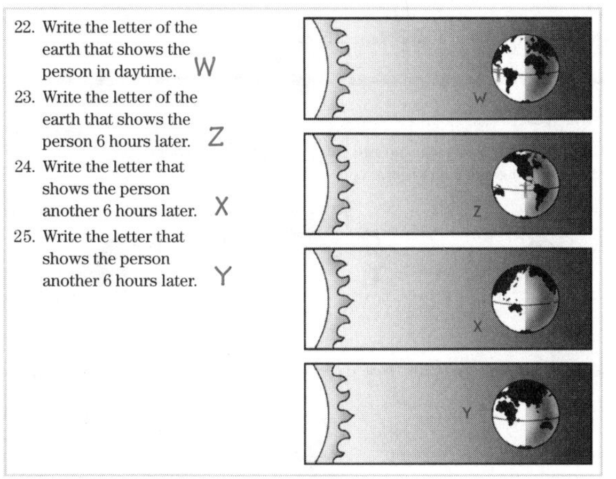

22. Write the letter of the earth that shows the person in daytime. W
23. Write the letter of the earth that shows the person 6 hours later. Z
24. Write the letter that shows the person another 6 hours later. X
25. Write the letter that shows the person another 6 hours later. Y

TEXTBOOK

Number your paper from 1 through 34.

Here's the rule about an electric eye: **Each time the beam of light is broken, the light changes.**

1. The light is off. The beam is broken 2 times. Is the light **on** or **off** at the end? off
2. The light is off. The beam is broken 5 times. Is the light **on** or **off** at the end? on
3. The light is off. The beam is broken 8 times. Is the light **on** or **off** at the end? off
4. How many electric eyes did Leonard use for his invention? 2
5. How many beams went across the doorway? 2

The picture shows two electric eye beams on the side of doors. The number **1** shows the beam that is broken first. The number **2** shows the beam that is broken next. Write the letter of the correct arrow for each doorway.

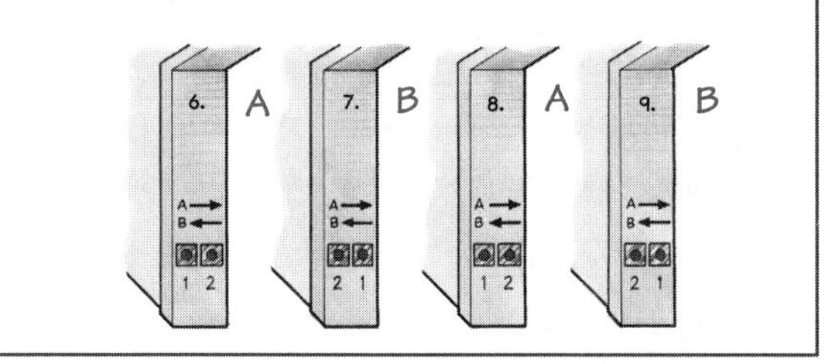

TEXTBOOK

Answer these questions about the counter on Leonard's device:

10. Every time somebody goes into the room, what does the counter do?
    - +1 (underlined)
    - -1
    - +0
11. Every time somebody goes out of the room, what does the counter do?
    - +1
    - -1 (underlined)
    - +0
12. What number does the counter end up at when the last person leaves the room? zero (0)
13. What happens to the lights when the counter gets to that number? Idea: They turn off.

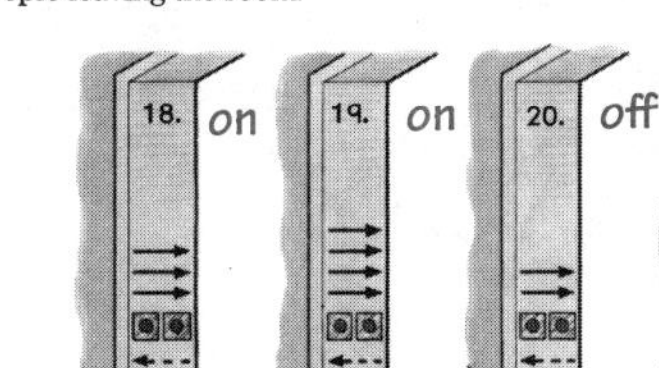

14. The solid arrows show how many times people went into the room. How many people went into the room? 5
15. The dotted arrows show how many times people left the room. How many people left the room? 2
16. Are the lights on in the room? yes
17. How many more people would have to leave the room before the lights go off? 3

For each picture, tell if the lights in the room are **on** or **off.** The solid arrows show people going into the room. The dotted arrows show people leaving the room.

18. on 19. on 20. off 21. on

TEXTBOOK

23. patent attorneys

22. What does an inventor get to protect an invention? patent
23. Special lawyers who get protection for inventions are called ▬.
24. What are businesses that make things called? manufacturers

Write the words that go in the blanks to tell about the steps you take to invent something.

25. You start with a ▬.
    - light
    - solution
    - need (underlined)

    Then you get an idea for an invention.
26. Then you build a ▬ of the invention to show how it works. model
27. Then you get a ▬ to protect your invention. patent

Skill Items

For each item, write the underlined word from the sentences in the box.

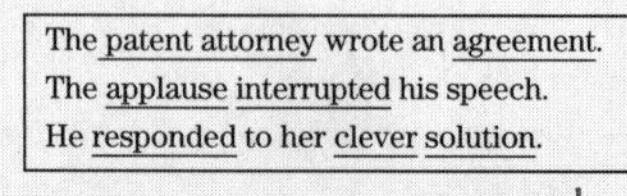

The patent attorney wrote an agreement.
The applause interrupted his speech.
He responded to her clever solution.

28. What underlining means **reacted?** responded
29. What underlining means **lawyer?** attorney
30. What underlining means **a promise made by people?** agreement
31. What underlining means **the clapping?** applause
32. What underlining means **very smart?** clever
33. What underlining names a lawyer whose special job is getting patents for new inventions? patent attorney
34. What underlining refers to solving a problem? solution

END OF TEST 5

WORKBOOK

51

Name ______

A Story Items

1. The slim woman in the gray coat said that not many people would be interested in Leonard's invention. Did she really think that? no
2. Why did she say it?
   - She didn't like the invention.
   - She didn't want to talk to her boss.
   - She didn't want to pay a lot for the invention. (underlined)
3. The woman in the gray coat made two offers. Tell about her **first** offer.
   10 thousand dollars for the invention and
   1 dollar for every copy that is sold.
4. Did Leonard like that offer? yes
5. Did Grandmother Esther like that offer? no
6. Tell about the offer everyone agreed on.
   10 thousand dollars for the invention and
   2 dollars for every copy that is sold.
7. **Underline** the 2 ways that tell how the slim woman changed after she made the deal.
   - Her voice was pleasant. (underlined)
   - She smiled. (underlined)
   - She yelled.
   - Her voice was loud.
   - Her voice was higher.
   - She closed her eyes.
8. What did Grandmother Esther and Leonard have to do to finish the deal?
   - win a prize
   - get another patent
   - sign papers (underlined)

WORKBOOK

9. Who did Grandmother Esther think would win first prize? them; Leonard
10. Who won first prize? Ronald Hogan
11. What was the person's invention? Idea: automatic list-writer
12. How much money did Leonard win for his prize? 10 thousand dollars
13. Why did Leonard want Grandmother Esther to go on the stage with him?
    - She wanted to go up there.
    - She helped with his invention. (underlined)
    - She knew Ronald Hogan.
14. Did she want to do that? no

Review Item

15. The picture shows the sun and two balls. Fix up the balls so that half of each ball is in sunlight and half is in shadow.

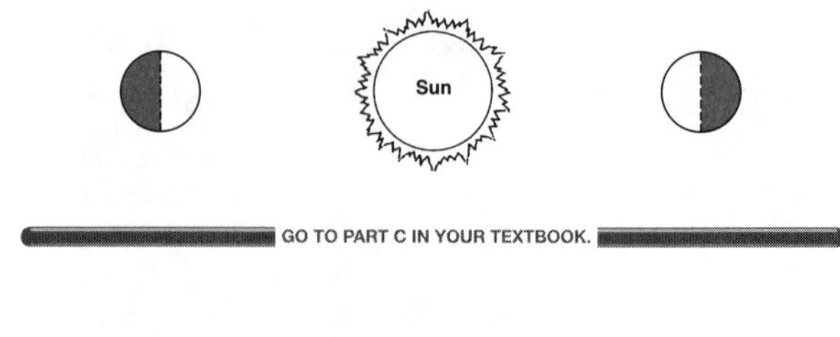

GO TO PART C IN YOUR TEXTBOOK.

TEXTBOOK

C Number your paper from 1 through 22.

Skill Items

Here are three events that happened in the story.
Write **beginning, middle** or **end** for each event.

1. The next thing Leonard knew, he was holding a check and people were clapping again. end
2. That evening at 8:30, the lights in the hall were dimmed. middle
3. The woman in the gray coat came back to Leonard's display with two men. beginning

Review Items

Use these names to answer the questions:
Tyrannosaurus, Triceratops.

4. What is animal **D?**
5. What is animal **E?**

4. Triceratops
5. Tyrannosaurus

E

D

Write the words that go in the blanks to tell about the steps you take to invent something.

6. You start with a ▬.
   - solution
   - electric eye
   - need

   Then you get an idea for an invention.
7. Then you build a ▬ of the invention to show how it works. model
8. Then you get a ▬ to protect your invention. patent

TEXTBOOK

9. Why don't smart manufacturers act interested in the inventions that they want? **Write the letter of the answer.** b
   a. because they want to pay more for the invention
   b. so they don't have to pay as much for the invention
   c. because they are at the fair all day long
10. Write the letter of the best deal for an inventor. c
11. Write the letter of the best deal for a manufacturer. a
    a. 5 thousand dollars and 5 dollars for every copy sold
    b. 8 thousand dollars and 5 dollars for every copy sold
    c. 12 thousand dollars and 5 dollars for every copy sold
12. Write the letters of the 2 kinds of places that are safe for geese. a, c
    a. places with no geese or ducks
    b. places with a few geese
    c. places with many geese
    d. places with a few ducks
13. The map shows a route. What state is at the north end of the route? Alaska
14. What country is at the south end of the route? Canada
15. About how many miles is the route? 2500 (miles)

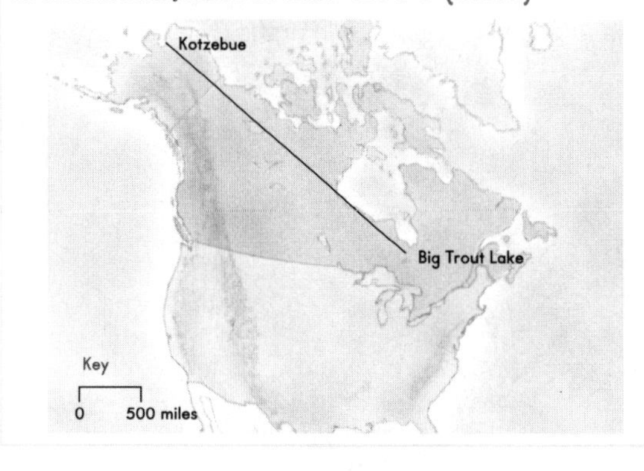

TEXTBOOK

16. Name 3 animals that are warm-blooded. (Any 3:) bears, humans, dogs, etc.
17. Name 3 animals that are cold-blooded. (Any 3:) fish, sharks, reptiles, etc.
18. Write the letter of the storm clouds. B
19. Write the letter of the clouds that may stay in the sky for days at a time. C
20. Write the letter of the clouds that have frozen drops of water. A

Study Items

Look in the Yellow Pages of your phone book to find out 2 things.

21. Find out if there are any electric-equipment manufacturers. The word **manufacturer** may be written like this in the Yellow Pages: **mfr.** If the Yellow Pages list any electric-equipment manufacturers, write down the name of one manufacturer. That would be the kind of company that would make copies of Leonard's invention.
22. Also look up the names of stores that might sell the copies that are manufactured. These are stores that would be listed under a heading like this: **Electric Equipment and Supplies—Retail.** The name **retail** tells you that you can buy things at that store. Write the name of an electric-equipment-and-supply retail store.
    (the name of one electric-equipment-and-supply retail store)

21. (the name of an electric-equipment manufacturer)

WORKBOOK

52

Name 8. Ideas: ABC Home Products dealer; electrical equipment and supplies; a specific retailer found in the Yellow Pages

A Story Items

1. The woman in the gray coat made two offers. Her first offer was 10 thousand dollars for the invention and 1 dollar for every copy that is sold.
2. Did Leonard like that offer? yes
3. Did Grandmother Esther like that offer? no
4. The offer that everyone agreed on was 10 thousand dollars for the invention and 2 dollars for every copy that is sold.
5. Name one reason Leonard didn't have much free time anymore. Ideas: He was talking to ABC Home Products a lot; he had more friends.
6. What name did ABC Home Products give to Leonard's invention? Mr. Light Saver

Answer these questions about the ad:

7. The ad said you should put a light saver in every room of your house.
8. Who should you see about getting some light savers? ____
9. Leonard's mother solved one problem she had with grocery shopping. She solved that problem by buying ▬.
   - a grocery cart
   - a Mr. Light Saver
   - an automatic list-writer
10. Leonard's mother still had a problem when she went grocery shopping. What was her problem?
    - opening the trunk while holding groceries
    - turning on lights while holding groceries
    - holding groceries and playing the drums

GO TO PART D IN YOUR TEXTBOOK.

TEXTBOOK

D Number your paper from 1 through 29.

1. The arrow on the map goes from San Francisco to ▬. Japan
2. Which ocean does the arrow cross? Pacific (Ocean)

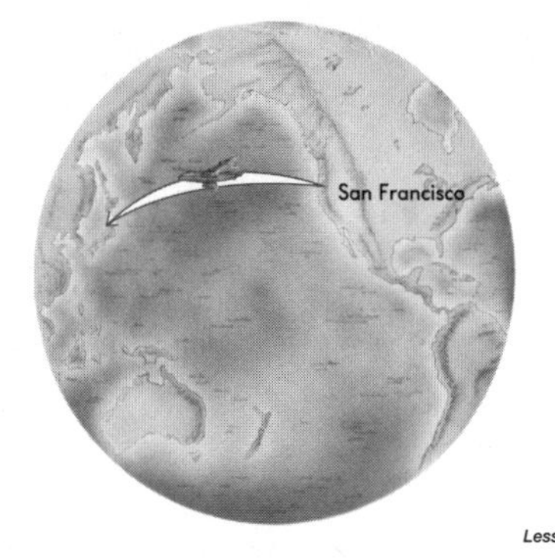

TEXTBOOK

3. Which is bigger, Alaska or Japan? Alaska
4. Is Japan a **state** or a **country?** country
5. How many people live in Japan?
   - <u>127 million</u>
   - 127 thousand
6. Write the letters of 3 types of products that are used in the United States and manufactured in Japan. b, e, f
   - a. furniture
   - b. TVs
   - c. books
   - d. Mr. Light Saver
   - e. CD players
   - f. cars
   - g. rugs

Skill Items

She selected a comfortable seat.

7. What word tells that the seat **felt** pleasant? comfortable
8. What word means **chose?** selected

Review Items

The solid arrows show people going into the room. The dotted arrows show people leaving the room. For each picture, tell if the lights in the room are **on** or **off.**

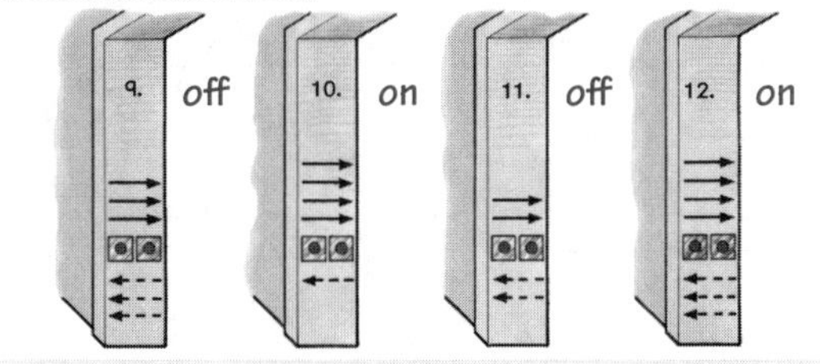

13. What runs an electric eye? electricity; current
14. What kind of boat do Eskimos use in the summer? kayak
15. Why don't they use those boats in the winter? Ideas: because the water is frozen; because of the ice floes; because the winds are too strong

TEXTBOOK

23. Idea: Killer whales are smaller than other whales.

Write the words that go in the blanks to tell about the steps you take to invent something.

16. You start with a ▬.
    - <u>need</u>
    - device
    - solution

    Then you get an idea for an invention.
17. Then you build a ▬ of the invention to show it works. model
18. Then you get a ▬ to protect your invention. patent
19. Write the letter of the best deal for an inventor. b
20. Write the letter of the best deal for a manufacturer. a
    - a. 15 thousand dollars and 4 dollars for every copy sold
    - b. 15 thousand dollars and 8 dollars for every copy sold
    - c. 15 thousand dollars and 5 dollars for every copy sold
21. If an invention wins a prize, would a manufacturer have to pay more money for it? yes
22. About how long are killer whales? about 12 meters
23. Compare the size of killer whales with the size of other whales.
24. Are killer whales fish? no
25. Tell if killer whales are **warm-blooded** or **cold-blooded.** warm-blooded
26. Which letter shows the place that has the warmest winters? L
27. Which letter shows the place that is closest to the equator? L
28. Which letter shows the place that is closest to a pole? R
29. Is the **North Pole** or the **South Pole** closer to that letter? North Pole

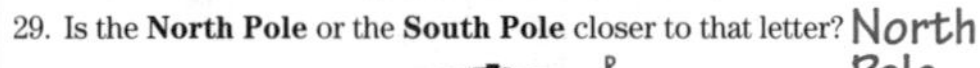

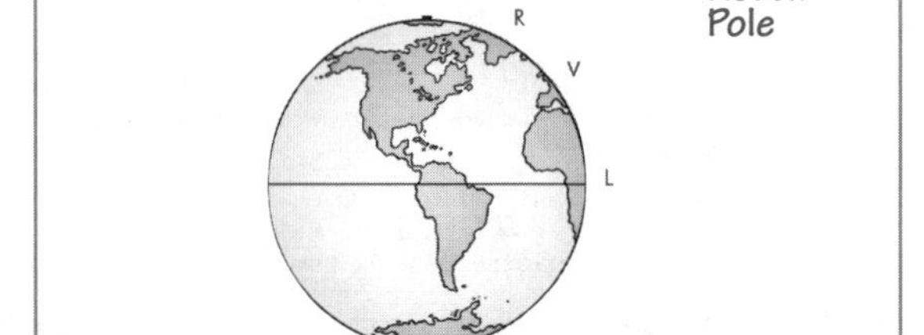

WORKBOOK

53

Name ______________________

A

1. How many suns are in the solar system? 1
2. How many planets are in the solar system? 9
3. Name the planet we live on. Earth
4. What's in the middle of the solar system? the sun
5. Name the only part of the solar system that's burning.
   - our moon
   - Earth
   - <u>the sun</u>
6. Is Earth the planet that is closest to the sun? no
7. The sun gives heat and light to all the planets.

8. Make an **X** on the sun.
9. Make a **Y** on Earth.

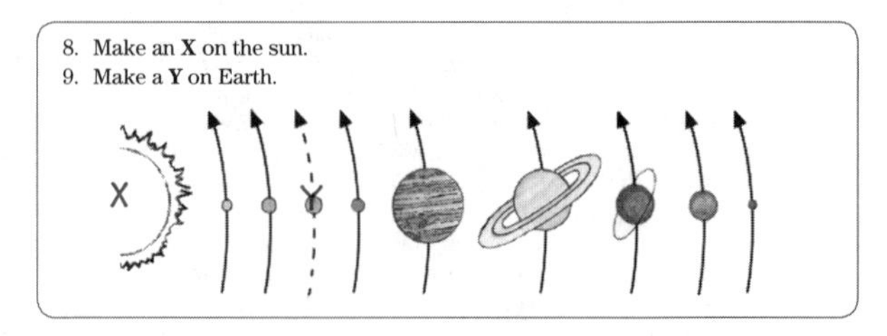

WORKBOOK

10. The planets are named below with Mercury first and Venus second.
Fill in the names of the missing planets.

Mercury, Venus, Earth, Mars, Jupiter, Saturn, Uranus, Neptune, Pluto.

11. Which planet is largest? Jupiter

12. Which planet is next-largest? Saturn

13. How many times larger than Earth is the sun?
- one hundred
- one thousand
- ten thousand

B Story Items

14. Does today's story take place in the past, the present, or the future?
future

15. Students who do well on the test will go on a trip. Where will they go?
Idea: across the solar system

16. About how many students are taking the test with Wendy?
30

17. How many students will go on the trip? 10

18. What country are those students from? Canada

19. How long will the test take? 4 hours

20. Why did Wendy feel sick at the end of the story? Idea: She couldn't remember the answer to a question.

GO TO PART D IN YOUR TEXTBOOK.

TEXTBOOK

Wendy wrote answers to the questions and moved to the next item. She read the item and started to feel a little sick. She couldn't remember the answer. She knew that if she missed more than one or two items on this whole test, she would not go on the trip.

Here was that item: Which planet has more moons, Jupiter or Saturn?

D Number your paper from 1 through 20.

Story Items

1. What kind of animals are in the picture? geese
2. In what country are most wild ones born? Canada
3. What is a **group** of these animals called? flock
4. How long do most of them live? about 30 years

Skill Items 5. The applause interrupted his speech.

Use the words in the box to write complete sentences.

interrupted	business	selected	applause
praised	excellent	comfortable	wandering

5. The ▬ ▬ his speech.
6. She ▬ a ▬ seat.

6. She selected a comfortable seat.

TEXTBOOK

Review Items

7. The solid arrows show how many times people went into the room. How many people went into the room? 4
8. The dotted arrows show how many times people left the room. How many people left the room? 1
9. Are the lights on in the room? Yes
10. How many more people would have to leave the room before the lights go off? 3

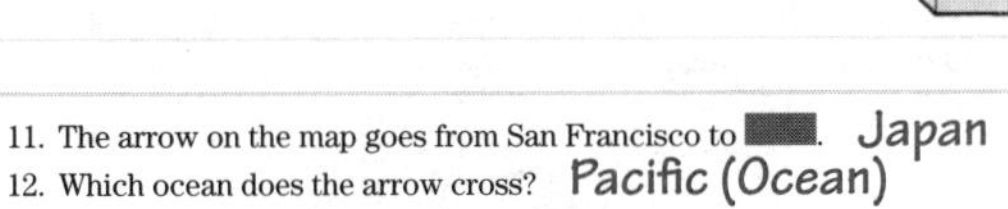

11. The arrow on the map goes from San Francisco to ▬. Japan
12. Which ocean does the arrow cross? Pacific (Ocean)

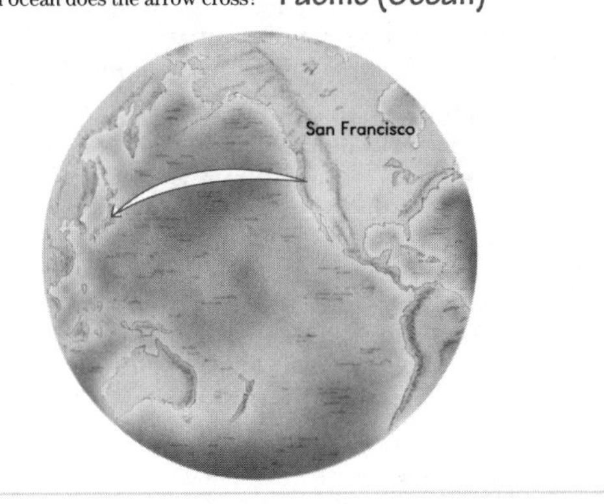

TEXTBOOK

13. What does an inventor get to protect an invention? patent
14. Special lawyers who get protection for inventions are called ▬. patent attorneys
15. If other people want to make copies of an invention, they have to make a deal with the ▬. inventor
16. What does the inventor usually make those people do? Idea: pay
17. Which is bigger, Alaska or Japan? Alaska
18. Is Japan a **state** or a **country?** country
19. How many people live in Japan?
    - 127
    - 127 million
    - 127 thousand
20. Write the letters of 3 types of products that are used in the United States and manufactured in Japan. d, e, f
    - a. furniture
    - b. Mr. Light Saver
    - c. books
    - d. TVs
    - e. CD players
    - f. cars
    - g. rugs

WORKBOOK

Name ________________

A

1. Write the present year on line C.
2. Then write **past** or **future** next to each of the other years.

A. future — 2230

B. future — 2020

C. (current year) — Present year

D. past — 1900

E. past — 1380

3. Write any **3** years that are in the past.
(Accept 3 past years.)

4. Write any **3** years that are in the future.
(Accept 3 future years.)

5. Things that have already happened are in the past
6. Things that are happening now are in the present (time)
7. Things that will happen are in the future (time)

B **Story Items**

8. How long is Traveler Four? 405 feet
9. How many people are in the crew? 30
10. How many passengers does it hold? 200
11. How fast can it travel? 1 thousand miles per second

WORKBOOK

12. How far is it from Earth to Jupiter?
    - 200 million miles
    - 400 thousand miles
    - 400 million miles

13. Here's a picture of Traveler Four. Label the lettered parts.

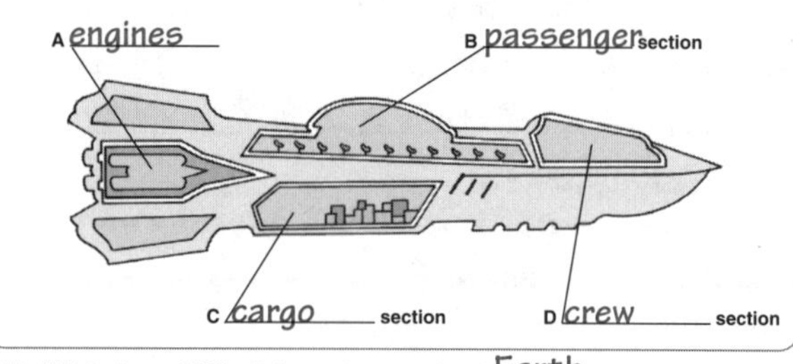

14. Which planet did Wendy know the most about? Earth
15. Which planet did she find the most interesting? Jupiter
16. Why did she think that planet was the most interesting?
    Idea: It was the largest.

Review Items

17. The planets are named below with Mercury first and Venus second. **Write the names of the missing planets.**
    Mercury, Venus, Earth, Mars, Jupiter, Saturn, Uranus, Neptune, Pluto.

GO TO PART D IN YOUR TEXTBOOK.

TEXTBOOK

Make sure that you know the answers to these questions:

How fast does Traveler Four travel?
1 thousand miles per second

How long would it take Traveler Four to go across the United States?
two-and-a-half seconds

How long would it take Traveler Four to go to the moon?
4 minutes

How long would it take Traveler Four to go to Jupiter?
four-and-a-half days

How far is it from Earth to Jupiter?
400 million miles

D Number your paper from 1 through 20.

Story Items

1. How many moons does Jupiter have? 63
2. How many moons does Saturn have? 47
3. If you went west from San Francisco, what country would you reach first? Japan
4. If you go west from the United States, what ocean do you cross? Pacific (Ocean)
5. Which is **larger** in size, Japan or Alaska? Alaska
6. Which has **colder** winter temperatures, the United States or Canada? Canada
7. In which direction would you go from Canada to reach the main part of the United States? south

TEXTBOOK

Review Items

8. Here's the rule: **People who don't show interest in an invention are manufacturers.**
   - Person A walked by the display without saying anything.
   - Person B watched the display and then praised Leonard on his wonderful invention.
   - Person C talked to Leonard for 15 minutes about the invention.
   - Person D listened to what Leonard had to say and then said, "Thank you," and walked away from the display.

   Write the letters of the 2 manufacturers. A, D

Write the words that go in the blanks to tell about the steps you take to invent something.

9. You start with a ___.
   - solution
   - need
   - light

   Then you get an idea for an invention.
10. Then you build a ___ of the invention to show how it works. model
11. Then you get a ___ to protect your invention. patent

12. Why don't smart manufacturers act interested in the inventions that they want? **Write the letter of the answer.** C
    a. because they want to pay more for the invention
    b. because they are at the fair all day long
    c. so they don't have to pay as much for the invention

13. Name the planet we live on. Earth
14. What's in the middle of the solar system? sun
15. Name the only part of the solar system that's burning. sun
16. Is Earth the planet that is closest to the sun? no
17. The sun gives ___ and ___ to all the planets. heat, light
18. Which planet is largest? Jupiter
19. Which planet is next-largest? Saturn
20. How many times larger than Earth is the sun?
    - 2 thousand
    - 1 hundred
    - 1 thousand

WORKBOOK

Name ______________________

A Story Items

Answer these questions about Traveler Four.

1. How many people are in the crew? 30
2. How many passengers does it hold? 200
3. How fast can it travel? 1 thousand miles per second
4. How long did the test take? 4 hours
5. Was Wendy sure that she had answered all the questions correctly?
   no
6. Name all the Travelers that were earlier than Traveler Four.
   Traveler One, Traveler Two, Traveler Three
7. How fast could Traveler One go? 1 mile per second
8. The woman told the students how they would find out whether they would go on the trip. How would they find out? Idea: They would get a letter.
9. Write the first name of the girl who sat behind Wendy during the test.
   Sidney
10. Did that girl think she did well on the test? no
11. What did Wendy do after math class every day?
    Idea: called home
12. Was Wendy selected for the trip? yes
13. What planet will she go to? Jupiter

WORKBOOK

Review Items

14. Name the planet we live on. Earth
15. What's in the middle of the solar system? sun
16. Name the only part of the solar system that's burning. sun
17. Which planet is largest? Jupiter
18. Which planet is next-largest? Saturn
19. How many moons does Saturn have? 47
20. How many moons does Jupiter have? 63
21. How far is it from Earth to Jupiter?
    - 400 miles
    - 400 million miles
    - 400 thousand miles

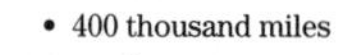

22. The picture shows half a hailstone. How many times did the stone go through a cloud? 6

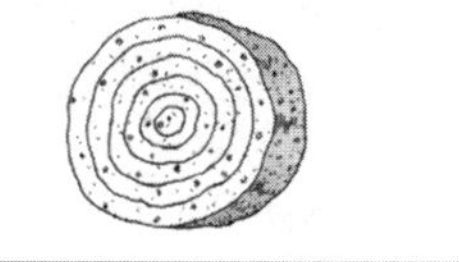

GO TO PART C IN YOUR TEXTBOOK.

TEXTBOOK

The mail usually came to Wendy's house about 11 each morning. By 11:15, Wendy's math class was over, so she ran to the phone and called her home. For the last five days, she had called home at 11:15 each morning. "Hi, Mom," she would say each day. She didn't have to tell her mother why she was calling. Her mother would say, "It hasn't come yet."

"Oh," Wendy would say. Each time her mother told her that the letter hadn't come, Wendy felt glad and sad. She felt sad because she hadn't found out whether she was going on the trip. She felt a little glad because she didn't want the letter to come if it said she wasn't going.

Then on November 19, Wendy's math teacher walked over to her desk just before the class was over. He bent over and said that there was an important message for her, and she should go to the office.

She felt so nervous that she hardly remembered leaving the classroom and going down the hall to the office. She was almost in a dream. The phone felt very heavy. She quickly moved it to her ear. "Mom," she said.

"You did it, honey," her mother said. "You're going."

C Number your paper from 1 through 22.

Skill Items

Without gravity, they were weightless.

1. What word means that something has no weight? weightless
2. What word names the force that pulls things back to Earth? gravity

Review Items

3. What is a person doing when the person makes an object for the first time? inventing
4. The person who makes an object for the first time is called an ▬. inventor
5. The object the person makes is called an ▬. invention

TEXTBOOK

6. How many times larger than Earth is the sun?
   - 1 hundred
   - 1 thousand
   - 10 thousand
7. What does an inventor get to protect an invention? patent
8. Special lawyers who get protection for inventions are called ▬. patent attorneys

The picture shows two electric eye beams on the side of doors. The number **1** shows the beam that is broken first. The number **2** shows the beam that is broken next. Write the letter of the correct arrow for each doorway.

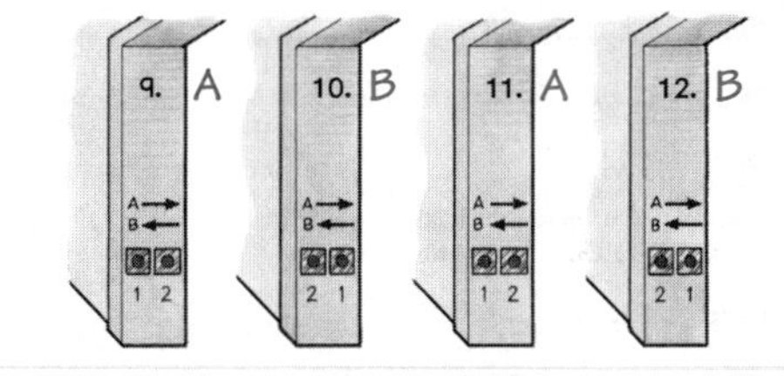

13. Which is smaller, Alaska or Japan? Japan
14. Is Japan a **state** or a **country?** country
15. How many people live in Japan?
    - 127
    - 127 million
    - 127 thousand
16. How old are geese when they mate for the first time? 3 years old
17. After male and female geese mate, how long do they stay together? Idea: until one dies
18. Most geese live for about ▬ years. 30

TEXTBOOK

Look at the map.
19. Which letter shows Big Trout Lake? X
20. Which letter shows Crooked Lake? Z
21. Write the name of the lake that's farther north. Big Trout Lake
22. What country is the **X** in? Canada

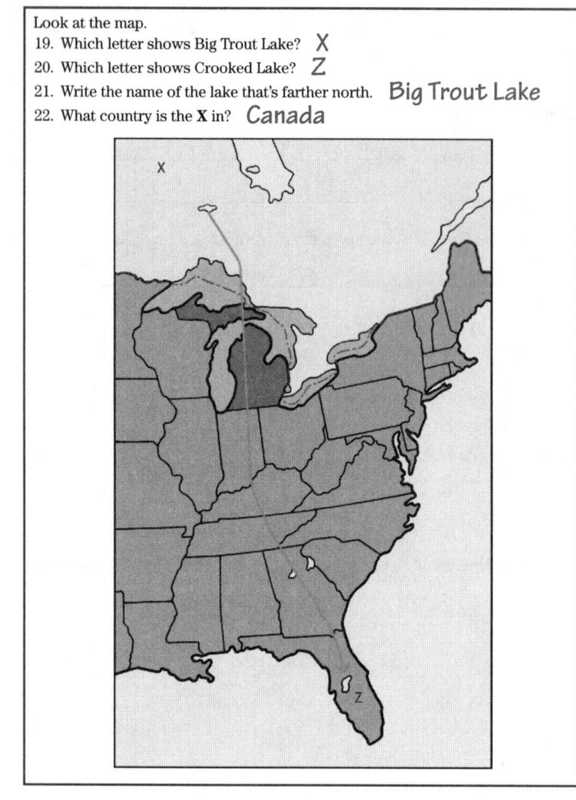

WORKBOOK

Name ____________________

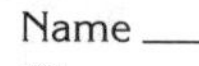

56

A

1. Which letter shows where Wendy's flight began? G
2. Which letter shows Tokyo? H
3. Draw a line to show the route that Wendy's jet plane took.
4. What's the largest city in Japan? Tokyo
5. In which direction did the jet fly from Canada to Tokyo? west

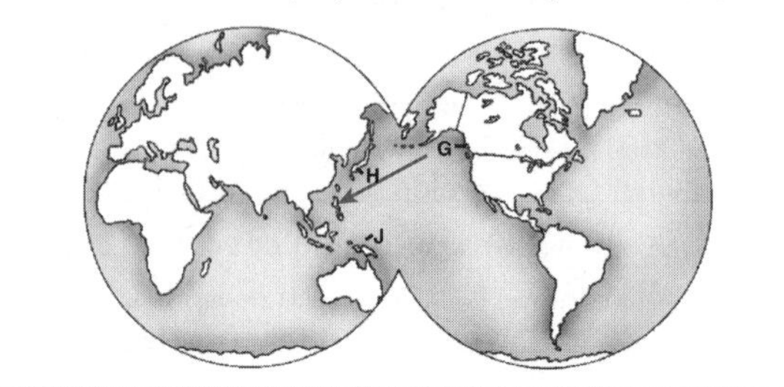

B **Story Items**

6. What city could Wendy see from the space station? Tokyo
7. What country is that city in? Japan
8. What country did Wendy's jet come from? Canada
9. What was Wendy's weight limit for her baggage?
   - 40 pounds
   - 100 pounds
   - 140 pounds
10. Was Wendy in good health? yes

WORKBOOK

11. What surprise did Wendy have at the space station?
    Idea: Sidney was there.
12. Was Sidney's name on the list of students who were going on the trip?
    no
13. Why did Sidney get to go on the trip?
    Ideas: A student (Tim) got sick; someone couldn't go.
14. Most of the other passengers were not students. Who were they?
    scientists

Review Items

15. The planets are named below with Mercury first and Venus second. **Write the names of the missing planets.**

    Mercury, Venus, Earth, Mars, Jupiter, Saturn, Uranus, Neptune, Pluto.

16. How many moons does Jupiter have? 63
17. How many moons does Saturn have? 47
18. How far is it from Earth to Jupiter?
    - 800 million miles
    - 40 million miles
    - 400 million miles
19. If other people want to make copies of an invention, they have to make a deal with the inventor
20. What does the inventor usually make those people do?
    Idea: pay

GO TO PART D IN YOUR TEXTBOOK.

TEXTBOOK

D **Number your paper from 1 through 20.**

Skill Items

Here are three events that happened in the story.
Write **beginning, middle,** or **end** for each event.
1. Wendy imagined how Sidney must have felt today, knowing that the other students were going on the trip. middle
2. Newspaper reporters met the students at the airport in Tokyo. beginning
3. The voice over the loudspeaker said, "Welcome aboard Traveler Four." end

Write the word from the box that means that same thing as the underlined part of each sentence.

concluded	moaned	ignore	practiced
glance	directed	divided	purchase

4. They will buy a new house next year. purchase
5. We finished our meal with apple pie. concluded
6. She worked on playing the piano. practiced

Use the words in the box to write complete sentences.

worried	gravity	weightless	comfortable	
final	equipment	nervous	magnetic	selected

7. She ___ a ___ seat.
8. Without ___, they were ___.

7. She selected a comfortable seat.
8. Without gravity, they were weightless.

TEXTBOOK

Review Items

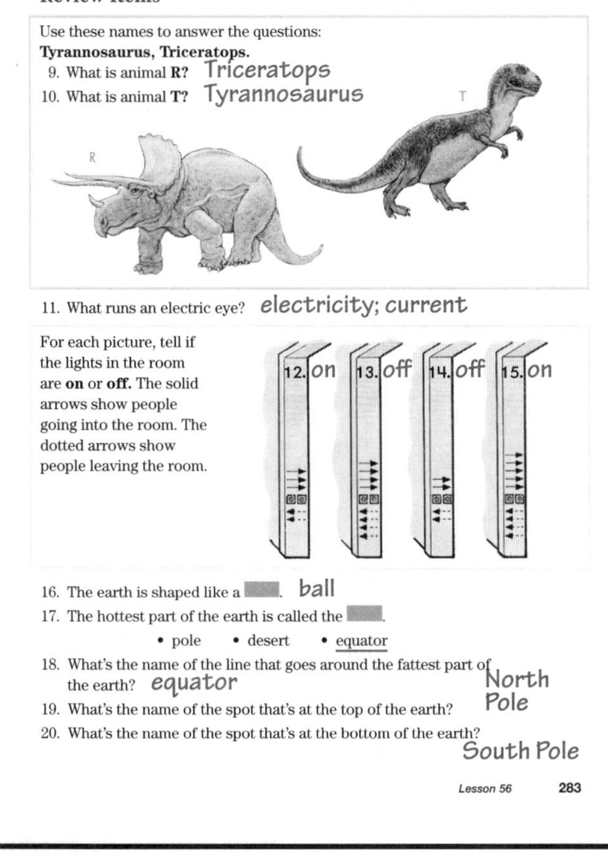

Use these names to answer the questions:
Tyrannosaurus, Triceratops.

9. What is animal **R**? Triceratops
10. What is animal **T**? Tyrannosaurus

11. What runs an electric eye? electricity; current

For each picture, tell if the lights in the room are **on** or **off.** The solid arrows show people going into the room. The dotted arrows show people leaving the room.

16. The earth is shaped like a ▬. ball
17. The hottest part of the earth is called the ▬.
    - pole
    - desert
    - equator
18. What's the name of the line that goes around the fattest part of the earth? equator
19. What's the name of the spot that's at the top of the earth? North Pole
20. What's the name of the spot that's at the bottom of the earth? South Pole

WORKBOOK

57

Name ____________________

A Story Items

1. **Underline 5** things that were in the cabinet in front of Wendy's seat.
   - space books
   - space food
   - writing table
   - space helmet
   - bed
   - TV screen
   - space suit
   - plates
   - keyboard
2. Why would everybody need tanks of oxygen when they got to Jupiter?
   Ideas: to breathe; to survive; because there is no oxygen on Jupiter
3. How far back did the passengers have to move their seats before they took off? halfway (back)
4. What was Wendy's idea about why the ship was shaking?
   - It was speeding through layers of air.
   - It was falling apart.
   - It was too old.
   - It was too heavy.
5. The pressure on Wendy felt like a person ________ sitting on her chest.
6. In what part of the spaceship were the engines?
   in the back/rear
7. The sound of the engines couldn't reach the passenger section because the spaceship Idea: was traveling faster than the sound.
8. What planet did Wendy see when she looked out the window?
   Earth

WORKBOOK

9. Make an **X** on a passenger seat.
10. Make a **P** on the space suit.
11. Make an **H** on the space helmet.
12. Make a **T** on the computer keyboard.
13. Make an **R** on the writing table.

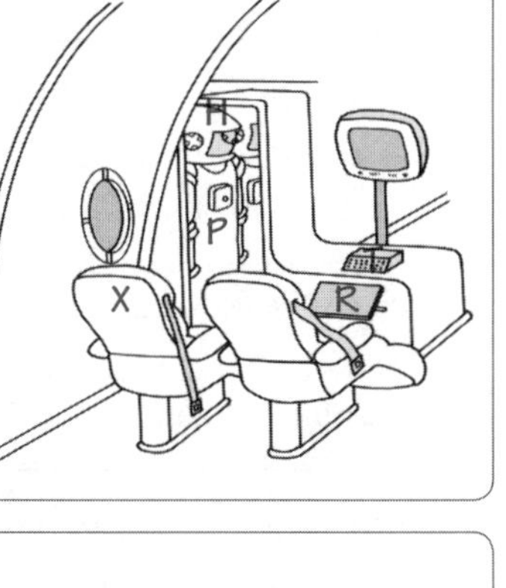

14. What planet is shown in the picture? Earth
15. Write **N** on the part of the planet that has night.
16. Write **D** on the part of the planet that has daylight.

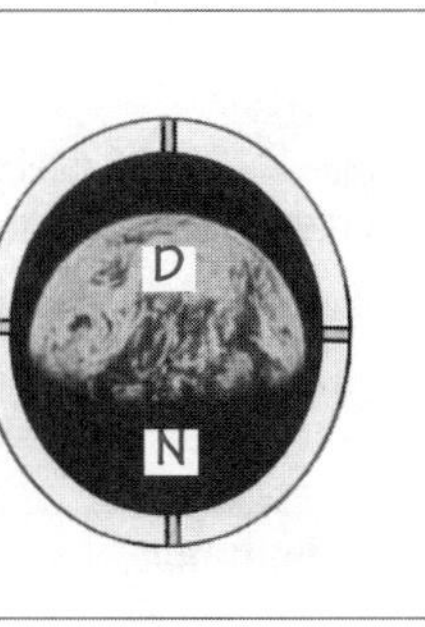

GO TO PART C IN YOUR TEXTBOOK.

TEXTBOOK

C Number your paper from 1 through 20.

Review Items

1. What's the largest city in Japan? Tokyo
2. How many heat lines are hitting place P on the map? 4
3. How many heat lines are hitting place R? 10
4. Write the letter of the place that's the hottest. R
5. Write the letter of the place that's the coldest. P
6. Write the letter of the place that has the warmest winters. R
7. Why is place R hotter than place P?

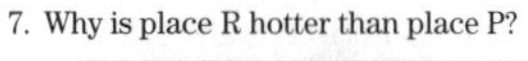

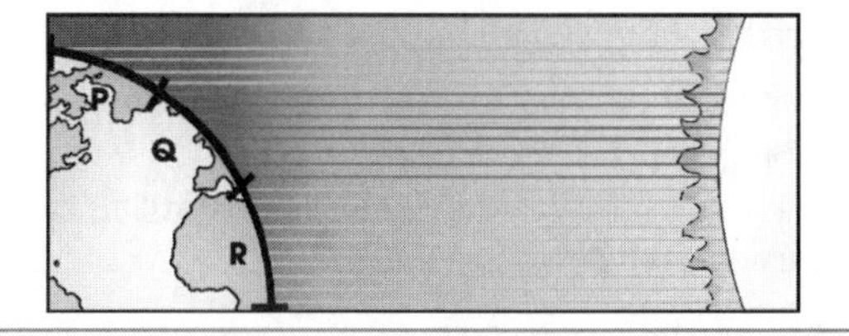

7. Ideas: It has more heat lines hitting it; it's closer to the equator.

TEXTBOOK

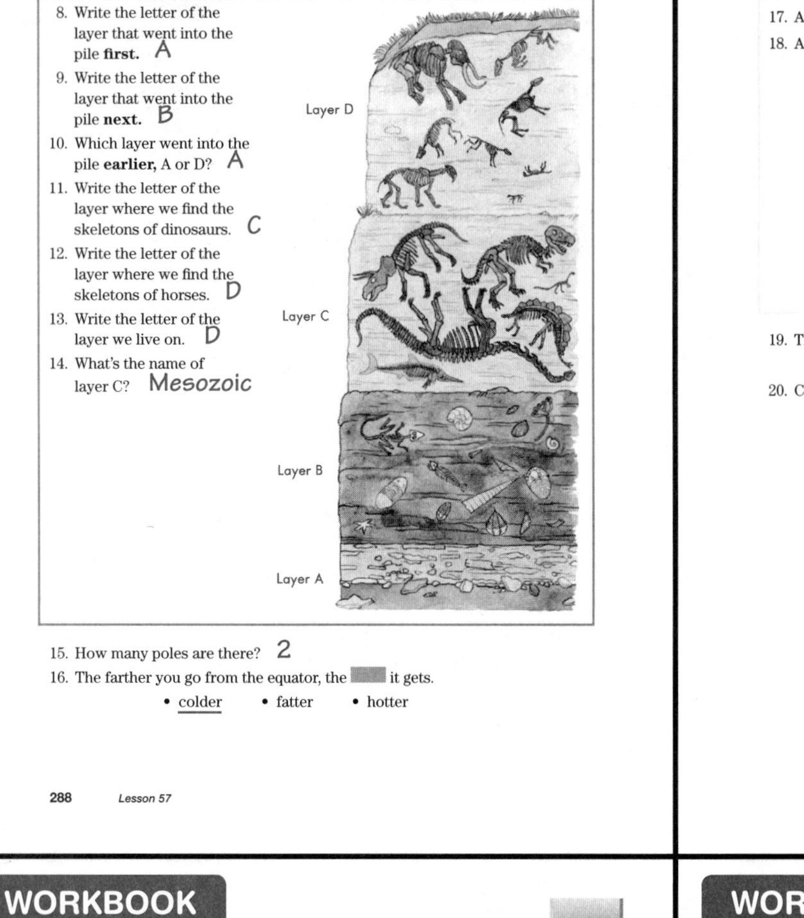

8. Write the letter of the layer that went into the pile **first.** A
9. Write the letter of the layer that went into the pile **next.** B
10. Which layer went into the pile **earlier,** A or D? A
11. Write the letter of the layer where we find the skeletons of dinosaurs. C
12. Write the letter of the layer where we find the skeletons of horses. D
13. Write the letter of the layer we live on. D
14. What's the name of layer C? Mesozoic

15. How many poles are there? 2
16. The farther you go from the equator, the ▒▒ it gets.
    - colder
    - fatter
    - hotter

TEXTBOOK

17. At which letter would the winters be very, very cold? D
18. At which letter would the winters be very, very hot? T

19. The sun shines ▒▒.
    - some of the time
    - all of the time
20. Can you see the sun all day long and all night long? no

WORKBOOK

58

Name ____________________

A

1. Gravity is the force that Idea: pulls things down.
2. If something weighed 100 pounds on Earth, how many pounds would it weigh on the moon? 17 pounds
3. If something weighed 20 pounds on Earth, would it weigh more than 20 pounds on Saturn? yes
4. Would it weigh more than 20 pounds on the moon? no
5. A person weighs 100 pounds on planet A and 300 pounds on planet B. Which planet has stronger gravity? (planet) B
6. A person weighs 100 pounds on planet A and 90 pounds on planet B. Which planet has stronger gravity? (planet) A
7. Planet A has weaker gravity than planet M. On which of those planets would you weigh more? (planet) M
8. Which planets have stronger gravity, the **bigger** planets or the **smaller** ones? the bigger planets

B Story Items

9. Why did Earth seem to get smaller? Idea: It was getting farther away.
10. What makes the sky around Earth look blue?
    - a layer of air
    - the sun
    - a layer of clouds

WORKBOOK

11. The pilot turned off the engines when the ship was out in space. Did the spaceship slow down? no
12. Was there any air outside the spaceship? no
13. What happens to people and things when there's no gravity?
    - They drop.
    - They float.
    - They survive.
14. When the gravity device is turned on, do things float in the air or fall to the floor? fall to the floor
15. The gravity device is off. What would happen if you hit a **big** blob of floating liquid? Idea: It would break into many little drops.
16. Do things fall to the floor when the gravity device is off? no
17. Did the gravity device come back on **fast** or **slowly?** slowly
18. If you drop something on Earth, it falls to the ground. What makes it fall? gravity

Review Item

19. **Fill in the blanks to show the four seasons.**
    winter, spring, summer, fall, winter, spring, summer, fall

GO TO PART D IN YOUR TEXTBOOK.

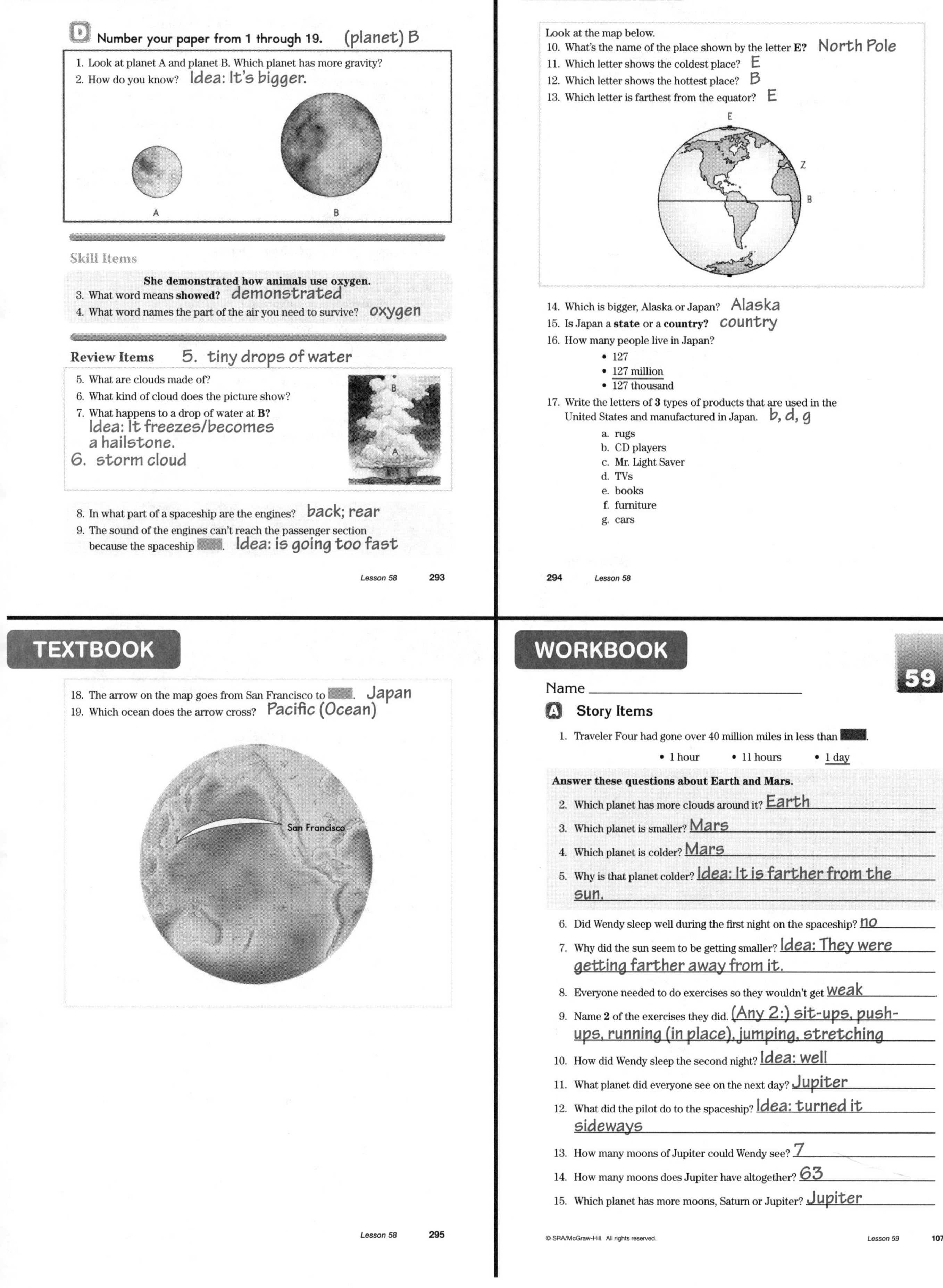

TEXTBOOK

D Number your paper from 1 through 19. (planet) B

1. Look at planet A and planet B. Which planet has more gravity?
2. How do you know? Idea: It's bigger.

Skill Items

She demonstrated how animals use oxygen.

3. What word means **showed?** demonstrated
4. What word names the part of the air you need to survive? oxygen

Review Items 5. tiny drops of water

5. What are clouds made of?
6. What kind of cloud does the picture show?
7. What happens to a drop of water at **B?**
   Idea: It freezes/becomes a hailstone.

6. storm cloud

8. In what part of a spaceship are the engines? back; rear
9. The sound of the engines can't reach the passenger section because the spaceship ▬. Idea: is going too fast

Lesson 58 293

TEXTBOOK

Look at the map below.

10. What's the name of the place shown by the letter **E?** North Pole
11. Which letter shows the coldest place? E
12. Which letter shows the hottest place? B
13. Which letter is farthest from the equator? E

14. Which is bigger, Alaska or Japan? Alaska
15. Is Japan a **state** or a **country?** country
16. How many people live in Japan?
    - 127
    - 127 million
    - 127 thousand
17. Write the letters of **3** types of products that are used in the United States and manufactured in Japan. b, d, g
    a. rugs
    b. CD players
    c. Mr. Light Saver
    d. TVs
    e. books
    f. furniture
    g. cars

294 Lesson 58

TEXTBOOK

18. The arrow on the map goes from San Francisco to ▬. Japan
19. Which ocean does the arrow cross? Pacific (Ocean)

Lesson 58 295

WORKBOOK

59

Name ____________________

A Story Items

1. Traveler Four had gone over 40 million miles in less than ▬.
   - 1 hour
   - 11 hours
   - 1 day

Answer these questions about Earth and Mars.

2. Which planet has more clouds around it? Earth
3. Which planet is smaller? Mars
4. Which planet is colder? Mars
5. Why is that planet colder? Idea: It is farther from the sun.
6. Did Wendy sleep well during the first night on the spaceship? no
7. Why did the sun seem to be getting smaller? Idea: They were getting farther away from it.
8. Everyone needed to do exercises so they wouldn't get weak.
9. Name **2** of the exercises they did. (Any 2:) sit-ups, push-ups, running (in place), jumping, stretching
10. How did Wendy sleep the second night? Idea: well
11. What planet did everyone see on the next day? Jupiter
12. What did the pilot do to the spaceship? Idea: turned it sideways
13. How many moons of Jupiter could Wendy see? 7
14. How many moons does Jupiter have altogether? 63
15. Which planet has more moons, Saturn or Jupiter? Jupiter

Lesson 59 107

WORKBOOK

16. **Underline** the 5 things that tell how Jupiter looked to Wendy.
    - It was small.
    - It was green and blue.
    - It was beautiful.
    - It had stripes.
    - She could see seven moons.
    - It was huge.
    - She could see twelve moons.
    - It was brown, orange and white.

Review Items

17. In which direction do geese migrate in the fall? south
18. In which direction do geese migrate in the spring? north
19. Write the directions **north, south, east** and **west** in the boxes.
20. Make a line that starts at the circle on the map and goes north.
21. If you start at the circle and move to the number 4, in which direction do you go? north

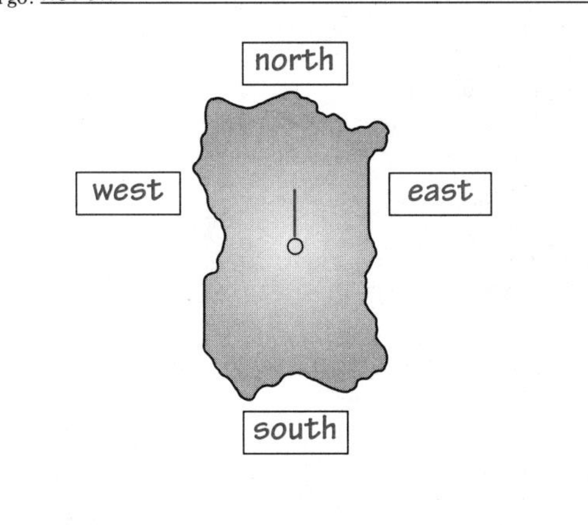

GO TO PART C IN YOUR TEXTBOOK.

TEXTBOOK

some more and took a nap in the afternoon. When she woke up, the pilot was talking over the loudspeaker. She said, "We're going to turn the spaceship sideways so that you can see Jupiter. It is quite a sight."

Slowly, the ship turned. It continued to move in the same direction it had been moving, but it was now moving sideways. Wendy pressed close to the window. And there it was, the largest planet in the solar system—Jupiter. It looked huge. Wendy could clearly see seven moons. She knew that there were 56 others, but she couldn't see them. The planet looked like a great striped ball, with the stripes circling the planet. Some stripes were dark brown, some were orange and some were white. For a moment, Wendy couldn't talk. She heard the other passengers saying things like, "Isn't that beautiful?" and "Incredible!"

C Number your paper from 1 through 21.

Skill Items

Write the word from the box that means the same thing as the underlined part of each sentence.

arithmetic	kneeled	device	tone	mentioned
pace	chuckle	hesitated	energy	suppose

1. He paused for a moment at the corner. hesitated
2. I think you know his mother. suppose
3. She quickly told about the movie. mentioned
4. The baby's little laugh woke me up. chuckle
5. They did their math homework after dinner. arithmetic

Use the words in the box to write complete sentences.

fancy	demonstrated	appeared	weightless
gravity	headline	oxygen	guessed

6. Without ___, they were ___. gravity, weightless
7. She ___ how animals use ___. demonstrated, oxygen

TEXTBOOK

Review Items

8. If something weighted 100 pounds on Earth, how many pounds would it weigh on our moon?
    - 10 pounds
    - 17 pounds
    - 47 pounds
9. If you drop something on Earth, it falls to the ground. What makes it fall? gravity
10. A person weighs 300 pounds on planet R and 200 pounds on planet T. Which planet has stronger gravity? R
11. Planet J has stronger gravity than planet K. On which of those planets would you weigh more? J
12. How many suns are in the solar system? 1
13. How many planets are in the solar system? 9
14. Write the letter of the best deal for an inventor. b
15. Write the letter of the best deal for a manufacturer. c
    a. 10 thousand dollars and 3 dollars for every copy sold
    b. 10 thousand dollars and 5 dollars for every copy sold
    c. 10 thousand dollars and 1 dollar for every copy sold
16. Write the letter of the footprint made by the heaviest animal. S
17. Write the letter of the footprint made by the lightest animal. R

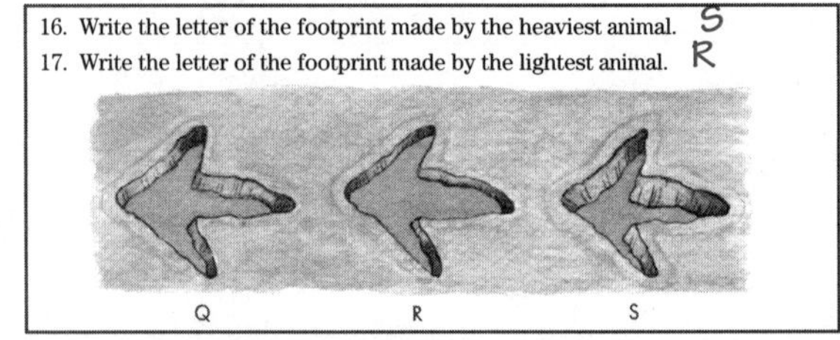

18. Which is larger, Earth or Saturn? Saturn
19. If an object weighed 20 pounds on Earth, would it weigh **more than 20 pounds** or **less than 20 pounds** on Saturn? more than 20 pounds
20. If an object weighed 20 pounds on Earth, would it weigh more than 20 pounds on our moon? no
21. Which planets have stronger gravities, the bigger planets or the smaller planets? bigger planets

TEXTBOOK

TEST 6 60

Number your paper from 1 through 36.

1. Name the planet we live on. Earth
2. What's in the middle of the solar system? sun
3. Name the only part of the solar system that's burning. sun
4. Is Earth the planet that is closest to the sun? no
5. The sun gives ___ and ___ to all the planets. heat, light
6. What's the largest city in Japan? Tokyo
7. The planets are named below with Mercury first and Venus second. **Write the names of all the planets, including the missing planets.**
   Mercury, Venus, Earth, ___, Jupiter, ___, Uranus, ___, Pluto. Mars, Saturn, Neptune
8. Which planet is largest? Jupiter
9. Which planet is next-largest? Saturn
10. How many moons does Saturn have? 47
11. How many moons does Jupiter have? 63
12. How far is it from Earth to Jupiter?
    - 40 million miles
    - 400 million miles
    - 800 million miles
13. How many times larger than Earth is the sun?
    - 500
    - 200
    - 100
14. How many suns are in the solar system? 1
15. How many planets are in the solar system? 9

TEXTBOOK

16. The arrow on the map goes from San Francisco to ▬. Japan
17. Which ocean does the arrow cross? Pacific (Ocean)

San Francisco

18. Which is smaller, Alaska or Japan? Japan
19. Is Japan a **state** or a **country?** country
20. If something weighed 20 pounds on Earth, would it weigh more than 20 pounds on our moon? no
21. Which is larger, Earth or Saturn? Saturn
22. If an object weighed 20 pounds on Earth, would it weigh **more than 20 pounds** or **less than 20 pounds** on Saturn? more than 20 pounds
23. A person weighs 100 pounds on planet A and 90 pounds on planet B. Which planet has stronger gravity? A
24. Planet P has stronger gravity than planet R. On which of those planets would you weigh more? P
25. Which planet has more clouds around it, Earth or Mars? Earth
26. Which planet is bigger? Earth
27. Which planet is warmer? Earth
28. Why is that planet warmer? Idea: It's closer to the sun.

TEXTBOOK

29. If something weighed 100 pounds on Earth, how many pounds would it weigh on our moon?
    - 57 pounds
    - 7 pounds
    - 17 pounds
30. If you drop something on Earth, it falls to the ground. What makes it fall? gravity

Skill Items

For each item, write the underlined word or words from the sentences in the box.

Without gravity, they were weightless.
She demonstrated how animals use oxygen.
She selected a comfortable seat.

31. What underlining tells that the seat felt pleasant? comfortable
32. What underlining means that something has no weight? weightless
33. What underlining means **chose?** selected
34. What underlining names the force that pulls things back to Earth? gravity
35. What underlining means **showed?** demonstrated
36. What underlining names the part of the air you need to survive? oxygen

END OF TEST 6

WORKBOOK

61

Name ______________

A Story Items

1. How much oxygen is on Io? Idea: none
2. What must people wear so they can breathe on Io? Ideas: space suits (with oxygen tanks); oxygen tanks
3. The automatic radio in the space suit tells people how to get back to the space station and how much oxygen; air they have left.
4. How well did Wendy sleep on the last night? Idea: not well
5. Name the moon where the ship will land. Io
6. What makes it dark on the surface of Jupiter? Idea: Jupiter is surrounded by gas.
7. Could you see very far on Jupiter with bright lights? no
8. Do gases surround Io? no
9. Does Io move around Jupiter **fast** or **slowly?** fast
10. It takes Io about 2 days to go all the way around Jupiter.
11. Where did the passengers keep their space suits? Idea: in the cabinets
12. The passengers tried on their space suits. Did the space suits feel **heavy** or **light?** heavy
13. Would they feel that way on Io? no
14. Tell why. Ideas: Io has less/little gravity; Io's gravity is weak.

WORKBOOK

15. Why did the engines of the spaceship start up again?
    - to slow the ship down
    - to speed the ship up
    - to turn in circles

16. What planet is shown? Jupiter
17. Make an **X** on the "eye" of the planet.
18. Which is bigger, the "eye" or Earth? the eye

X

19. The planets are named below with Mercury first. **Write the names of the missing planets.**

Mercury, Venus, Earth, Mars, Jupiter, Saturn, Uranus, Neptune, Pluto.

GO TO PART C IN YOUR TEXTBOOK.

TEXTBOOK

C Number your paper from 1 through 18.

Story Items

Answer these questions about Jupiter and Io.

1. Which has **more** gravity? Jupiter
2. Which is **smaller** than Earth? Io
3. Where can you jump 8 feet high? Io
4. Which has a stronger gravity, Earth or Jupiter? Jupiter
5. So where would you feel lighter? Earth

Review Items

6. How many moons does Saturn have? 47
7. How many moons does Jupiter have 63
8. How far is it from Earth to Jupiter?
   - 400 million miles
   - 800 million miles
   - 40 million miles
9. If something weighed 40 pounds on Earth, would it weigh more than 40 pounds on our moon? no
10. Which is larger, Earth or Saturn? Saturn
11. If an object weighed 40 pounds on Earth, would it weigh **more than 40 pounds** or **less than 40 pounds** on Saturn? more than
12. When a gravity device is turned on, do things float in the air or fall to the floor? fall to the floor
13. Planet Q has stronger gravity than planet R. On which of those planets would you weigh less? Planet R
14. Which planets have stronger gravities, the bigger planets or the smaller planets? bigger planets
15. Which planet has more clouds around it, Earth or Mars? Earth
16. Which planet is smaller? Mars
17. Which planet is colder? Mars
18. Why is that planet colder? Idea: It's farther from the sun.

WORKBOOK

Name ______________________

A Story Items

1. As Traveler Four approached Io, the engines came on with great force. Tell why. Idea: to slow down the spaceship
2. Did Wendy **feel** the engines or **hear** the engines? Idea: feel them
3. Why were the passengers glad to leave the spaceship? Ideas: They wanted to get off the ship; they wanted to see Io.
4. Did Wendy feel **light** or **heavy** when she left the ship? light
5. Tell why.
   - Io has weaker gravity.
   - Io has stronger gravity.
   - Io has no oxygen.
6. Wendy jumped 5 feet high. Could she jump that high on Earth? no
7. Tell about the size of Wendy's room. Ideas: very small; just enough space for a bed and chair
8. Name 2 things that were in the room. (Any 2:) bed, chair, closet
9. There were maps and lots of other things at the space station to teach visitors about Jupiter. Name 2 other things. (Any 2:) telescopes, pictures of Jupiter, books, computer games, map

WORKBOOK

10. How big is Jupiter compared to the other planets in the solar system?
    - bigger
    - smaller
    - the same size
11. How long does it take Jupiter to spin around one time? 10 hours
12. What place on Io did Wendy and Sidney want to visit? a volcano; Soup Pot
13. How far from the space station was the volcano?
    - 30 miles
    - half a mile
    - 100 meters

Review Items

14. What planet is shown? Jupiter
15. Which is bigger, the "eye" of the planet or Earth? the eye

GO TO PART D IN YOUR TEXTBOOK.

TEXTBOOK

"Me, neither," Wendy said.

Rod Samson told about other things that people might look at on Io. Then he pointed to a row of telescopes near the windows of the space station. "Of course, you may want to look at Jupiter. Through those telescopes you can get a close-up view of the clouds that surround the great planet. Also, we have thousands of pictures of Jupiter. And we have hundreds of books and CD-ROMs that show and tell everything we know about the planet. If you look on the back of your map, you'll find a list of the more important facts about Jupiter. The planet is bigger than all the other planets in the solar system put together. It spins around one time every ten hours. The gases that surround it are poisonous."

When the meeting was over, Sidney said, "Let's go see the volcano."

D Number your paper from 1 through 22.

Skill Items

Lava erupted from the volcano's crater.

1. What word means **coughed out** or **spit out?** erupted
2. What word means **melted rock?** lava
3. What do we call the enormous dent at the top of a volcano? crater

Review Items

4. The gravity device is off. What would happen if you hit a big blob of floating liquid? Idea: It would break into many drops.
5. Do things fall to the floor when the gravity device is off? no
6. A person weighs 100 pounds on planet A and 300 pounds on planet B. Which planet has stronger gravity? B
7. Which planets have stronger gravities, the bigger planets or the smaller planets? bigger planets
8. Which has a stronger gravity, Earth or Jupiter? Jupiter
9. So where would you feel **lighter?** Earth
10. Could you see very far on Jupiter with bright lights? no
11. Does Io move around Jupiter **fast** or **slowly?** fast
12. It takes Io about ▬▬ to go all the way around Jupiter. 2 days

TEXTBOOK

13. When a person makes an object for the first time, the person ▬ the object. invents

14. Write the letter of the clouds that have frozen drops of water. B
15. Write the letter of the clouds that may stay in the sky for days at a time. C
16. Write the letter of the storm clouds. A

17. Female animals fight in the spring to protect ▬. their babies
18. Name **2** kinds of Alaskan animals that are dangerous in the spring. (Any 2:) polar bears, wolves, walruses
19. Which came **earlier** on Earth, dinosaurs or horses? dinosaurs
20. Which came **earlier** on Earth, strange sea animals or dinosaurs? strange sea animals

- On planet A you can jump 10 feet high.
- On planet B you can jump 30 feet high.
- On planet C you can jump 5 feet high.
- On planet D you can jump 20 feet high.
- On planet E you can jump 3 feet high.

21. Write the letter of the planet that has the most gravity. E
22. Write the letter of the planet that has the least gravity. B

WORKBOOK

63

Name ____________________

A Story Items

1. What was the temperature outside the space station? 200 degrees below zero
2. Did it feel cold to Wendy? no
3. Tell why. Idea: She was wearing her space suit.
4. Wendy and Sidney were running and leaping when they first left the space station. The automatic radio told Wendy if she kept doing what she was doing, she would run out of oxygen in ▬.
   - 5 minutes
   - 35 minutes (underlined)
   - 25 minutes
5. Which uses up more oxygen, **walking** or **running?** running
6. The girls were heading toward the volcano. What marked the path? (red) flags
7. What's another name for hot melted rock? lava
8. What name did the volcano have? Soup Pot
9. What color is lava when it's very hot? orange
10. What color is lava after it cools a little bit? brown
11. What color is lava after it's completely cooled? gray
12. The inside of the volcano was larger than a city block.
13. As the girls started to walk around the rim of the volcano, the voice came over Wendy's radio again. How long would Wendy's oxygen last if she kept using it as fast as she had been using it?
   - 45 minutes (underlined)
   - 35 minutes
   - 25 minutes

WORKBOOK

14. What did the girls walk onto to look down into the volcano?
   - a sidewalk
   - an overhang (underlined)
   - a slide
15. What happened while they were standing on it? Ideas: It broke; it fell.
16. What did Wendy grab? a rock
17. What happened to Sidney? Ideas: She fell.; She couldn't hold on to Wendy.

Review Items

18. Which planet in the picture has more gravity? (Planet) D
19. How do you know? Idea: It is larger.

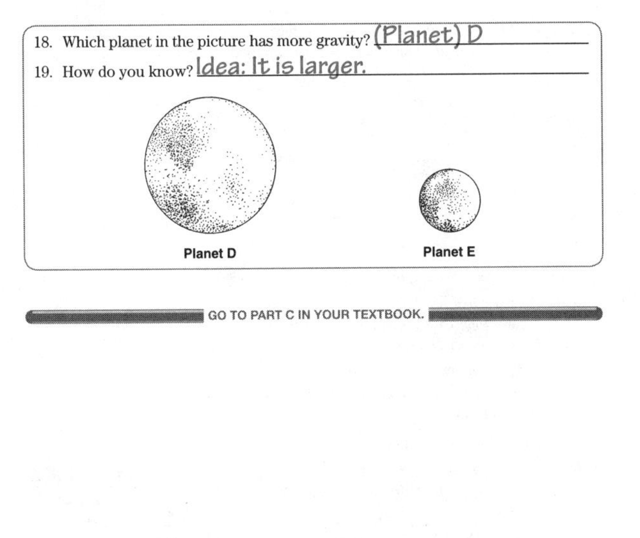

GO TO PART C IN YOUR TEXTBOOK.

TEXTBOOK

The overhang looked scary. Wendy thought for a moment, then said, "Okay. Let's go out there."

So the girls walked onto the overhang. They walked to the end of it and looked down. They were almost above the lava. When Wendy looked down, she got a little dizzy looking at the boiling hot rock. Then suddenly, she felt the ground move. She quickly turned around and saw that the overhang was cracking off and starting to fall into the crater.

She started to run back to the rim, but it was too late. The overhang broke off with Wendy and Sidney standing on it. Wendy reached out and grabbed a rock on the edge of the rim. She felt Sidney behind her, trying to grab on to her. But Sidney could not hold on. She fell. Wendy could hear her yelling something over the radio, but Wendy couldn't turn around. She was hanging on to the rock with all her might.

C Number your paper from 1 through 18.

Skill Items

Use the words in the box to write complete sentences.

oxygen	crater	assigned	area	erupted
impressive	demonstrated		crackle	lava

1. She ▬ how animals use ▬.
2. ▬ ▬ from the volcano's ▬.

Here are 3 events that happened in the story. Write **beginning, middle** or **end** for each event.

3. Wendy and Sidney started walking toward the volcano. beginning
4. She quickly turned around and saw that the overhang was cracking off and starting to fall into the crater. end
5. Within half an hour, the girls were standing on the huge rim that circled the volcano. middle

1. She demonstrated how animals use oxygen.
2. Lava erupted from the volcano's crater.

TEXTBOOK

Review Items

6. Name the largest city in Japan. Tokyo
7. After Traveler Four took off, the pilot turned off the engines. Did the spaceship slow down? no
8. Was there any air outside the spaceship? no
9. Do gases surround Io? no
10. How much oxygen surrounds Io? Idea: none
11. Name the largest planet in the solar system. Jupiter
12. How long does it take Jupiter to spin around one time? 10 hours
13. Which has **more** gravity, Jupiter or Io? Jupiter
14. Which is **smaller** than Earth? Io
15. Where can you jump 8 feet high? Io
16. In what season are animals most dangerous in Alaska? spring
17. During what season do female animals in Alaska have babies? spring
18. Write the letters of the 5 things that tell about Jupiter. a, c, d, f, h
    - a. It has stripes.
    - b. It has 15 moons.
    - c. It has more gravity than Earth.
    - d. It's brown, orange and white.
    - e. It's small.
    - f. It's huge.
    - g. It's green and blue.
    - h. It's beautiful.

WORKBOOK

Name ____________________

A Story Items

1. After the overhang fell, Wendy pulled herself up onto the rim of the volcano. Was this **hard** or **easy?** easy
2. Tell why.
    - The gravity was weak.
    - There wasn't any oxygen.
    - She was in a space suit.
3. Was Sidney in the lava? no
4. How close were Sidney's feet to the lava? Idea: a couple of meters
5. Where did Wendy go to get help for Sidney? space station
6. On the way to get help, the automatic voice came over Wendy's radio. Why?
    - She was using up oxygen too fast.
    - She was not running fast enough.
    - Her space suit was getting too hot.
7. Whose voice came over Wendy's radio next? Rod's/Rod Samson's
8. What did he tell her to do? Ideas: stop; sit down; rest; take it easy; etc.
9. Wendy ran out of oxygen. **Underline 3** things that happened to Wendy.
    - Her arms became stiff.
    - Her arms became tingly.
    - Her voice wouldn't work.
    - Her voice was loud.
    - She saw Rod.
    - She saw spots.
10. About how far from the space station was Wendy when she passed out?
    - 200 centimeters
    - 10 yards
    - 200 meters

WORKBOOK

11. Where was Wendy when she woke up? Idea: inside a vehicle
12. How many people were in the vehicle with Wendy? 3
13. Who was driving? Rod (Samson)
14. What did the woman attach to Wendy's space suit? (fresh) oxygen tanks
15. Where did the vehicle stop? Ideas: on the rim of Soup Pot; near where the overhang had been

Review Items

Here's the rule about an electric eye: **Each time the beam of light is broken, the light changes.**

16. The light is off. The beam is broken 4 times. Shade the bulbs that are off.

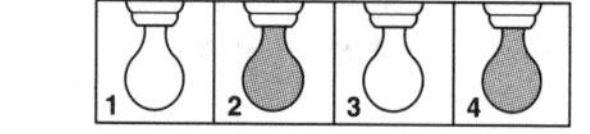

17. Is the light **on** or **off** at the end? off
18. The light is off. The beam is broken 3 times. Shade the bulbs that are off.

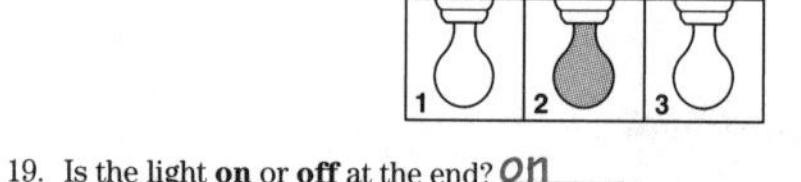

19. Is the light **on** or **off** at the end? on
20. The light is off. The beam is broken 6 times. Shade the bulbs that are off.

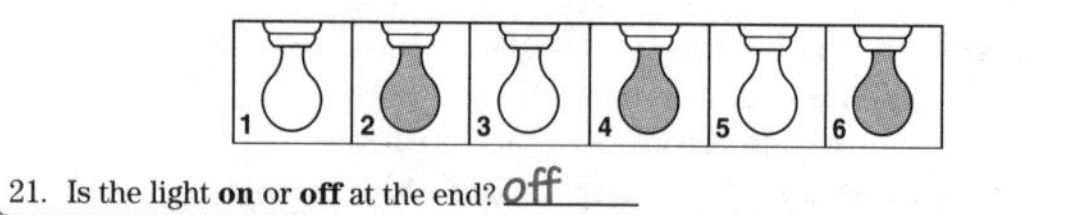

21. Is the light **on** or **off** at the end? off

GO TO PART C IN YOUR TEXTBOOK.

TEXTBOOK

surface of Io. Wendy's helmet was off. There was air inside the vehicle. Rod Samson was driving the vehicle. Another man was sitting next to him. A woman was in back with Wendy. The woman was attaching fresh oxygen tanks to Wendy's space suit.

Wendy tried to sit up, but the woman gently pushed her back down. The woman said, "Take it easy. We'll be up at the top of Soup Pot in just a minute."

"You've got to get there fast," Wendy said. "Sidney is just hanging on. She's . . ."

"We're going as fast as we can," the woman said. "Everything is going to be all right."

Wendy looked at the woman's face. The woman looked worried.

The woman said, "I'll put your helmet back on. You have fresh tanks of oxygen now."

Rod said to the woman, "Fasten her helmet. We're almost there."

The woman helped Wendy put on the helmet. The vehicle stopped. Wendy looked outside. The vehicle had stopped on the rim of Soup Pot, right near the place where the overhang had been.

C Number your paper from 1 through 19.

Review Items

1. Which planet is largest? Jupiter
2. Which planet is next-largest? Saturn
3. How many times larger than Earth is the sun? 100
4. Write the names of the 9 planets, starting with Mercury. Mercury, Venus, Earth, Mars, Jupiter, Saturn, Uranus, Neptune, Pluto
5. If something weighed 100 pounds on Earth, how many pounds would it weigh on our moon?
    - 25 pounds
    - 100 pounds
    - 17 pounds
6. If something weighed 50 pounds on Earth, would it weigh more than 50 pounds on our moon? no
7. Which is larger, Earth or Jupiter? Jupiter
8. If an object weighed 50 pounds on Earth, would it weigh **more than 50 pounds** or **less than 50 pounds** on Jupiter? more than 50 pounds
9. If you drop something on Earth, it falls to the ground. What makes it fall? gravity

TEXTBOOK

10. What color is lava when it's very hot?
 • gray • orange • brown
11. What color is lava after it cools a little bit?
 • gray • orange • brown
12. What color is lava after it's completely cooled?
 • gray • orange • brown

Use these names to answer the questions:
Tyrannosaurus, Triceratops.
13. What is animal **A?** Triceratops
14. What is animal **B?** Tyrannosaurus

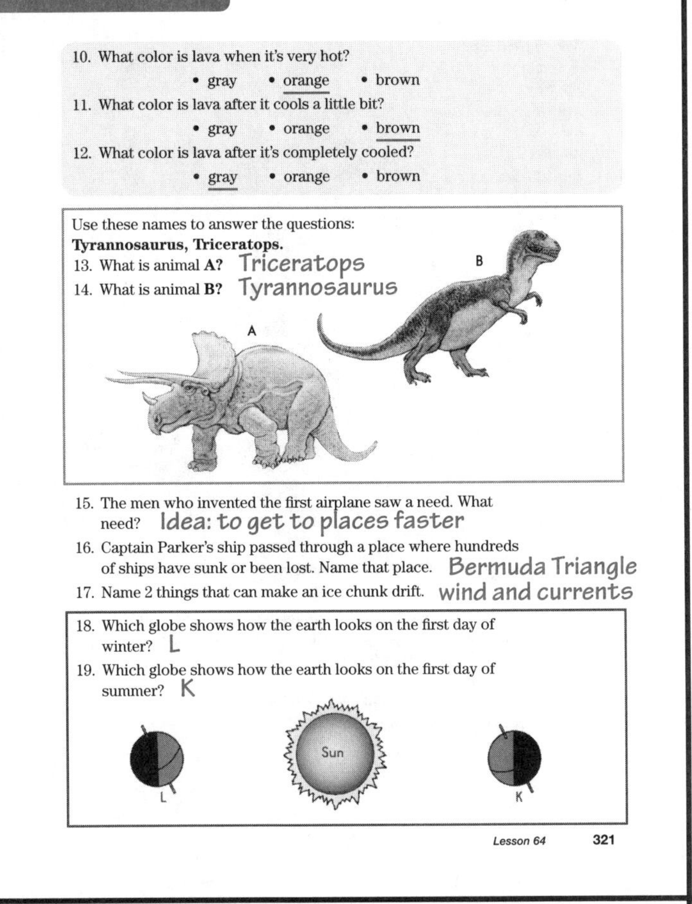

15. The men who invented the first airplane saw a need. What need? Idea: to get to places faster
16. Captain Parker's ship passed through a place where hundreds of ships have sunk or been lost. Name that place. Bermuda Triangle
17. Name 2 things that can make an ice chunk drift. wind and currents

18. Which globe shows how the earth looks on the first day of winter? L
19. Which globe shows how the earth looks on the first day of summer? K

Sun L K

WORKBOOK

65

Name ______________________

A Story Items

1. What was Sidney hanging on to when Wendy left for help? a rock
2. Where was Sidney when Wendy came back? Idea: in a cave
3. What did Wendy think had happened to Sidney? Idea: that she had fallen into the lava
4. What happened to the end of the rope that fell into the lava? Idea: It burned.
5. Who slid down the rope? Rod (Samson)
6. What did he tell Sidney to do? Ideas: climb onto his back; put her arm around his neck; hang on
7. When Sidney reached the top of the rim, how did she look?
 • healthy • pale • sad
8. Why could everybody take their helmets off inside the space station? Idea: because it has oxygen
9. **Underline 2** words that tell how Sidney felt at the end of the story.
 • thirsty • tired • cold • glad

Review Items

10. How many moons does Jupiter have? 63
11. Which planet has more moons, Saturn or Jupiter? Jupiter
12. How much oxygen surrounds Io? Idea: none
13. Does Io move around Jupiter **fast** or **slowly?** fast

WORKBOOK

14. It takes Io about 2 days to go all the way around Jupiter.

15. Which planet in the picture has more gravity? (Planet) G
16. How do you know? Idea: It's larger.

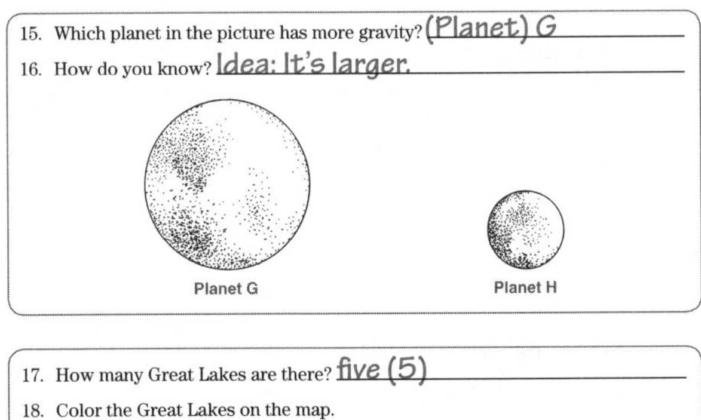

17. How many Great Lakes are there? five (5)
18. Color the Great Lakes on the map.

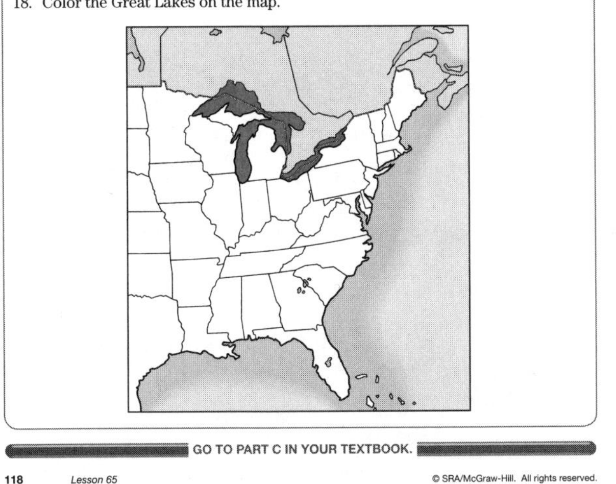

GO TO PART C IN YOUR TEXTBOOK.

TEXTBOOK

Everybody got into the vehicle. The vehicle moved slowly down the side of the volcano and along the row of flags back to the space station. A door opened in the space station and the vehicle went inside. The door closed behind the vehicle.

The woman helped Sidney from the vehicle. Then the others got out. They walked through a door to the meeting place in the space station. When they were inside, they took off their helmets. The woman helped Sidney to one of the chairs. Sidney slumped into the chair.

"I don't feel scared anymore," Sidney said. Then she added, "But am I ever tired. I feel as if I've been working for a hundred years."

Wendy said, "When we came back to the volcano and didn't see you, I thought I was going to die. I thought you had fallen into that lava."

"I was close," Sidney said. "I was hanging on to that rock. Then after a while I got one foot into a little crack in the rocks and I pushed up. I climbed into that cave."

"I'm glad," Wendy said.

Rod handed Sidney a cup of tea. "Sip this," he said. "Watch out. It's hot."

Sidney sipped the tea, looked up, and smiled. Then she said, "Oh, am I glad to be back here."

C Number your paper from 1 through 19.

Review Items

1. What planet is shown in the picture? Jupiter
2. Which is bigger, the "eye" of the planet or Earth? the eye

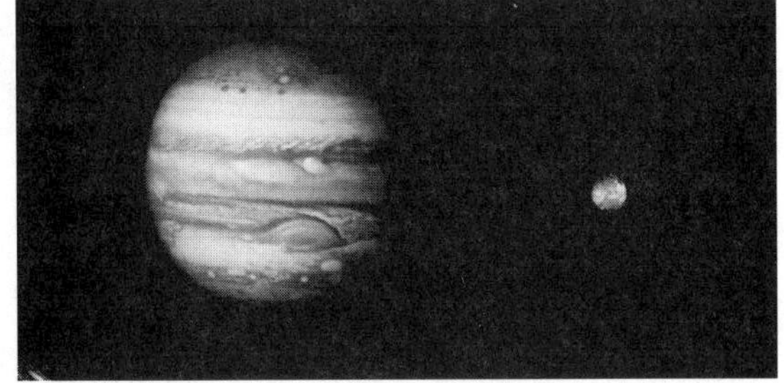

TEXTBOOK

3. Which uses up more oxygen, jumping or sitting? jumping
4. What's another name for hot, melted rock? lava
5. Write the names of the 9 planets, starting with the planet that's closest to the sun.

Write the name of each numbered object in the picture. Choose from these names:

- kayak
- spear
- Eskimo
- fishing pole
- sled
- sled dogs

5. Mercury, Venus, Earth, Mars, Jupiter, Saturn, Uranus, Neptune, Pluto
6. sled dogs
7. sled
8. fishing pole
9. spear
10. Eskimo
11. kayak

TEXTBOOK

12. Write the letter of the layer that went into the pile **first.** A
13. Write the letter of the layer that went into the pile **next.** B
14. Write the letter of the layer that went into the pile **last.** D
15. Which layer went into the pile **earlier,** A or B? A
16. Which layer went into the pile **earlier,** C or B? B
17. Write the letter of the layer we live on. D

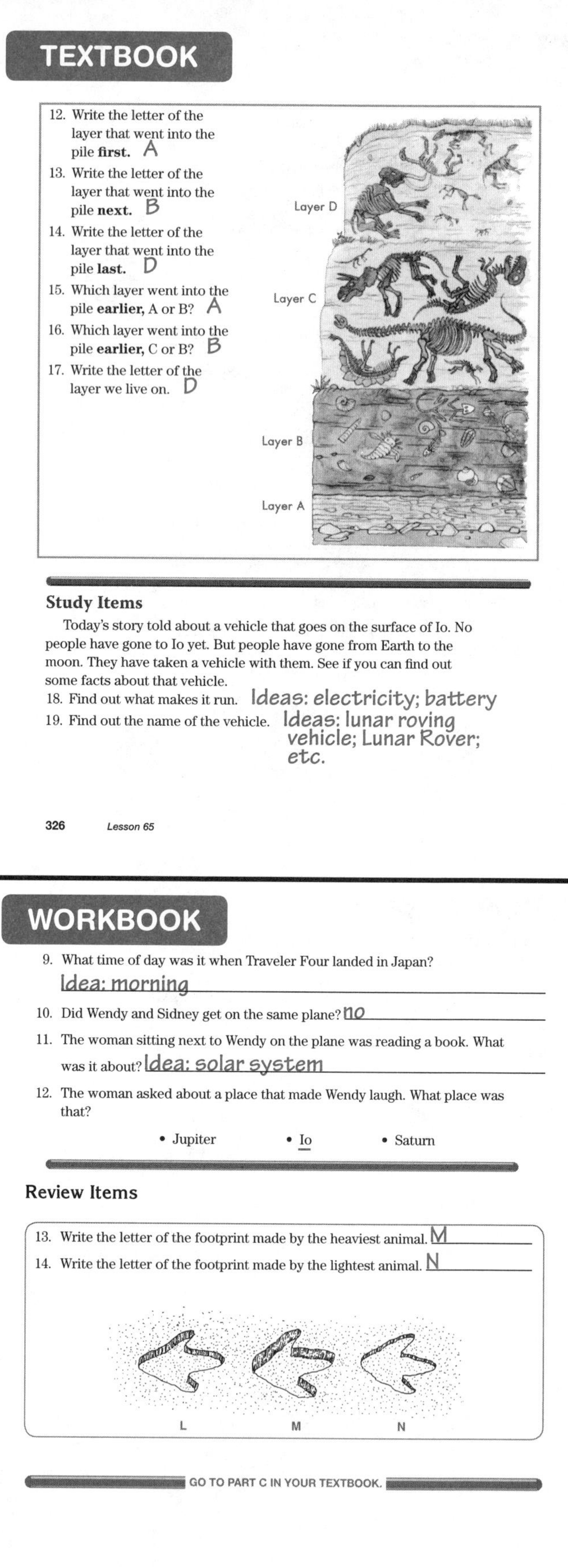

Study Items

Today's story told about a vehicle that goes on the surface of Io. No people have gone to Io yet. But people have gone from Earth to the moon. They have taken a vehicle with them. See if you can find out some facts about that vehicle.

18. Find out what makes it run. Ideas: electricity; battery
19. Find out the name of the vehicle. Ideas: lunar roving vehicle; Lunar Rover; etc.

WORKBOOK

Name ____________________

A Story Items

1. How long did the students stay on Io? 5 days
2. Name 3 things Wendy did after her adventure at Soup Pot.
   1. Idea: studied rocks;
   2. took a (200-mile) trip to see volcanos;
   3. took (over 200) pictures
3. When it was time to go back home to Earth, Wendy felt both happy and sad. She felt happy because she would see Idea: friends and family.
4. She felt sad because she would have to say goodbye to Ideas: her new friends; Rod; Io.
5. Wendy took lots of pictures of the things she saw. Which pictures did Wendy want more than all the rest? Idea: pictures of Soup Pot
6. How far away were the big volcanos the girls visited?
   - 200 miles
   - 100 miles
   - 1 mile
7. Name 2 ways these volcanoes were different from Soup Pot.
   1. (any 2 ideas:) they were bigger; they were much
   2. farther from the station; one was erupting.
8. Name 2 things Wendy planned to do when she got back to her home town.
   1. (any 2 ideas:) visit her friends; visit her family;
   2. show them her pictures; tell about her adventure

WORKBOOK

9. What time of day was it when Traveler Four landed in Japan? Idea: morning
10. Did Wendy and Sidney get on the same plane? no
11. The woman sitting next to Wendy on the plane was reading a book. What was it about? Idea: solar system
12. The woman asked about a place that made Wendy laugh. What place was that?
    - Jupiter
    - Io
    - Saturn

Review Items

13. Write the letter of the footprint made by the heaviest animal. M
14. Write the letter of the footprint made by the lightest animal. N

L M N

GO TO PART C IN YOUR TEXTBOOK.

TEXTBOOK

C Number your paper from 1 through 23.

Skill Items

The incredible whales made them anxious.

1. What word names warm-blooded animals that look like fish? whales
2. What word means **nervous** or **scared?** anxious
3. What word means **amazing?** incredible

Review Items

4. If you drop something on Earth, it falls to the ground. What makes it fall? gravity
5. A person weighs 200 pounds on planet X and 100 pounds on planet Y. Which planet has stronger gravity? X
6. Planet P has stronger gravity than planet R. On which of those planets would you weigh more? P
7. Which planet has fewer clouds around it, Earth or Mars? Mars
8. Which planet is bigger? Earth
9. Which planet is colder? Mars
10. Why is that planet colder? Idea: It's farther from the sun.
11. Which has **more** gravity, Jupiter or Io? Jupiter
12. Which is **smaller** than Earth? Io
13. Where can you jump 8 feet high? Io
14. Write the names of the 9 planets, starting with the planet that's closest to the sun.
15. What is a person doing when the person makes an object for the first time? inventing
16. The person who makes an object for the first time is called an ▆▆. inventor
17. The object the person makes is called an ▆▆. invention

14. Mercury, Venus, Earth, Mars, Jupiter, Saturn, Uranus, Neptune, Pluto

TEXTBOOK

18. How old are geese when they mate for the first time? 3 (years old)
19. After male and female geese mate, how long do they stay together? Idea: until one goose dies
20. Most geese live for about ▆▆ years. 30
21. Geese live in large groups called ▆▆. flocks
22. Where are most wild geese born? Canada
23. The ▆▆s are the coldest places on the earth and the ▆▆ is the hottest place on the earth. pole, equator

END OF LESSON 66 INDEPENDENT WORK

SPECIAL PROJECT

Make a wall chart that shows these planets:
Mercury, Venus, Earth, Mars, Jupiter.

For each planet, find the answers to these questions:

- How big is the planet?
- How many hours does it take to turn around? (How long is a day on that planet?)
- How long does it take to circle the sun?
- How many moons does it have?
- How far from the sun is it?

WORKBOOK

Name ____________________

A

Here are animal names in alphabetical order. Label each animal in the picture below.

bear	giraffe	lion	sheep
cow	goat	parrot	squirrel
eagle	hamster	pigeon	tiger
elephant	horse	rabbit	zebra

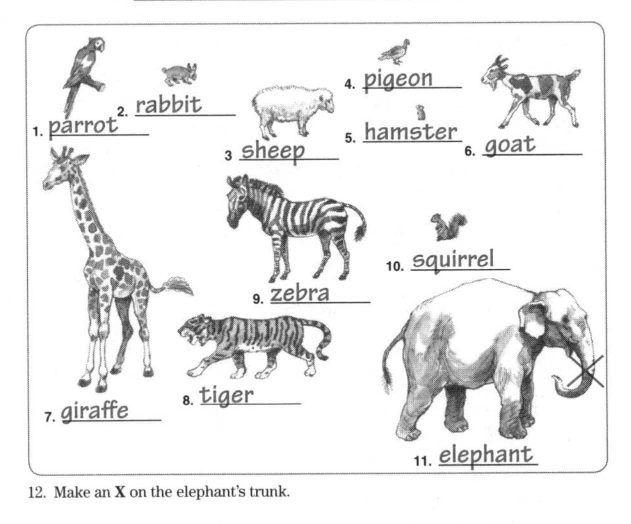

12. Make an **X** on the elephant's trunk.

WORKBOOK

B Story Items

13. How old was Waldo when he started cooking? 10 (years old)
14. Did people like Waldo's cooking? no
15. Who like Waldo's cooking? Idea: animals
16. When the circus animals gathered in Waldo's yard, the weather was warm and the windows were open.
17. How did Waldo's family feel about having so many animals in the yard? Idea: They didn't like it.
18. What did Waldo use to get the animals back into the truck? Idea: some of his food
19. Which animals did Waldo feed in the truck—the circus animals or the other animals? the circus animals
20. What did Waldo do after the other animals followed him out of the truck? Idea: He fed them.
21. Did the animals need to eat a lot of Waldo's food to make them happy? no
22. When the trainers saw how Waldo handled the animals, they were ▆▆.
    - angry
    - amazed
    - tired

Review Item

23. Draw arrows at **X,** at **Y** and at **Z** to show the way the melted rock moves.

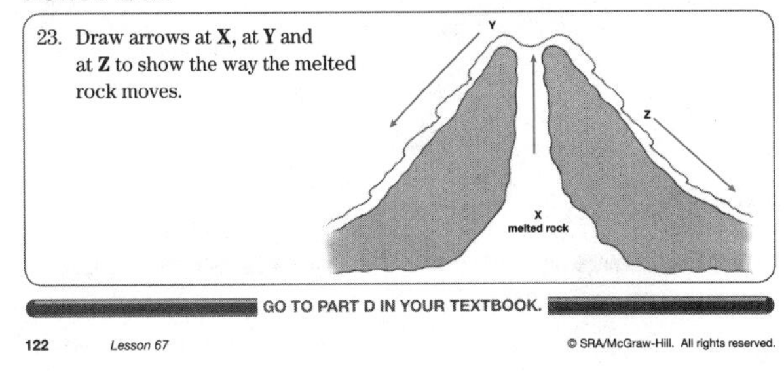

GO TO PART D IN YOUR TEXTBOOK.

TEXTBOOK

D Number your paper from 1 through 16.

Skill Items

Use the words in the box to write complete sentences.

numb	whales	vehicle	lava	pale
managed	anxious	crater	incredible	erupted

1. ▬ ▬ from the volcano's ▬. lava, erupted, crater
2. The ▬ ▬ made them ▬. incredible, whales, anxious

Review Items

3. Write the letters of **3** types of products that are used in the United States and manufactured in Japan. c, e, g
   - a. rugs
   - b. Mr. Light Saver
   - c. CD players
   - d. furniture
   - e. TVs
   - f. books
   - g. cars
4. Which planet has more clouds around it, Earth or Mars? Earth
5. Which planet is bigger? Earth
6. Which planet is hotter? Earth
7. Why is that planet hotter? Idea: It's closer to the sun.
8. Which has more gravity, Jupiter or Io? Jupiter
9. Which is smaller than Earth? Io
10. Where can you jump 8 feet high? Io
11. Which has a stronger gravity, Earth or Jupiter? Jupiter
12. So where would you feel lighter? Earth
13. Does Io move around Jupiter **fast** or **slowly?** fast
14. It takes Io about ▬ to go all the way around Jupiter. 2 days
15. How long does it take Jupiter to spin around one time? 10 hours
16. Which uses up more oxygen, sitting or jumping? jumping

WORKBOOK

68

Name ____________

A Story Items

1. Why did people stay in Waldo's yard after the circus animals left? Ideas: because more animals were gathering; to watch the animals; to see what happened
2. Why couldn't those people see Waldo's legs? Idea: because there were so many animals around him
3. How did those people **feel** about the show the animals were putting on? Idea: They liked it.
4. Why did people from all over make phone calls to Waldo's house? Idea: to see if their animals were there
5. Waldo's sister thought it was ridiculous when somebody asked her if she'd seen a striped cat. Why did she think it was ridiculous? Idea: because she'd seen so many striped cats
6. Waldo came up with a solution to solve a problem with his cooking. What was his solution? Idea: to earn money to pay for the food
7. Did his parents agree with his solution? no
8. What decision did Waldo's parents make? Idea: that Waldo should stop cooking

WORKBOOK

Review Items

9. Write **north, south, east** and **west** in the correct boxes.
10. In which direction is ocean current **R** moving? east
11. In which direction is ocean current **S** moving? north
12. Which direction is the wind coming from? west
13. Make an arrow above ice chunk **T** to show the direction the current will move the ice chunk.
14. Make an arrow next to ice chunk **U** to show the direction the current will move the ice chunk.

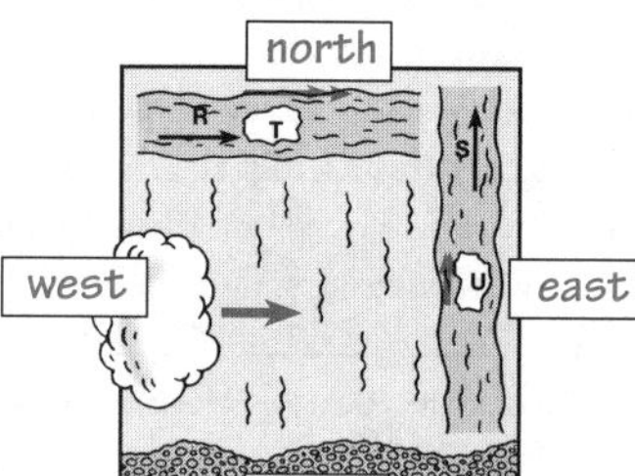

15. Write the missing seasons on the picture below.
16. Shade half of earth **J** and half of earth **L.**

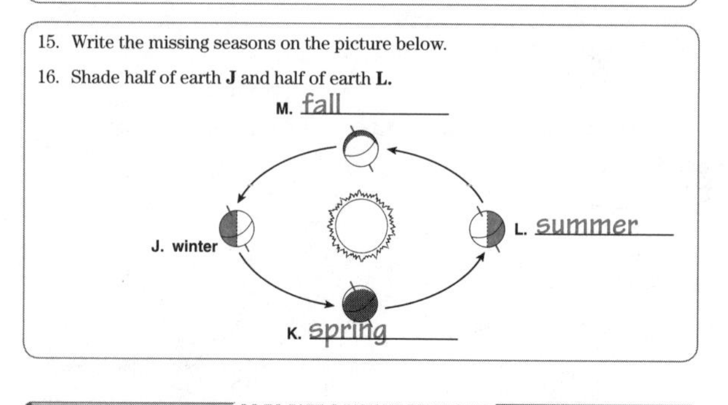

GO TO PART C IN YOUR TEXTBOOK.

TEXTBOOK

"Yes, Dad," Waldo said.

"Make him stop cooking," his sister said. "Make him stop."

His brother said, "Yeah, make him stop. Or make him answer all the phone calls."

"That's enough from you two," Waldo's mother said. She continued, "Waldo is a good boy. We just have to figure out some way to solve this problem."

His sister said, "I know how to solve the problem. We could make Waldo . . ."

"Go into the other room," Waldo's mother said. Then his mother added, "We'll work out a solution to this problem."

So Waldo, his mother, and his father sat in the kitchen and talked about the problem. There were still many animals outside. Two big dogs were standing on their hind legs, looking through the kitchen window. One of them kept howling. The phone was ringing in the other room. Every now and then, one of the neighbors would yell something like, "Get out of here. Go home."

After Waldo and his parents talked for a while, Waldo's father said, "I don't see any solution except one. You're going to have to stop cooking."

Waldo's mother said, "I'm afraid that's right. It costs a lot of money to cook all that food. Then nobody can eat it except those animals."

Waldo said, "But I'll pay for the food. I'll get a job and make enough to pay for my own food. And I'll . . ."

"I'm sorry, son," his father said. "I think you'll just have to stop cooking."

C Number your paper from 1 through 22.

Skill Items

Here are three events that happened in the story. Write **beginning, middle** or **end** for each event.

1. After Waldo and his parents talked for a while, Waldo's father said, "I don't see any solution except one." end
2. Most of those people remained in the yard after the circus truck left with the circus animals. beginning
3. Waldo walked up the back steps of his house and the crowd of animals followed him. middle

TEXTBOOK

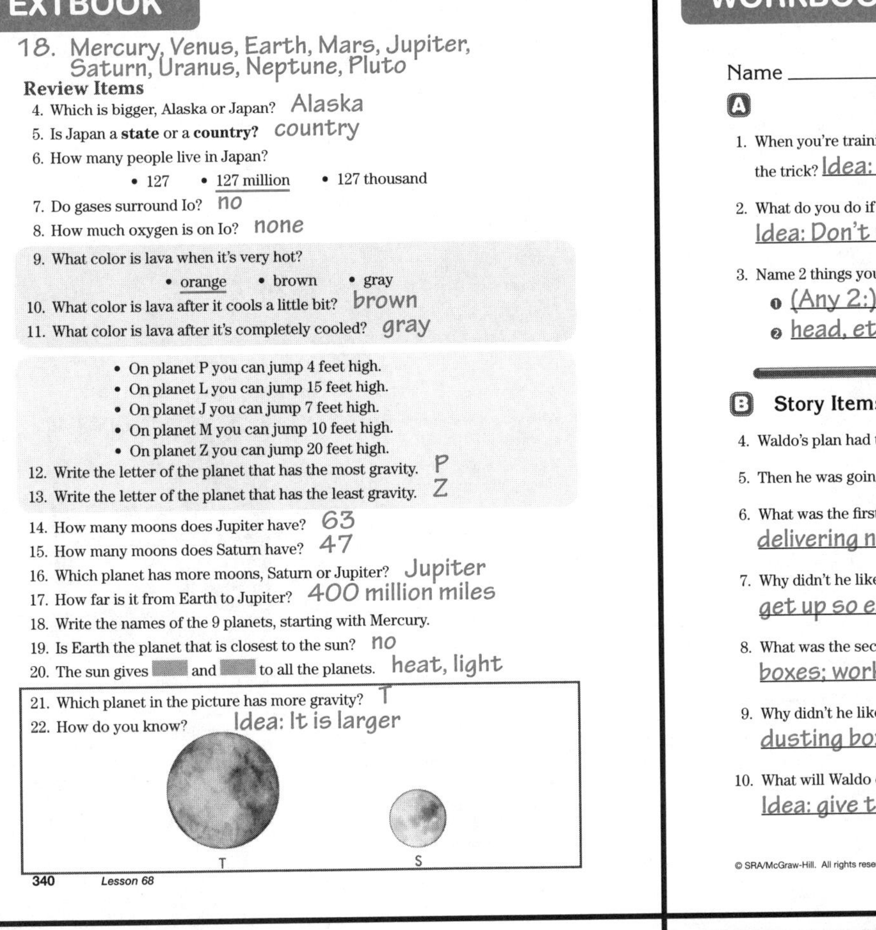

18. Mercury, Venus, Earth, Mars, Jupiter, Saturn, Uranus, Neptune, Pluto

Review Items

4. Which is bigger, Alaska or Japan? Alaska
5. Is Japan a **state** or a **country?** country
6. How many people live in Japan?
   - 127
   - 127 million
   - 127 thousand
7. Do gases surround Io? no
8. How much oxygen is on Io? none
9. What color is lava when it's very hot?
   - orange
   - brown
   - gray
10. What color is lava after it cools a little bit? brown
11. What color is lava after it's completely cooled? gray

- On planet P you can jump 4 feet high.
- On planet L you can jump 15 feet high.
- On planet J you can jump 7 feet high.
- On planet M you can jump 10 feet high.
- On planet Z you can jump 20 feet high.

12. Write the letter of the planet that has the most gravity. P
13. Write the letter of the planet that has the least gravity. Z
14. How many moons does Jupiter have? 63
15. How many moons does Saturn have? 47
16. Which planet has more moons, Saturn or Jupiter? Jupiter
17. How far is it from Earth to Jupiter? 400 million miles
18. Write the names of the 9 planets, starting with Mercury.
19. Is Earth the planet that is closest to the sun? no
20. The sun gives ▬ and ▬ to all the planets. heat, light
21. Which planet in the picture has more gravity? T
22. How do you know? Idea: It is larger

T S

340 Lesson 68

WORKBOOK

Name ____________________

69

A

1. When you're training an animal, what do you do each time the animal does the trick? Idea: Reward the animal.
2. What do you do if the animal does not do the trick? Idea: Don't reward the animal.
3. Name 2 things you could give to a dog to reward it.
   ❶ (Any 2:) a bone, a dog treat, a pat on the
   ❷ head, etc.

B Story Items

4. Waldo's plan had two parts. First, Waldo was going to get a job.
5. Then he was going to fix up the garage.
6. What was the first job that Waldo got? delivering newspapers
7. Why didn't he like that job? Idea: because he had to get up so early
8. What was the second job that Waldo got? Ideas: dusting boxes; working in a shoe store
9. Why didn't he like that job? Idea: because he hated dusting boxes
10. What will Waldo do to make the animals in the pet shop happy? Idea: give them some of his food

Lesson 69 125

WORKBOOK

11. While Waldo was cooking, the pet shop owner opened a window. Why did she do that? Idea: because Waldo's food smelled so bad
12. Why did Waldo tell her to close the window? Idea: because animals would come in through the window

Review Items

13. Shade the part of the earth where it is nighttime.
14. Which side of the earth is closer to the sun, **J** or **F?** J
15. Which side of the earth is in nighttime? F
16. Which side of the earth is in daytime? J

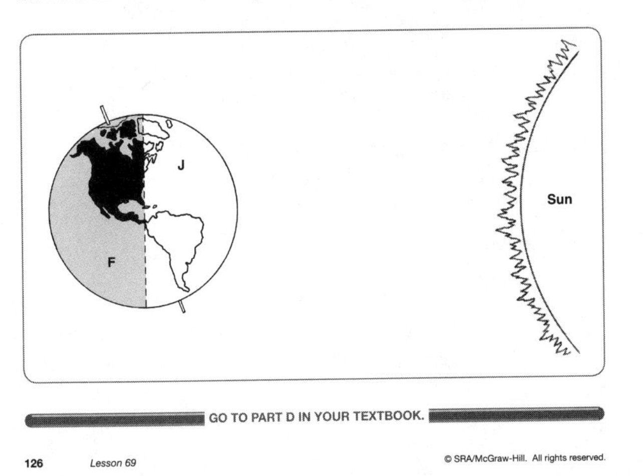

GO TO PART D IN YOUR TEXTBOOK.

126 Lesson 69

TEXTBOOK

"Close the window," Waldo said, "or they'll come inside."

"I've never seen anything like this," the owner said.

The animals inside the pet shop were starting to howl and screech and run around in circles and jump up and down. The owner of the pet shop said, "My, my. I've never seen anything like this in my whole life."

Waldo smiled and said, "Just wait and see what they do when I bring the food out to them."

D Number your paper from 1 through 19.

Skill Items

The boring speaker disturbed the audience.

1. What's another word for **bothered?** disturbed
2. What word is the opposite of **interesting?** boring
3. What do we call all the people who watch an event? audience

Review Items

4. The map shows a route. What state is at the north end of the route? Alaska
5. What country is at the south end of the route? Canada
6. About how many miles is the route? 2500 (miles)

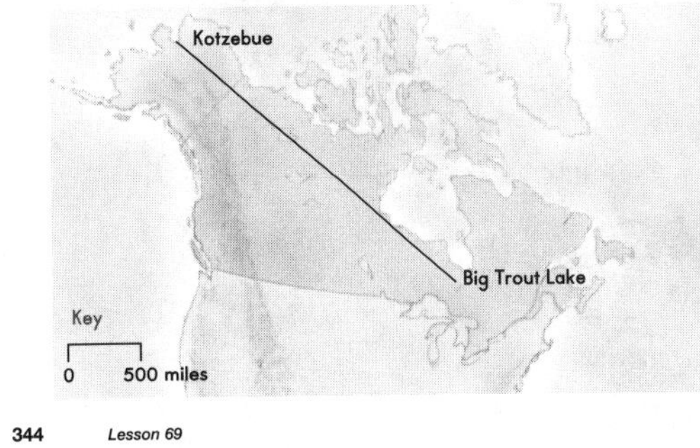

344 Lesson 69

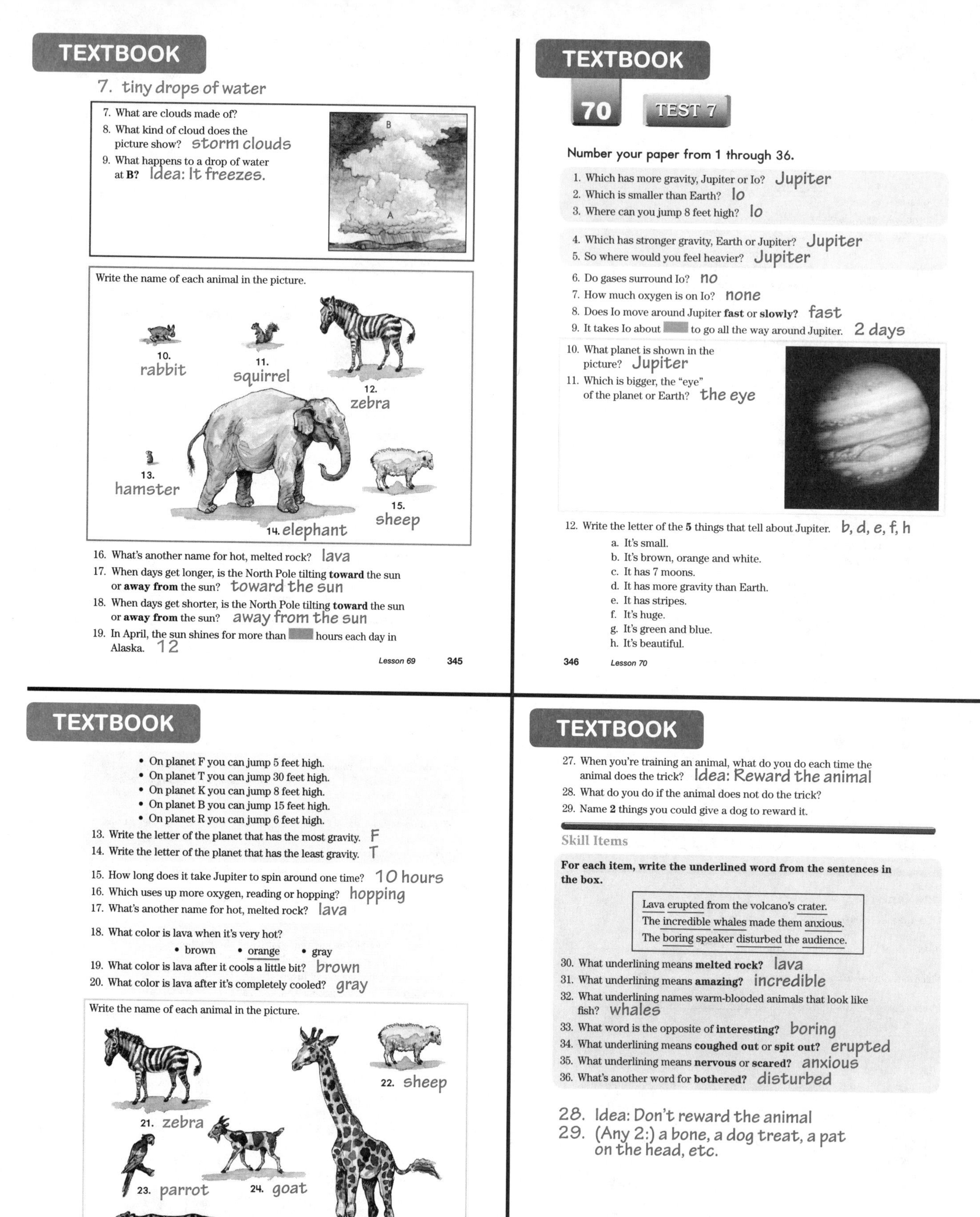

TEXTBOOK

7. tiny drops of water

7. What are clouds made of?
8. What kind of cloud does the picture show? storm clouds
9. What happens to a drop of water at **B?** Idea: It freezes.

Write the name of each animal in the picture.

10. rabbit
11. squirrel
12. zebra
13. hamster
14. elephant
15. sheep

16. What's another name for hot, melted rock? lava
17. When days get longer, is the North Pole tilting **toward** the sun or **away from** the sun? toward the sun
18. When days get shorter, is the North Pole tilting **toward** the sun or **away from** the sun? away from the sun
19. In April, the sun shines for more than ▬ hours each day in Alaska. 12

TEXTBOOK

70 TEST 7

Number your paper from 1 through 36.

1. Which has more gravity, Jupiter or Io? Jupiter
2. Which is smaller than Earth? Io
3. Where can you jump 8 feet high? Io
4. Which has stronger gravity, Earth or Jupiter? Jupiter
5. So where would you feel heavier? Jupiter
6. Do gases surround Io? no
7. How much oxygen is on Io? none
8. Does Io move around Jupiter **fast** or **slowly?** fast
9. It takes Io about ▬ to go all the way around Jupiter. 2 days
10. What planet is shown in the picture? Jupiter
11. Which is bigger, the "eye" of the planet or Earth? the eye
12. Write the letter of the **5** things that tell about Jupiter. b, d, e, f, h
    a. It's small.
    b. It's brown, orange and white.
    c. It has 7 moons.
    d. It has more gravity than Earth.
    e. It has stripes.
    f. It's huge.
    g. It's green and blue.
    h. It's beautiful.

TEXTBOOK

- On planet F you can jump 5 feet high.
- On planet T you can jump 30 feet high.
- On planet K you can jump 8 feet high.
- On planet B you can jump 15 feet high.
- On planet R you can jump 6 feet high.

13. Write the letter of the planet that has the most gravity. F
14. Write the letter of the planet that has the least gravity. T
15. How long does it take Jupiter to spin around one time? 10 hours
16. Which uses up more oxygen, reading or hopping? hopping
17. What's another name for hot, melted rock? lava
18. What color is lava when it's very hot?
    - brown
    - orange
    - gray
19. What color is lava after it cools a little bit? brown
20. What color is lava after it's completely cooled? gray

Write the name of each animal in the picture.

21. zebra
22. sheep
23. parrot
24. goat
25. tiger
26. giraffe

TEXTBOOK

27. When you're training an animal, what do you do each time the animal does the trick? Idea: Reward the animal
28. What do you do if the animal does not do the trick?
29. Name **2** things you could give a dog to reward it.

Skill Items

For each item, write the underlined word from the sentences in the box.

Lava erupted from the volcano's crater.
The incredible whales made them anxious.
The boring speaker disturbed the audience.

30. What underlining means **melted rock?** lava
31. What underlining means **amazing?** incredible
32. What underlining names warm-blooded animals that look like fish? whales
33. What word is the opposite of **interesting?** boring
34. What underlining means **coughed out** or **spit out?** erupted
35. What underlining means **nervous** or **scared?** anxious
36. What's another word for **bothered?** disturbed

28. Idea: Don't reward the animal
29. (Any 2:) a bone, a dog treat, a pat on the head, etc.

WORKBOOK

Name ____________

A

1. When you teach an animal a simple trick, when do you reward the animal? Idea: when the animal does the trick
2. When don't you reward the animal? Idea: when the animal doesn't do the trick
3. Let's say that you want to teach an animal a very hard trick. Can the animal do the trick at first? no
4. What will happen if the animal doesn't receive any rewards until it does the trick? Idea: The animal will stop trying to do the trick.
5. When you're teaching the animal a hard trick, what do you reward the animal for doing? Idea: for trying to do the trick

Let's say you're training a dog to jump up in the air and do a backward somersault. **Use the words below to finish each sentence.**

- jumping up and turning upside down
- jumping up in the air
- jumping up and leaning backward

6. At first you would reward the dog for jumping up in the air
7. Later you would reward the dog for jumping up and leaning backward
8. Later you would reward the dog for jumping up and turning upside down

WORKBOOK

B Story Items

9. What's the name of the pet shop owner? Maria (Sanchez)
10. Why wasn't the pet shop making money? Ideas: because people weren't buying/didn't like pets; it wasn't interesting.
11. When Waldo let the cats out of their cages, what did Maria think the cats would do? Idea: chase the birds
12. Did the cats do that? no
13. What did they do? (Any 2:) rubbed against Waldo's legs; meowed; purred loudly; put their tails high in the air
14. After Waldo let all the animals out of their cages, where did he sit down? Idea: He sat in the front window of the pet shop.
15. Which animals did he feed first? birds
16. What was happening outside the pet shop window? Idea: A crowd was gathering.

GO TO PART D IN YOUR TEXTBOOK.

TEXTBOOK

four or five people standing in front of the window. But soon there was a large crowd of more than thirty people.

Waldo was now feeding the animals. He held a little bit of food high in the air. The birds flew from his shoulders and his head. They flew around and took the food from his hand. Maria watched. The other animals watched. The people outside the window watched. The birds went back to Waldo's shoulders and head. Then Waldo fed the dogs and cats and rabbits and hamsters and all the other animals. The people outside were laughing and pointing.

D Number your paper from 1 through 21.

Skill Items

Use the words in the box to write complete sentences.

deserved	boring	adult	anxious	aimed
audience	incredible	fancy	disturbed	whales

1. The ▬ ▬ made them ▬. incredible, whales, anxious
2. The ▬ speaker ▬ the ▬. boring, disturbed, audience

Review Items

3. What runs an electric eye? electricity; current
4. Which planet is largest? Jupiter
5. Which planet is the next largest? Saturn
6. How many times larger than the earth is the sun? 100
7. How many suns are in the solar system? 1
8. How many planets are in the solar system? 9
9. What's the largest city in Japan? Tokyo
10. When you're training an animal, what do you do each time the animal does the trick? Idea: give the animal a reward
11. What do you do if the animal does not do the trick? Idea: don't give the animal a reward

TEXTBOOK

12. Gravity is the force that ▬. Idea: pulls things down
13. What happens to people and things when there's no gravity? Idea: They float.
14. If something weighed 100 pounds on Earth, how many pounds would it weigh on our moon? 17 pounds
15. The pilot of Traveler Four turned off the engines when the spaceship was out in space. Did the ship slow down? no
16. If you drop an object on Earth, it falls to the ground. What makes it fall? gravity
17. The arrow on the map goes from San Francisco to ▬. Japan
18. Which ocean does the arrow cross? Pacific (Ocean)

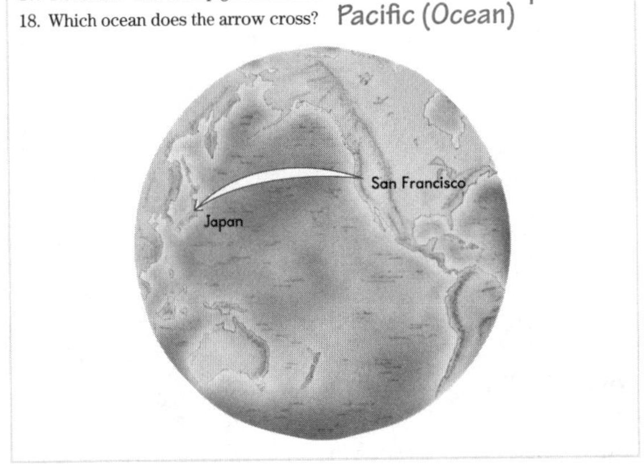

TEXTBOOK

19. What planet is shown in the picture? Jupiter
20. Which is bigger, the "eye" of the planet or Earth? the eye

21. Write the letters of the 5 things that tell about Jupiter. b, d, e, f, h
    a. It's small.
    b. It's beautiful.
    c. It has 4 moons.
    d. It's huge.
    e. It has stripes.
    f. It has more gravity than Earth.
    g. It's green and blue.
    h. It's brown, orange and white.

WORKBOOK

Name ____________________

A Story Items

1. How many pets did Maria usually sell in a week? 8
2. How many did she sell on the day that Waldo cooked? 17
3. Why did she sell so many more pets when Waldo cooked? Idea: because the animals looked so cute
4. Maria said that she would give Waldo some money for every dollar she makes by selling pets. How much money? 20 cents
5. How did Waldo feel about that deal? Idea: He loved it.
6. When Waldo got home, he was out of breath. Tell why. Idea: because he ran home
7. Why was he late? Ideas: because he'd been at the pet shop; he was talking to Maria.
8. Waldo changed his plans about cooking in the garage. Where will he cook? Idea: at the pet shop
9. Did his parents like that idea? yes
10. Did Waldo know a lot about training animals? no
11. How will he learn about training animals? Idea: He will get books.
12. What will he use as a reward when he trains animals? Idea: his food

WORKBOOK

B Review Items

13. In which direction do geese migrate in the fall? south
14. In which direction do geese migrate in the spring? north
15. Write the directions **north, south, east** and **west** in the boxes.
16. Make a line that starts at the circle on the map and goes north.
17. If you start at the circle and move to the number 4, in which direction do you go? west

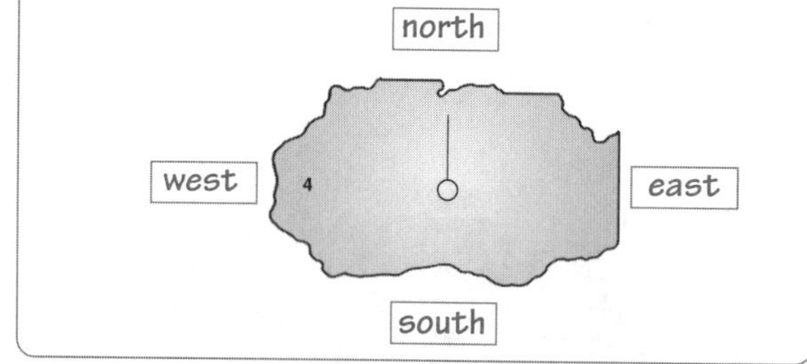

18. **Fill in the blanks to show the four seasons.**
    winter, spring, summer, fall, winter
    spring, summer, fall.

GO TO PART C IN YOUR TEXTBOOK.

TEXTBOOK

Waldo started to get angry. "I'm a good cook," he said. "I can't help it if the only people who like my food are not people."

Waldo's sister laughed and said, "Oh, that makes a lot of sense. The only people are not people. Make him stop cooking."

Waldo's father said to Fran, "Just be quiet and give Waldo a chance to tell us about his job."

Waldo explained, "I'll cook at the pet shop and I'll make a lot of money. The owner of the pet shop told me that she would give me 20¢ for every dollar that she made from selling a pet. I'll be rich."

"Yeah," his brother said. "But how are people going to buy pets if they're holding their noses all the time?"

"Be quiet," Waldo's mother said. "I think Waldo deserves a chance to cook again if he cooks at the pet shop."

Waldo said, "There's a kitchen in the back of the pet shop and I can cook everything I need there. And I did it today." Waldo went on to explain how he had cooked the food, let the animals out of their cages, and sat in the window with them. "The pet shop was mobbed," he concluded. "And people were buying pets like crazy."

"I think that's very nice," his mother said.

"I think it stinks," his sister said. "You should make him..."

"That's enough," Waldo's father said.

Waldo said, "I think I'm going to start training some of the animals to do tricks. I don't know much about training animals, but I'll get some books and read them. I know that the animals will do anything to get my food. So I'll use the food as a reward. And I think I can train the animals to do some really good tricks."

Waldo's father said, "As long as you don't cook around the house, I think your plan sounds very good. You may work in the pet shop."

A Number your paper from 1 through 18.

Review Items

1. Name the planet we live on. Earth
2. What's in the middle of the solar system? the sun
3. Name the only part of the solar system that's burning. the sun

TEXTBOOK

4. Ideas: the back; the tail; behind the passenger section

4. In what part of a spaceship are the engines?
5. The sound of the engines can't reach the passenger section because the spaceship ▬. Ideas: moves faster than the (speed of) sound
6. If an object weighed 20 pounds on Earth, would it weigh more than 20 pounds on our moon? no
7. Which is larger, Earth or Saturn? Saturn
8. If an object weighed 20 pounds on Earth, would it weigh **more than 20 pounds** or **less than 20 pounds** on Saturn? more than 20 pounds
9. A person weighs 100 pounds on Planet A and 300 pounds on Planet B. Which planet has stronger gravity? B
10. Planet A has stronger gravity than Planet R. On which of those planets would you weigh more? A
11. When you teach an animal a simple trick, when do you reward the animal? Idea: when the animal does the trick
12. When don't you reward the animal? Idea: when the animal doesn't do the trick
13. Let's say that you want to teach an animal a very hard trick. Can the animal do the trick at first? no
14. What will happen if the animal doesn't receive any rewards until it does the trick? Idea: It will stop trying to do the trick.
15. So when you're teaching the animal a hard trick, what do you reward the animal for doing? Idea: for trying to do the trick

Let's say you're training a dog to jump up in the air and do a backward somersault. **Use the words below to finish each sentence.**

- jumping up and leaning backward
- jumping up in the air
- jumping up and turning upside down

16. At first, you would reward the dog for ▬. jumping up in the air
17. Later you would reward the dog for ▬.
18. Later you would reward the dog for ▬.

17. jumping up and leaning backward
18. jumping up and turning upside down

WORKBOOK

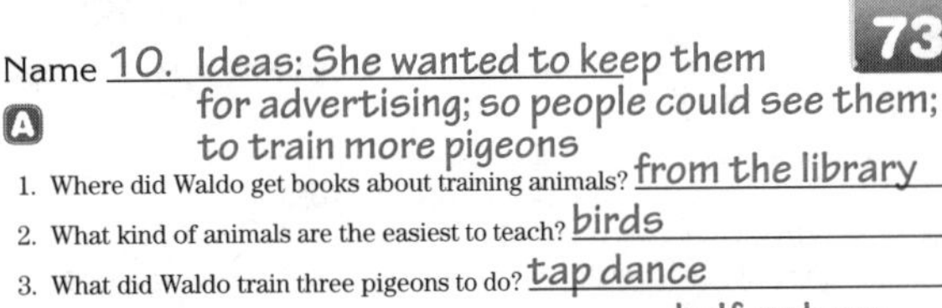

Name 10. Ideas: She wanted to keep them for advertising; so people could see them; to train more pigeons

A

1. Where did Waldo get books about training animals? from the library
2. What kind of animals are the easiest to teach? birds
3. What did Waldo train three pigeons to do? tap dance
4. How long did it take the first pigeon to learn that trick? half an hour
5. Did it take **more time** or **less time** to train the second pigeon? less time
6. What did Waldo attach to the pigeon's feet? buttons
7. Why did he do that? Idea: so they'd make tapping sounds
8. Where did Waldo put the pigeons after he finished training them? Idea: in the front of the pet shop
9. Why did he do that? Ideas: to show them off; so a crowd would gather
10. Maria didn't sell the first three pigeons that Waldo trained. Why not?
11. How many dancing pigeons did people order the first day? 8
12. Waldo trained a rabbit to walk on a tightrope. Where did he put the ropes at first? on a table
13. What kind of ropes were they? thick
14. When Waldo put the ropes a few centimeters above the table, he did something so the rabbit wouldn't fall. What did he do? Idea: He put a belt around the rabbit.
15. What did Waldo do to make a super trick? Idea: trained some mice to sit on the rabbit's back

WORKBOOK

B Review Items

16. How many Great Lakes are there? five (5)
17. Color the Great Lakes on the map.

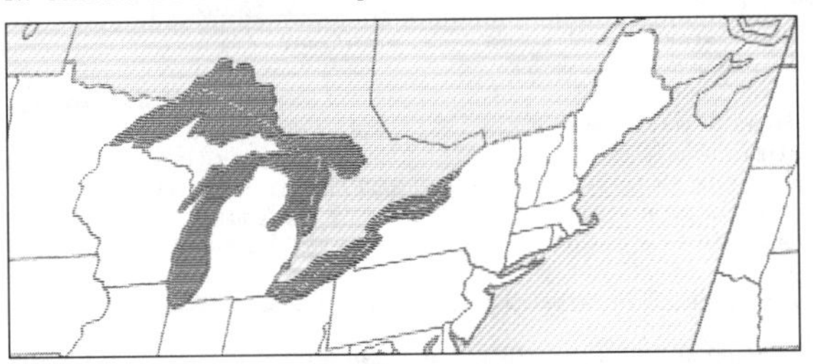

Here's the rule about an electric eye: **Each time the beam of light is broken, the light changes.**

18. The light is off. The beam is broken 5 times. Is the light **on** or **off** at the end? on
19. The light is off. The beam is broken 7 times. Is the light **on** or **off** at the end? on
20. The light is off. The beam is broken 2 times. Is the light **on** or **off** at the end? off

GO TO PART C IN YOUR TEXTBOOK.

TEXTBOOK

C Number your paper from 1 through 16.

Skill Items

A lot of folks mobbed around the cute singer.

1. What's another word for **good-looking and charming?** cute
2. What's another word for **people?** folks
3. What's another word for **crowded around?** mobbed

Review Items

4. How long ago did dinosaurs live on the earth?
   - a hundred years ago
   - a hundred million years ago
   - a million years ago
5. Here's how an electric eye at a store works. When somebody walks in the door, the person's body stops the beam of light from reaching the ▬. electric eye

The picture shows two electric eye beams on the side of doors. The number **1** shows the beam that is broken first. The number **2** shows the beam that is broken next. Write the letter of the correct arrow for each doorway.

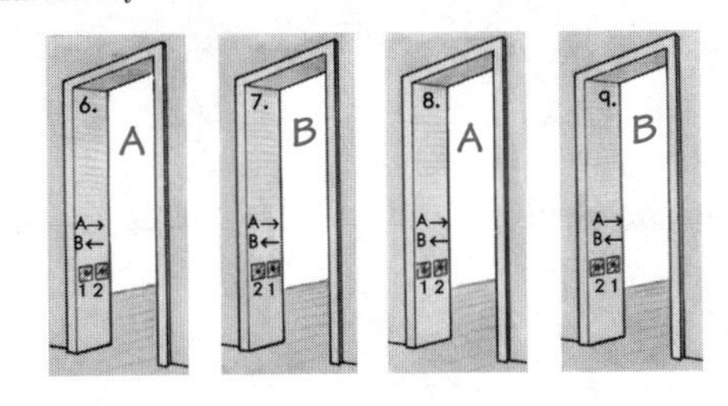

TEXTBOOK

Write the words that go in the blanks to tell about the steps you take to invent something.

10. You start with a ▬.
  • need • electric eye • solution
  Then you get an idea for an invention.
11. Then you build a ▬ of the invention to show how it works. model
12. Then you get a ▬ to protect your invention. patent
13. What are businesses that make things called? manufacturers
14. Write the letter of the best deal for an inventor. b
15. Write the letter of the best deal for a manufacturer. a
  a. 8 thousand dollars and two dollars for every copy sold
  b. 8 thousand dollars and six dollars for every copy sold
  c. 8 thousand dollars and four dollars for every copy sold
16. Name 2 things you could give a dog to reward it. (Any 2:) a bone, a dog treat, a pat on the head, etc.

WORKBOOK

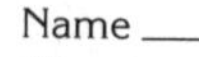

Name ______________________

A Story Items

1. Where will the animal show take place? Samson High School
2. On what day of the week will it be held? Friday
3. At what time will it start? 7 o'clock (in the evening)
4. How much is the admission? 1 dollar
5. Name **3** acts that will be in the animal show.
  (Any 3:) rabbit walking tight ropes; cat riding a bicycle; dog playing water glasses; etc.
6. The more water the glass has, the ▬ the sound it makes.
  • higher • lower
7. **Cross out** the glass that will make the **highest** ring.
8. **Circle** the glass that will make the **lowest** ring.

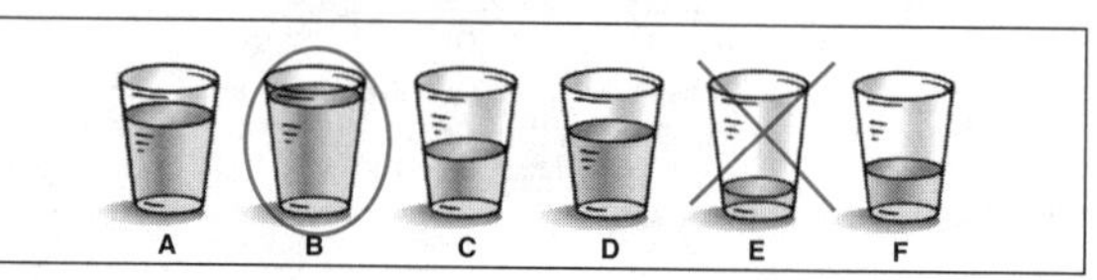

9. What object did the dog use to tap the glasses? hammer
10. What did the dog do with that object at the end of the trick?
  Idea: tossed it into the air
11. What trick would Gormer the rabbit do? walk a tight rope
12. What trick would Henry the cat do? ride a bicycle
13. What song did Homer the dog play? Mary Had a Little Lamb

WORKBOOK

14. Waldo and Maria decided to cook the food for the show at the high school.
  Why didn't they want to cook it at the pet shop? Idea: because many animals would follow them
15. Why wasn't Waldo able to cook his food at the high school?
  Idea: because the stove wouldn't work
16. What food will they use for rewards? Ideas: regular animal food; food from the pet shop

B Review Item

17. Draw arrows at **D**, at **E** and at **F** to show the way the melted rock moves.

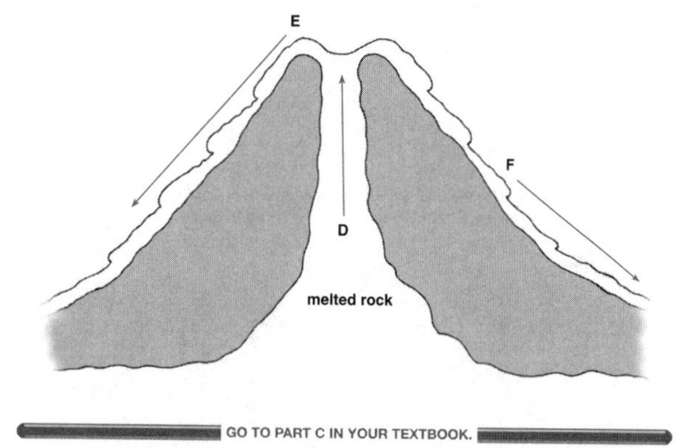

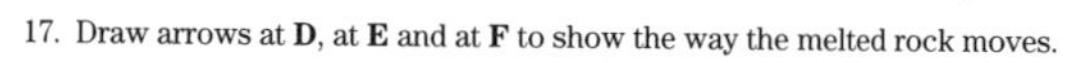

TEXTBOOK

plan would be better than cooking in the pet shop and then bringing the food over in a car. Maria had pointed out, "If you cook at the high school, we won't have a thousand animals following the car over to the high school."

So Waldo went to the kitchen of the high school. He laid out the things that he wanted to cook. Then he turned on the stove and waited for it to get hot. He waited and waited. Suddenly, he realized that the stove was not working. He ran from the kitchen and found Maria. "I can't cook," he said. "The stove doesn't work."

Maria didn't say anything for a moment. Then she said, "I'll go back to the pet shop and get some pet food that is supposed to be really good. I just hope the animals will work for that food."

"Me, too," Waldo said.

C Number your paper from 1 through 20.

Skill Items

Use the words in the box to write complete sentences.

folks	disturbed	screeched	cute	audience
delivered	boring	peppy	mobbed	attract

1. The ▬ speaker ▬ the ▬.
2. A lot of ▬ ▬ around the ▬ singer.

Review Items

3. What's the name of geese that are gray and black and white? Canada geese
4. What's the name of geese that are all white? Snow geese
5. What color are all geese when they are born? yellow
6. In which direction do geese fly in the fall? south
7. What is this trip called? migration

1. The boring speaker disturbed the audience.
2. A lot of folks mobbed around the cute singer.

TEXTBOOK

8. When geese learn to fly, do they start in the water or on the land? *on the land*
9. They run with their ▬ out to the side. *wings*

10. The earth is shaped like a ▬. *ball*
11. The hottest part of the earth is called the ▬.
    - pole
    - desert
    - equator

12. How long ago did dinosaurs live on the earth?
    - a hundred years ago
    - a hundred million years ago
    - a million years ago
13. Most of the things that we use everyday were invented after the year ▬.
    - 1900 • 2000 • 1800

14. What does an inventor get to protect an invention? *patent*
15. Special lawyers who get protection for inventions are called ▬.
    - patents
    - dentists
    - patent attorneys

16. Why don't smart manufacturers act interested in the inventions that they want? **Write the letter of the answer.**
    a. because they are at the fair all day long
    b. because they want to pay more for the invention
    c. so they don't have to pay as much for the invention
17. If an invention wins a prize, would a manufacturer have to pay money for it? *yes*

TEXTBOOK

Study Items

- Get two glasses that look the same. The glasses must be made of glass, not plastic or paper.
- Fill one glass half full of water.
- Tap the glass and listen to the sound it makes.
- Now fix up the second glass so that it makes the same sound as the first glass.

Write the answers to these items.

18. How much water is in the second glass when both glasses make the same sound? *Ideas: half full of water; the same amount as the first glass*
19. Change the amount of water in the second glass so it makes a sound that is lower than the sound of the first glass. Did you **add water** to the second glass or **take water away?** *add water*
20. Find out how a xylophone works and tell how its keys are like glasses of water.

Idea: The larger keys make lower sounds and smaller keys make higher sounds, just like more water makes a lower sound and less water makes a higher sound.

WORKBOOK

75

Name ____________________

A Skill Items

east	attorney
north	million
muff	inventors
Mercury	hundred
admission	off
Venus	liquid
funnel	rocket
thousand	walrus
museum	
manufacturers	

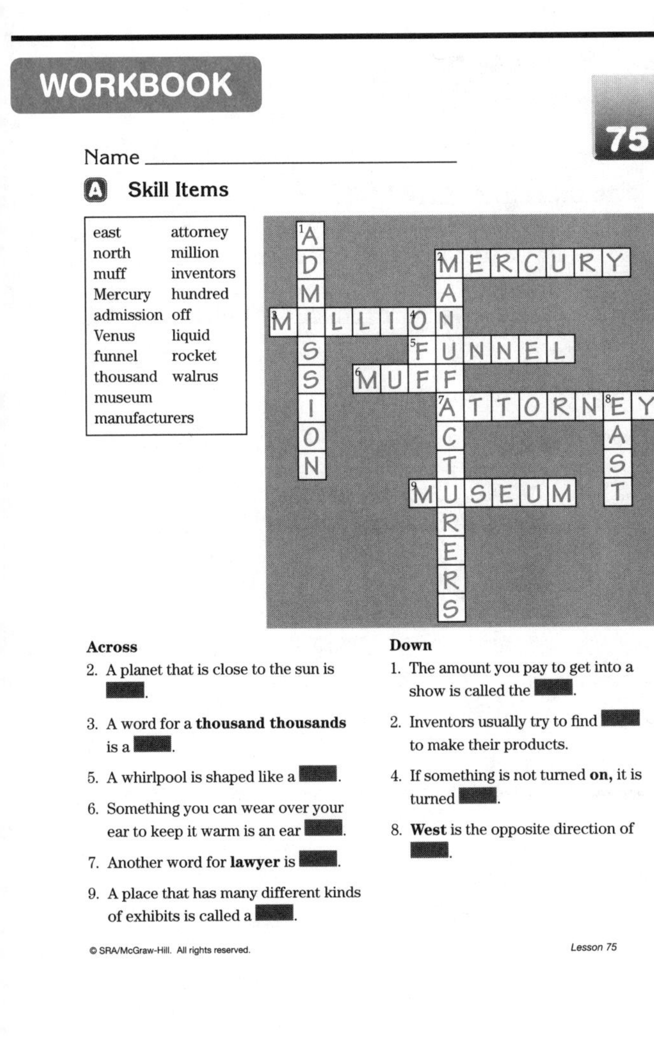

Across

2. A planet that is close to the sun is ▬.
3. A word for a **thousand thousands** is a ▬.
5. A whirlpool is shaped like a ▬.
6. Something you can wear over your ear to keep it warm is an ear ▬.
7. Another word for **lawyer** is ▬.
9. A place that has many different kinds of exhibits is called a ▬.

Down

1. The amount you pay to get into a show is called the ▬.
2. Inventors usually try to find ▬ to make their products.
4. If something is not turned **on,** it is turned ▬.
8. **West** is the opposite direction of ▬.

WORKBOOK

B Story Items

1. About how many people came to see the animal show? *Two thousand (2,000)*
2. Was the show a **flop** or a **success**? *a flop*
3. Why did the animals act the way they did? *Idea: because they didn't get any of Waldo's special food*
4. What trick does Homer the dog usually do? *Idea: plays a song on glasses of water*
5. How well did Homer do his trick the first time he did it in the show? *Ideas: perfectly; very well*
6. What did Waldo use to reward Homer? *Idea: an ordinary dog treat*
7. Did Homer like that reward? *no*
8. Did Homer perform well again? *no*
9. What did Waldo **usually** use to reward the tap-dancing pigeons? *Idea: his special food*
10. What did Waldo use during the show to reward the pigeons? *bird seed*
11. Did the pigeons keep doing their trick for that reward? *no*

GO TO PART C IN YOUR TEXTBOOK.

TEXTBOOK

Maria came onto the stage again. "Sorry about that, folks," she said. She was trying to smile. "But you know how animals are. Let's hope our next act will do a little better. This act is one of the most amazing acts you will ever see. If you've never seen pigeons tap dance, this act will be a real treat for you. And here they are, ladies and gentlemen, the tap-dancing pigeons."

The crowd applauded. Some people were saying, "I've seen this act and it is great."

The tap-dancing pigeons weren't very great this time. Waldo brought out the pigeons, turned on the peppy music and gave the birds the signal to start dancing. And they danced quite well, at least for a while. Usually, Waldo would toss them little bits of special food as they danced. This time, he tossed them little bits of bird seed. The birds blinked and spit out the seeds. Before the song was half over, one of them stopped dancing and started to peck at the buttons that were attached to its feet. Then one of the other birds started dancing out of time with the music. Soon that pigeon stopped dancing. It pecked at the third bird. The third bird pecked the first bird. The first bird flew to the back of the hall and landed on top of a picture.

"This is a bad act," somebody shouted from the back of the audience. Again, the people in the audience began to talk to each other. Maria came out on the stage and smiled. She tried to talk, but the people in the audience did not listen. They were busy talking to each other. They were saying things like, "Who said this was a good show?" and "These animals aren't even trained well."

Waldo was thinking, "I hope this show will be over soon."

C Number your paper from 1 through 16.

Skill Items

Here are 3 events that happened in the story. Write **beginning, middle** or **end** for each event.

1. Maria told Waldo that there were nearly two thousand people in the hall. beginning
2. The first bird flew to the back of the hall and landed on top of a picture. end
3. Waldo gave Gormer a little piece of carrot. middle

TEXTBOOK

Review Items

4. The more water the glass has, the ___ the sound it makes.
   - lower
   - higher
5. Write the letter of the glass that will make the lowest ring. F
6. Write the letter of the glass that will make the highest ring. C

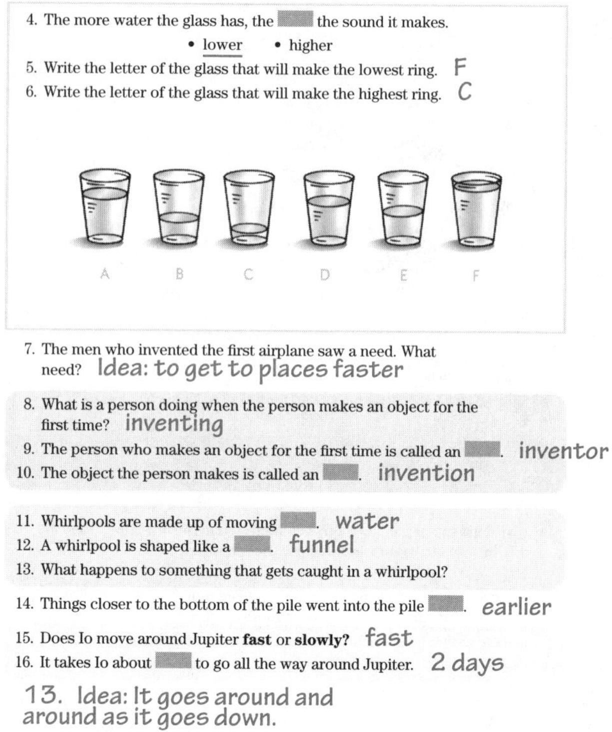

7. The men who invented the first airplane saw a need. What need? Idea: to get to places faster
8. What is a person doing when the person makes an object for the first time? inventing
9. The person who makes an object for the first time is called an ___. inventor
10. The object the person makes is called an ___. invention
11. Whirlpools are made up of moving ___. water
12. A whirlpool is shaped like a ___. funnel
13. What happens to something that gets caught in a whirlpool?
14. Things closer to the bottom of the pile went into the pile ___. earlier
15. Does Io move around Jupiter **fast** or **slowly?** fast
16. It takes Io about ___ to go all the way around Jupiter. 2 days

13. Idea: It goes around and around as it goes down.

WORKBOOK

76

Name ______________________

A Skill Items

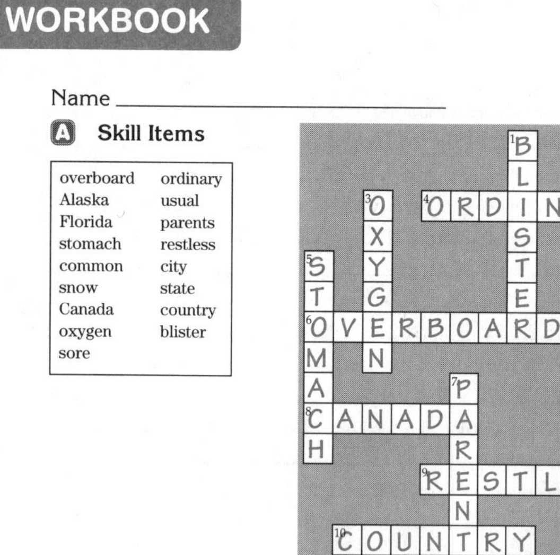

Across

4. Things you see all the time in different places are ___ things.
6. When things go over the side of a ship, they go ___.
8. Geese that are gray and black and white are called ___ geese.
9. When you feel ___, you don't want to keep doing what you're doing.
10. Japan is a ___.

Down

1. You may get a ___ on your foot if your shoe doesn't fit well.
2. Oomoo and Oolak lived in the state of ___.
3. When Wendy was on Io, she had to wear an ___ tank so she could breathe.
5. If you are hungry, your ___ may make noise.
7. Your mother and father are called your ___.

WORKBOOK

B Story Items

1. How did the people in the audience feel about the animal show? Idea: They didn't like it.
2. People returned their trained animals to the pet shop. Why wouldn't those animals do their tricks? Idea: because they didn't get Waldo's special food
3. What did the people want? Ideas: a refund; their money
4. Did Waldo eat very much dinner? no
5. What was he thinking about during dinner? Idea: how to train animals for new rewards
6. Where did he go right after dinner? to his bedroom
7. Waldo's father said that Waldo had a training problem.
8. The animals would work for Idea: Waldo's special food but they would not work for Idea: any other rewards.
9. Waldo could solve this problem by training the animals to work for Idea: other rewards

GO TO PART C IN YOUR TEXTBOOK.

TEXTBOOK

C Number your paper from 1 through 19.

Skill Items

The tour to the islands was a fantastic experience.

1. What word describes each thing you do? experience
2. What's another word for a **trip to several places?** tour
3. What's another word for **wonderful?** fantastic

Review Items

4. Which is smaller, Alaska or Japan? Japan
5. Is Japan a **state** or a **country?** country
6. How many people live in Japan?
   - 127
   - 127 million
   - 127 thousand
7. Which planet has more clouds around it, Earth or Mars? Earth
8. Which planet is smaller? Mars
9. Which planet is colder? Mars
10. Why is that planet colder? Idea: It is farther from the sun.

Use these names to answer the questions:
Tyrannosaurus, Triceratops.

11. What is animal **G?** Triceratops
12. What is animal **H?** Tyrannosaurus

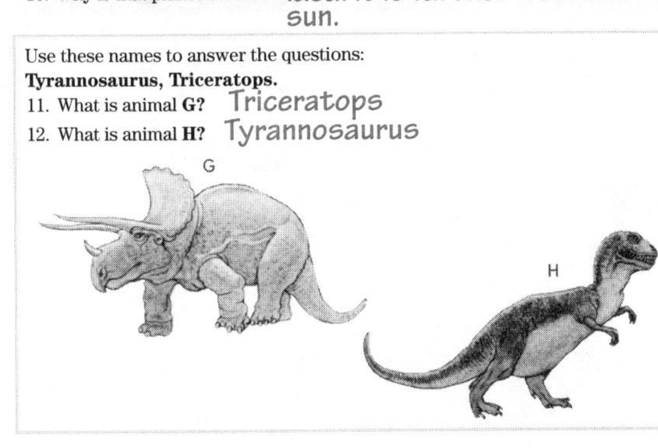

TEXTBOOK

13. Captain Parker's ship passed through a place where hundreds of ships have sunk or been lost. Name that place. Bermuda Triangle
14. Which came **earlier** on Earth, dinosaurs or horses? dinosaurs
15. Which came **earlier** on Earth, strange sea animals or dinosaurs? strange sea animals
16. Name 3 animals that are warm-blooded. (Any 3:) bears, humans, dogs, etc.
17. Name 3 animals that are cold-blooded. (Any 3:) fish, sharks, reptiles, etc.
18. The picture shows half a hailstone. How many times did the stone go through a cloud? 3

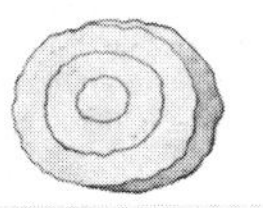

19. How long does it take Jupiter to spin around one time? 10 hours

WORKBOOK

77

Name ____________________

A Skill Items

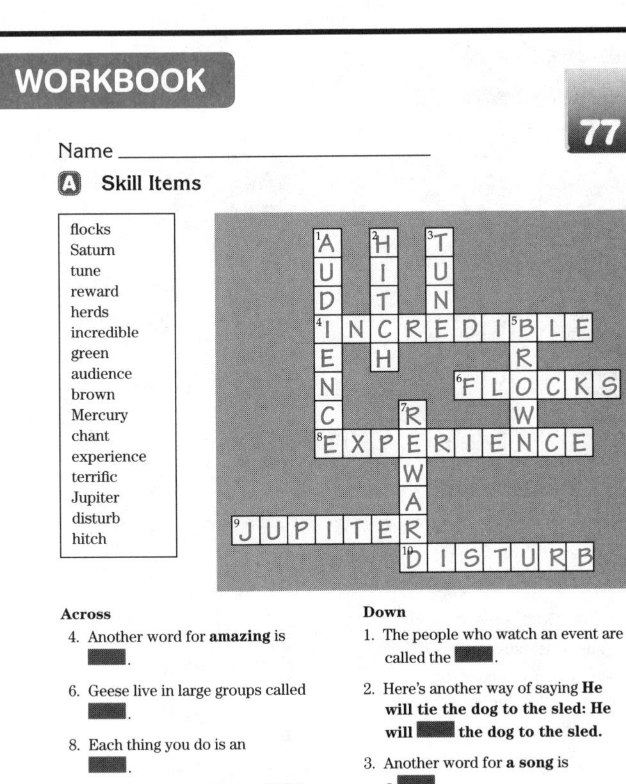

Across

4. Another word for **amazing** is ▬.
6. Geese live in large groups called ▬.
8. Each thing you do is an ▬.
9. Io is a moon of the planet ▬.
10. Another word for **bother** is ▬.

Down

1. The people who watch an event are called the ▬.
2. Here's another way of saying **He will tie the dog to the sled: He will ▬ the dog to the sled.**
3. Another word for **a song** is a ▬.
5. Jupiter is orange, white and ▬.
7. Something you get for doing a good job is a ▬ for doing that job.

WORKBOOK

B Story Items

1. Waldo read until late at night and then went to bed. Why didn't he go to sleep right away? Ideas: He was thinking about what he'd read/retraining the animals.
2. When you teach animals to work for new rewards, do you change the reward **quickly** or **slowly?** slowly
3. When you teach an animal to work for a new reward, what kind of reward do you start with? Idea: one the animal will work for
4. Then what do you do to that reward? Idea: slowly change it
5. When do you stop changing the reward? ____________
6. What reward do Waldo's animals work for? Idea: his special food
7. When Waldo teaches his animals to work for new rewards, what reward will he start with? Idea: his special food
8. Then what will he do to that reward? Idea: change it slowly
9. How long did the school day seem to Waldo? ____________
10. Where did he go right after school? Idea: to the pet shop
11. What did he start doing as soon as he got there? Idea: cooking some special food

GO TO PART C IN YOUR TEXTBOOK.

5. Ideas: when it becomes the new reward; when the animal will work for the new reward
9. Ideas: very long; a year long

TEXTBOOK

The school day seemed to drag on and on. Waldo looked at his watch every five or ten minutes. Each time, he said to himself, "Will this school day ever be over?"

It seemed as if a whole year passed before the last bell of the school day rang. The kids rushed from their classroom. Waldo was one of the first outside. He ran to the pet shop. When he arrived there, he was out of breath. But he didn't waste a second. He went into the kitchen and fixed some food. He didn't pay much attention to the three dogs and the goat that were looking in the kitchen window. Then he took his food inside the pet shop. The animals were jumping around and making a lot of noise.

Maria looked at him, and he looked at her. With a smile, he said, "Well, I sure hope it works."

Maria said, "We'll soon find out." And they did.

C Number your paper from 1 through 17.

Skill Items

Use the words in the box to write complete sentences.

waste	cute	fantastic	refund	folks
shortly	deserved	experience	tour	mobbed

1. A lot of ▬ ▬ the ▬ singer.
2. The ▬ to the islands was a ▬ ▬.

Review Items

3. Write the letters of 3 types of products that are used in the United States and manufactured in Japan. b, d, f
   - a. books
   - b. cars
   - c. rugs
   - d. TVs
   - e. furniture
   - f. CD players
   - g. Mr. Light Saver

1. A lot of folks mobbed the cute singer.
2. The tour to the islands was a fantastic experience.

TEXTBOOK

4. Two things happen to melted rock when it moves down the sides of a volcano. Name those two things. Idea: It gets cooler and it hardens.
5. What is it called when the earth shakes and cracks? earthquake; quake
6. Which uses up more oxygen, sleeping or jumping? jumping
7. What's another name for hot, melted rock? lava
8. What color is lava when it's very hot?
   - brown
   - orange
   - gray
9. What color is lava after it cools a little bit? brown
10. What color is lava after it's completely cooled? gray
11. Which has more gravity, Jupiter or Io? Jupiter
12. Which is smaller than Earth? Io
13. Where can you jump 8 feet high? Io
14. Which has a stronger gravity, Earth or Jupiter? Jupiter
15. So where would you feel lighter? Earth
16. The earth makes a circle around the sun one time every ▬. year
17. How many days does it take the earth to make one full circle around the sun? 365

WORKBOOK

Name ______________________

A Story Items

Fill in each blank with the word **regular** or the word **coated.**

1. Waldo trained the pigeons to work for a new reward. First Waldo rewarded the pigeons with his special food. Next, Waldo rewarded the pigeons with two coated seeds.
2. Next, Waldo rewarded the pigeons with two coated seeds and one regular seed.
3. Next, Waldo rewarded the pigeons with two regular seeds and one coated seed.
4. At the end, Waldo rewarded the pigeons with three regular seeds.
5. Waldo trained the rabbit to work for a new reward. First, Waldo rewarded the rabbit with his special food. Next, Waldo rewarded the rabbit with two pieces of coated carrots.
6. Next, Waldo rewarded the rabbit with two pieces of coated carrots and one piece of regular carrot.
7. At the end, Waldo rewarded the rabbit with three pieces of regular carrots.
8. Which people did Maria call after Waldo retrained the animals? Idea: the people who had returned their animals to the pet shop
9. What did she tell those people about the animals? Idea: that the animals would work for regular food

Fill in each blank with the word **top** or the word **bottom.**

10. A **regular pyramid** has one animal at the top of the pyramid.
11. An **upside-down pyramid** has one animal at the bottom of the pyramid.

WORKBOOK

B Skill Items

truck
kayak
pole
boring
crater
Canada
Alaska
volcano
intelligent
drifting
equator
clever
hotter
ignore
colder
earthquake
automobile

Crossword answers: 1 DRIFTING, 2 VOLCANO, 3 KAYAK, 4 COLDER, 5 AUTOMOBILE, 6 CLEVER, 7 BORING, 8 IGNORE, 9 EQUATOR, CANADA

Across

5. Another word for **car** is ▬.
6. Most wild geese are born in ▬.
7. **Interesting** is the opposite of ▬.
9. The part of the earth that receives more heat than any other part is the ▬.

Down

1. When an ice chunk is being moved by a current, we say that the ice chunk is ▬.
2. A mountain that erupts is called a ▬.
3. The kind of boat that Eskimos use is a ▬.
4. The farther you go from the equator, the ▬ it gets.
6. Another word for **very smart** is ▬.
8. When you don't pay attention to something you ▬ that thing.

GO TO PART C IN YOUR TEXTBOOK.

TEXTBOOK

C Number your paper from 1 through 21.

Story Items

1. Why didn't Waldo like his idea of making a regular pyramid? Idea: It was too easy.
2. What super trick is Waldo training the animals to do? an upside-down pyramid
3. What animal will be at the bottom of that pyramid? Ideas: a huge dog; a St. Bernard
4. What was the first animal that Waldo trained for the super trick? Ideas: a huge dog; a St. Bernard
5. The two smaller dogs had to jump to a special place on the big dog's back. Which dog stood with its paws on the huge dog's head? the black dog
6. Which dog stood on the huge dog's rear end? the spotted dog

Review Items

7. When you teach animals to work for new rewards, do you change the reward **quickly** or **slowly?** slowly
8. When you teach an animal to work for a new reward, what kind of reward do you start with? Idea: one the animal will work for
9. Then what do you do to that reward? Idea: slowly change it
10. When do you stop changing the reward?
11. When you teach an animal a simple trick, when do you reward the animal? Idea: when it does the trick;
12. When don't you reward the animal? Idea: when it doesn't do the trick
13. Let's say that you want to teach an animal a very hard trick. Can the animal do the trick at first? no
14. What will happen if the animal doesn't receive any rewards until it does the trick? Idea: The animal will stop trying to do the trick.
15. When you're teaching the animal a hard trick, what do you reward the animal for doing? Idea: for trying to do the trick

10. Ideas: when it becomes the new reward; when the animal will work for the new reward

TEXTBOOK

Write the name of each animal in the picture.

WORKBOOK

79

Name ______________________

A Story Items

1. In what country are the states of Colorado and Utah? United States
2. Name the mountains you drive over to get from Colorado to Utah. Rocky Mountains
3. In which direction do you go to get from Colorado to Utah? west
4. Name 2 cities in Colorado. Denver, Greeley
5. Name one city in Utah. Salt Lake City

6. Write **north, south, east** and **west** in the correct boxes.
7. Make an **R** on the state of Colorado.
8. Make a **T** on the state of Utah.

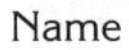

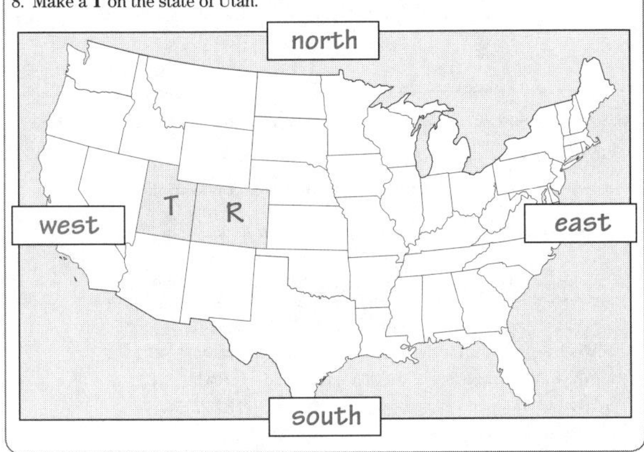

WORKBOOK

B Story Items

9. What animal was at the bottom of the upside-down pyramid? Ideas: a huge dog; a St. Bernard
10. Which dog stood on the huge dog's rear end? the spotted dog
11. Which dog stood with its paws on the huge dog's head? the black dog
12. How many cats were in the pyramid? 4
13. What animals did the cats stand on? Idea: the smaller dogs
14. How many squirrels were in the pyramid? 8
15. What animals did the squirrels stand on? the cats
16. How many pigeons were in the pyramid? 16
17. What animals did the pigeons stand on? the squirrels
18. Waldo and Maria didn't show the upside-down pyramid before the animal show. Why not? ______________________
19. How many times did the dancing pigeons do their act? 2 times
20. How well did they do their act? Ideas: perfectly; very well
21. How did the audience respond to the dancing pigeons? Ideas: They loved it; they went wild.
22. What did the audience do while Homer played "Mary Had a Little Lamb"? Ideas: clapped in time with the music; applauded

18. Ideas: because they wanted the pyramid to be a surprise; because it was a super trick

GO TO PART D IN YOUR TEXTBOOK.

TEXTBOOK

Next was the dog that did backward somersaults in the air. First Waldo held out a stick and signaled the dog to jump over the stick. Then Waldo signaled the dog to roll over, to sit up, to speak and to walk on its hind legs. Then Waldo signaled the dog to do the backward somersaults. When the dog started to do the somersaults, the people in the audience counted together, "One . . . two . . . three . . . four . . . five . . . six." Then the people applauded, as Waldo tossed some dog treats to the dog.

Now came the super act.

D Number your paper from 1 through 16.

Story Items

1. Did Waldo use his special food to reward the animals during the animal show? no
2. What did he use? regular food
3. One act was the dog that did backward somersaults. What did the audience do while that dog did somersaults?
4. How many somersaults did the dog do? 6
5. What act comes right after the dog that does somersaults? The upside-down pyramid

Skill Items

Here are 3 events that happened in the story. Write **beginning, middle** or **end** for each event.

6. Waldo gave the pigeons the signal to dance again. middle
7. Just before the pet shop closed, Waldo showed Maria the animals he had just trained. beginning
8. Next was the dog that did backward somersaults in the air. end

3. Idea: counted the somersaults

TEXTBOOK

Review Items

Fill in each blank with the word **top** or the word **bottom.**

9. A regular pyramid has one animal at the ____ of the pyramid. top
10. An upside-down pyramid has one animal at the ____ of the pyramid. bottom

Let's say you're training a dog to jump up in the air and do a backward somersault. Use the words below to finish each sentence.

- jumping up and turning upside down
- jumping up and leaning backward
- jumping up in the air

11. At first, you would reward the dog for ____. jumping up in the air
12. Later you would reward the dog for ____.
13. Later you would reward the dog for ____.

- On planet A you can jump 10 feet high.
- On planet B you can jump 30 feet high.
- On planet C you can jump 5 feet high.
- On planet D you can jump 20 feet high.
- On planet E you can jump 3 feet high.

14. Write the letter of the planet that has the most gravity. E
15. Write the letter of the planet that has the least gravity. B
16. Could you see very far on Jupiter with bright lights? no

12. jumping up and leaning backward
13. jumping up and turning upside-down

TEXTBOOK

TEST 8 80

1. Idea: when the animal does the trick

Number your paper from 1 through 26.

1. When you teach an animal a simple trick, when do you reward the animal?
2. When don't you reward the animal? Idea: when the animal doesn't do the trick
3. Let's say that you want to teach an animal a very hard trick. Can the animal do the trick at first? no
4. What will happen if the animal doesn't receive any rewards until it does the trick? Idea: It will stop trying to do the trick.
5. So when you're teaching the animal a hard trick, what do you reward the animal for doing? Idea: for trying to do the trick

6. The more water the glass has, the ____ the sound it makes.
   - lower
   - higher
7. Which glass will make the lowest ring? A
8. Which glass will make the highest ring? F

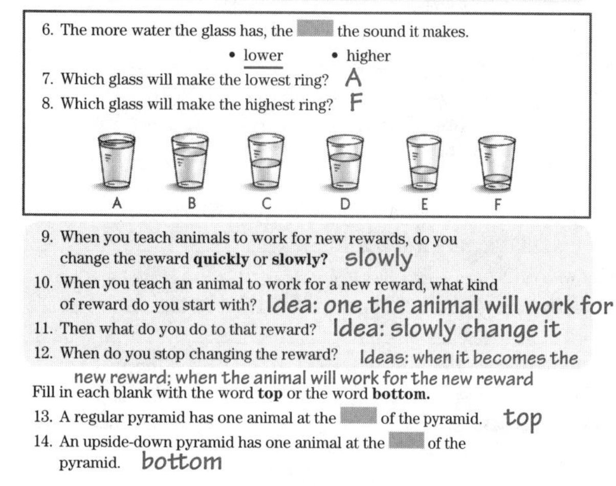

9. When you teach animals to work for new rewards, do you change the reward **quickly** or **slowly?** slowly
10. When you teach an animal to work for a new reward, what kind of reward do you start with? Idea: one the animal will work for
11. Then what do you do to that reward? Idea: slowly change it
12. When do you stop changing the reward? Ideas: when it becomes the new reward; when the animal will work for the new reward

Fill in each blank with the word **top** or the word **bottom.**

13. A regular pyramid has one animal at the ____ of the pyramid. top
14. An upside-down pyramid has one animal at the ____ of the pyramid. bottom

TEXTBOOK

15. In what country are the states of Colorado and Utah? United States
16. Name the mountains you drive over to get from Colorado to Utah. Rocky Mountains
17. In which direction do you go to get from Colorado to Utah? west
18. Name **2** cities in Colorado. Denver, Greeley
19. Name one city in Utah. Salt Lake City

20. Which letter shows Colorado? J
21. Which letter shows Utah? K

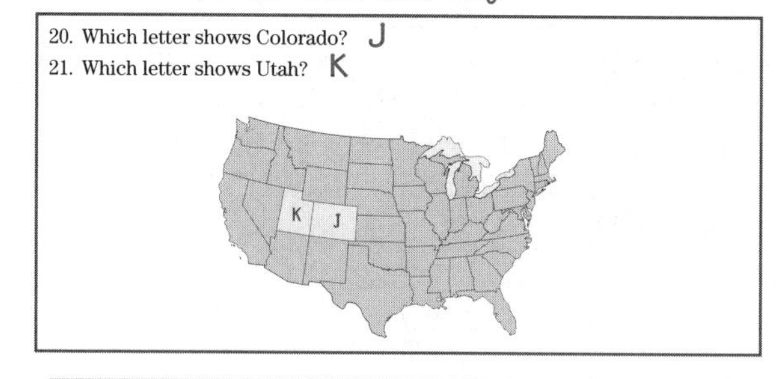

Skill Items

For each item, write the underlined word from the sentences in the box.

A lot of folks mobbed the cute singer.
The tour to the islands was a fantastic experience.

22. What underlining means **wonderful?** fantastic
23. What underlining means **good-looking and charming?** cute
24. What underlining describes each thing you do? experience
25. What underlining means **crowded around?** mobbed
26. What underlining means **people?** folks

WORKBOOK

4. Ideas: a cat that would ring a bell; a dog that would keep rabbits and birds out of her garden; a cat that would honk a truck horn

Name ______________________

A Story Items

1. When the animals did the super trick at Samson High School, what did the birds do before they landed on the squirrels? Ideas: flew over the audience; circled the hall 3 times
2. How did Waldo signal the birds to land on the squirrels? He whistled (loudly).
3. How did the audience feel about the pyramid act? Ideas: They loved it; they thought it was great.
4. Some people put in special orders for trained animals. Name one of those special orders. ______________________
5. What time of year is usually the busiest for the pet shop? Christmas time
6. Did the pet shop have **more business** or **less business** than it had at Christmas? more business
7. What's a tour? Idea: a traveling show
8. How long would Waldo's tour last? about a month
9. How many shows is Maria planning for the tour? over 30
10. How will Waldo keep up with his school work while he's on the tour? Idea: Maria will be his teacher.
11. What will Waldo and Maria ride in when they travel from city to city? a small truck
12. What will the animals travel in? a big trailer
13. Who will drive? Idea: Maria will hire a driver.
14. Before Waldo could go, he would need permission from his parents.

WORKBOOK

B Skill Items

involve	lower	Triceratops	gravity	tire	shortly
Rocky	higher	Tyrannosaurus	selected	regular	waste
contacted	clever	information	hire	deserve	

													G			
											L		R			
											O		A			
				C	L	E	V	E	R		W		V			D
									O		E		I			E
			W			T	R	I	C	E	R	A	T	O	P	S
			A						K				Y			E
			S	H	O	R	T	L	Y							R
			T													V
S	E	L	E	C	T	E	D						H	I	R	E

Across

3. Another word for **very smart** is ▇▇.
7. The name of the dinosaur that had horns and armor was ▇▇.
8. Another word for **soon** is ▇▇.
9. Another word for **chose** is ▇▇.
10. When you give someone a job, you ▇▇ that person.

Down

1. The more water the glass has, the ▇▇ the sound it makes.
2. Bigger planets have more ▇▇ than smaller planets.
4. To get from Colorado to Utah, you cross the ▇▇ Mountains.
5. Something you should receive is something you ▇▇.
6. When we use something the wrong way, we ▇▇ that thing.

GO TO PART C IN YOUR TEXTBOOK.

TEXTBOOK

over that work with you. I'll be your teacher."

Waldo smiled. "Do you mean we'll study on the tour?"

"Sure," she said. "We're going to take a small truck and a big trailer. The animals will be in the trailer. You and I will be in the truck. We'll hire a driver to drive the truck. So you and I can study as we go from city to city."

Maria went on to explain that a person who puts on tours for good shows contacted her and set up the places they would go. "And we'll make a lot of money," Maria said. "All we need now is permission from your parents."

• • •

"Waldo, you're hardly eating," Waldo's mother said. "What's the matter?"

Waldo's sister said, "Oh, he doesn't eat any food unless he . . ."

"That's enough," Waldo's father said. Then he turned to Waldo and said, "I feel that you're trying to tell us something. What is it?"

"Well," Waldo said slowly. "Can I go on a tour and put on shows in over thirty cities with the animals?"

Waldo's mother sat up very straight and put her fork down. "What are you talking about?" she said. "What tour? Which cities?"

So Waldo explained the tour. Then he added, "I'll get my schoolwork done. The school has given permission. Everything is all set if you give me permission. Can I go?"

C Number your paper from 1 through 11.

Skill Items

She will contact the person we want to hire.

1. What word tells about giving somebody a job? hire
2. What word tells about getting in touch with somebody? contact

Review Items

3. When you're training an animal, what do you do each time the animal does the trick? Idea: give the animal a reward
4. What do you do if the animal does not do the trick? Idea: don't give the animal a reward
5. Name **2** things you could give a dog to reward it. (Any 2:) a bone, a dog treat, a pat on the head, etc.

TEXTBOOK

Write the name of each animal in the picture.

6. elephant

7. goat

8. tiger

9. sheep

10. squirrel

11. parrot

WORKBOOK

Name ____________ **82**

A Story Items

1. Who did Waldo's father want to talk to before he gave Waldo permission to go on the tour? Maria
2. What did Waldo's father think after he talked to Maria? Idea: that it sounded like a very good tour
3. How many shows did Waldo and Maria do **before** they got to Denver? 5
4. Which city did Waldo and Maria go to **after** Denver? Greeley
5. Which brakes stopped working first—the truck brakes or the trailer brakes? trailer brakes
6. Where was the truck when the brakes failed? in the mountains

- Write **B** in front of each thing that happened **before** the tour.
- Write **D** in front of each thing that happened **during** the tour.

7. B The driver hooked up the line for the trailer brakes.
8. D Waldo saw a mountain goat.
9. B Waldo's parents gave permission for Waldo to go on the trip.
10. B The driver explained why the trailer needed brakes.
11. D Maria and Waldo stopped studying and looked at the mountains.
12. D Waldo and Maria did a show in Denver, Colorado.
13. B Waldo and Maria did a show at Samson High School.
14. How did the truck engine sound to Waldo at the end of the story?
15. What did Waldo smell at the end of the story? Idea: burnt-out brakes

14. Ideas: It was screaming; like it was going to fall apart

WORKBOOK

B Review Items

Look at the picture.

16. Shade the part of the earth where it is nighttime.
17. Which side of the earth is closer to the sun, J or K? K
18. Which side of the earth is in nighttime? J
19. Which side of the earth is in daytime? K

20. Write **north, south, east** and **west** in the correct boxes.
21. In which direction is ocean current **L** moving? west
22. In which direction is ocean current **M** moving? north
23. Which direction is the wind coming from? south
24. Make an arrow above ice chunk **N** to show the direction the current will move the ice chunk.
25. Make an arrow above ice chunk **P** to show the direction the current will move the ice chunk.

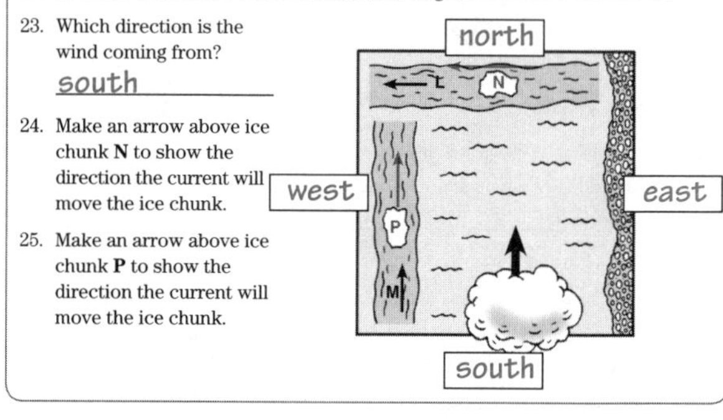

GO TO PART C IN YOUR TEXTBOOK.

TEXTBOOK

brakes, the pickup truck would have a hard time stopping.

Now the truck was going very fast down the mountain. The tires screeched as the truck went around a sharp curve. For a moment, it seemed as if the truck would go over the edge. In fact, the truck went through some stones on the side of the road. Then it came back on the road and continued to gain speed.

The driver said, "The trailer is pushing us, and the truck brakes are gone now."

The truck seemed to be flying down the road. It came up behind a car that was loaded with camping gear. The driver of the pickup truck honked the horn and went around the car like it was standing still. Faster, faster, faster. The truck was now on a long, straight part of the road, but the grade was very steep and the truck was going so fast that the engine sounded as if it was ready to fly apart. Waldo could smell the burnt-out brakes.

Waldo was almost afraid to look outside, so he watched the driver. The driver had his foot pressed down hard on the brake pedal, but the pickup truck continued to speed down the long, straight part of the road. The driver turned on the truck lights and pressed his hand against the horn. Waldo understood what the driver was trying to do. He was trying to warn the other cars on the road that the truck was in trouble. The sounds were terrible—the engine screaming, the horn blasting, the air rushing outside the truck. And the smell of the burnt-out brakes was strong. Waldo felt sick. He tried not to think about what was happening. He tried not to think about his animals in the trailer and what might happen to them.

C Number your paper from 1 through 8.

Skill Items

Use the words in the box to write complete sentences.

experience	regular	fastened	fantastic	hire
couple	tour	contact	remind	difficult

1. The ▆ to the islands was a ▆ ▆. tour, fantastic, experience
2. She will ▆ the person we want to ▆. contact, hire

TEXTBOOK

Review Items

3. The pilot of Traveler Four turned off the engines when the spaceship was out in space. Did the ship slow down? no
4. Was there any air outside the spaceship? no
5. Which planets have stronger gravities, the bigger planets or the smaller planets? bigger planets
6. A person weighs 100 pounds on Planet A and 90 pounds on Planet B. Which planet has stronger gravity? A

7. The arrow on the map goes from San Francisco to ▆. Japan
8. Which ocean does the arrow cross? Pacific (Ocean)

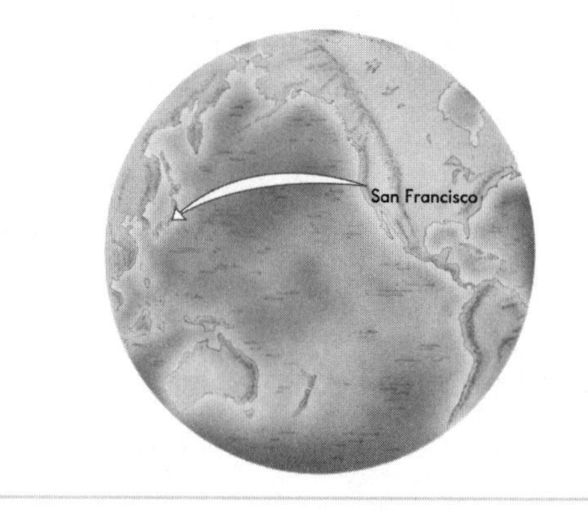

WORKBOOK

Name

83

A Story Items

1. Why couldn't the driver stop the truck? Idea: because the brakes weren't working
2. How many pounds of weight do you have to push down with to make the emergency brake work? at least 80 pounds
3. If the huge dog had **all** its weight on the brake, would the brake work? yes
4. Did the huge dog weigh **more than 100 pounds** or **less than 100 pounds?** more than 100 pounds
5. How many paws did the huge dog have on the brake? 2
6. Was the weight of the three dogs enough to make the brake work? yes
7. Was that enough weight to make the brake stop the trailer very fast? no
8. Why was it important for the trailer to stop fast? Ideas: They might crash; they might go over the edge; the animals might get hurt.
9. What did Waldo do to get more weight on the brake? Ideas: He told the cats to get on the pyramid; he signaled the cats.

B Review Items

10. Write the names of the 9 planets, starting with the planet closest to the sun. Mercury, Venus, Earth, Mars, Jupiter, Saturn, Uranus, Neptune, Pluto

WORKBOOK

11. In which direction do geese migrate in the fall? south
12. In which direction do geese migrate in the spring? north
13. Write the directions **north, south, east** and **west** in the boxes.
14. Make a line that starts at the circle on the map and goes north.
15. If you start at the circle and move to the number 5, in which direction do you go? north

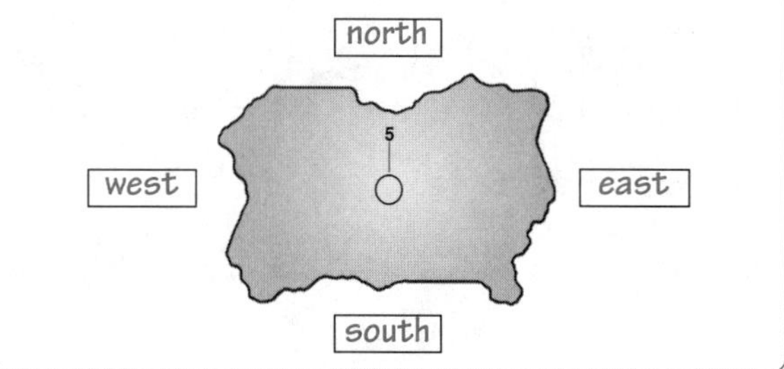

16. How many moons does Jupiter have? 63
17. How many moons does Saturn have? 47
18. Which planet has more moons, Saturn or Jupiter? Jupiter
19. How far is it from Earth to Jupiter? 400 million miles
20. Do gases surround Io? no
21. How much oxygen is on Io? Idea: none

GO TO PART C IN YOUR TEXTBOOK.

TEXTBOOK

"Cats," Waldo yelled. "Cats, get on the pyramid." He signaled the cats. For a moment, they stood without moving. Then, with one great leap, the first cat jumped onto the back of the spotted dog. Then another cat, and another. Finally, the last cat got on the pyramid.

The truck was almost to the curve.

C Number your paper from 1 through 15.

Review Items

1. Does Io move around Jupiter **fast** or **slowly?** fast
2. It takes Io about ▬ to go all the way around Jupiter. 2 days

3. What planet is shown in the picture? Jupiter
4. Which is bigger, the "eye" of the planet or Earth? the eye

5. How long does it take Jupiter to spin around one time? about 10 hours

TEXTBOOK

6. The more water the glass has, the ▬ the sound it makes.
   - lower
   - higher
7. Write the letter of the glass that will make the lowest ring. E
8. Write the letter of the glass that will make the highest ring. B

A B C D E F

9. In what country are the states of Colorado and Utah? United States
10. Name the mountains you drive over to get from Colorado to Utah. Rocky Mountains
11. In which direction do you go to get from Colorado to Utah? west
12. Name **2** cities in Colorado. Denver; Greeley
13. Name one city in Utah. Salt Lake City
14. Which letter shows Colorado? F
15. Which letter shows Utah? G

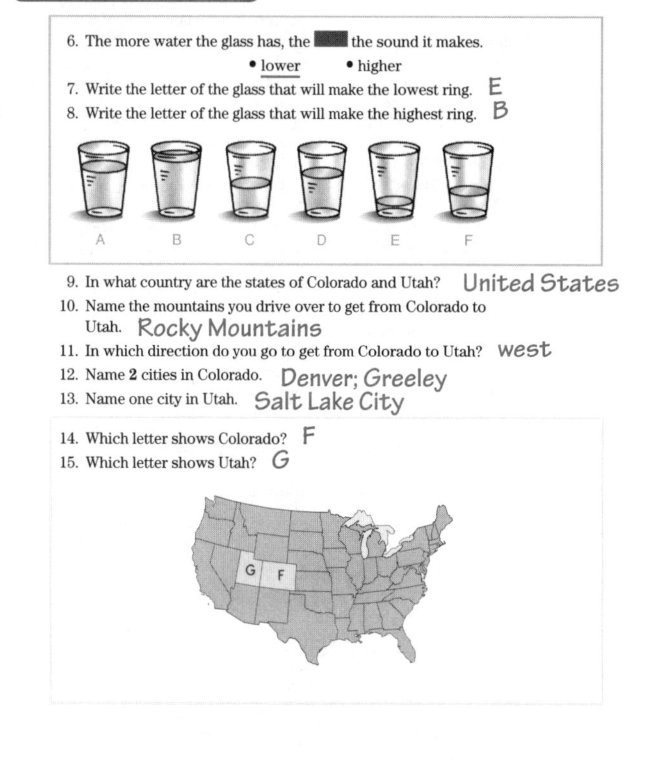

WORKBOOK

Name ______________________

84

A

Write the name of each kind of coral below the correct picture.

• **red coral** • **staghorn coral** • **brain coral**

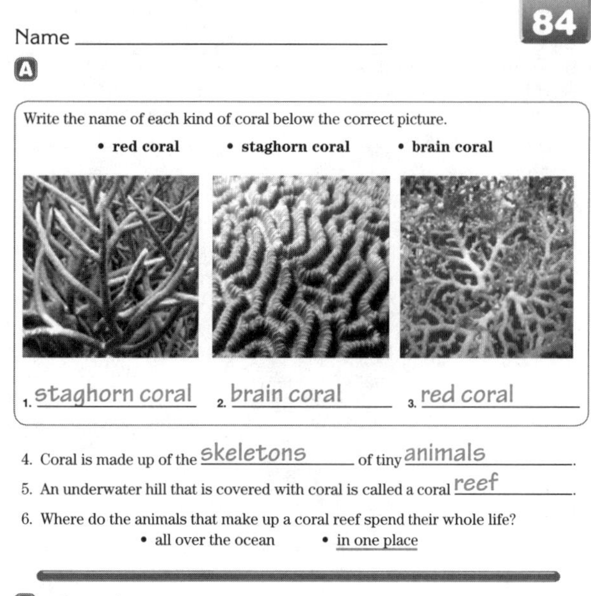

1. staghorn coral 2. brain coral 3. red coral

4. Coral is made up of the skeletons of tiny animals.
5. An underwater hill that is covered with coral is called a coral reef.
6. Where do the animals that make up a coral reef spend their whole life?
   • all over the ocean • in one place

B **Story Items**

7. The weight of three dogs and four cats was on the emergency brake. Was that more than 80 pounds? yes
8. Was that enough weight to stop the truck? yes

WORKBOOK

9. To keep the brake locked in place, the driver turned a screw.
10. After the truck had stopped, what treat did Waldo give the animals? Idea: some of his special food
11. Why did he give them a treat? Ideas: because they had done the trick/saved everyone/stopped the truck
12. What trick did the animals do for the people who gathered around the truck? upside-down pyramid
13. How long did it take to get the brakes fixed? Idea: less than an hour
14. Where did the truck and trailer go after the brakes were fixed? Ideas: Utah; Salt Lake City
15. What followed the truck and trailer? Idea: a line of cars
16. Waldo remembered one show as the greatest show his animals ever did. Where did that show take place? Ideas: in the trailer; on the mountain road

C **Skill Items**

Here are 3 events that happened in the story. Write **beginning, middle** or **end** for each event.

17. The show in Utah was a great success. end
18. The truck was at the curve now, but it was hardly moving. beginning
19. Two other policemen were directing traffic around the truck and trailer. middle

GO TO PART D IN YOUR TEXTBOOK.

TEXTBOOK

Waldo looked at Maria. She smiled. "I'll show you the trick that I like best," Waldo said.

Waldo signaled the huge dog to stand next to the road. Then he signaled the two smaller dogs. They jumped onto the back of the huge dog. Then came the cats. Then came the squirrels. Finally, Waldo whistled and sixteen pigeons landed on the squirrels. For a moment, the crowd was silent. Then people began to clap and cheer. "That's amazing," some of them shouted.

"Yes," Waldo said. "That's the best trick in the world." It was the best trick in the world because it saved so many lives.

Waldo signaled the pigeons and they flew from the pyramid. The squirrels jumped down, the cats jumped down, followed by the two smaller dogs.

Within an hour, the brakes on the trailer and the truck were fixed, and the truck continued on its way to Utah. A long line of cars followed the trailer.

The show in Utah was a great success. The newspapers carried stories about the experience that Waldo and Maria had in the Rocky Mountains.

Waldo was very pleased with the show. But the show that he remembered as the greatest one his animals ever did took place in a trailer that was speeding down a mountain road.

D Number your paper from 1 through 20.

Review Items

1. If you can see the sun, it is ▬ on your side of the earth. daytime
2. What is it on the other side of the earth? nighttime
3. The earth turns around one time every ▬ hours. 24
4. What kind of boat do Eskimos use in the summer? kayak
5. Why don't they use those boats in the winter?
6. How long ago did dinosaurs live on the earth?
   • a hundred years ago
   • a hundred million years ago
   • a million years ago

5. Ideas: because the water is frozen; because of the ice floes; because the winds are too strong

TEXTBOOK

7. Which planet in the picture has more gravity? R
8. How do you know? It's larger.

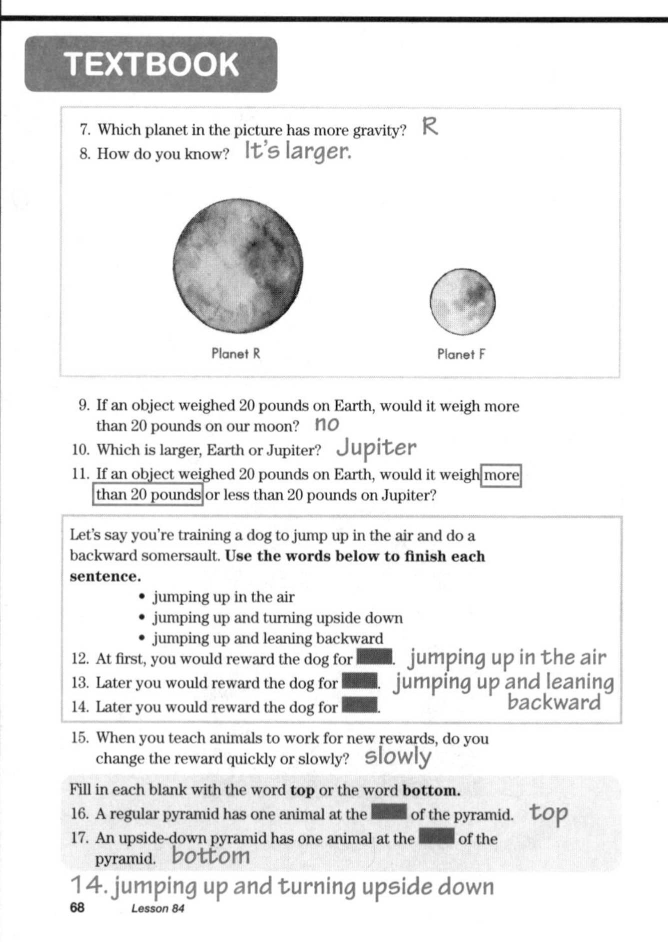

9. If an object weighed 20 pounds on Earth, would it weigh more than 20 pounds on our moon? no
10. Which is larger, Earth or Jupiter? Jupiter
11. If an object weighed 20 pounds on Earth, would it weigh more than 20 pounds or less than 20 pounds on Jupiter?

Let's say you're training a dog to jump up in the air and do a backward somersault. **Use the words below to finish each sentence.**

• jumping up in the air
• jumping up and turning upside down
• jumping up and leaning backward

12. At first, you would reward the dog for ▬. jumping up in the air
13. Later you would reward the dog for ▬. jumping up and leaning backward
14. Later you would reward the dog for ▬.

15. When you teach animals to work for new rewards, do you change the reward quickly or slowly? slowly

Fill in each blank with the word **top** or the word **bottom**.

16. A regular pyramid has one animal at the ▬ of the pyramid. top
17. An upside-down pyramid has one animal at the ▬ of the pyramid. bottom

14. jumping up and turning upside down

TEXTBOOK

18. Write the letter of the clouds that have frozen drops of water. B
19. Write the letter of the clouds that may stay in the sky for days at a time. C
20. Write the letter of the storm clouds. A

END OF LESSON 84 INDEPENDENT WORK

SPECIAL PROJECT

For this project, your group may either decide to train an animal a new trick or write a report that tells how you would train an animal.

If the group decides to train an animal, think about training a pigeon to do a dance. Pigeons learn to dance quite fast. If you train a hamster or a white rat, the training will take more time because these animals will not learn the trick as fast as a pigeon learns to dance. But you may teach a rat to walk a rope or teach a hamster to climb to the top of a tower that you make.

If you train an animal, write a report that tells how you did it. Tell about the rewards that you used to train the animal and tell about the steps that you used in training the animal.

If you do not train an animal, write a report that tells which rewards you would use and how you would use them. Tell all the things you would do to train the animal. Remember, the animal will not be able to do the trick the first time it tries, so you have to reward the animal for trying.

WORKBOOK

85

Name ____________________

A Story Items

1. What was Darla deathly afraid of? water
2. Name 2 things Darla wasn't afraid of. (Any 2:) snakes; the dark; high places; mice; beetles; spiders
3. How would Darla feel when water got up to her neck? Ideas: very afraid; like it would choke her
4. Name 2 acts of bravery. (Any 2:) saving someone from a burning building; climbing a mountain; etc.
5. Complete the rule about being brave. To be brave, you must do things that are hard for you to do.
6. Was holding snakes an act of bravery for Darla? no
7. Tell why. Idea: because holding snakes wasn't hard for her to do
8. Was swimming an act of bravery for Darla? yes
9. Tell why. Ideas: because she was afraid of water; because it was hard for her to do
10. Where was Darla going to take swimming lessons? at the high school
11. What sign did Darla have to show that she became frightened when she thought about swimming? Idea: Her palms were sweaty.

WORKBOOK

B Review Items

12. Write the missing seasons on the picture below.
13. Shade half of earth **R** and half of earth **T**.

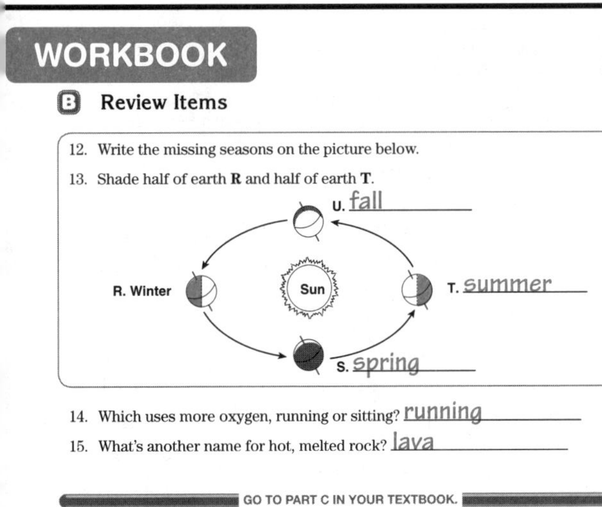

14. Which uses more oxygen, running or sitting? running
15. What's another name for hot, melted rock? lava

GO TO PART C IN YOUR TEXTBOOK.

TEXTBOOK

decided that I won't like myself very much unless I'm brave."

Julie said, "I think they're going to give swimming lessons at the high school. I hear that the instructor is very good."

Darla made a face. "Every time I think about it, I get scared. Feel the palms of my hands." The palms were sweaty. Darla said, "I'm scared. But I'll do it."

C Number your paper from 1 through 18.

Skill Items

I have confidence that we can avoid a long conversation.

1. What word describes people talking to each other about something? conversation
2. What word tells what you do when you stay away from something? avoid
3. What word tells that you are sure about something? confidence

Review Items

4. Which globe shows how the earth looks on the first day of winter? X
5. Which globe shows how the earth looks on the first day of summer? Q

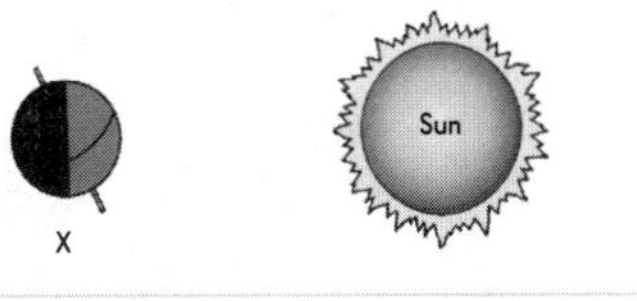

TEXTBOOK

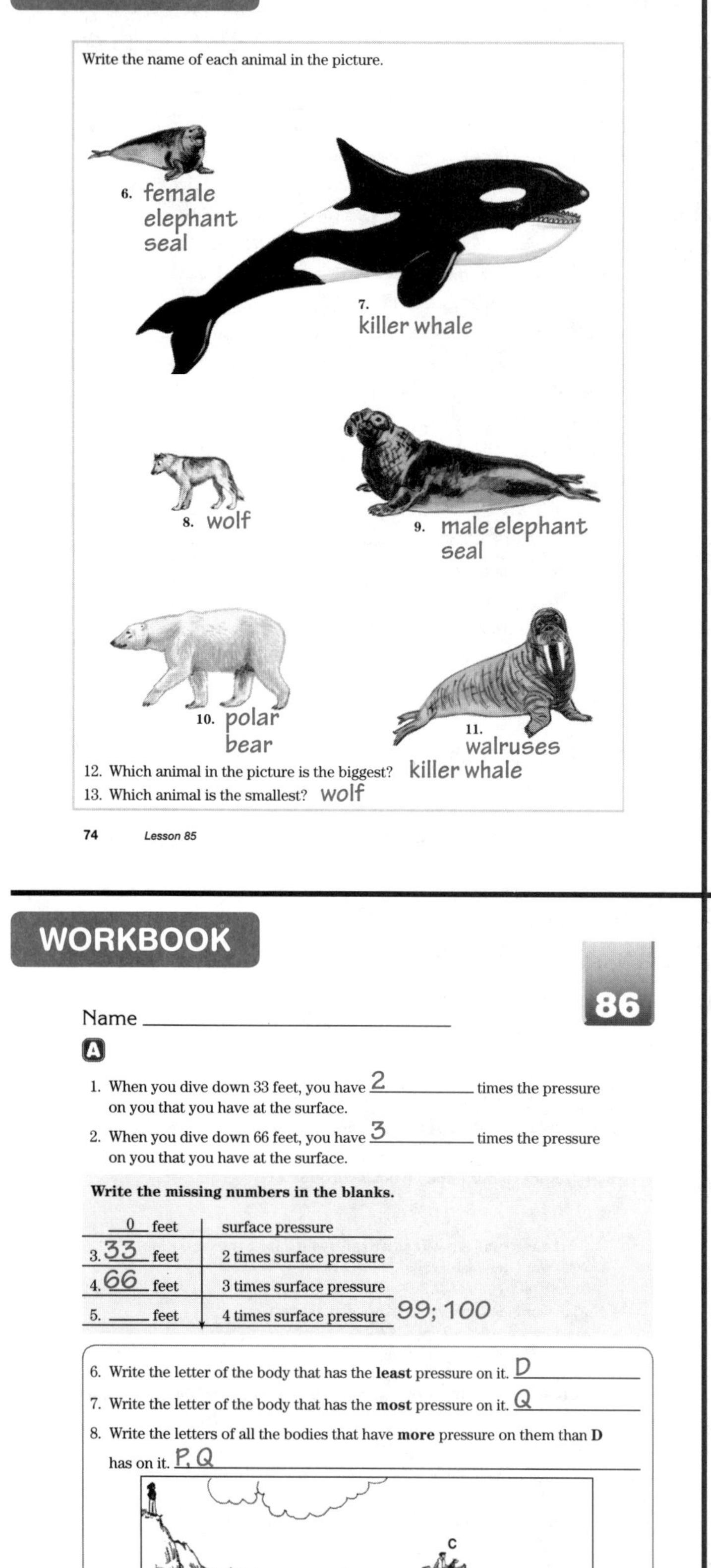

Write the name of each animal in the picture.

6. female elephant seal
7. killer whale
8. wolf
9. male elephant seal
10. polar bear
11. walruses
12. Which animal in the picture is the biggest? killer whale
13. Which animal is the smallest? wolf

TEXTBOOK

Write the name of each kind of coral.

14. staghorn coral
15. brain coral
16. red coral

17. Coral is made up of the ▬ of tiny ▬. skeletons; animals
18. An underwater hill that is covered with coral is called a coral ▬. reef

WORKBOOK

86

Name ____________________

A

1. When you dive down 33 feet, you have 2 times the pressure on you that you have at the surface.
2. When you dive down 66 feet, you have 3 times the pressure on you that you have at the surface.

Write the missing numbers in the blanks.

0 feet	surface pressure
3. 33 feet	2 times surface pressure
4. 66 feet	3 times surface pressure
5. ____ feet	4 times surface pressure

99; 100

6. Write the letter of the body that has the **least** pressure on it. D
7. Write the letter of the body that has the **most** pressure on it. Q
8. Write the letters of all the bodies that have **more** pressure on them than **D** has on it. P, Q

C
D
P
Q

WORKBOOK

B Story Items

12. Ideas: Water leaked inside her mask; she breathed water through her nose.

9. What does the color of water tell you about the water? Idea: how deep the water is
10. Name **2** things Darla did when she was learning to swim. (Any 2:) how to float; how to breathe while she swam; how to kick; how to pull with her arms
11. What was Darla getting ready to do in this story? Ideas: go scuba diving; dive off a diving boat
12. What problem did Darla have with her scuba mask the first time she tried to wear it? ____________
13. How did she **feel** when that happened? Idea: panicky
14. What was the deepest dive Darla had ever made? 50 feet
15. How deep will she dive this time? (about) 100 feet

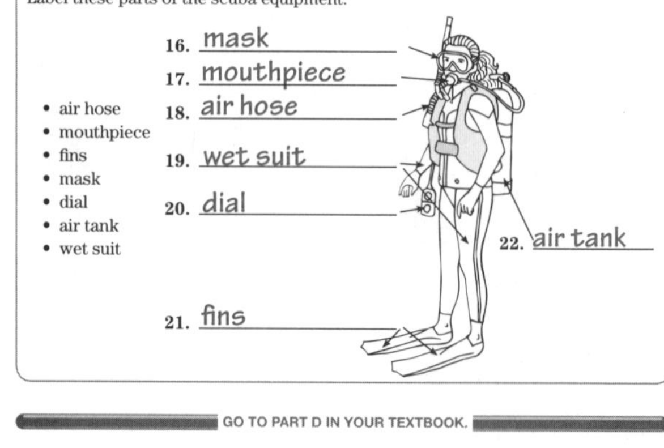

Label these parts of the scuba equipment.

- air hose
- mouthpiece
- fins
- mask
- dial
- air tank
- wet suit

16. mask
17. mouthpiece
18. air hose
19. wet suit
20. dial
21. fins
22. air tank

GO TO PART D IN YOUR TEXTBOOK.

TEXTBOOK

8. Ideas: when it becomes the new reward; when the animal will work for the new reward

D Number your paper from 1 through 17.

Skill Items

success	avoid	instructor	hire	conversation
confidence	panic	separate	contact	directing

1. She will ▇▇ the person we want to ▇▇. contact, hire
2. I have ▇▇ that we can ▇▇ a long ▇▇. confidence, avoid, conversation

Review Items

3. How old are geese when they mate for the first time? 3 (years old)
4. After male and female geese mate, how long do they stay together? Idea: until one dies
5. Most geese live for about ▇▇ years. 30
6. When you teach an animal to work for a new reward, what kind of reward do you start with? Idea: one the animal will work for
7. Then what do you do to that reward? Idea: slowly change it
8. When do you stop changing the reward?
9. Which has stronger gravity, Earth or Jupiter? Jupiter
10. So where would you feel heavier? Jupiter
11. Which uses up more oxygen, hopping or sleeping? hopping
12. What's another name for hot, melted rock? lava
13. Write the letters of the 6 things that tell about Jupiter. a, b, d, e, f, h
    a. It has more gravity than Earth.
    b. It's brown, orange and white.
    c. It's small.
    d. It's huge.
    e. It has stripes.
    f. It has 16 moons.
    g. It's green and blue.
    h. It's beautiful.
14. Let's say that you want to teach an animal a very hard trick. Can the animal do the trick at first? no
15. What will happen if the animal doesn't receive any rewards until it does the trick? Idea: The animal will stop trying to do the trick.
16. So when you're teaching the animal a hard trick, what do you reward the animal for doing? Idea: for trying to do the trick
17. Name **2** acts of bravery. (Any 2:) Saving someone from a burning building; climbing a mountain, etc.

WORKBOOK

Name ____________________

A Story Items

1. The diving boat was about 1,000 miles east of the United States.
2. Name the islands that are near the place they are diving. Bermuda Islands
3. Were the divers **north** or **south** of those islands? south
4. In what ocean are they diving? Atlantic (Ocean)
5. What did the guide tell the divers to do if they got separated? Idea: return to the surface
6. How deep were the divers at the end of the story? 66 feet
7. How deep are the divers going to go? (about) 100 feet
8. If you go underwater that deep, the pressure is much greater than it is on land. How many times greater is it? 4 times
9. When divers are that deep, how long should they take to return to the surface of the water? at least/about 2 minutes
10. What may happen to the divers if they go up faster than that? Idea: They may get the bends.
11. What made Darla's ears hurt? the pressure
12. How deep was she when they started to hurt? 15 feet
13. If you move up too fast from very deep water, you may get the bends.
14. What forms in your blood as you go up too fast? bubbles
15. When you go up very fast, is there **more pressure** or **less pressure** on your body? less pressure

WORKBOOK

Fill in the blanks to show how deep the divers would be.

16. When the diver is 33 feet underwater, the pressure is two times as great as it is on land.
17. When the diver is 66 feet underwater, the pressure is three times as great as it is on land.
18. When the diver is 100 feet underwater, the pressure is four times as great as it is on land.
19. Could Darla feel the weight of her air tank underwater? no
20. Could Darla feel the pressure of the water? yes
21. Name **2** things that were part of the incredible scene that Darla and Julie saw. ____________
22. When Darla looked at the other divers below her, what did she think they looked like? insects
23. What happened each time a diver breathed? Ideas: A great mass of bubbles came out; they made a hissing sound.
24. What did the diving guide point out to the group? a (giant) ray fish
25. When you open a bottle of soda pop, what happens to the pressure inside the bottle? Idea: It goes down.
26. What forms in the soda pop? bubbles

GO TO PART C IN YOUR TEXTBOOK.

21. (Any 2:) a great reef; lots of plants; silver fish; plants like domes; etc.

TEXTBOOK

C Number your paper from 1 through 12.

Review Items

1. What's the name of the line that goes around the fattest part of the earth? equator
2. What's the name of the spot that's at the top of the earth? North Pole
3. What's the name of the spot that's at the bottom of the earth? South Pole
4. When you dive down 33 feet, you have ▇▇ times the pressure on you that you have at the surface. 2
5. When you dive down 66 feet, you have ▇▇ times the pressure on you that you have at the surface. 3

6. What part of the scuba equipment does the **A** show?
7. What part does the **B** show?
8. What part does the **C** show?
9. What part does the **D** show?
10. What part does the **E** show?
11. What part does the **F** show?
12. What part does the **G** show?

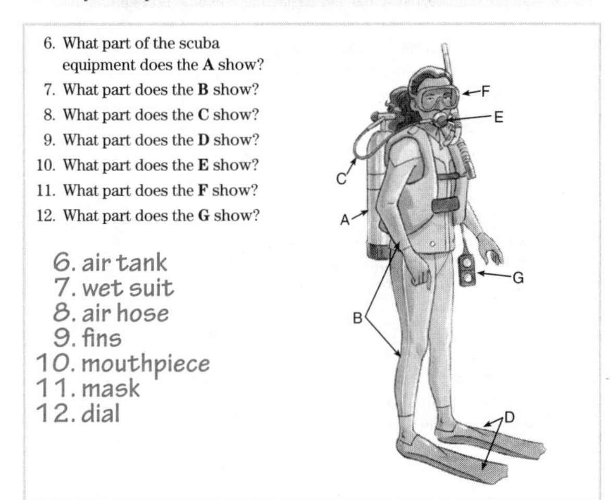

6. air tank
7. wet suit
8. air hose
9. fins
10. mouthpiece
11. mask
12. dial

WORKBOOK

Name ______________________

A Story Items

1. How deep did the divers go? 100 feet
2. About how long did it take them to get there? ten minutes
3. Did things look **darker** or **lighter** at the bottom? darker
4. There weren't as many plants down there because there wasn't as much light
5. Name **3** things the great water pressure was doing to Darla. Ideas (any 3): The mask pressed against her face; her ears rang; her mouth was dry; she had trouble swallowing.
6. Why did the bubbles following the divers look dark gray? Idea: because the water was so dark
7. What is the name of the arrow-shaped fish that Darla saw? barracuda
8. Write **2** facts Darla knew about these fish. Ideas (any 2): They're very dangerous; their mouths are filled with sharp teeth; they grow to almost 2 meters long.
9. Is the water cooler at **100 feet down** or **at the surface?** at 100 feet down
10. Is all the water at 100 feet down the same temperature? no
11. What should a diver's bubbles look like? large masses
12. What did Julie's bubbles look like? a small trail
13. What did that mean? Idea: Julie wasn't getting enough air.

WORKBOOK

14. Julie started to go to the surface very fast. Why did Darla want to catch Julie? Ideas: to stop her; so she wouldn't get the bends
15. Who could swim faster, Darla or Julie? Julie

Answer these questions about a buoyancy device:

16. What do you fill it with? air
17. When it is filled up, what happens to the diver? Idea: The diver moves up/floats/goes to the surface.
18. When it is empty, what happens to the diver? Idea: The diver moves down/sinks.
19. What hard decision did Darla have to make after she caught up with Julie? Idea: if she should share her air hose with Julie.
20. What did Darla decide to do? Idea: share her air hose
21. Did Julie want to share the air hose with Darla? no
22. Julie didn't know what she was doing because she was in a state of panic

GO TO PART C IN YOUR TEXTBOOK.

TEXTBOOK

C Number your paper from 1 through 16.

Skill Items

The scuba diver and her partner surfaced near the reef.

1. What word describes a person you do something with? partner
2. What word tells about a ridge that forms underwater? reef
3. What words tell about someone who goes underwater with a mask and a tank of air? scuba diver
4. What word tells that a person swam to the surface? surfaced

Here are 3 events that happened in the story. Write **beginning, middle** or **end** for each event.

5. About ten minutes after the dive began, the group of divers had reached the bottom of the valley between two long reefs. beginning
6. Darla was starting to feel a little nervous, especially as she moved through a current of very cool water. middle
7. Now Darla was faced with one of the most difficult decisions she had ever made in her life. end

Review Items

8. What does the color of water tell you about the water? Idea: how deep the water is
9. If you're underwater 100 feet deep, the pressure is much greater than it is on land. How many times greater is it? 4 times
10. When divers are that deep, how long should they take to return to the surface of the water? at least/about 2 minutes
11. What may happen to the divers if they go up faster than that? Idea: The diver may get the bends.
12. When you open a bottle of soda pop, what happens to the pressure inside the bottle? Idea: It goes down.
13. What forms in the soda pop? bubbles

TEXTBOOK

14. Write the letter of the body that has the least pressure on it. D
15. Write the letter of the body that has the most pressure on it. Q
16. Write the letters of all the bodies that have more pressure on them than **P** has on it. Q

Name ____________________

89

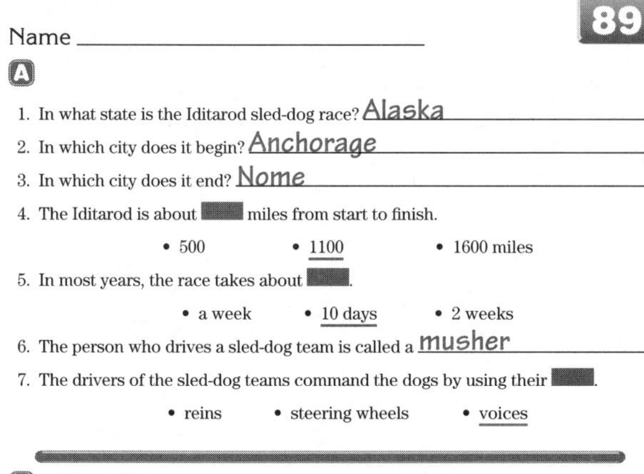

A

1. In what state is the Iditarod sled-dog race? Alaska
2. In which city does it begin? Anchorage
3. In which city does it end? Nome
4. The Iditarod is about ▬ miles from start to finish.
   • 500 • 1100 • 1600 miles
5. In most years, the race takes about ▬.
   • a week • 10 days • 2 weeks
6. The person who drives a sled-dog team is called a musher
7. The drivers of the sled-dog teams command the dogs by using their ▬.
   • reins • steering wheels • voices

B Story Items

8. As Darla and Julie moved up to the surface of the water, they had to stop ten feet below the surface. How long did they wait there? 1 minute
9. Why didn't the girls go straight up to the surface? Idea: because they might get the bends
10. How did the water pressure change as the girls moved toward the surface?
11. How did the light around them change as they moved toward the surface? Idea: It got brighter.

10. Idea: The water pressure went down/pushed against them with less force.

C Skill Items

coral	overcome	Colorado	understand	emergency	instructor
bends	reef	California	surface	buoyant	suffer
oxygen	Utah	bare	success	bubbles	musher

Crossword answers: 1 SUCCESS, 2 INSTRUCTOR, 3 REEF, 4 OVERCOME, 5 MUSHER, 6 EMERGENCY, 7 CORAL, 8 BUBBLES, 9 BENDS, 10 COLORADO

Across

2. Another word for **teacher** is ▬.
4. When you solve a problem, you ▬ the problem.
6. A brake you use if the regular brake doesn't work is called an ▬ brake.
8. When you open a bottle of soda pop, ▬ form in the pop.
10. One of the states in the western part of the United States is ▬.

Down

1. When you do very well at something, you have ▬.
3. An underwater hill that's covered with coral is called a coral ▬.
5. The person who drives a sled-dog team is called a ▬.
7. ▬ is made up of the shells of tiny animals.
9. If divers move up too fast from very deep water, they may get the ▬.

GO TO PART D IN YOUR TEXTBOOK.

understand scuba diving you must understand water pressure. The pressure on your body becomes very great when you dive. When you go down 33 feet in water, the pressure on your body is two times as great as it is when you're standing on land. When you go down 66 feet, the pressure on your body is three times as great as it is on land."

As Darla talked, her mind went back to the first time she had gone down 100 feet. Since that dive, she had gone down much farther. She had already taken ten dives below 130 feet and thirty dives below 100 feet. She had gone diving with her sister in the Pacific Ocean and the Atlantic Ocean. She had been swimming with seals, whales and even sharks. She no longer had fear of the water, but she remembered how she had felt on her first deep dive.

"Oh, yes," she said to the group. "Some of you may be afraid of the water. You can overcome that fear if you train yourself to think about the things you must do. I know that you can overcome the fear because when I started out, I was as afraid of the water as anybody that ever lived."

The people in the group smiled, and Darla went on with the instruction.

D Number your paper from 1 through 19.

Story Items

1. What did Darla realize about **herself** when she got to the surface of the water? Idea: that she was brave
2. What kind of job did Darla have at the end of the story?
3. Name **2** oceans where Darla and Julie have gone diving. Pacific, Atlantic
4. Darla told her students, "To understand scuba diving, you must understand ▬. water pressure

Skill Items

partner	twilight	confidence	especially
surfaced	rapidly	conversation	overcame
avoid	scuba diver	mass	reef

5. I have ▬ that we can ▬ a long ▬. confidence, avoid, conversation
6. The ▬ and her ▬ ▬ near the ▬. scuba diver, partner, surfaced, reef

2. Ideas: scuba diving instructor; swimming instructor

14. (Any 3:) the bends; ear pain; mask pushed tight against face; trouble swallowing

Review Items

7. In what ocean is the **X?** Atlantic (Ocean)
8. About how many miles is it from Florida to the **X?** 1000 (miles)

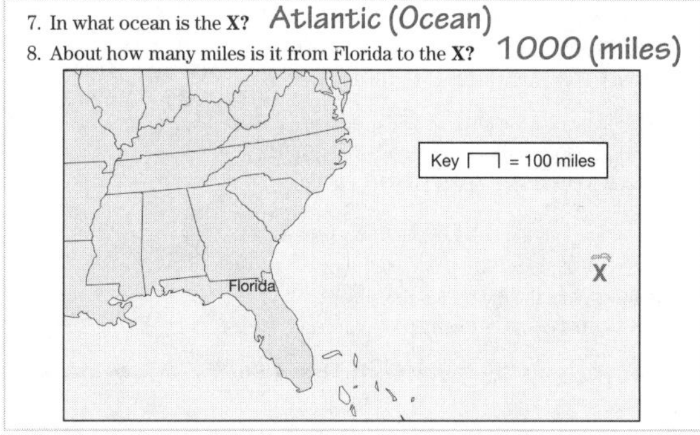

9. If you move up too fast from very deep water, you may get the ▬. bends
10. What forms in your blood as you go up too fast? bubbles
11. When you go up very fast, is there **more pressure** or **less pressure** on your body? less pressure
12. Do things look **light** or **dark** when you're 100 feet below the surface of the ocean? dark
13. There aren't as many plants down there because there isn't as much ▬. light
14. Name 3 things that great water pressure can do to you.
15. Name an arrow-shaped fish. barracuda
16. Write **2** facts about those fish. Ideas (any 2): They're very dangerous; their mouths are filled with sharp teeth; they grow to almost 2 meters long, etc.
17. What do you fill a buoyancy device with? air
18. When it is filled up, what happens to the diver?
19. When it is empty, what happens to the diver? Idea: The diver moves down/sinks.

18. Idea: The diver moves up/floats/goes to the surface.

TEXTBOOK

90

Number your paper from 1 through 36.

1. Coral is made up of the ____ of tiny ____. skeletons, animals
2. An underwater ridge that is covered with coral is called a coral ____. reef
3. When you dive down 33 feet, you have ____ times the pressure on you that you have at the surface. 2
4. When you dive down 66 feet, you have ____ times the pressure on you that you have at the surface. 3
5. What does the color of water tell you about the water? Idea: how deep the water is
6. In what ocean is the **X**? Atlantic (Ocean)
7. About how many miles is it from Florida to the **X**? 1000 (miles)

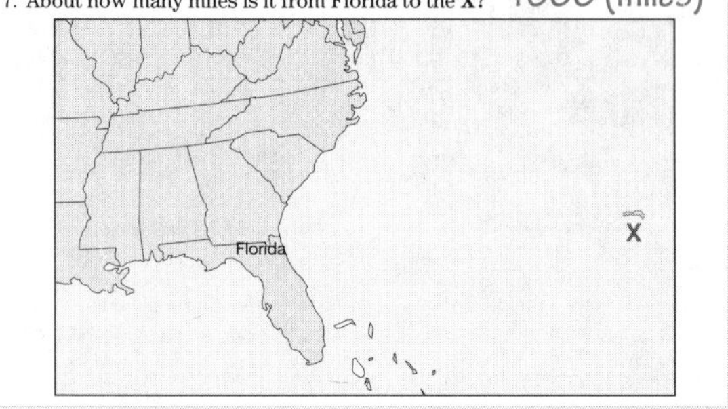

8. Do things look **light** or **dark** when you're 100 feet below the surface of the ocean? dark
9. There aren't as many plants down there because there isn't as much ____. light
10. Name **3** things that great water pressure can do to you. Ideas (any 3): make mask press against face; cause ears to ring; cause trouble swallowing; make mouth dry

TEXTBOOK

11. Write the letter of the body that has the **least** pressure on it. P
12. Write the letter of the body that has the **most** pressure on it. R
13. Write the letters of all the bodies that have more pressure on them than **M** has on it. R

14. If you move up too fast from very deep water, you may get the ____. bends
15. What forms in your blood as you go up too fast? bubbles
16. When you go up very fast, is there **more pressure** or **less pressure** on your body? less pressure
17. When you open a bottle of soda pop, what happens to the pressure inside the bottle? It goes down.
18. What forms in the soda pop? bubbles
19. Name an arrow-shaped fish. barracuda
20. Write **2** facts about those fish. (Any 2 ideas:) They're very dangerous; their mouths are filled with sharp teeth; they grow to almost 2 meters long, etc.

TEXTBOOK

24. Idea: The diver moves up/floats/goes to the surface.

21. Is the water cooler at 100 feet down or at the surface? 100 feet down
22. Is all the water at 100 feet down the same temperature? no
23. What do you fill a buoyancy device with? air
24. When it is filled up, what happens to the diver?
25. When it is empty, what happens to the diver? Idea: The diver moves down/sinks.
26. In what state is the Iditarod sled-dog race? Alaska
27. In which city does it begin? Anchorage
28. In which city does it end? Nome
29. The Iditarod is about ____ miles from start to finish.
    • 1600 • 500 • <u>1100</u>
30. In most years the race takes about ____.
    • <u>10 days</u> • 2 weeks • a week

Skill Items

For each item, write the underlined word or words from the sentences in the box.

> I have <u>confidence</u> that we can <u>avoid</u> a long <u>conversation</u>.
> The <u>scuba diver</u> and her <u>partner</u> <u>surfaced</u> near the <u>reef</u>.

31. What underlining tells what you do when you stay away from something? avoid
32. What underlining describes a person you do something with? partner
33. What underlining tells about someone who goes underwater with a mask and a tank of air? scuba diver
34. What underlining describes people talking to each other about something? conversation
35. What underlining tells that you are sure about something? confidence
36. What underlining tells that people swam to the surface? surfaced

WORKBOOK

91

Name ______________________

A

1. Most sled-dog teams have an ____ number of dogs.
   • <u>even</u> • odd
2. For the Iditarod, a sled-dog team can't have more than 16 dogs.
3. Which letter shows the swing dogs? B
4. Which letter shows the wheel dogs? E
5. Which letter shows the lead dogs? A
6. Which letter shows where the musher is most of the time? H
7. Which letter shows the gang line? J
8. Which letter shows tug lines? R

A R B C D E J F G H

WORKBOOK

Use these words to answer items 9–11:

- **wheel dogs** • **lead dogs** • **swing dogs**

9. These dogs are responsible for freeing the sled when it gets stuck. wheel dogs
10. These dogs are very smart, and other dogs obey them. lead dogs
11. These dogs are very good followers, and they are smart. swing dogs

B Story Items

17. Ideas: wheel dog; Alaskan husky

12. What town does Susie live near? Knik
13. In what state does she live? Alaska
14. What's the name of her dog? Denali
15. Susie's Uncle Chad was getting ready for the Iditarod
16. Susie went to Chad's place on a sled
17. What kind of sled dog was Susie's dog? _____
18. Was he going to be part of Chad's regular sled-dog team? no
19. How many times had Chad entered the Iditarod before? once
20. How many times had he finished the race at Nome? none
21. What was his goal for the Iditarod this year? Idea: to finish
22. This year's race would begin in a little more than 2 weeks.
23. Chad drove the dogs and his sled to ▬.
    - Eagle Claw Valley • Beaver River Valley • Eagle River Valley
24. Chad wanted to find out what the team would do in really ▬.
    - cold weather • rough country • flat country

GO TO PART D IN YOUR TEXTBOOK.

TEXTBOOK

they were all very strong, and they were all tough. They would need that toughness when they ran the Iditarod because then they would have to pull the sled all day long—sometimes for more than fourteen hours a day.

Susie had gone on more than a hundred practice runs with Chad, and she knew every dog that he owned—all fifteen of them. Although she knew a lot about mushing, she was always amazed at how much more Chad knew about it. He had been in the Iditarod once before, but he didn't do very well. The sled broke down about 200 miles from Nome, and he didn't finish the race. His goal for this year was to finish. He wasn't thinking about being in first or second place, just finishing. Susie had once told him, "You know so much about mushing, you could win first place!"

He had laughed and said, "Some mushers in that race know more about mushing than I'll ever learn. It's just an honor to be in the same race they are in."

The truck pulled off the road. Down below was Eagle River Valley. It looked very steep. Chad said, "We'll take the sled down into the valley and around the rocky parts."

Chad jumped out of the truck and told the dogs, "Everybody out of the truck." The dogs were glad to obey that command. Some of them looked like they were flying as they jumped out of the truck bed. Through the snow they raced, yapping and running in circles. Then Chad whistled, and they all crowded around him with their tails wagging.

D Number your paper from 1 through 14.

Review Items

1. In what state is the Iditarod sled-dog race? Alaska
2. In which city does it begin? Anchorage
3. In which city does it end? Nome
4. The Iditarod is about ▬ miles from start to finish.
    - 1600 • 500 • 1100
5. In most years, the race takes about ▬.
    - 10 days • 2 weeks • a week
6. The person who drives a sled-dog team is called a ▬. musher
7. The drivers of the sled-dog teams command the dogs by using their ▬.
    - voices • reins • steering wheels

TEXTBOOK

8. How does water pressure change as you move from deep water toward the surface? Idea: The pressure becomes less.
9. How does the light around you change as you move toward the surface? Idea: There is more light.

10. When the diver is ▬ feet underwater, the pressure is **two** times as great as it is on land. 33
11. When the diver is ▬ feet underwater, the pressure is **three** times as great as it is on land. 66
12. When the diver is ▬ feet underwater, the pressure is **four** times as great as it is on land. 100

13. Which letter shows Colorado? D
14. Which letter shows Utah? E

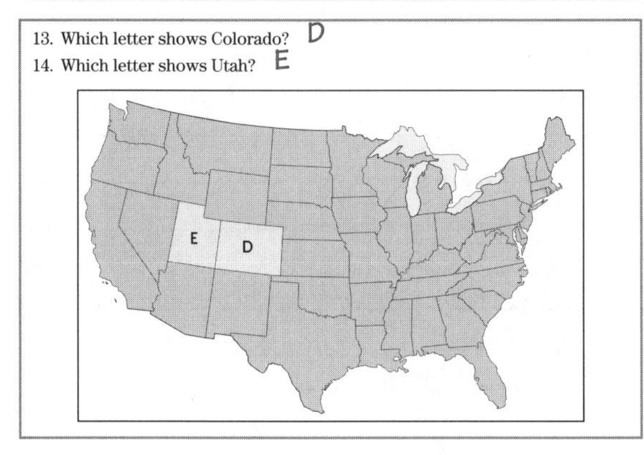

WORKBOOK

92

Name _____

A

1. What do sled dogs wear to protect their feet? booties
2. **Underline** the 4 items that tell what could happen to a sled dog's feet if they didn't have protection.
    - snowballs between the pads
    - slipping on hard snow
    - stiff legs
    - icicles on their ankles
    - cuts from ice and frozen snow
    - long claws
    - cuts that do not heal well
3. The booties that Chad prefers are made of canvas
4. If booties are too tight, what could happen? Ideas: The dog's blood cannot circulate around the paws; the dog's ankles could swell up.
5. If booties are too loose, what could happen? Idea: They could fall off.

B Story Items

6. How many dogs did Chad plan to run in the Iditarod? 14
7. How many dogs did Chad start with at Eagle River Valley? 14
8. How many dogs did Susie keep on leashes? 2
9. Why did Chad put bags of dirt on the sled? Idea: because the dogs will have to pull a lot of weight in the race
10. The dogs wore something they didn't usually wear for practice runs. What was that? booties
11. Why did they wear them for this run? Idea: because today would be a tough run
12. What command tells sled dogs to turn left? haw

WORKBOOK

13. What command tells them to turn right? gee
14. What command tells them to move straight ahead? mush
15. What did Chad do to test the dogs?
    - He got the sled stuck against rocks.
    - He ran the dogs along the road.
    - He did not tell the dogs what to do.

Review Items

16. Write **north, south, east** and **west** in the correct boxes.
17. In which direction is ocean current **B** moving? east
18. In which direction is ocean current **C** moving? north
19. Which direction is the wind coming from? west
20. Make an arrow above ice chunk **D** to show the direction the current will move the chunk.
21. Make an arrow next to ice chunk **E** to show the direction the current will move the chunk.

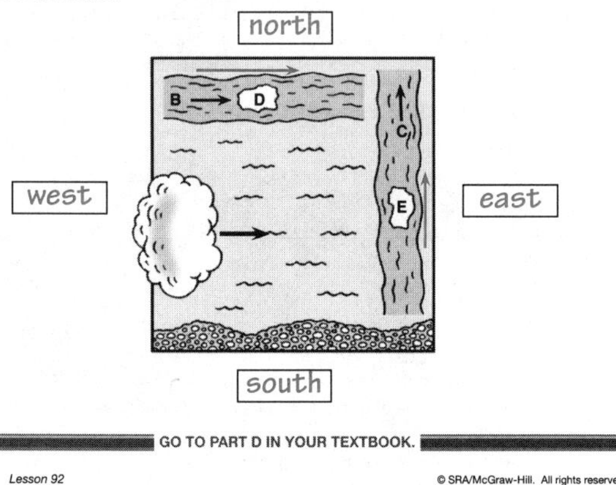

GO TO PART D IN YOUR TEXTBOOK.

TEXTBOOK

D Number your paper from 1 through 16.

Review Items

1. What are clouds made of?
2. What kind of cloud does the picture show?
3. What happens to a drop of water at **B**?
   Idea: It freezes.

1. tiny drops of water
2. storm cloud

4. Which object went into the pile **first?** shoe
5. Which object went into the pile **last?** rock
6. Which object went into the pile **earlier**, the cup or the pencil? cup
7. Which object went into the pile **just after** the bone? cup

TEXTBOOK

Use these words to answer items 8—10:

- **swing dogs** • **wheel dogs** • **lead dogs**

8. These dogs are very smart, and other dogs obey them. lead dogs
9. These dogs are responsible for freeing the sled when it gets stuck. wheel dogs
10. These dogs are very good followers, and they are smart. swing dogs

11. Which letter in the picture shows the wheel dogs? T
12. Which letter shows the lead dogs? P
13. Which letter shows the swing dogs? J
14. Which letter shows where the musher is most of the time? G
15. Which letter shows the tug lines? K
16. Which letter shows the gang line? M

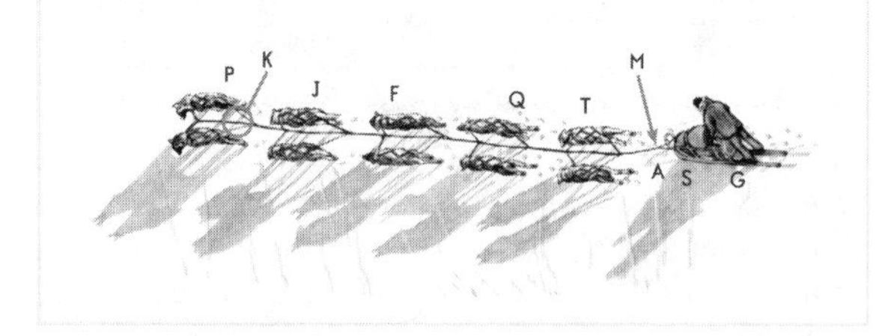

WORKBOOK

93

Name ____________

A Story Items

1. To get the sled free, Chad first gave commands to the wheel dogs.
2. When the sled tipped over, the dogs on leashes thought Chad was ▬.
   - awkward
   - playing
   - angry
3. Why didn't some of the dogs on the gang line run over to Chad?
   Idea: because the lead dogs did not move
4. During most of the practice, how many dogs were on the gang line?
   14
5. At the end of the practice, how many dogs were on the gang line?
   16
6. Which number of dogs was easier to handle? 14
7. Which number of dogs made a more powerful team? 16
8. When were the dogs going to be examined?
   Ideas: tomorrow; the next day; in the morning
9. What happens if a dog does not pass the examination? Idea: It can't run in the Iditarod.

WORKBOOK

B Skill Items

avoid	strain	barracuda	booties	shark
leash	gang	left	gee	lead
tug	swing	haw	wheel	mush
Alaska	Nome	equator	Anchorage	purpose

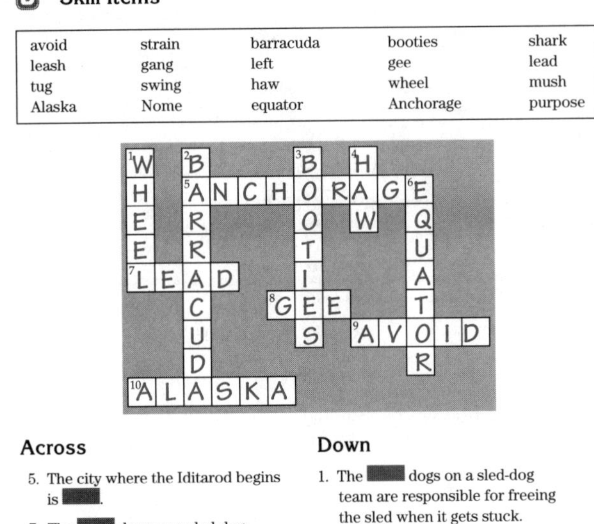

Across

5. The city where the Iditarod begins is ▬.
7. The ▬ dogs on a sled-dog team are very smart, and other dogs obey them.
8. The command that tells sled dogs to turn right is ▬.
9. When you stay away from something, you ▬ that thing.
10. The Iditarod is held in the state of ▬.

Down

1. The ▬ dogs on a sled-dog team are responsible for freeing the sled when it gets stuck.
2. An arrow-shaped fish is a ▬.
3. Sled dogs wear ▬ to protect their feet.
4. The command that tells sled dogs to turn left is ▬.
6. The make-believe line around the middle of the earth is called the ▬.

GO TO PART C IN YOUR TEXTBOOK.

TEXTBOOK

Number your paper from 1 through 21.

Skill Items

The veterinarian gave the dogs a thorough examination.

1. What word means **checkup?** examination
2. What word means **animal doctor?** veterinarian
3. What word means that nothing is overlooked? thorough

Write the word from the box that means the same thing as the underlined part of each sentence.

harness	partner	deadly	anchored
boxing	separated	mobbed	instructor

4. The teacher wrote a problem on the board. instructor
5. He has a great fear of snakes. deadly
6. The children were no longer together. separated

Review Items

7. How long does it take Jupiter to spin around one time? (about) 10 hours
8. What's another name for hot, melted rock? lava

- On planet M you can jump 15 feet high.
- On planet Q you can jump 5 feet high.
- On planet G you can jump 12 feet high.
- On planet X you can jump 20 feet high.
- On planet T you can jump 2 feet high.

9. Write the letter of the planet that has the most gravity. T
10. Write the letter of the planet that has the least gravity. X

TEXTBOOK

11. When you teach an animal a simple trick, when do you reward the animal? Idea: when it does the trick
12. When don't you reward the animal? Idea: when the animal doesn't do the trick
13. Most sled-dog teams have an ▬ number of dogs.
    - odd
    - even
14. For the Iditarod, a sled-dog team can't have more than ▬ dogs. 16
15. What do sled dogs wear to protect their feet? booties
16. Name **2** cities in Colorado. Greeley, Denver
17. Name one city in Utah. Salt Lake City
18. **Write the letters of the 4 items that tell what could happen to a sled dog's feet if they didn't have protection.** b, c, e, g
    a. long claws
    b. snowballs between the pads
    c. cuts that do not heal well
    d. stiff legs
    e. slipping on hard snow
    f. icicles on their ankles
    g. cuts from ice and frozen snow
19. What command tells sled dogs to move straight ahead? mush
20. What command tells sled dogs to turn right? gee
21. What command tells sled dogs to turn left? haw

WORKBOOK

94

Name ______

A Story Items

1. At the beginning of today's story, who was late in the morning? Chad
2. Susie was surprised to see which dog in the truck? Butch
3. Chad told Susie that he planned to run sixteen dogs.
4. How did that make Susie feel? Ideas: excited; happy
5. Which 2 dogs would now be on the team? Butch and Denali
6. What does a musher have to do with any dogs that are injured during the Iditarod? Idea: leave the dog at the next checkpoint
7. What did Chad plan to do with some dogs if he had trouble with a team of sixteen? Idea: leave some of them at the next checkpoint
8. According to the rules, there must be at least how many dogs on the gang line at the end of the Iditarod? 5
9. The veterinarian found out that one dog had a problem. Which dog? Chugger
10. What was the problem? Idea: Her hip was weak.
11. What job does that dog have on Chad's team? wheel dog

WORKBOOK

B Review Items

Write the missing numbers in the blanks.

0 feet	surface pressure
12. 33 feet	2 times surface pressure
13. 66 feet	3 times surface pressure
14. 100 feet	4 times surface pressure

15. Write the missing seasons on the picture below.
16. Shade half of earth **W** and half of earth **Y**.

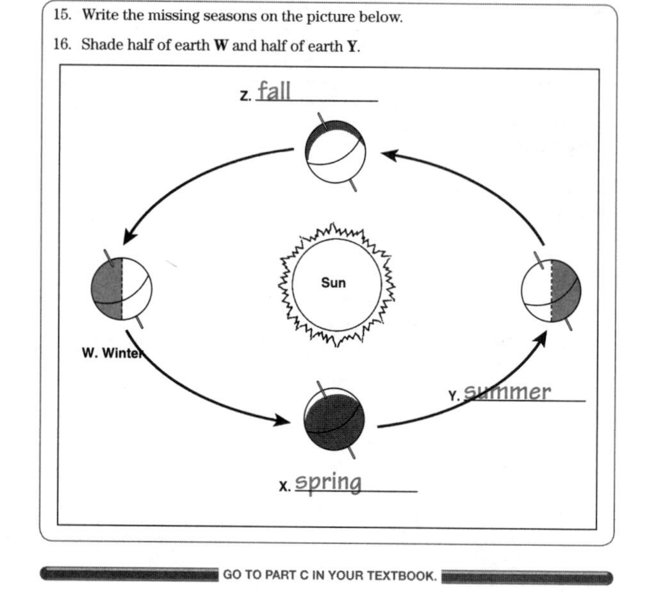

GO TO PART C IN YOUR TEXTBOOK.

TEXTBOOK

1. scuba diver, partner, surfaced, reef

C Number your paper from 1 through 19.

Skill Items

Use the words in the box to write complete sentences.

exchanged	truck driver	alarm	thorough
partner	demanded	replaced	reef
veterinarian	scuba diver	surfaced	examination

1. The ▬ and her ▬ ▬ near the ▬.
2. The ▬ gave the dogs a ▬ ▬. veterinarian, thorough, examination

Write the word from the box that means the same thing as the underlined part of each sentence.

tune	replaced	according	strained
overcame	pest	shortly	alarm

3. He solved his fear of storms. overcame
4. Darla learned a new song for the party. tune
5. We're going to eat soon. shortly

Review Items

6. What happens if a sled dog doesn't pass the Iditarod's health examination? Idea: The dog cannot run in the race.
7. If booties on a sled dog are too tight, what could happen?
8. If booties are too loose, what could happen? Idea:They could fall off.
9. In what country are the states of Colorado and Utah? United States
10. Name the mountains you drive over to get from Colorado to Utah. Rocky Mountains
11. In which direction do you go to get from Colorado to Utah? west

7. Ideas: The dog's blood cannot circulate around the paws; the dog's ankles could swell up.

TEXTBOOK

12. When you teach animals to work for new rewards, do you change the reward **quickly** or **slowly?** slowly
13. When you teach an animal to work for a new reward, what kind of reward do you start with? Idea: one the animal will work for
14. Then what do you do to that reward? Idea: slowly change it
15. When do you stop changing the reward?
16. Name 3 things that great water pressure can do to you.
17. The more water the glass has, the ▬ the sound it makes.
    - lower
    - higher
18. Write the letter of the glass that will make the lowest ring. A
19. Write the letter of the glass that will make the highest ring. F

15. Ideas: when it becomes the new reward; when the animal will work for the new reward
16. Ideas (any 3): make ears ring; make mouth dry; make mask press against face; have trouble swallowing

WORKBOOK

95

Name ____________________

A

1. The rules for the Iditarod require the musher to have certain things. **Underline** those things.
   - enough food for a day
   - firewood
   - an ax
   - enough food for a week
   - extra shoes
   - booties
   - a tent
   - a good sleeping bag
   - snowshoes
   - extra dogs
2. How much food does each dog need every day?
   - 3 pounds
   - 2 pounds
   - 1 pound
3. The sled must have room to hold ▬.
   - another musher
   - an injured dog
   - a spare sled

B Story Items

4. What did Chad decide to do with Chugger? Idea: keep her on the team
5. He gave some reasons for his decision. **Underline** 2 reasons.
   - She had always been the fastest runner.
   - She had never had any hip problems.
   - She was frequently sick.
   - Neither of her parents had hip problems.
   - She was only three years old.
6. What's the name of the woman whose picture was on Susie's wall? Susan Butcher
7. How many times did she enter the Iditarod? 17
8. How many times did she finish in first place? 4
9. On March 15, what was the weather like when the race began? Ideas: miserable; the temperature was near freezing and thick, wet snow was falling.

WORKBOOK

10. How many mushers start the race at the same time?
   • 1 • 2 • 10 • all
11. How much time passes before the next musher starts? 2 minutes
12. What number was Chad? 61
13. The musher in front of Chad was from Sweden.
14. When mushers are on the trail, how much help can they get from someone else? Idea: none

Review Items

Look at the picture below.

15. Shade the part of the earth where it is nighttime.
16. Which side of the earth is closer to the sun, **W** or **X**? W
17. Which side of the earth is in nighttime? X
18. Which side of the earth is in daytime? W

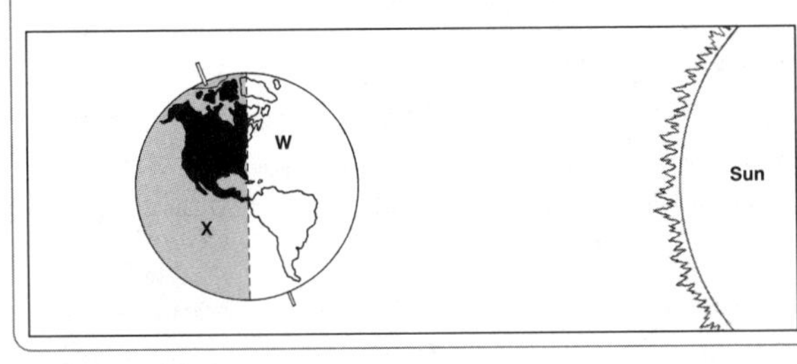

GO TO PART D IN YOUR TEXTBOOK.

TEXTBOOK

1. Idea: carry the dog in the sled to the next checkpoint

said, "Now there's a team with some real power. Think of how well they're going to do when Mr. Martin unties them from his truck." Everybody laughed.

It was now after 11 A.M., but Chad hadn't started yet. He was the 61st musher in the race. Just ahead of him was a musher from Sweden. Behind Chad was a musher from Michigan. That musher had run the Iditarod six times.

Chad and Susie were busy getting ready. They were putting booties on the dogs' feet. Chad brought along more than a thousand booties. He figured that he would change booties about every two days and more often if the snow was hard and frozen.

"Number 59," the announcer called from the start line. "Terry North from Colorado. It's your turn, Terry. Good luck." Terry tipped his hat and shouted, "Mush," so loudly that some of the dogs that were not in his team tried to run. One of them was Hoover, a dog in Chad's team.

Chad said, "Take it easy, Hoover. It won't be long now."

Chad and Susie checked the supplies one last time. They had already done it three times earlier, and if something was missing now, there wasn't much they could do about it because of the most important rule of the Iditarod. Once the race starts, all mushers are on their own. They can't try to get help from anybody who is not in the race. They can't use a phone, a radio or any other device that would allow others to help them. When they are on the trail, they must do the best they can without help from anybody.

D Number your paper from 1 through 25.

Review Items

1. During the Iditarod, what does a musher have to do with any dogs that are injured?
2. According to the Iditarod rules, there must be at least how many dogs on the gang line at the end of the race? (at least) 5
3. If you're underwater 100 feet deep, the pressure is much greater than it is on land. How many times greater is it? 4 times
4. When divers are that deep, how long should they take to return to the surface of the water? at least/about 2 minutes
5. What may happen to the divers if they go up faster than that? Idea: They may get the bends.

TEXTBOOK

6. Is the water cooler at **100 feet down** or **at the surface?** 100 feet down
7. Is all the water at 100 feet down the same temperature? no
8. Name 2 acts of bravery.
9. What do you fill a buoyancy device with? air
10. When it is filled up, what happens to the diver?
11. When it is empty, what happens to the diver? Idea: The diver moves down/sinks.

12. What part of the scuba equipment does the **J** show?
13. What part does the **K** show?
14. What part does the **L** show?
15. What part does the **M** show?
16. What part does the **N** show?
17. What part does the **O** show?
18. What part does the **P** show?

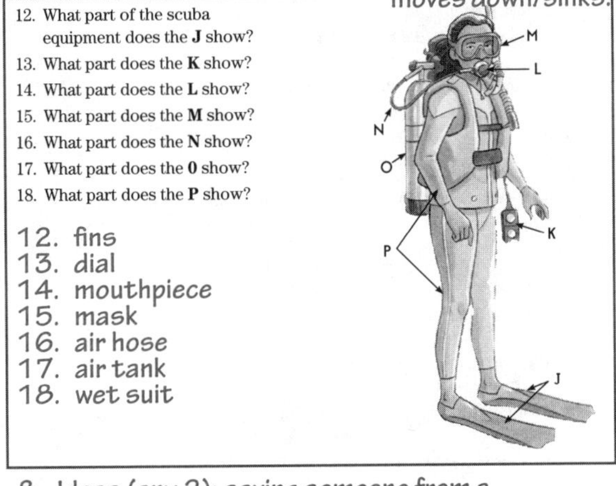

12. fins
13. dial
14. mouthpiece
15. mask
16. air hose
17. air tank
18. wet suit

8. Ideas (any 2): saving someone from a burning building; climbing a mountain; etc.
10. Idea: The diver moves up/floats/goes to the surface.

TEXTBOOK

Write the name of each kind of coral.

19. staghorn coral
20. brain coral
21. red coral

22. Name **2** things you could give a dog to reward it.
23. What color is lava when it's very hot?
   • brown • orange • gray
24. What color is lava after it cools a little bit? brown
25. What color is lava after it's completely cooled? gray

22. (Any 2:) a bone, a dog treat, a pat on the head, etc.

WORKBOOK

96

Name ____________

A Idea: because race officials must check that

1. Why are checkpoints called checkpoints? all mushers pass through each checkpoint
2. Name **3** things a musher does at checkpoints. (Any 3:) rest their teams; make repairs; feed their dogs; drop off injured or sick dogs; get food; have a veterinarian check all the dogs
3. How does food get to the checkpoints? Idea: Airplanes deliver it.
4. About how far apart are the checkpoints? 50 miles
5. About how many checkpoints are there between Anchorage and Nome? 24

B Story Items

Ideas: The race was too dangerous;

6. Just before Chad left, Susie became worried. What worried her? something could happen to Chad and Denali.
7. Was Chad **calm** or **nervous?** nervous
8. What was the name of the woman who left just before Chad? Siri Carlson
9. How do mushers get water for their dogs? Ideas: heat snow to melt it; haul water from a stream
10. What do mushers often use to make beds for their dogs? Idea: branches from evergreen trees

WORKBOOK

11. **Underline** the items that tell what it was like on the third day of the race.
    - frozen lakes
    - 10 degrees below zero
    - rough country
    - hard, icy snow
    - blowing snow
    - soft snow
    - blasting wind
    - flat trail
    - mountains
    - warm
    - sunny
    - 10 degrees above zero
12. What was the name of the pass Chad was going through? Rainy Pass
13. Why did he think that name was funny? Idea: because it's always frozen and cold
14. What's the name of the first woman to win the Iditarod? Libby Riddles
15. In what year did she win it? 1985
16. Where were she and most of the mushers when the race was stopped the first time? Rainy Pass
17. Why did Susie write a different letter after she heard the TV report? ____________
18. In the letter she didn't send, what did she write about? Denali's birthday
19. What did the race officials think they would have to do if the bad weather continued? Idea: send out search parties for the missing teams

GO TO PART D IN YOUR TEXTBOOK.

17. Ideas: because the TV report made her worry about Chad's safety; because Denali's birthday didn't seem very important anymore

TEXTBOOK

part of the letter she was writing now:

Do you know that in two days, it will be Denali's birthday? He'll be three years old.

Suddenly, the TV program stopped and an announcer said, "Here's a special report on the Iditarod from Rainy Pass." The picture on the TV showed snow blowing and a reporter who was yelling over the wind. He told about the high winds at Rainy Pass. He said, "The winds are blowing so hard that some of the mushers are lost because they can't see the trail. The race officials may have to send out search parties if some of the teams don't show up at the checkpoint pretty soon."

Susie didn't finish the letter she had started. Denali's birthday didn't seem very important anymore. Instead, she wrote another letter.

Dear Uncle Chad,

The weather report from Rainy Pass is scary. I hope you are not one of those mushers who got lost. I hope they found all the mushers who got lost. And I hope their dogs are okay. I hope that your team is doing well.

With love,

Susie

What she really wanted to say in her letter was, "Oh please make sure that Denali is all right. Oh please don't get lost. And if you do get lost, please find your way to the next checkpoint."

D Number your paper from 1 through 19.

Review Items

1. The rules for the Iditarod require each musher to have certain things. Write the letters of those things. a, b, e, g, i
   - a. an ax
   - b. snowshoes
   - c. a tent
   - d. firewood
   - e. a good sleeping bag
   - f. extra shoes
   - g. enough food for a day
   - h. enough food for a week
   - i. booties
   - j. extra dogs

TEXTBOOK

2. During the Iditarod, how much food does each dog need every day?
   - 1 pound
   - 2 pounds
   - 3 pounds
3. Each sled in the Iditarod must have room to hold ____.
   - a spare sled
   - another musher
   - an injured dog
4. Name the woman who finished the Iditarod sixteen times. Susan Butcher
5. How many times did she **enter** the Iditarod? 17
6. How many times did she finish in first place? 4
7. How many mushers start the Iditarod at the same time? 1
8. How much time passes before the next musher starts? 2 minutes
9. When Iditarod mushers are on the trail, how much help can they get from someone else? none
10. Is the water cooler at **100 feet down** or **at the surface?** 100 feet down
11. Is all the water at 100 feet down the same temperature? no
12. What do you fill a buoyancy device with? air
13. When it is filled up, what happens to the diver?
14. When it is empty, what happens to the diver?
15. If you move up too fast from very deep water, you may get the ____. bends
16. What forms in your blood as you go up too fast? bubbles
17. When you go up very fast, is there **more pressure** or **less pressure** on your body? less pressure
18. When you're training an animal, what do you do each time the animal does the trick? Idea: give the animal a reward
19. What do you do if the animal does not do the trick? Idea: don't give the animal a reward

13. Idea: The diver moves up/floats/goes to the surface.
14. Idea: The diver moves down/sinks.

WORKBOOK

97

Name ____________________

A Story Items

1. Would the snow be deeper **on the trail** or **off the trail**? off the trail
2. Why? Idea: No one had been over the snow recently.
3. If Chad had stayed on the trail, he would have gone in which direction? west
4. How did he figure out which direction he was going? Idea: He used his compass.
5. Did he turn **left** or **right** in order to go in the correct direction? left
6. When the wind finally died down, how much daylight was there? Idea: almost none
7. What could Chad see? Ideas: the mountains; lights from the lodge
8. How did the dogs know they were near the checkpoint? ____________________
9. How did they act? Ideas: happy; they seemed to pep up.
10. When Chad arrived at the lodge, how many mushers were missing? 2
11. What was the name of one of those mushers? Siri Carlson
12. How did Chad show the officials the route he had taken? Idea: He went with them on snowmobiles.
13. When did Chad see one of the missing mushers? the next morning

8. Idea: They could see the lights/smell the food coming from the checkpoints.

WORKBOOK

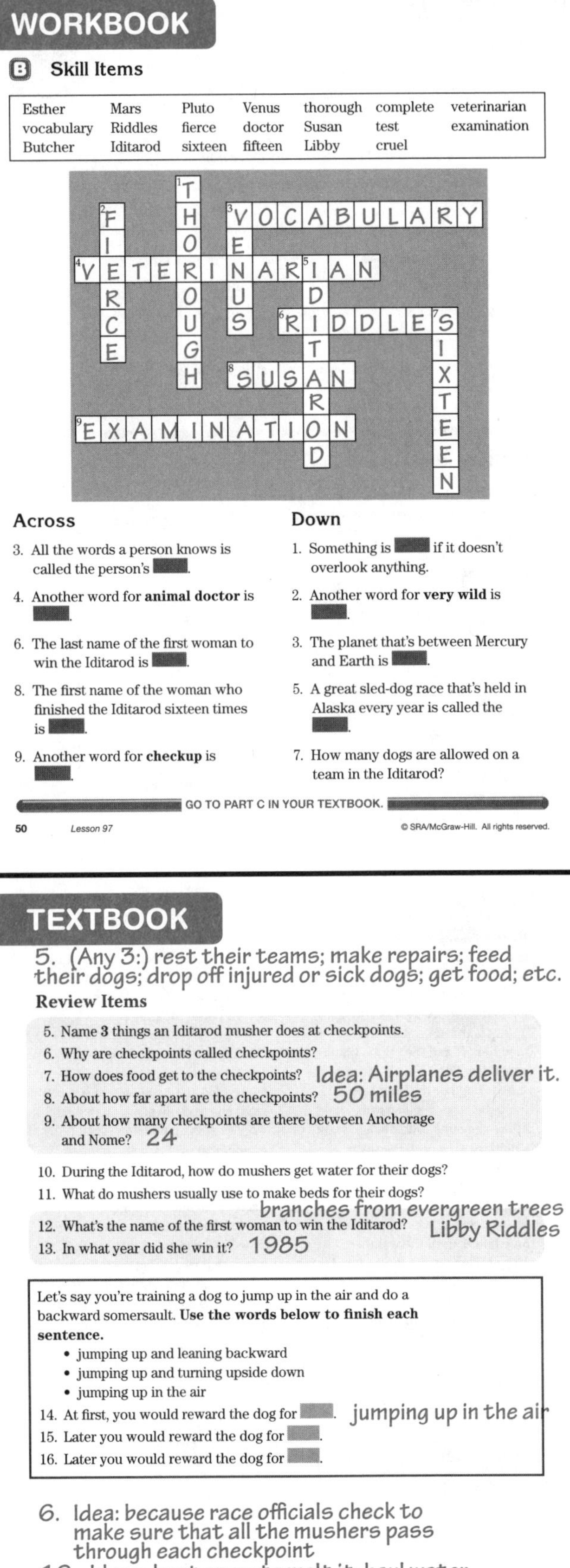

B Skill Items

Esther	Mars	Pluto	Venus	thorough	complete	veterinarian
vocabulary	Riddles	fierce	doctor	Susan	test	examination
Butcher	Iditarod	sixteen	fifteen	Libby	cruel	

Across

3. All the words a person knows is called the person's ▬.
4. Another word for **animal doctor** is ▬.
6. The last name of the first woman to win the Iditarod is ▬.
8. The first name of the woman who finished the Iditarod sixteen times is ▬.
9. Another word for **checkup** is ▬.

Down

1. Something is ▬ if it doesn't overlook anything.
2. Another word for **very wild** is ▬.
3. The planet that's between Mercury and Earth is ▬.
5. A great sled-dog race that's held in Alaska every year is called the ▬.
7. How many dogs are allowed on a team in the Iditarod?

GO TO PART C IN YOUR TEXTBOOK.

TEXTBOOK

C Number your paper from 1 through 16.

Skill Items

Visibility was miserable in the fierce blizzard.

1. What word means **terrible?** miserable
2. What word refers to how well you can see things? visibility
3. What word means **very wild?** fierce
4. What word names a snowstorm that is windy and very cold? blizzard

TEXTBOOK

5. (Any 3:) rest their teams; make repairs; feed their dogs; drop off injured or sick dogs; get food; etc.

Review Items

5. Name **3** things an Iditarod musher does at checkpoints.
6. Why are checkpoints called checkpoints?
7. How does food get to the checkpoints? Idea: Airplanes deliver it.
8. About how far apart are the checkpoints? 50 miles
9. About how many checkpoints are there between Anchorage and Nome? 24
10. During the Iditarod, how do mushers get water for their dogs?
11. What do mushers usually use to make beds for their dogs? branches from evergreen trees
12. What's the name of the first woman to win the Iditarod? Libby Riddles
13. In what year did she win it? 1985

Let's say you're training a dog to jump up in the air and do a backward somersault. **Use the words below to finish each sentence.**

- jumping up and leaning backward
- jumping up and turning upside down
- jumping up in the air

14. At first, you would reward the dog for ▬. jumping up in the air
15. Later you would reward the dog for ▬.
16. Later you would reward the dog for ▬.

6. Idea: because race officials check to make sure that all the mushers pass through each checkpoint
10. Ideas: heat snow to melt it; haul water from a stream
15. jumping up and leaning backward
16. jumping up and turning upside down

WORKBOOK

Name ______________________ **98**

A

1. The rules of the Iditarod state that every musher must rest for 24 hours at one checkpoint and must rest for eight hours at two other checkpoints.
2. This rule was put in to protect the ▬.
   - mushers • dogs • race officials
3. In what year was the first Iditarod? • 1973 • 1963 • 1993
4. During the first running of the Iditarod, how many dogs died during the race? • 10 • 20 • 30
5. During more recent years, how many dogs die during each race?
   - 5 to 8 • 8 to 10 • 2 to 3

B Story Items

6. Write **3** on the map to show where Chad was on day 3.
7. Write **9** on the map to show where he was on day 9.

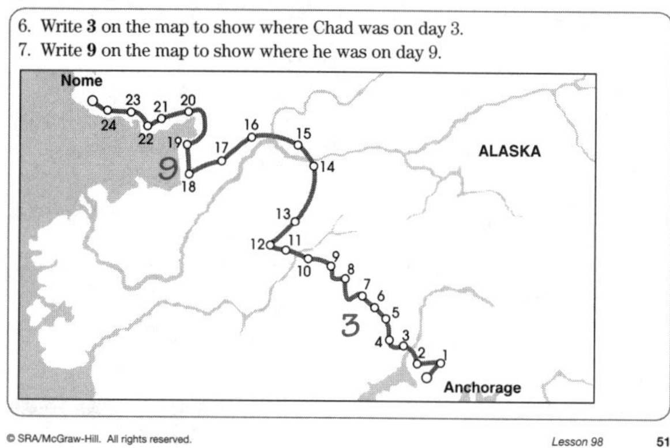

WORKBOOK

8. Something was the same on day 3 of the race and day 9 of the race. What was that? Ideas: Chad was lost; the weather was very bad.
9. What happened as the sled was going over a thick crust of frozen snow? Idea: The sled broke through the ice/fell in the water.
10. Which dog let out a yelp? Chugger
11. Chad was in the water up to his chest.
12. Name the 2 dogs that had to do most of the pulling to get the sled out of the water. Denali and Butch
13. What did Chad do with the tarp? Idea: made a tent
14. What did Chad do first, take care of the injured dog or take care of himself? took care of himself
15. How much time did he have to get dry and warm? Idea: a few minutes
16. What would have happened if he took too much time? Idea: He would freeze.
17. Name **3** things he did inside the tent that he built. (Any 3:) started a fire; took off his wet clothes; put on dry clothes; brought Chugger into the tent
18. What did Chad do to find the trail? Idea: climbed a hill
19. Whose sled did he see? Siri Carlson's
20. When he harnessed the dogs, which 2 dogs were the wheel dogs? Denali and Butch
21. Which dog walked behind the sled? Buck
22. Where was Chugger? in the sled

GO TO PART D IN YOUR TEXTBOOK.

TEXTBOOK

dogs. Chugger could not walk on all four legs. Her back left leg did not work because her hip had failed.

Chad took Chugger off the gang line and carried her into the tent. He dried her off and then put a blanket around her. She licked his face as he was tucking her in. Then he took Buck, the other regular wheel dog, off the gang line. Buck would walk behind the sled until the team reached the next checkpoint. Denali and Butch would be the wheel dogs for the rest of the race.

Chad stayed at the grove for three hours, until the weather cleared. Then he climbed a nearby hill so he could look in all directions for the trail. He didn't have much hope of seeing it, but he thought it was worth trying. To his surprise, he saw a dog sled as soon as he got to the top of the hill. It was a few hundred yards to the east. When he took a closer look, he said, "I know who that is." It was Siri Carlson. Chad whistled and waved.

She waved back and shouted something, but he couldn't hear what she said. He signaled that he would catch up with her. Then he ran back to his team and hitched them to the gang line. He put Chugger in the sled. When Chad told the team to mush, Chugger tried to stand up. Chad patted her and said, "Not you, Chugger. You just take it easy." The team went east over the hills until it reached the trail. Chad could see Siri's team about half a mile ahead of him.

D Number your paper from 1 through 16.

Skill Items

Use the words in the box to write complete sentences.

thorough	courage	examination	visibility
included	injured	purpose	veterinarian
officials	blizzard	miserable	fierce

1. The ▬ gave the dogs a ▬ ▬.
2. ▬ was ▬ in the ▬ ▬.

1. veterinarian, thorough, examination
2. visibility, miserable, fierce, blizzard

TEXTBOOK

Review Items

3. During the Iditarod, is the snow deeper **on the trail** or **off the trail?** on the trail
4. Why? Idea: No one had been over the snow recently.
5. How does water pressure change as you move from deep in the water toward the surface?
6. How does the light around you change as you move toward the surface? Idea: It gets brighter.
7. In what state is the Iditarod sled-dog race? Alaska
8. In which city does it begin? Anchorage
9. In which city does it end? Nome
10. The Iditarod is about ▬ miles from start to finish.
    - 1600 • 500 • 1100
11. In most years, the race takes about ▬.
    - 10 days • 2 weeks • a week
12. Name an arrow-shaped fish. barracuda
13. Write **2** facts about those fish.
14. What command tells sled dogs to turn right? gee
15. What command tells sled dogs to move straight ahead? mush
16. What command tells sled dogs to turn left? haw

5. Idea: It goes down/pushes with less force.

13. Ideas (any 2): They're very dangerous; their mouths are filled with sharp teeth; they grow almost 2 meters long; etc.

WORKBOOK

99

Name ______

A Story Items

1. Where did Chad leave Chugger before going on to finish the race? Idea: at a checkpoint
2. How many dogs were now on the gang line? 15
3. Which dog did not have a partner? Buck
4. Chad finished the race in 35 th place.
5. Siri Carlson finished in 34 th place.
6. Did Chad meet his main goal for this race? yes
7. What was that goal? Idea: to finish the race
8. How did the mushers and their teams get back to Anchorage from Nome? Idea: by plane
9. Who met Chad at the airport? Susie
10. Susie had a lot of questions. Most of them were about Denali.
11. What had the vet told her the day before about Chugger? ______
12. What did Chad say he wanted to do with Denali for the next Iditarod? Idea: make him a regular wheel dog
13. Who did Chad plan to practice with during the summer? Siri Carlson
14. Denali ran in six more Iditarods. Who was the musher for five of them? Chad
15. Who was the other musher? Susie

11. Ideas: There wasn't much the vet could do for Chugger's hip; she would probably be ok as long as she didn't pull sleds or do heavy work.

WORKBOOK

B Review Items

16. Most sled-dog teams have an ▬ number of dogs. • <u>even</u> • odd
17. For the Iditarod, a sled-dog team can't have more than 16 dogs.
18. Which letter in the picture shows the wheel dogs? C
19. Which letter shows the swing dogs? H
20. Which letter shows the lead dogs? B
21. Which letter shows where the musher is most of the time? W
22. Which letter shows tug lines? L
23. Which letter shows the gang line? E

B L H Y U C E R W D

Use these words to answer items 24–26:
• swing dogs • wheel dogs • lead dogs

24. These dogs are very good followers, and they are smart. swing dogs
25. These dogs are responsible for freeing the sled when it gets stuck. wheel dogs
26. These dogs are very smart, and other dogs obey them. lead dogs

GO TO PART C IN YOUR TEXTBOOK.

TEXTBOOK

11. Ideas: The dog's blood cannot circulate around the paws; the dog's ankles could swell up.

C Number your paper from 1 through 13.

Skill Items

Write the word from the box that means the same thing as the underlined part of each sentence.

sheltered	darted	plunged	peered
rapidly	recently	trailed	victory

1. The fish <u>moved very fast</u> in the fish tank. darted
2. We ran down the hill <u>quickly</u>. rapidly
3. The kittens <u>followed</u> their mother across the yard. trailed

Review Items

4. The rules of the Iditarod state that every musher must rest for ▬ hours at one checkpoint and must rest for ▬ hours at two other checkpoints. 24/8
5. This rule was put in to protect the ▬.
   • race officials • mushers • <u>dogs</u>
6. In what year was the first Iditarod? 1973
7. During the first running of the Iditarod, how many dogs died during the race? 30
8. During more recent years, how many dogs die during each race? 2 to 3
9. What do sled dogs wear to protect their feet? booties
10. **Write the letters of the 4 items that tell what could happen to a sled dog's feet if they didn't have protection.** b, c, e, g
    a. stiff legs
    b. snowballs between the pads
    c. cuts from ice and frozen snow
    d. long claws
    e. slipping on hard snow
    f. icicles on their ankles
    g. cuts that do not heal well
11. If booties on a sled dog are too tight, what could happen?
12. If booties are too loose, what could happen? Idea: The booties could fall off.
13. What happens if a sled dog doesn't pass the Iditarod's health examination? Idea: It cannot run in the race.

TEXTBOOK

100 TEST 10

Number your paper from 1 through 34.

1. Most sled-dog teams have an ▬ number of dogs.
   • odd • <u>even</u>
2. For the Iditarod, a sled-dog team can't have more than ▬ dogs. 16

Use these words to answer items 3–5:
• swing dogs • wheel dogs • lead dogs

3. These dogs are very good followers, and they are smart. swing dogs
4. These dogs are responsible for freeing the sled when it gets stuck. wheel dogs
5. These dogs are very smart, and other dogs obey them. lead dogs
6. If booties on a sled dog are too tight, what could happen?
7. If booties are too loose, what could happen? Idea: The booties could fall off.
8. What command tells sled dogs to turn right? gee
9. What command tells sled dogs to move straight ahead? mush
10. What command tells sled dogs to turn left? haw
11. What happens if a sled dog doesn't pass the Iditarod's health examination? Idea: The dog cannot run in the race.
12. During the Iditarod, what does a musher have to do with any dogs that are injured?
13. According to the Iditarod rules, there must be at least how many dogs on the gang line at the end of the race? 5

6. Ideas: The dog's blood cannot circulate around the paws; the dog's ankles could swell up.
12. Idea: leave them at the checkpoint

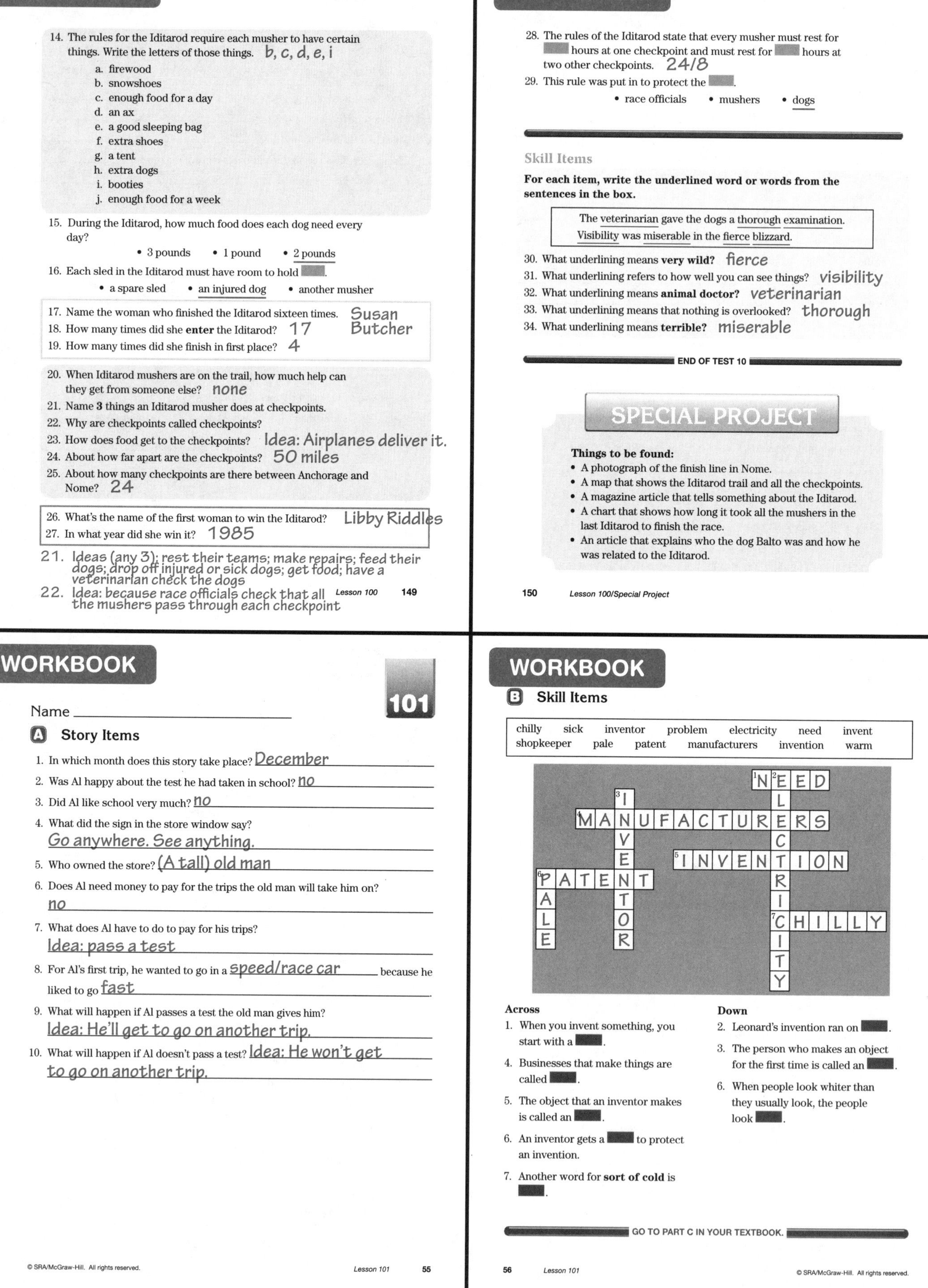

TEXTBOOK

14. The rules for the Iditarod require each musher to have certain things. Write the letters of those things. b, c, d, e, i
    a. firewood
    b. snowshoes
    c. enough food for a day
    d. an ax
    e. a good sleeping bag
    f. extra shoes
    g. a tent
    h. extra dogs
    i. booties
    j. enough food for a week
15. During the Iditarod, how much food does each dog need every day?
    • 3 pounds • 1 pound • 2 pounds
16. Each sled in the Iditarod must have room to hold ▬.
    • a spare sled • an injured dog • another musher
17. Name the woman who finished the Iditarod sixteen times. Susan Butcher
18. How many times did she **enter** the Iditarod? 17
19. How many times did she finish in first place? 4
20. When Iditarod mushers are on the trail, how much help can they get from someone else? none
21. Name **3** things an Iditarod musher does at checkpoints.
22. Why are checkpoints called checkpoints?
23. How does food get to the checkpoints? Idea: Airplanes deliver it.
24. About how far apart are the checkpoints? 50 miles
25. About how many checkpoints are there between Anchorage and Nome? 24
26. What's the name of the first woman to win the Iditarod? Libby Riddles
27. In what year did she win it? 1985

21. Ideas (any 3): rest their teams; make repairs; feed their dogs; drop off injured or sick dogs; get food; have a veterinarian check the dogs
22. Idea: because race officials check that all the mushers pass through each checkpoint

Lesson 100 149

TEXTBOOK

28. The rules of the Iditarod state that every musher must rest for ▬ hours at one checkpoint and must rest for ▬ hours at two other checkpoints. 24/8
29. This rule was put in to protect the ▬.
    • race officials • mushers • dogs

Skill Items

For each item, write the underlined word or words from the sentences in the box.

> The veterinarian gave the dogs a thorough examination.
> Visibility was miserable in the fierce blizzard.

30. What underlining means **very wild?** fierce
31. What underlining refers to how well you can see things? visibility
32. What underlining means **animal doctor?** veterinarian
33. What underlining means that nothing is overlooked? thorough
34. What underlining means **terrible?** miserable

END OF TEST 10

SPECIAL PROJECT

Things to be found:
- A photograph of the finish line in Nome.
- A map that shows the Iditarod trail and all the checkpoints.
- A magazine article that tells something about the Iditarod.
- A chart that shows how long it took all the mushers in the last Iditarod to finish the race.
- An article that explains who the dog Balto was and how he was related to the Iditarod.

150 Lesson 100/Special Project

WORKBOOK

101

Name ____________________

A Story Items

1. In which month does this story take place? December
2. Was Al happy about the test he had taken in school? no
3. Did Al like school very much? no
4. What did the sign in the store window say? Go anywhere. See anything.
5. Who owned the store? (A tall) old man
6. Does Al need money to pay for the trips the old man will take him on? no
7. What does Al have to do to pay for his trips? Idea: pass a test
8. For Al's first trip, he wanted to go in a speed/race car because he liked to go fast.
9. What will happen if Al passes a test the old man gives him? Idea: He'll get to go on another trip.
10. What will happen if Al doesn't pass a test? Idea: He won't get to go on another trip.

Lesson 101 55

WORKBOOK

B Skill Items

chilly	sick	inventor	problem	electricity	need	invent
shopkeeper	pale	patent	manufacturers	invention	warm	

Across

1. When you invent something, you start with a ▬.
4. Businesses that make things are called ▬.
5. The object that an inventor makes is called an ▬.
6. An inventor gets a ▬ to protect an invention.
7. Another word for **sort of cold** is ▬.

Down

2. Leonard's invention ran on ▬.
3. The person who makes an object for the first time is called an ▬.
6. When people look whiter than they usually look, the people look ▬.

GO TO PART C IN YOUR TEXTBOOK.

56 Lesson 101

TEXTBOOK

C Number your paper from 1 through 20.

Skill Items

Write the word from the box that means the same thing as the underlined part of each sentence.

rocket	whether	incredible	silly
suppose	business	device	however

1. She made a machine for making snowballs. device
2. They decided if they would have a party. whether
3. He saw an amazing animal. incredible

Review Items

4. What's another name for hot, melted rock? lava
5. During the Iditarod, how do mushers get water for their dogs?
6. What do mushers usually use to make beds for their dogs? Idea: branches from evergreen trees
7. During the Iditarod, is the snow deeper **on the trail** or **off the trail?** on the trail
8. Why? Idea: No one has been over the snow recently.
9. In what year was the first Iditarod? 1973
10. During the first running of the Iditarod, how many dogs died during the race? 30
11. During more recent years, how many dogs die during each race? 2 to 3
12. Which is bigger, Alaska or Japan? Alaska
13. Is Japan a **state** or a **country?** country
14. How many people live in Japan?
    - 127
    - 127 million
    - 127 thousand

5. Ideas: heat snow to melt it; haul water from a stream

TEXTBOOK

15. Write the letters of 3 types of products that are used in the United States and manufactured in Japan. a, c, f
    a. TVs
    b. books
    c. cars
    d. rugs
    e. furniture
    f. CD players
    g. Mr. Light Saver
16. The person who drives a sled-dog team is called a ▬. musher
17. The drivers of the sled-dog teams command the dogs by using their ▬.
    - voices
    - reins
    - steering wheels
18. How many mushers start the Iditarod at the same time? 1
19. How much time passes before the next musher starts? 2 minutes
20. The ▬s are the coldest places on the earth and the ▬ is the hottest place on the earth. pole, equator

WORKBOOK

Name ____________________

A

1. How far does light travel in one second?
    - 86 miles
    - 186 thousand miles
    - 186 miles
2. What else travels as fast as light? Idea: nothing
3. How long does it take light to travel from the sun to Earth?
   8 minutes

B Story Items

4. What does Al have to do to pay for his trips?
   Idea: pass a test
5. Name the first vehicle Al and the old man rode in.
   Idea: (red) race car
6. What was the fastest speed they went in that vehicle?
    - 500 miles per hour
    - 130 miles per hour
    - 200 miles per hour
7. Why did Al and the old man have to shout in the racing car?
   Idea: The car was very noisy.
8. Name the second vehicle Al and the old man rode in.
   jet (plane)

WORKBOOK

9. How fast did they go in that vehicle?
   500 miles per hour
10. If the speedometer needle on the red racer is pointing to 70, how **fast** is the vehicle going?
    70 miles per hour
11. How **far** will that vehicle go in one hour? 70 miles

Review Items

12. Write the names of the 9 planets, starting with the planet that's closest to the sun.
    Mercury, Venus, Earth, Mars, Jupiter,
    Saturn, Uranus, Neptune, Pluto
13. During the Iditarod, what does a musher have to do with any dogs that are injured?
    Idea: take them to the next checkpoint
14. According to the Iditarod rules, there must be at least how many dogs on the gang line at the end of the race? 5
15. During the Iditarod, how much food does each dog need every day?
    - 1 pound
    - 2 pounds
    - 3 pounds
16. Each sled in the Iditarod must have room to hold ▬.
    - a spare sled
    - another musher
    - an injured dog

GO TO PART D IN YOUR TEXTBOOK.

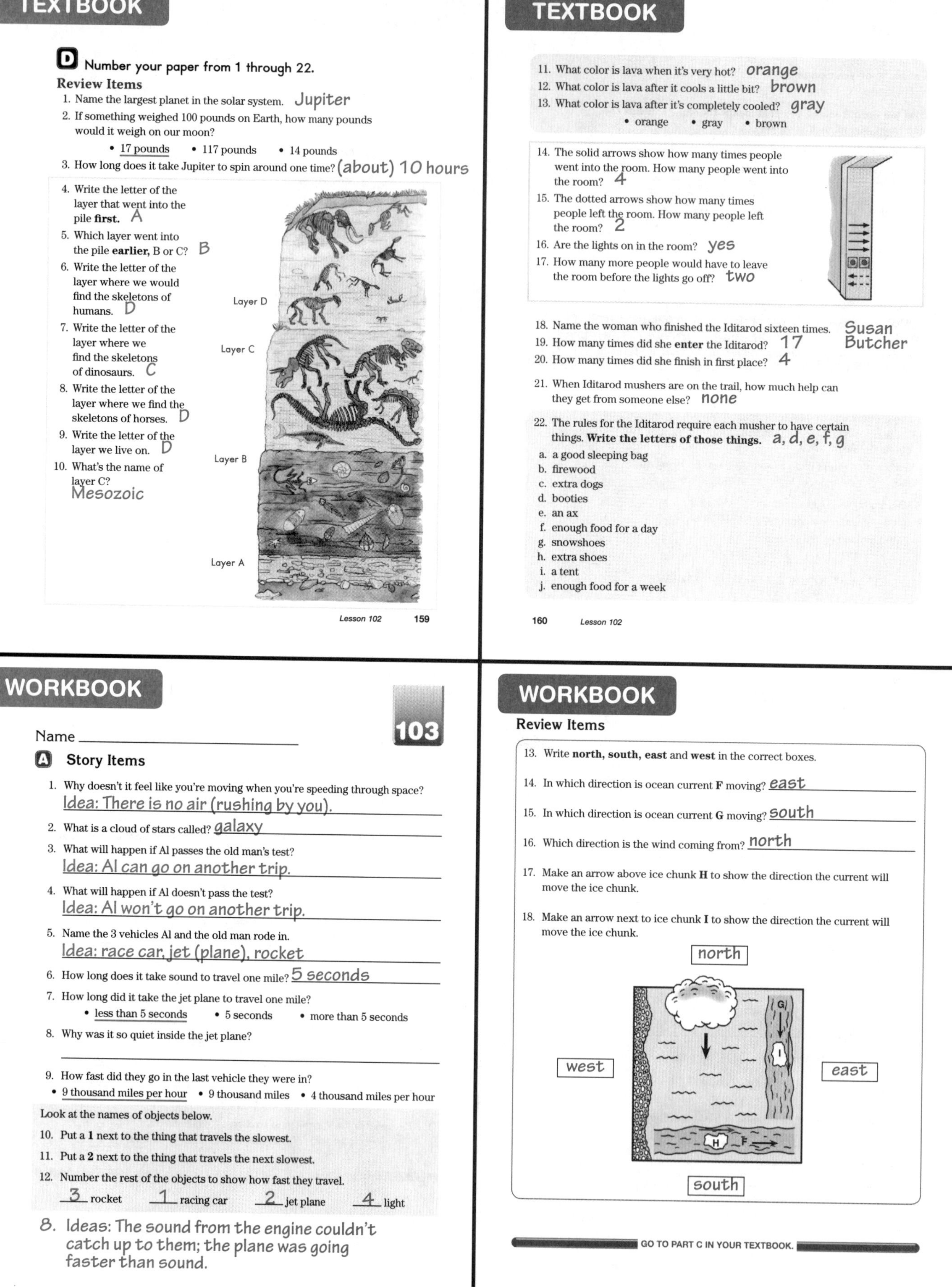

TEXTBOOK

D Number your paper from 1 through 22.

Review Items

1. Name the largest planet in the solar system. Jupiter
2. If something weighed 100 pounds on Earth, how many pounds would it weigh on our moon?
   - 17 pounds • 117 pounds • 14 pounds
3. How long does it take Jupiter to spin around one time? (about) 10 hours
4. Write the letter of the layer that went into the pile **first.** A
5. Which layer went into the pile **earlier,** B or C? B
6. Write the letter of the layer where we would find the skeletons of humans. D
7. Write the letter of the layer where we find the skeletons of dinosaurs. C
8. Write the letter of the layer where we find the skeletons of horses. D
9. Write the letter of the layer we live on. D
10. What's the name of layer C? Mesozoic

TEXTBOOK

11. What color is lava when it's very hot? orange
12. What color is lava after it cools a little bit? brown
13. What color is lava after it's completely cooled? gray
    - orange • gray • brown
14. The solid arrows show how many times people went into the room. How many people went into the room? 4
15. The dotted arrows show how many times people left the room. How many people left the room? 2
16. Are the lights on in the room? yes
17. How many more people would have to leave the room before the lights go off? two
18. Name the woman who finished the Iditarod sixteen times. Susan Butcher
19. How many times did she **enter** the Iditarod? 17
20. How many times did she finish in first place? 4
21. When Iditarod mushers are on the trail, how much help can they get from someone else? none
22. The rules for the Iditarod require each musher to have certain things. **Write the letters of those things.** a, d, e, f, g
    a. a good sleeping bag
    b. firewood
    c. extra dogs
    d. booties
    e. an ax
    f. enough food for a day
    g. snowshoes
    h. extra shoes
    i. a tent
    j. enough food for a week

WORKBOOK

Name ____________________ **103**

A **Story Items**

1. Why doesn't it feel like you're moving when you're speeding through space?
   Idea: There is no air (rushing by you).
2. What is a cloud of stars called? galaxy
3. What will happen if Al passes the old man's test?
   Idea: Al can go on another trip.
4. What will happen if Al doesn't pass the test?
   Idea: Al won't go on another trip.
5. Name the 3 vehicles Al and the old man rode in.
   Idea: race car, jet (plane), rocket
6. How long does it take sound to travel one mile? 5 seconds
7. How long did it take the jet plane to travel one mile?
   - less than 5 seconds • 5 seconds • more than 5 seconds
8. Why was it so quiet inside the jet plane?
9. How fast did they go in the last vehicle they were in?
   - 9 thousand miles per hour • 9 thousand miles • 4 thousand miles per hour

Look at the names of objects below.

10. Put a **1** next to the thing that travels the slowest.
11. Put a **2** next to the thing that travels the next slowest.
12. Number the rest of the objects to show how fast they travel.
    3 rocket 1 racing car 2 jet plane 4 light

8. Ideas: The sound from the engine couldn't catch up to them; the plane was going faster than sound.

WORKBOOK

Review Items

13. Write **north, south, east** and **west** in the correct boxes.
14. In which direction is ocean current **F** moving? east
15. In which direction is ocean current **G** moving? south
16. Which direction is the wind coming from? north
17. Make an arrow above ice chunk **H** to show the direction the current will move the ice chunk.
18. Make an arrow next to ice chunk **I** to show the direction the current will move the ice chunk.

GO TO PART C IN YOUR TEXTBOOK.

TEXTBOOK

C Number your paper from 1 through 27.

Skill Items

Write the word from the box that means the same thing as the underlined part of each sentence.

happy	attached	prepared	thick
level	approached	comfortable	clever

1. The road was flat for many miles. level
2. They got ready for the big party. prepared
3. The truck moved toward the cliff. approached

Review Items

4. In what ocean is the **X?** Atlantic (Ocean)
5. About how many miles is it from Florida to the **X?** 1,000 (miles)

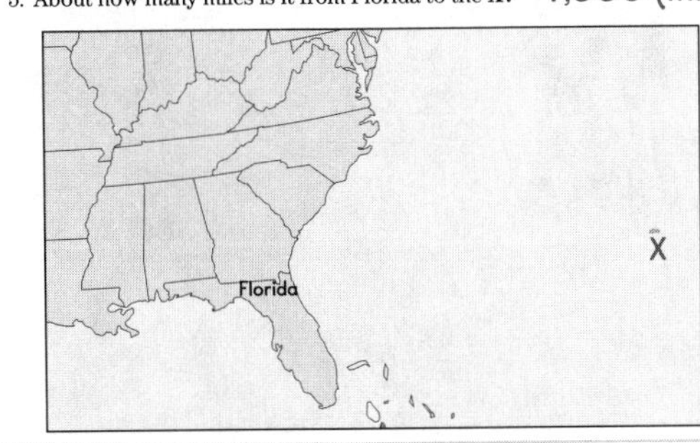

6. A person weighs 400 pounds on planet M and 200 pounds on planet B. Which planet has stronger gravity? M
7. Which planets have stronger gravities, the bigger planets or the smaller planets? bigger

TEXTBOOK

11. (Any 2:) saving someone from a burning building; climbing a mountain, etc.

8. How many miles does light travel in one second?
   - 186 miles
   - 186 thousand miles
   - 86 thousand miles
9. What else travels as fast as light? Idea: nothing
10. How long does it take light to travel from the sun to Earth?
    - 5 seconds
    - 8 seconds
    - 8 minutes
11. Name 2 acts of bravery.
12. What does the color of water tell you about the water? Idea: how deep the water is
13. When you open a bottle of soda pop, what happens to the pressure inside the bottle? Idea: It goes down.
14. What forms in the soda pop? bubbles
15. Do things look **light** or **dark** when you're 100 feet below the surface of the ocean? dark
16. There aren't as many plants down there because there isn't as much ▬. light
17. Name 3 things that great water pressure can do to you.
18. In what state is the Iditarod sled-dog race? Alaska
19. In which city does it begin? Anchorage
20. In which city does it end? Nome
21. The Iditarod is about ▬ miles from start to finish.
    - 1600
    - 500
    - 1100
22. In most years, the race takes about ▬.
    - 10 days
    - 2 weeks
    - a week
23. How does water pressure change as you move from deep in the water toward the surface? Idea: It goes down/pushes with less force.
24. How does the light around you change as you move toward the surface? Idea: It gets brighter.
25. When the diver is ▬ feet underwater, the pressure is **two** times as great as it is on land. 33
26. When the diver is ▬ feet underwater, the pressure is **three** times as great as it is on land. 66
27. When the diver is ▬ feet underwater, the pressure is **four** times as great as it is on land. 100

17. (Any 3:) ear pain; mask pushed against face; trouble swallowing, etc.

WORKBOOK

104

Name ____________

A Story Items

1. Al had trouble going to sleep because ▬.
   - he wasn't tired.
   - he kept thinking about his trip.
   - he was hungry.
2. Why did Al leave for school early?
   - to read the newspaper
   - to read his science book
   - to talk to his teacher
3. Why was Al's teacher surprised when he raised his hand in school? Ideas: Al never raises his hand/answers.
4. It is so quiet in a jet plane that is going 900 miles per hour because the plane is moving faster than sound (of the engines).
5. What was the name of the street the store was on? Anywhere Street
6. What question did the old man ask Al? What does it mean to go fast?
7. Why did the old man say he would take Al on another trip? Idea: He'd passed the test.
8. What did Al want to learn about on his next trip? matter
9. Al's teacher had told the class that all things are made of matter.
10. How many forms of matter are there? 3

WORKBOOK

Review Items

11. Write the missing seasons on the picture below.
12. Shade half of earth D and half of earth F.

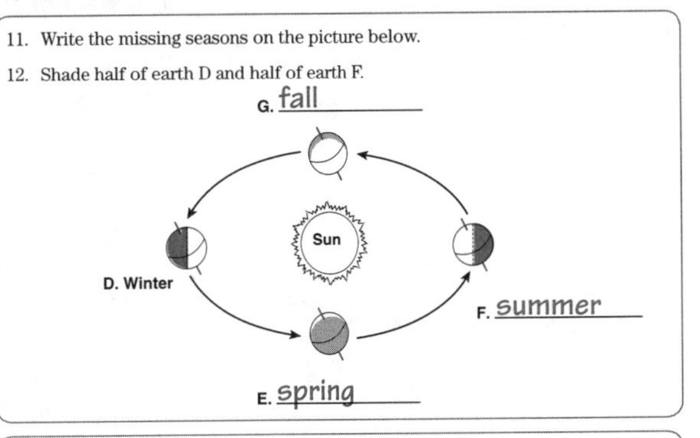

Look at the picture below.

13. Which side of the earth is closer to the sun, P or Q? Q
14. Which side of the earth is in nighttime? P
15. Which side of the earth is in daytime? Q

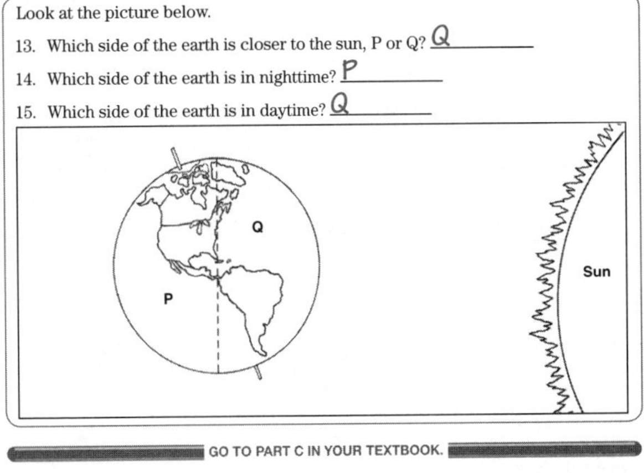

GO TO PART C IN YOUR TEXTBOOK.

TEXTBOOK

serious. Maybe Al's answer was wrong.

Al decided to explain what he meant. He continued, "Light travels 186 thousand miles every second. But at the speed of light it would take us millions of years to reach the galaxy we saw. So light isn't very fast at all. And so I don't know what it means to say that something is fast."

The old man's face looked very cold. Then the old man smiled and said, "You are a smart boy. You are a thinking boy. You have passed your test. You have paid for your trip."

The old man bent over so that his face was very close to Al's face. "And where do you want to go for your next trip? Go anywhere. See anything."

Al thought back to the things that his class had been studying. One thing was matter. His teacher had told the class that all things are made of matter and that there are three forms of matter. But Al didn't understand the three forms of matter.

Al looked at the old man and said, "I would like to find out about matter."

C Number your paper from 1 through 21.

Skill Items

At midnight, he saw a familiar galaxy.

1. What word refers to something that is well known to you? familiar
2. What word means **12 o'clock at night?** midnight
3. What word names a group of millions and millions of stars? galaxy

Review Items

4. When a person makes an object for the first time, the person ▬ the object. invents
5. How many miles does light travel in one second?
   - 186 million miles
   - 186 miles
   - 186 thousand miles
6. What else travels as fast as light? Idea: nothing
7. How long does it take light to travel from the sun to Earth?
   - 12 minutes
   - 8 minutes
   - 12 seconds

TEXTBOOK

8. Idea: because there's no air (rushing by you)

8. Why doesn't it feel like you're moving when you're speeding through space?
9. What is a cloud of stars called? galaxy
10. How long does it take sound to travel one mile? 5 seconds

Write the name of each animal in the picture.

TEXTBOOK

17. **Write the letter** of the thing that travels the slowest. b
18. **Write the letter** of the thing that travels the fastest. a
    a. light
    b. racing car
    c. jet plane
    d. sound
    e. rocket
19. When you're training an animal, what do you do each time the animal does the trick? Idea: give the animal a reward
20. What do you do if the animal does not do the trick? Idea: don't give the animal a reward
21. Name **2** things you could give a dog to reward it. (Any 2:) a bone, a dog treat, a pat on the head, etc.

WORKBOOK

105

Name ____________________

A Story Items

1. When things are hard, what form of matter are they? solid
2. When hard matter gets hotter, which form does it change into first? liquid
3. When matter gets still hotter, which form does it change into? gas
4. At first, the frying pan was matter in the solid form.
5. How can you change a solid form of matter into a liquid? Idea: Heat it.
6. To change a liquid form of matter into a gas, you make the liquid hotter.
7. What is the coldest form of matter? solid
8. The sun is matter in the gas form.
9. What form of matter is a rock? solid
10. What form of matter is the air around you? gas
11. What form of matter did the rock turn into when the old man let go of it? gas

WORKBOOK

12. Look at the list below. Put an **M** in front of everything that is matter.

M air gas

M water liquid

M ice solid

M brick solid

M wood solid

M steam gas

M glass solid

M tea liquid

M smoke gas

M juice liquid

Look at the list above.

13. Write **solid** after everything that is matter in the solid form.
14. Write **liquid** after everything that is matter in the liquid form.
15. Write **gas** after everything that is matter in the gas form.

GO TO PART C IN YOUR TEXTBOOK.

TEXTBOOK

C Number your paper from 1 through 24.

Story Items

1. Where did Al and the old man go after they left the sun? to Earth (then to Saturn)
2. What was inside the bottle that the old man was holding? air; gas
3. In which form of matter is the air around you? gas
4. If you make air cold enough, what form of matter does it turn into first? liquid
5. If you make air still colder, what form of matter does it turn into? solid
6. Name a planet that has huge rings around it. Saturn

Skill Items

Use the words in the box to write complete sentences.

familiar	anxious	experience	miserable
galaxy	blizzard	surprised	fierce
midnight	visibility	level	demand

7. ▬ was ▬ in the ▬ ▬.
8. At ▬, he saw a ▬ ▬. midnight, familiar, galaxy

Review Items

9. Which planet has more clouds around it, Earth or Mars? Earth
10. Which planet is larger? Earth
11. Which planet is hotter? Earth
12. Why is that planet hotter? Idea: It's closer to the sun.
13. How long does it take light to travel from the sun to Earth?
    - 8 hours
    - 8 seconds
    - 8 minutes
14. How long does it take sound to travel one mile? 5 seconds

7. visibility, miserable, fierce blizzard

TEXTBOOK

15. It is quiet inside a jet plane that is going 900 miles per hour because the plane is moving faster than ▬. sound (of the engines)
16. How many forms of matter are there? 3
17. How many miles does light travel in one second? 186 thousand (miles)
18. Name **2** cities in Colorado. Greeley, Denver
19. Name one city in Utah. Salt Lake City
20. When you teach an animal a simple trick, when do you reward the animal?
21. When don't you reward the animal?
22. Let's say that you want to teach an animal a very hard trick. Can the animal do the trick at first? no
23. What will happen if the animal doesn't receive any rewards until it does the trick?
24. So when you're teaching the animal a hard trick, what do you reward the animal for doing? Idea: for trying to do the trick

20. Idea: when it does the trick
21. Idea: when the animal doesn't do the trick
23. Idea: The animal will stop trying to do the trick.

WORKBOOK

106

Name ____________________

A Story Items

1. Al and the old man were on several planets with the bottle of air. On which planet did they fill the bottle with air? Earth
2. Then Al and the old man took the bottle of air to a planet that has rings. Which planet was that? Saturn
3. Which planet did Al and the old man go to next? Pluto
4. In what form of matter is air on Saturn? liquid
5. In what form of matter is air on Earth? gas
6. In what form of matter is air on Pluto? solid
7. Which planet is colder, Saturn or Pluto? Pluto
8. Why is that planet colder? Idea: It is farther from the sun.
9. What form of matter is water? liquid
10. What form of matter is steam? gas
11. What form of matter is ice? solid
12. How can you change a liquid form of matter into a solid? Ideas: Cool it; make it colder.
13. How can you change a liquid form of matter into a gas? Ideas: Heat it; make it hotter.
14. What was strange about Anywhere Street? Ideas: It was empty; no cars; no people
15. How did Al feel about himself when he realized that he understood matter? Ideas: smart; good; proud; happy

WORKBOOK

B Review Items

16. **Write the letters** of the 5 things that are matter in the solid form.
a, b, c, f, j

17. **Write the letters** of the 4 things that are matter in the liquid form.
d, e, h, k

18. **Write the letters** of the 3 things that are matter in the gas form.
g, i, l

a. brick	d. juice	g. smoke	j. wood
b. glass	e. milk	h. tea	k. water
c. ice	f. rock	i. air	l. steam

19. The sun is matter in the gas form.

20. What form of matter is the air around you? gas

GO TO PART C IN YOUR TEXTBOOK.

TEXTBOOK

Suddenly Al realized that he was very smart. That made him feel excited. "Wow!" he said, and laughed out loud. Then he started to run home.

C Number your paper from 1 through 18.

Skill Items

Here are 3 events that happened in the story. Write **beginning**, **middle** or **end** for each event.

1. Al suddenly realized that he was standing on a floor, not on the planet Pluto. middle
2. Al looked at cars and at buildings, and he realized that everything he looked at was matter. end
3. The old man said, "Saturn is very far from the sun." beginning

Review Items

4. Name the largest planet in the solar system. Jupiter
5. How long does it take Jupiter to spin around one time? (about) 10 hours

TEXTBOOK

6. How many miles does light travel in one second? 186 thousand (miles)
7. What else travels as fast as light? Idea: nothing

8. How many forms of matter are there? 3
9. When things are hard, what form of matter are they? solid
10. When hard matter gets hotter, which form does it change into? liquid
11. When matter gets still hotter, which form does it change into? gas

12. How can you change a solid form of matter into a liquid?
13. To change a liquid form of matter into a gas, you make the liquid ▓▓▓. hotter

14. **Write the letters** of the 5 things that are matter in the solid form.
a, b, g, j, k
15. **Write the letters** of the 5 things that are matter in the liquid form.
e, f, h, i, l
16. **Write the letters** of the 3 things that are matter in the gas form.
c, d, m

a. rock	h. soda pop
b. glass	i. tea
c. smoke	j. ice
d. air	k. wood
e. water	l. juice
f. milk	m. steam
g. brick	

17. The sun is matter in the ▓▓▓ form. gas
18. What form of matter is the air around you? gas

12. Idea: Heat it.

WORKBOOK

107

Name ______________________

A Story Items

1. Why didn't Al tell his mother he had gone to Saturn and Pluto?
Idea: She wouldn't believe him.

2. Why did Al stay up so late?
Idea: He watched a movie.

3. What did Al do in school that showed he was very tired?
Idea: He fell asleep.

4. The old man asked Al two questions. Write one of those questions.
____

5. Why did the old man disappear from the store? Idea: because Al didn't know the answers to the questions

6. What is the hottest form of any matter? gas

7. What is the next-hottest form of any matter? liquid

8. What is the coldest form of any matter? solid

9. Why didn't Al know the answers to the old man's questions?
Idea: because he hadn't studied

10. What did the sign in the store window usually say?
Go anywhere. See anything.

11. What did the sign in the store window say after Al failed the test?
Store for sale

4. (Any 1:) Which form of matter is the hottest?; Which form of matter is the coldest?

WORKBOOK

12. Where did Al go to find the answers to the questions the old man asked? to the library

13. Where did Al go after he left that place? Idea: to the old man's store

14. Why did he go there? Idea: He wanted to take the test again.

B Review Items

15. Draw arrows at **J,** at **K** and at **L** to show the way the melted rock moves.

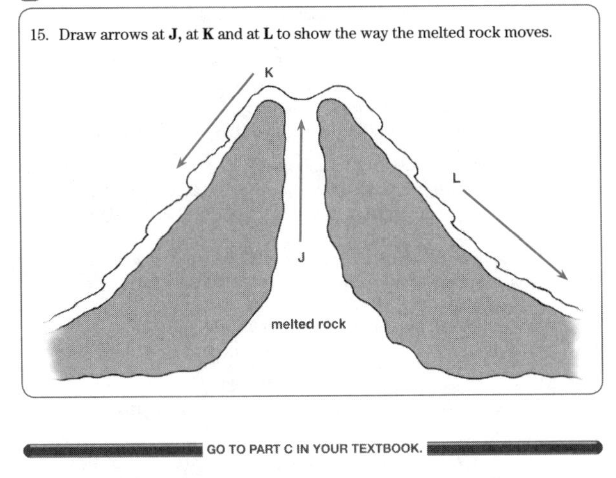

GO TO PART C IN YOUR TEXTBOOK.

TEXTBOOK

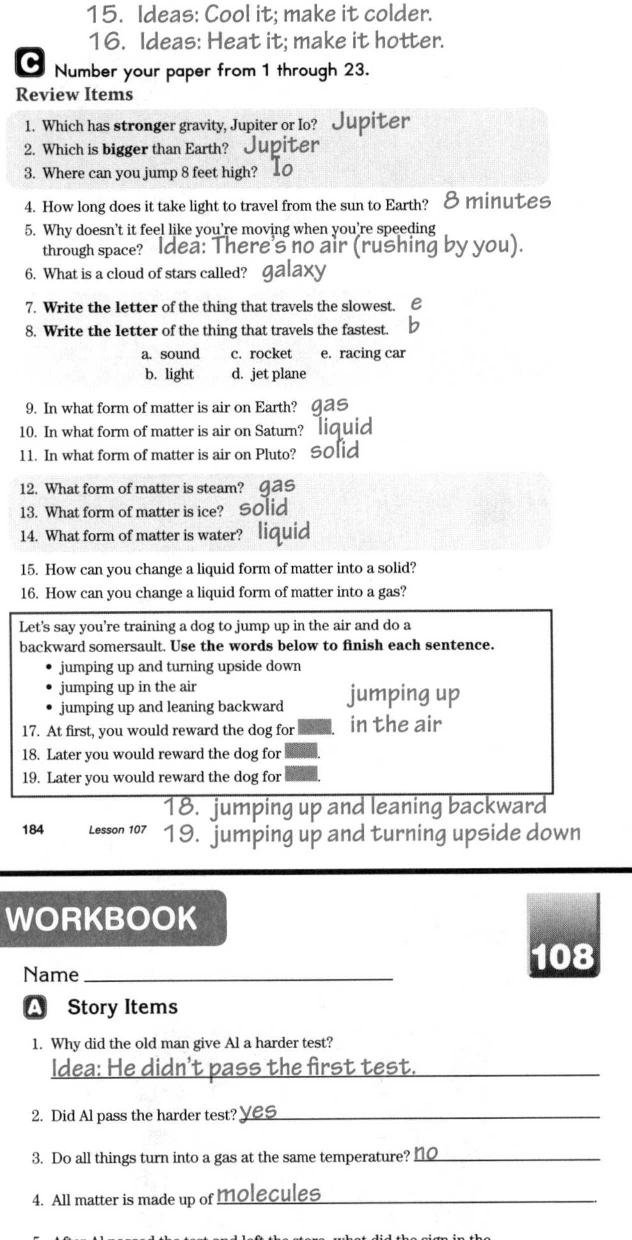

15. Ideas: Cool it; make it colder.
16. Ideas: Heat it; make it hotter.

C Number your paper from 1 through 23.

Review Items

1. Which has **stronger** gravity, Jupiter or Io? Jupiter
2. Which is **bigger** than Earth? Jupiter
3. Where can you jump 8 feet high? Io
4. How long does it take light to travel from the sun to Earth? 8 minutes
5. Why doesn't it feel like you're moving when you're speeding through space? Idea: There's no air (rushing by you).
6. What is a cloud of stars called? galaxy
7. **Write the letter** of the thing that travels the slowest. e
8. **Write the letter** of the thing that travels the fastest. b

   a. sound c. rocket e. racing car
   b. light d. jet plane

9. In what form of matter is air on Earth? gas
10. In what form of matter is air on Saturn? liquid
11. In what form of matter is air on Pluto? solid
12. What form of matter is steam? gas
13. What form of matter is ice? solid
14. What form of matter is water? liquid
15. How can you change a liquid form of matter into a solid?
16. How can you change a liquid form of matter into a gas?

Let's say you're training a dog to jump up in the air and do a backward somersault. **Use the words below to finish each sentence.**

- jumping up and turning upside down
- jumping up in the air
- jumping up and leaning backward

17. At first, you would reward the dog for ___. jumping up in the air
18. Later you would reward the dog for ___.
19. Later you would reward the dog for ___.

18. jumping up and leaning backward
19. jumping up and turning upside down

TEXTBOOK

20. The more water the glass has, the ___ the sound it makes.
    - <u>lower</u> • higher
21. Write the letter of the glass that will make the lowest ring. D
22. Write the letter of the glass that will make the highest ring. A

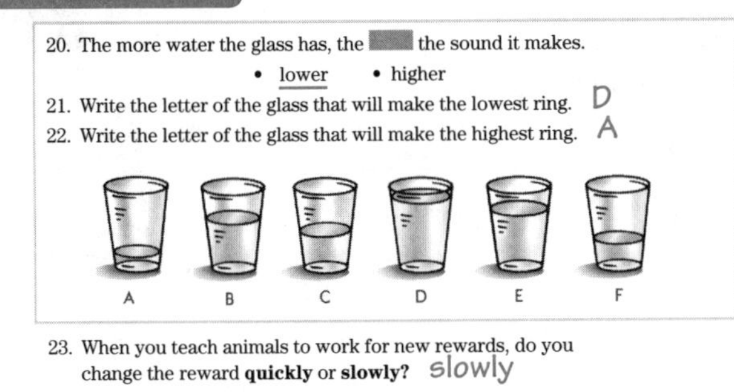

23. When you teach animals to work for new rewards, do you change the reward **quickly** or **slowly?** slowly

WORKBOOK

108

Name ______________________

A Story Items

1. Why did the old man give Al a harder test? Idea: He didn't pass the first test.
2. Did Al pass the harder test? yes
3. Do all things turn into a gas at the same temperature? no
4. All matter is made up of molecules.
5. After Al passed the test and left the store, what did the sign in the window say? Go anywhere. See anything.
6. Do sugar molecules look like air molecules? no
7. Do all sugar molecules look the same? yes
8. What did Al do that surprised his class? Ideas: raised his hand; answered a hard question; told about matter
9. What did Al want to see on his next trip? molecules
10. Name 5 things that are made up of molecules. Ideas: water, air, rock, glass, iron, etc.
11. Why can't you see molecules when you look at an object? Idea: because the molecules are too small

WORKBOOK

B Skill Items

Earth	binoculars
pressure	light
planets	stars
sun	Jupiter
Pluto	Saturn
moon	gravity
telescope	Io
sunshine	Mars
Neptune	

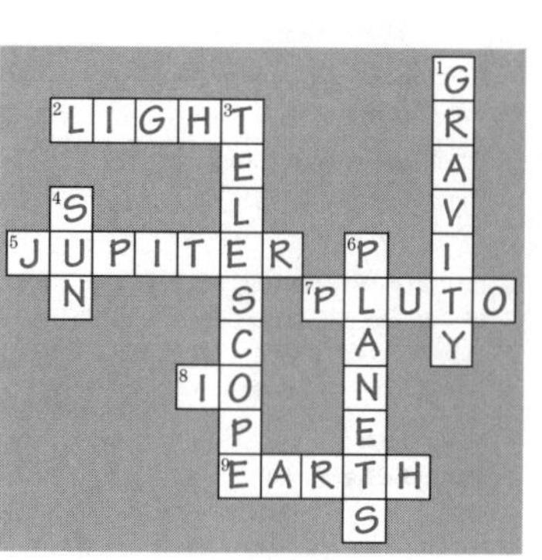

Across

2. The sun gives heat and ▬ to all the planets.
5. The largest planet in the solar system is ▬.
7. The planet that is farthest from the sun is ▬.
8. One of Jupiter's moons is named ▬.
9. The planet we live on is called ▬.

Down

1. The force that makes things fall to the ground is ▬.
3. You can look through a ▬ to see some planets.
4. The ▬ is in the middle of the solar system.
6. There are nine ▬ in the solar system.

GO TO PART C IN YOUR TEXTBOOK.

TEXTBOOK

C Number your paper from 1 through 19.

Skill Items

The crystal contained more than a billion molecules.

1. What word means **a thousand millions?** billion
2. What word means **the smallest parts of a material?** molecules
3. What word names a shiny material that has flat sides and sharp edges? crystal

Review Items

4. Write the names of the 9 planets, starting with the planet closest to the sun.
5. How many moons does Jupiter have? 63
6. Which planet has more moons, Saturn or Jupiter? Jupiter
7. Does Io move around Jupiter **fast** or **slowly?** fast
8. It takes Io about ▬ to go all the way around Jupiter. 2 days
9. When things are hard, what form of matter are they? solid
10. When hard matter gets hotter, which form does it change into? liquid
11. When matter gets still hotter, which form does it change into? gas
12. Which planet is colder, Saturn or Pluto? Pluto
13. Why is that planet colder? Idea: It is farther from the sun.
14. What is the hottest form of any matter? gas
15. What is the next-hottest form of any matter? liquid
16. What is the coldest form of any matter? solid
17. Which uses up more oxygen, jumping or walking? jumping

4. Mercury, Venus, Earth, Mars, Jupiter, Saturn, Uranus, Neptune, Pluto

TEXTBOOK

18. What planet is shown in the picture? Jupiter
19. Which is bigger, the "eye" or Earth? the eye

WORKBOOK

109

Name ______________

A Story Items

1. How did Al and the old man change to go inside the grain of sand? Ideas: shrank; grew smaller
2. The old man told Al, "A grain of sand is made of space and molecules."
3. How were the sand molecules arranged? Idea: in rows
4. The sand molecules that Al saw were in the solid form of matter.
5. **Underline** 2 things that tell about any molecules in the solid form.
   - They fly around.
   - They stay in place.
   - They are hot.
   - They are lined up.
6. The old man planned to make the grain of sand colder than room temperature.

Review Items

Use these names to answer the questions: **Tyrannosaurus, Triceratops.**

7. What is animal G? Triceratops
8. What is animal H? Tyrannosaurus

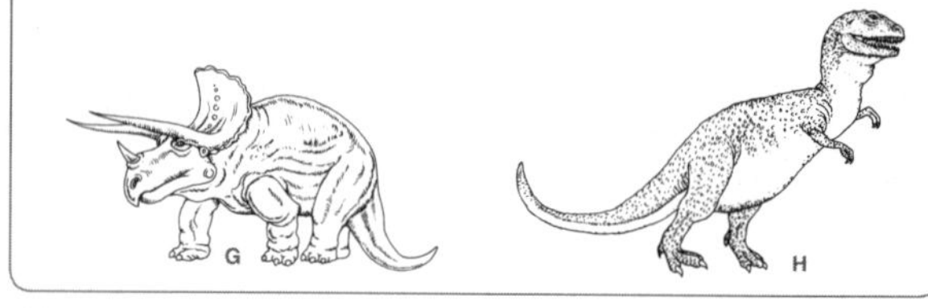

WORKBOOK

9. Name an arrow-shaped fish. barracuda
10. Write **2** facts about those fish.
11. Is the water cooler at **100 feet down** or **at the surface?** 100 feet down
12. Is all the water at 100 feet down the same temperature? no
13. What do you fill a buoyancy device with? air
14. When it is filled up, what happens to the diver? Idea: The diver moves up/floats/goes to the surface.
15. When it is empty, what happens to the diver? Idea: The diver moves down/sinks.

GO TO PART C IN YOUR TEXTBOOK.

10. Ideas (any 2): They're very dangerous; their mouths are filled with sharp teeth; they grow to almost 2 meters long; etc.

TEXTBOOK

Al looked. "I see it," he said. Then Al saw another molecule and another molecule. The molecules seemed to be in a row. Now Al could see another row of molecules above the first row. Every molecule was vibrating very fast.

Al said, "The molecules are all lined up in rows."

The old man said, "These molecules are in the solid form of matter. That is why they are lined up. Remember this rule: When molecules are in the solid form, they are lined up and they stay in place."

"That's really interesting," Al said, looking above the top row of vibrating molecules.

The old man continued, "These molecules are the same temperature as the room. If we make the grain of sand colder and colder, you will see a change in the molecules."

"I don't understand," Al said. "These molecules are in the solid form of matter. The solid form of matter is the coldest form. So how could the molecules change if the matter gets colder? The molecules will still be in the solid form."

The old man smiled. "I see that you are using the information you have learned. Good for you, my friend. And you are right. The molecules will remain in the solid form of matter, but watch what happens to them when the temperature gets lower than the temperature on Pluto."

C Number your paper from 1 through 24.

Skill Items

Use the words in the box to write complete sentences.

billion	vibrating	galaxy	chilly	familiar
library	molecules	midnight	crystal	confused

1. At ___, he saw a ___ ___.
2. The ___ contained more than a ___ ___.

1. At midnight, he saw a familiar galaxy.
2. The crystal contained more than a billion molecules.

TEXTBOOK

3. What is a person doing when the person makes an object for the first time? inventing
4. The person who makes an object for the first time is called an ___. inventor
5. The object the person makes is called an ___. invention
6. How can you change a solid form of matter into a liquid? Ideas: Heat it; make it hotter.
7. To change a liquid form of matter into a gas, you make the liquid ___. hotter
8. **Write the letters** of the 5 things that are matter in the solid form. a, c, g, i, l
9. **Write the letters** of the 4 things that are matter in the liquid form. e, f, h, k
10. **Write the letters** of the 3 things that are matter in the gas form. b, d, j

a. glass
b. smoke
c. brick
d. air
e. water
f. milk
g. rock
h. tea
i. wood
j. steam
k. juice
l. ice

11. Do all things turn into a gas at the same temperature? no
12. All matter is made of ___. molecules
13. Do sugar molecules look like air molecules? no
14. Do all sugar molecules look the same? yes
15. Why can't you see molecules when you look at an object? Idea: They are too small.
16. Most sled-dog teams have an ___ number of dogs.
    - odd
    - even
17. For the Iditarod, a sled-dog team can't have more than ___ dogs. 16

TEXTBOOK

18. Which letter in the picture shows the wheel dogs? O
19. Which letter shows the lead dogs? I
20. Which letter shows the swing dogs? N
21. Which letter shows where the musher is most of the time? X
22. Which letter shows the tug lines? S
23. Which letter shows the gang line? Z

24. What happens if a sled dog doesn't pass the Iditarod's health examination? Idea: It cannot run the race.

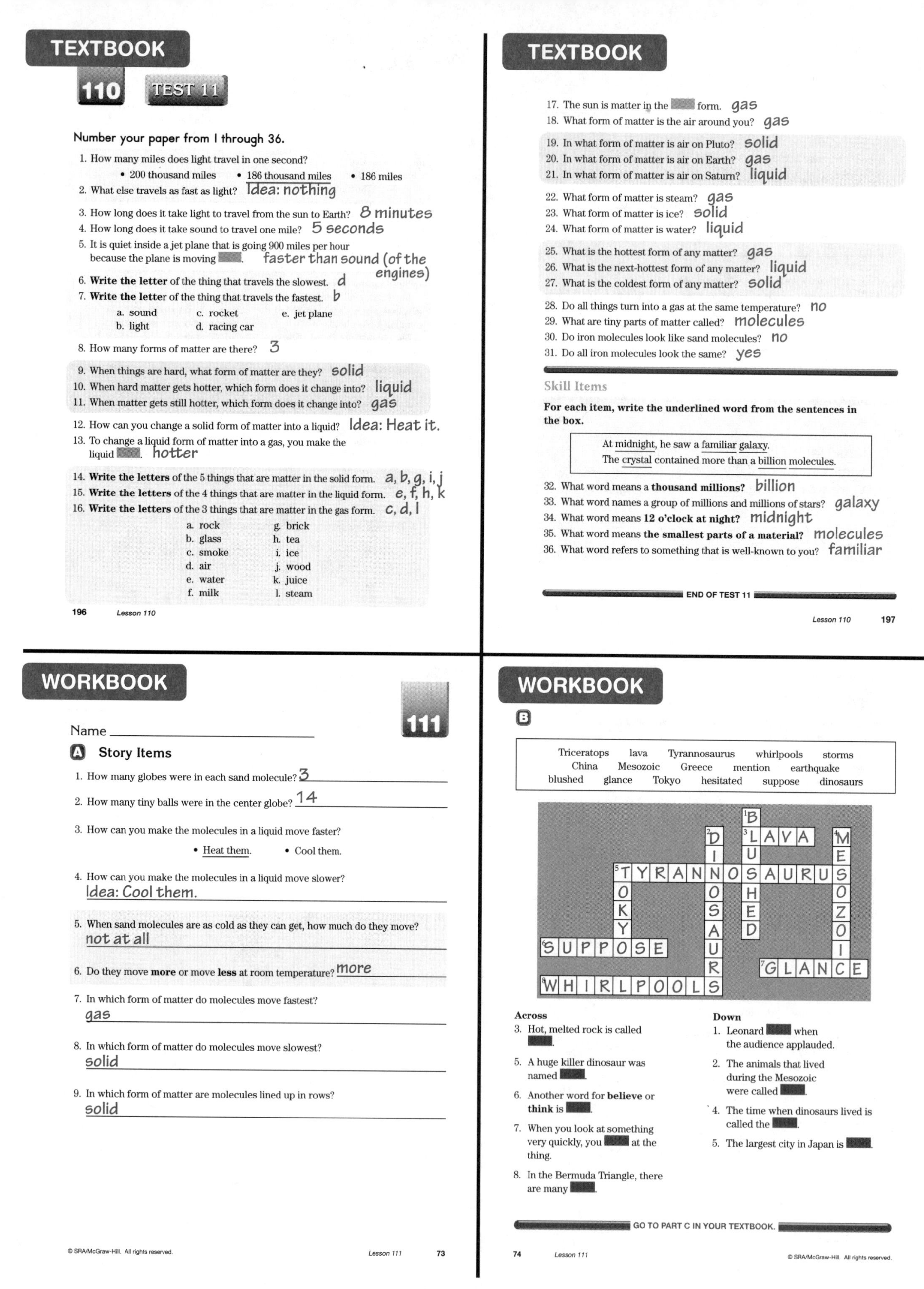

TEXTBOOK

110 TEST 11

Number your paper from 1 through 36.

1. How many miles does light travel in one second?
   - 200 thousand miles
   - 186 thousand miles
   - 186 miles
2. What else travels as fast as light? Idea: nothing
3. How long does it take light to travel from the sun to Earth? 8 minutes
4. How long does it take sound to travel one mile? 5 seconds
5. It is quiet inside a jet plane that is going 900 miles per hour because the plane is moving ▬. faster than sound (of the engines)
6. **Write the letter** of the thing that travels the slowest. d
7. **Write the letter** of the thing that travels the fastest. b
   - a. sound
   - b. light
   - c. rocket
   - d. racing car
   - e. jet plane
8. How many forms of matter are there? 3
9. When things are hard, what form of matter are they? solid
10. When hard matter gets hotter, which form does it change into? liquid
11. When matter gets still hotter, which form does it change into? gas
12. How can you change a solid form of matter into a liquid? Idea: Heat it.
13. To change a liquid form of matter into a gas, you make the liquid ▬. hotter
14. **Write the letters** of the 5 things that are matter in the solid form. a, b, g, i, j
15. **Write the letters** of the 4 things that are matter in the liquid form. e, f, h, k
16. **Write the letters** of the 3 things that are matter in the gas form. c, d, l
   - a. rock
   - b. glass
   - c. smoke
   - d. air
   - e. water
   - f. milk
   - g. brick
   - h. tea
   - i. ice
   - j. wood
   - k. juice
   - l. steam

196 Lesson 110

TEXTBOOK

17. The sun is matter in the ▬ form. gas
18. What form of matter is the air around you? gas
19. In what form of matter is air on Pluto? solid
20. In what form of matter is air on Earth? gas
21. In what form of matter is air on Saturn? liquid
22. What form of matter is steam? gas
23. What form of matter is ice? solid
24. What form of matter is water? liquid
25. What is the hottest form of any matter? gas
26. What is the next-hottest form of any matter? liquid
27. What is the coldest form of any matter? solid
28. Do all things turn into a gas at the same temperature? no
29. What are tiny parts of matter called? molecules
30. Do iron molecules look like sand molecules? no
31. Do all iron molecules look the same? yes

Skill Items

For each item, write the underlined word from the sentences in the box.

> At midnight, he saw a familiar galaxy.
> The crystal contained more than a billion molecules.

32. What word means a **thousand millions?** billion
33. What word names a group of millions and millions of stars? galaxy
34. What word means **12 o'clock at night?** midnight
35. What word means **the smallest parts of a material?** molecules
36. What word refers to something that is well-known to you? familiar

END OF TEST 11

Lesson 110 197

WORKBOOK

111

Name ____________

A Story Items

1. How many globes were in each sand molecule? 3
2. How many tiny balls were in the center globe? 14
3. How can you make the molecules in a liquid move faster?
   - Heat them.
   - Cool them.
4. How can you make the molecules in a liquid move slower? Idea: Cool them.
5. When sand molecules are as cold as they can get, how much do they move? not at all
6. Do they move **more** or move **less** at room temperature? more
7. In which form of matter do molecules move fastest? gas
8. In which form of matter do molecules move slowest? solid
9. In which form of matter are molecules lined up in rows? solid

 Lesson 111 73

WORKBOOK

B

> Triceratops lava Tyrannosaurus whirlpools storms
> China Mesozoic Greece mention earthquake
> blushed glance Tokyo hesitated suppose dinosaurs

Across

3. Hot, melted rock is called ▬.
5. A huge killer dinosaur was named ▬.
6. Another word for **believe** or **think** is ▬.
7. When you look at something very quickly, you ▬ at the thing.
8. In the Bermuda Triangle, there are many ▬.

Down

1. Leonard ▬ when the audience applauded.
2. The animals that lived during the Mesozoic were called ▬.
4. The time when dinosaurs lived is called the ▬.
5. The largest city in Japan is ▬.

GO TO PART C IN YOUR TEXTBOOK.

74 Lesson 111

TEXTBOOK

floated, he tried to make sure that he would remember the things he had seen. He remembered how the molecules looked when they were as cold as they could get. He remembered how they looked in the solid form at room temperature. He remembered how they changed when they got hot enough to go into the liquid form. And he remembered how they looked in the gas form.

Suddenly Al noticed that everything was getting darker and darker. Now Al could see that he was no longer small. He was standing inside the old man's store.

The old man said, "You wanted molecules. You got molecules. Remember everything that you have seen. Pass the test and pay for your trip. Then you can go on another trip. Go anywhere. See anything."

Al said, "Don't worry. I'll pass the test."

C Number your paper from 1 through 22.

Story Items

1. Write the letters of the 2 ways that molecules charge when they go from a solid to a liquid. b, d
   - a. They move slower.
   - b. They move faster.
   - c. They stay in rows.
   - d. They do not stay in rows.
2. Did Al see many molecules when the sand was in the gas form? no
3. In which form of matter are molecules closest together? solid
4. In which form of matter are molecules farthest apart? gas

Review Items

5. Which planet has more gravity? B
6. How do you know? Idea: It's

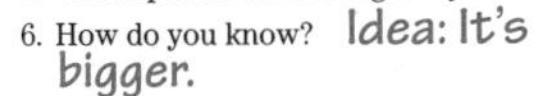

bigger.

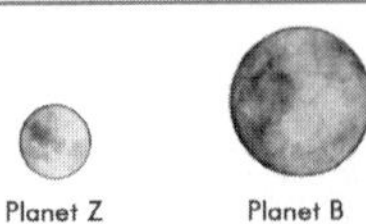

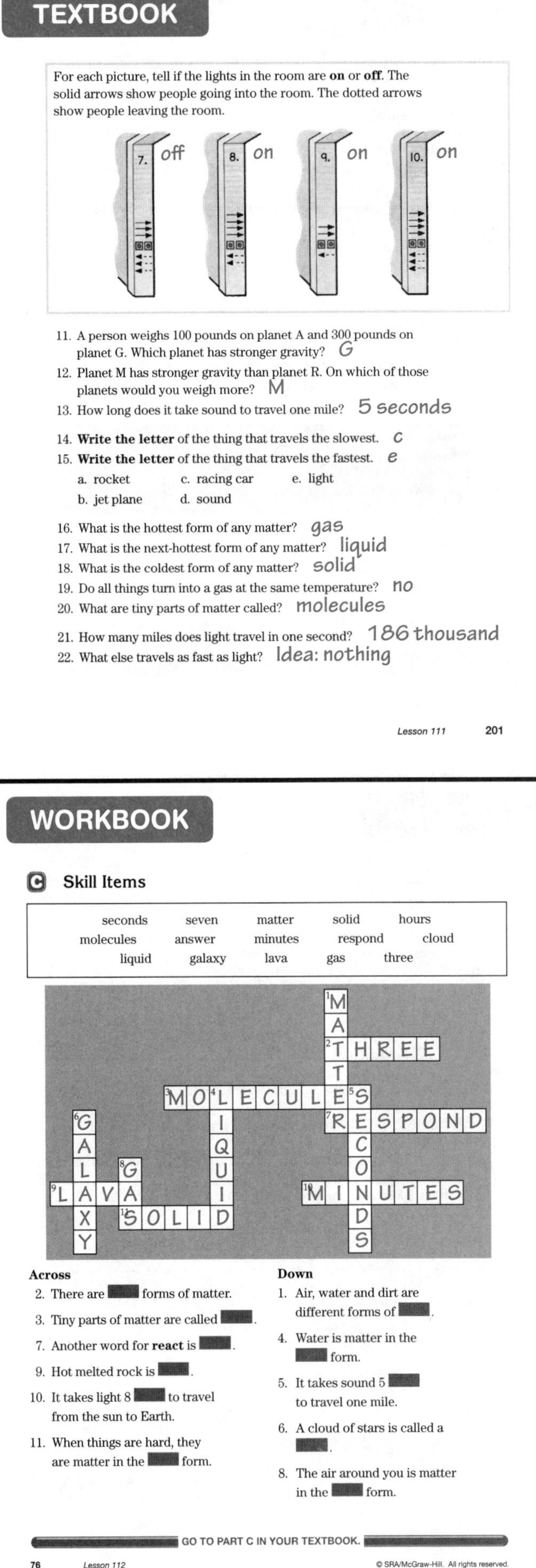

TEXTBOOK

For each picture, tell if the lights in the room are **on** or **off**. The solid arrows show people going into the room. The dotted arrows show people leaving the room.

7. off
8. on
9. on
10. on

11. A person weighs 100 pounds on planet A and 300 pounds on planet G. Which planet has stronger gravity? G
12. Planet M has stronger gravity than planet R. On which of those planets would you weigh more? M
13. How long does it take sound to travel one mile? 5 seconds
14. **Write the letter** of the thing that travels the slowest. c
15. **Write the letter** of the thing that travels the fastest. e
    - a. rocket
    - b. jet plane
    - c. racing car
    - d. sound
    - e. light
16. What is the hottest form of any matter? gas
17. What is the next-hottest form of any matter? liquid
18. What is the coldest form of any matter? solid
19. Do all things turn into a gas at the same temperature? no
20. What are tiny parts of matter called? molecules
21. How many miles does light travel in one second? 186 thousand
22. What else travels as fast as light? Idea: nothing

WORKBOOK

4. Ideas: because the old man told him about molecules; because Al went on a trip/saw molecules

Name ________ **112**

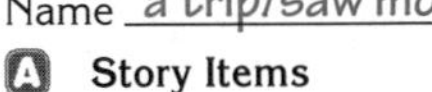

A Story Items

1. Al wanted to tell Angela his secret about Anywhere Street, but part of his mind told him that Angela Idea: would not believe him.
2. Did she believe Al's story about the old man and the trips? no
3. Did Angela believe that Al knew a lot about molecules? yes
4. Why did Al know so much about molecules?
5. Where did he go after school? to the (old man's) store
6. The old man gave Al a test on molecules. Write the 2 questions the old man asked. Then write the answers to the questions.

   Question 1: Idea: How can we make molecules stand still?

   Answer 1: Ideas: Cool them; make them as cold as they can get.

   Question 2: Idea: How can you make molecules go very fast?

   Answer 2: Ideas: Heat them; make the molecules hotter.
7. After the test, Al asked the old man a question. What did he want the old man to do? Idea: take Angela on a trip (with them)
8. How will Angela pay for her trip?

   Idea: She'll have to pass a test on what she sees.

B Review Items

9. How many moons does Saturn have? 47
10. How many moons does Jupiter have? 63
11. How far is it from Earth to Jupiter? 400 million miles

WORKBOOK

C Skill Items

seconds, seven, matter, solid, hours, molecules, answer, minutes, respond, cloud, liquid, galaxy, lava, gas, three

												1M						
												A						
												2T	H	R	E	E		
												T						
					3M	O	4L	E	C	U	L	E	5S					
	6G						I					7R	E	S	P	O	N	D
	A						Q						C					
	L		8G				U						O					
9L	A	V	A				I				10M	I	N	U	T	E	S	
	X		11S	O	L	I	D						D					
	Y												S					

Across

2. There are ▬ forms of matter.
3. Tiny parts of matter are called ▬.
7. Another word for **react** is ▬.
9. Hot melted rock is ▬.
10. It takes light 8 ▬ to travel from the sun to Earth.
11. When things are hard, they are matter in the ▬ form.

Down

1. Air, water and dirt are different forms of ▬.
4. Water is matter in the ▬ form.
5. It takes sound 5 ▬ to travel one mile.
6. A cloud of stars is called a ▬.
8. The air around you is matter in the ▬ form.

GO TO PART C IN YOUR TEXTBOOK.

TEXTBOOK

The old man straightened up and waved his hand. "Now where do you want to go? Remember—go anywhere. See anything."

Al asked, "Could I take my sister with me on the next trip? She's smart and she'd really love to go on these trips."

The old man smiled. He said, "Bring her with you. But remember—she'll have to pass a test on what she sees."

"She'll pass the test," Al said.

Al ran from the store. The bell went ding, ding. Al could hardly wait to tell Angela.

C Number your paper from 1 through 17.

Review Items

1. How can you make the molecules in a liquid move slower?
   - Heat them.
   - Cool them.
2. How can you make the molecules in a liquid move faster? Idea: Heat them.
3. In which form of matter do molecules move fastest? gas
4. In which form of matter do molecules move slowest? solid
5. In which form of matter are molecules lined up in rows? solid
6. In which form of matter are molecules farthest apart? gas
7. In which form of matter are molecules closest together? solid
8. When sand molecules are as cold as they can get, how much do they move? Idea: not at all
9. Do they move **more** or **less** at room temperature? more
10. Write the letters of the **2** ways that molecules change when they go from a solid to a liquid. b, c
    a. They stay in rows.
    b. They do not stay in rows.
    c. They move faster.
    d. They move slower.

TEXTBOOK

11. What are clouds made of? (tiny) drops of water
12. What kind of cloud does the picture show? storm clouds
13. What happens to a drop of water at **B?** Idea: It freezes.

Use these words to answer items 14–16:
- **swing dogs**
- **wheel dogs**
- **lead dogs**

14. These dogs are very smart, and other dogs obey them. lead dogs
15. These dogs are very good followers, and they are smart. swing dogs
16. These dogs are responsible for freeing the sled when it gets stuck. wheel dogs
17. Why can't you see molecules when you look at an object? Idea: They are too small.

WORKBOOK

113

Name ____________________

A Story Items

1. After supper, Al said to Angela, "Let's go for a walk. I want to tell you something." What did he want to tell her? Idea: that she could go on a trip
2. Al kept making a picture of what Angela's face would look like when she found out that Al had been telling the truth. He imagined that her mouth would Idea: fall open.
3. He imagined that her eyes would Idea: get wide.
4. How did the picture that Al imagined compare to the one that he actually saw? Idea: It was the same as what actually happened.
5. Was Angela surprised that there really was an Anywhere Street? yes
6. How did Angela feel when the old man first appeared? Ideas: surprised; scared; etc.
7. Where did the old man take Al and Angela? Ideas: to Africa; to a jungle
8. Why did Al take off his jacket and open his shirt? Idea: because it was very hot
9. What animal charged at Al and Angela? elephant

WORKBOOK

B Review Items

10. What do sled dogs wear to protect their feet? booties
11. **Underline the 4 items that tell what could happen to a sled dog's feet if they didn't have protection.**
    a. slipping on hard snow
    b. snowballs between the pads
    c. icicles on their ankles
    d. stiff legs
    e. long claws
    f. cuts that do not heal well
    g. cuts from ice and frozen snow
12. If booties on a sled dog are too tight, what could happen? ____________________
13. If booties are too loose, what could happen? Idea: They could fall off.
14. What command tells sled dogs to turn right? gee
15. What command tells sled dogs to move straight ahead? mush
16. What command tells sled dogs to turn left? haw
17. During the Iditarod, what does a musher have to do with any dogs that are injured? ____________________
18. According to the Iditarod rules, there must be at least how many dogs on the gang line at the end of the race? at least 5

GO TO PART C IN YOUR TEXTBOOK.

12. Ideas: The dog's blood cannot circulate around the paws; the dog's ankles could swell up.
17. Idea: Drop off the dog at the next checkpoint.

TEXTBOOK

3. Mercury, Venus, Earth, Mars, Jupiter, Saturn, Uranus, Neptune, Pluto

C Number your paper from 1 through 22.

Skill Items

12. Ideas: heat snow to melt it; haul water from a stream

The poem they created was nonsense.

1. What word means **no sense at all?** nonsense
2. What word means **made?** created

Review Items

13. branches from evergreen trees

3. Write the names of the 9 planets, starting with the planet closest to the sun.
4. In which form of matter is air on Saturn? liquid
5. In which form of matter is air on Pluto? solid
6. In which form of matter is air on Earth? gas
7. In which form of matter do molecules move fastest? gas
8. In which form of matter do molecules move slowest? solid
9. In which form of matter are molecules lined up in rows? solid
10. How many miles does light travel in one second? 186 thousand (miles)
11. What else travels as fast as light? Idea: nothing
12. During the Iditarod, how do mushers get water for their dogs?
13. What do mushers usually use to make beds for their dogs?
14. What's the name of the first woman to win the Iditarod? Libby Riddles
15. In what year did she win it? 1985
16. During the Iditarod, is the snow deeper **on the trail** or **off the trail?** off the trail
17. Why? Idea: No one had been over the snow recently.
18. The rules of the Iditarod state that every musher must rest for ___ hours at one checkpoint and must rest for ___ hours at two other checkpoints. 24/8
19. This rule was put in to protect the ___.
    - dogs
    - race officials
    - mushers
20. In what year was the first Iditarod? 1973
21. During the first running of the Iditarod, how many dogs died during the race? 30
22. During more recent years, how many dogs die during each race? 2 or 3

WORKBOOK

Name ____________________

A Story Items

1. What happened to the elephant that was chasing Angela? Idea: It disappeared.
2. Where did the old man take Al and Angela after they left the jungle? Idea: the ocean
3. Who wanted to go there? Al
4. How deep was the **bottom** of the ocean where Al and Angela were?
   - 200 feet
   - 2 miles
   - 20 feet
5. What covers some of the rocks? coral
6. What is coral made of?
   - animal shells
   - rocks
   - insects
7. When the old man blew up the balloon, it was about as big as an apple
8. The old man stopped at 30 feet from the surface. As he went up, did the balloon have **more** or **less** air pressure on it? less (pressure)
9. So did the balloon get **bigger** or **smaller?** bigger
10. Then what happened to the balloon? Idea: It burst.

WORKBOOK

11. Where would a balloon be bigger—at 60 feet below the surface or at 120 feet below the surface? 60 feet below (the surface)

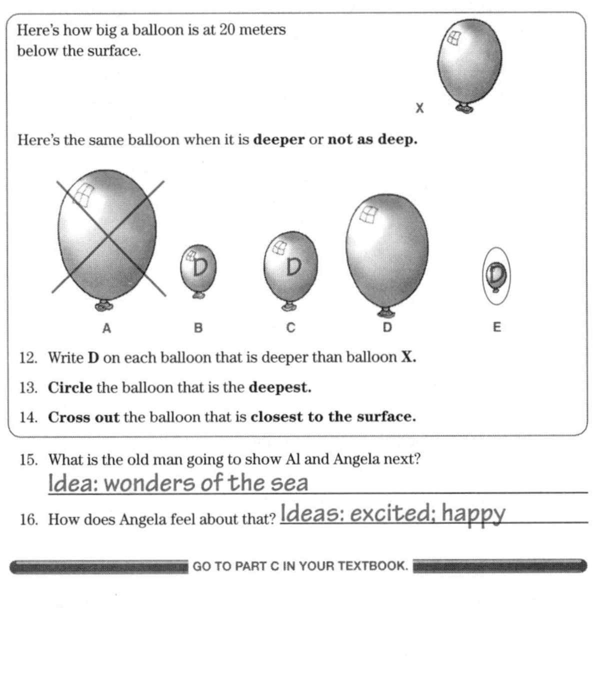

Here's how big a balloon is at 20 meters below the surface.
X
Here's the same balloon when it is **deeper** or **not as deep.**
A
B
C
D
E
D
D
D

12. Write **D** on each balloon that is deeper than balloon **X.**
13. **Circle** the balloon that is the **deepest.**
14. **Cross out** the balloon that is **closest to the surface.**

15. What is the old man going to show Al and Angela next? Idea: wonders of the sea
16. How does Angela feel about that? Ideas: excited; happy

GO TO PART C IN YOUR TEXTBOOK.

TEXTBOOK

less pressure on it. After a few moments, Al said, "I'll remember everything."

"Me too," his sister said.

"Good," the old man said. "Now let's go back down and see some of the wonders of the sea."

Al was ready to see them. Angela said, "That sounds great."

C Number your paper from 1 through 22.

Story Items

1. There's a fish at each letter. Write the letter of the fish with the **greatest pressure** on it. F
2. Write the letter of the fish with the **least pressure** on it. H

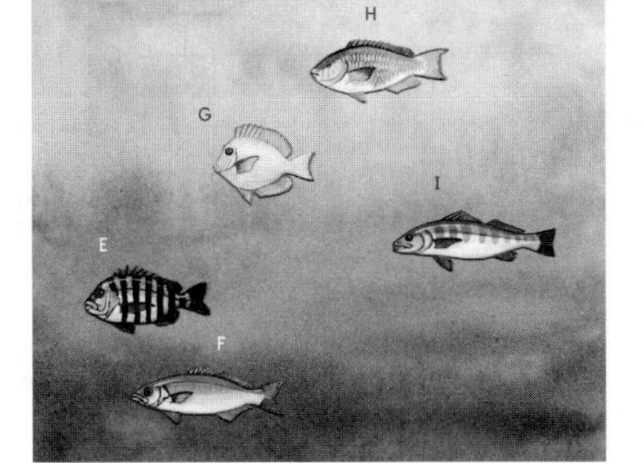

TEXTBOOK

Skill Items

Write the word from the box that means the same thing as the underlined part of each sentence.

survives	section	daydreamed	concluded
however	surrounds	experience	demonstrated

3. The fence goes all the way around the yard. surrounds
4. He cleaned his part of the room. section
5. They showed how the machine works. demonstrated

Use the words in the box to write complete sentences.

usual	nonsense	insisted	molecules	created
impressive	crystal	honest	billion	

6. The ▬ contained more than a ▬ ▬. crystal, billion, molecules
7. The poem they ▬ was ▬. created, nonsense

Review Items

8. If something weighed 50 pounds on Earth, would it weigh more than 50 pounds on our moon? no
9. Which is larger, Earth or Jupiter? Jupiter
10. If something weighed 20 pounds on Earth, would it weigh **more than 20 pounds** or **less than 20 pounds** on Jupiter?

11. Write the letter of the footprint made by the lightest animal. K
12. Write the letter of the footprint made by the heaviest animal. L

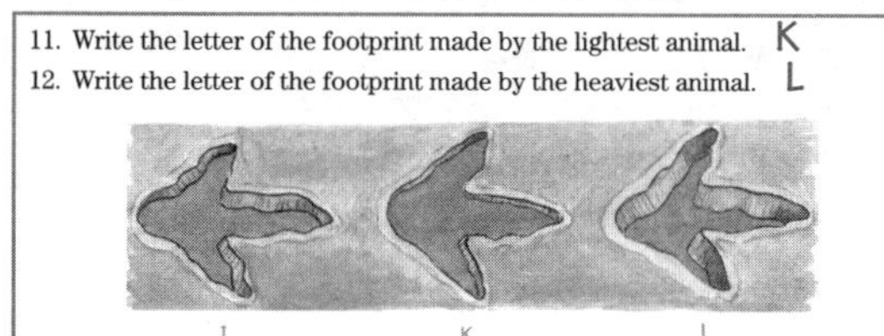

10. more than 20 pounds

TEXTBOOK

13. What color is lava when it's very hot? orange
14. What color is lava after it cools a little bit? brown
15. What color is lava after it's completely cooled? gray

- brown
- gray
- orange

Write the name of each kind of coral.

16. brain coral

17. staghorn coral

18. red coral

19. An underwater hill that is covered with coral is called a coral ▬. reef
20. Name the woman who finished the Iditarod sixteen times. Susan Butcher
21. How many times did she **enter** the Iditarod? 17
22. How many times did she finish in first place? 4

WORKBOOK

115

Name ______________________

A Story Items

1. Al and Angela saw a huge whale. Name that whale. blue whale
2. The old man told Al and Angela, "The squid moves by squirting out water."
3. Name the largest animal in the world. blue whale
4. That animal weighs more than 10 elephants.
5. Are whales fish? no
6. What's the name of a smaller whale that is black and white? killer whale
7. Are whales **warm-blooded** or **cold-blooded?** warm-blooded

8. Name the animal in the picture. squid
9. Which arrow shows the way the animal squirts water out? B
10. Which arrow shows the way the animal will move? A
11. Make a **T** on a tentacle.

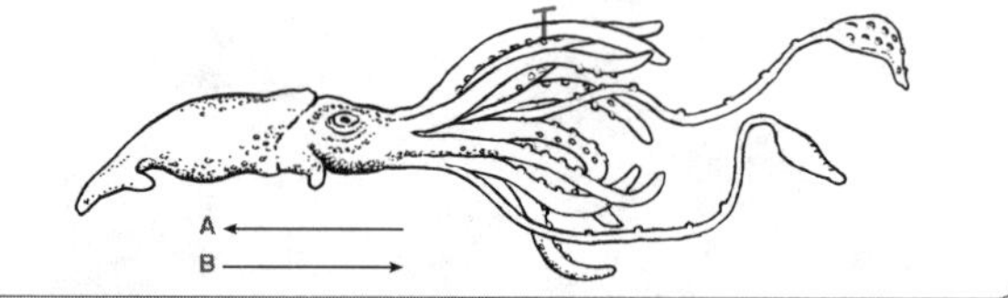

WORKBOOK

B Review Items

The picture shows marks left by an animal.

12. Which arrow shows the direction the animal is moving? G
13. Write the letter of the part that shows the mark left by the animal's tail. E
14. Write the letter of the part that shows a footprint. D

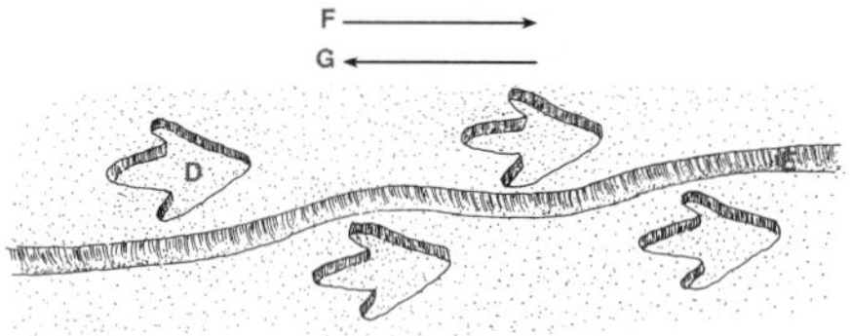

F ⟶
G ⟵

D

15. In which form of matter are molecules lined up in rows? solid
16. In which form of matter do molecules move slowest? solid
17. In which form of matter do molecules move fastest? gas
18. Where would a balloon be bigger—at 90 feet below the surface or at 60 feet below the surface? 60 feet below (the surface)

GO TO PART C IN YOUR TEXTBOOK.

TEXTBOOK

C Number your paper from 1 through 21.

Story Items

1. What animal did the giant squid attack? blue whale
2. Did the squid kill that animal? no
3. What kind of animals scared the blue whale? killer whales
4. Why was the blue whale afraid of those animals? Idea: because killer whales can kill blue whales
5. At the beginning of today's story, the old man blew up a balloon. That balloon was the size of a ___. watermelon
6. What happened to the balloon as the old man went deeper and deeper? Idea: It got smaller (and smaller).
7. Why did that happen? Idea: There was more pressure on it.
8. How many feet deep did the old man take Al and Angela? 300 (feet)
9. What color was the water down there?
   - light blue
   - dark purple
   - green
10. Al and Angela saw an animal that looked like a giant tube with many arms. Name that animal. giant squid
11. About how long was the animal? 50 feet
12. What are the animal's arms called? tentacles
13. The animal's arms stick to things because they are covered with ___. Idea: small cups

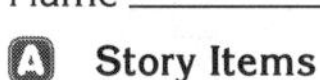

Review Items

14. Name **3** things an Iditarod musher does at checkpoints.
15. Why are checkpoints called checkpoints?
16. How does food get to the checkpoints? Idea: airplanes deliver it
17. About how far apart are the checkpoints? 50 miles
18. About how many checkpoints are there between Anchorage and Nome? 24

14. (Any 3:) rest their teams; make repairs; feed their dogs; drop off injured or sick dogs; get food; have veterinarians check the dogs
15. Idea: because race officials check that all mushers pass through each checkpoint

TEXTBOOK

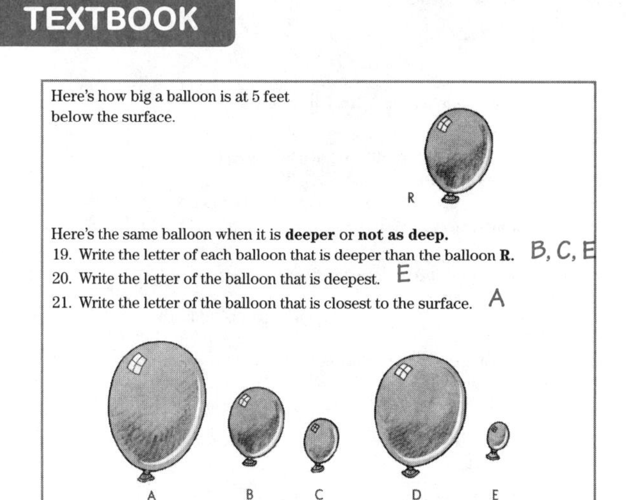

Here's how big a balloon is at 5 feet below the surface.

Here's the same balloon when it is **deeper** or **not as deep.**

19. Write the letter of each balloon that is deeper than the balloon **R.** B, C, E
20. Write the letter of the balloon that is deepest. E
21. Write the letter of the balloon that is closest to the surface. A

WORKBOOK

116

Name ______________________

A Story Items

1. The old man made a high sound. What did that tell the killer whales to do? Idea: swim away (fast)
2. Did the killer whales kill the blue whale? no
3. How deep is the deepest part of the ocean?
   - 60 miles
   - 10 miles
   - 6 miles
4. Do plants grow on the bottom of the deepest part of the ocean? no
5. Tell why. Idea: because there is no sunlight
6. Do the fish on the bottom of the ocean look like fish near the surface? no
7. What is animal A? giant squid
8. What is animal B? killer whale
9. What is animal C? blue whale

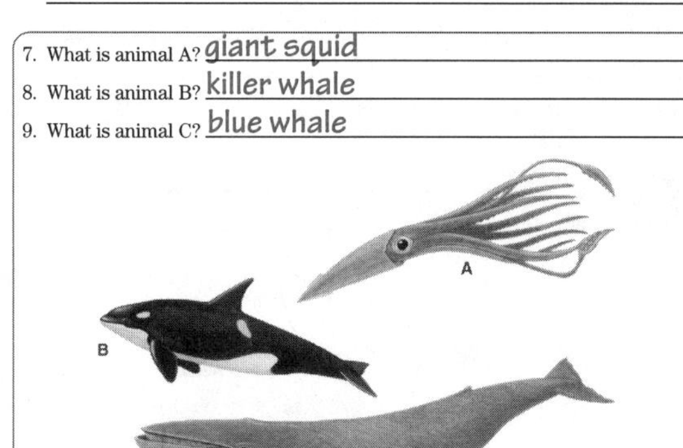

WORKBOOK

10. When Al and Angela got home, their mother was holding a package. Who was the package from? the old man
11. What was inside the package? a book
12. What was shown in the picture on the cover? Idea: a blue whale and a giant squid
13. Some pictures in the book showed things that Al and Angela had seen on their trip. Name **2** of those things. (Any 2:) blue whale; giant squid; killer whales; strange deep-sea fish; balloon rising and getting bigger
14. Where did Al take the book the next day? to school
15. Who made fun of Al in school? Homer
16. How did the students in Al's class like his explanations of the things in the book? Idea: They liked him.
17. What did the students do when Al finished his talk? Idea: applauded

GO TO PART C IN YOUR TEXTBOOK.

TEXTBOOK

C Number your paper from 1 through 22.

Skill Items

The squid wriggled its tentacles.

1. What word names a sea animal? squid
2. What word means **squirmed around in all directions?** wriggled
3. What word refers to arms that are like huge snakes? tentacles

Here are 3 events that happened in the story. Write **beginning, middle** or **end** for each event.

4. Here's what somebody said: "That sound is part of the language killer whales use." beginning
5. After Al and Angela left the store, Angela asked, "Did we really go to the bottom of the ocean?" middle
6. Al showed the book to his class and started to explain. end

Review Items

7. In what state is the Iditarod sled-dog race? Alaska
8. In which city does it begin? Anchorage
9. In which city does it end? Nome
10. The Iditarod is about ▬ miles from start to finish.
    - 500 • 1600 • <u>1100</u>
11. In most years, the race takes about ▬.
    - a week • <u>10 days</u> • 2 weeks
12. The person who drives a sled-dog team is called a ▬. musher
13. The drivers of the sled-dog teams command the dogs by using their ▬.
    - reins • <u>voices</u> • steering wheels

TEXTBOOK

14. There's a fish at each letter. Write the letter of the fish with the **greatest pressure** on it. D
15. Write the letter of the fish with the **least pressure** on it. A

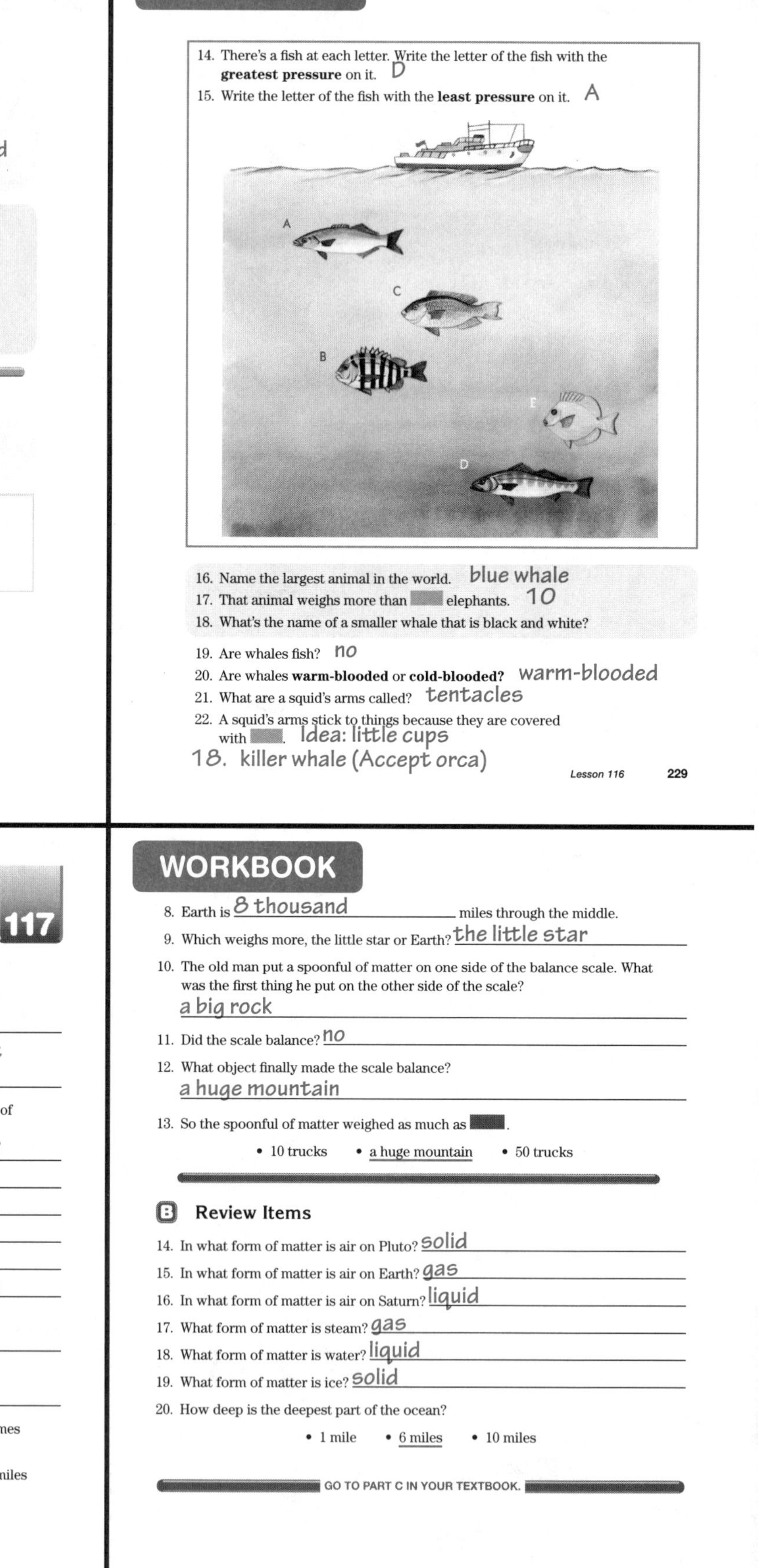

16. Name the largest animal in the world. blue whale
17. That animal weighs more than ▬ elephants. 10
18. What's the name of a smaller whale that is black and white?
19. Are whales fish? no
20. Are whales **warm-blooded** or **cold-blooded?** warm-blooded
21. What are a squid's arms called? tentacles
22. A squid's arms stick to things because they are covered with ▬. Idea: little cups

18. killer whale (Accept orca)

WORKBOOK

117

Name ______________________

A Story Items

1. Where did Al and Angela go after school?
   Idea: to the old man's store
2. Why was Angela walking so fast? Idea: She wanted to get to the store/to go on a trip.
3. The old man asked Al and Angela many questions about the sea. Write 2 of those questions. Then write the answers. (Any 2:)
   Question 1: A. How does a squid make itself move? B. How deep is the ocean?
   Answer 1: A. by squirting out water B. 6 miles
   Question 2: C. What's the largest animal? D. How big is the largest animal?
   Answer 2: C. blue whale D. as big as 10 elephants
4. Where did Angela want to go on their next trip?
   Idea: to the stars
5. Name the first star that the old man showed Al and Angela.
   (our) sun
6. Al and Angela saw flames on the sun that were 12 times bigger than Earth.
7. Al and Angela went to a little star. That star was 8 miles through the middle.

WORKBOOK

8. Earth is 8 thousand miles through the middle.
9. Which weighs more, the little star or Earth? the little star
10. The old man put a spoonful of matter on one side of the balance scale. What was the first thing he put on the other side of the scale?
    a big rock
11. Did the scale balance? no
12. What object finally made the scale balance?
    a huge mountain
13. So the spoonful of matter weighed as much as ▬.
    - 10 trucks • <u>a huge mountain</u> • 50 trucks

B Review Items

14. In what form of matter is air on Pluto? solid
15. In what form of matter is air on Earth? gas
16. In what form of matter is air on Saturn? liquid
17. What form of matter is steam? gas
18. What form of matter is water? liquid
19. What form of matter is ice? solid
20. How deep is the deepest part of the ocean?
    - 1 mile • <u>6 miles</u> • 10 miles

GO TO PART C IN YOUR TEXTBOOK.

TEXTBOOK

C Number your paper from 1 through 21.

Skill Items

Use the words in the box to write complete sentences.

expensive	wriggled	shocked	created
tentacles	nonsense	addressed	universe

1. The poem they ▬ was ▬. *created, nonsense*
2. The squid ▬ its ▬. *wriggled, tentacles*

Review Items

3. Name the animal in the picture. *giant squid*
4. Which arrow shows the way the animal squirts water out? *X*
5. Which arrow shows the way the animal will move? *Y*

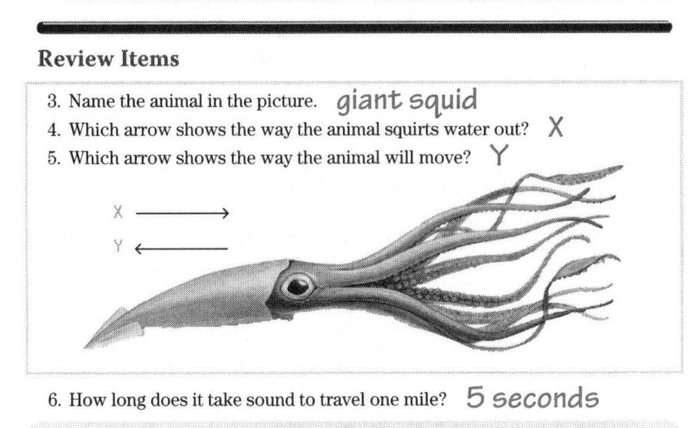

6. How long does it take sound to travel one mile? *5 seconds*
7. Do plants grow on the bottom of the deepest part of the ocean? *no*
8. Tell why. *Idea: There's no sunlight.*
9. Do all things turn into a gas at the same temperature? *no*
10. What are tiny parts of matter called? *molecules*
11. Do wood molecules look like air molecules? *no*
12. Do all air molecules look the same? *yes*
13. Where would a balloon be bigger—at 100 feet below the surface of the ocean or at 40 feet below the surface? *40 feet below*

TEXTBOOK

14. What is animal N? *blue whale*
15. What is animal O? *killer whale*

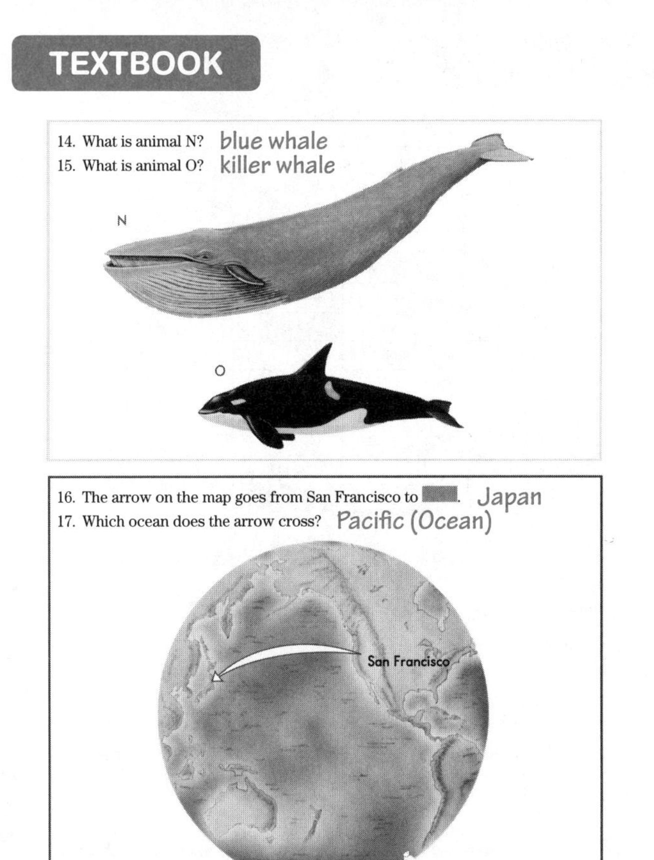

16. The arrow on the map goes from San Francisco to ▬. *Japan*
17. Which ocean does the arrow cross? *Pacific (Ocean)*

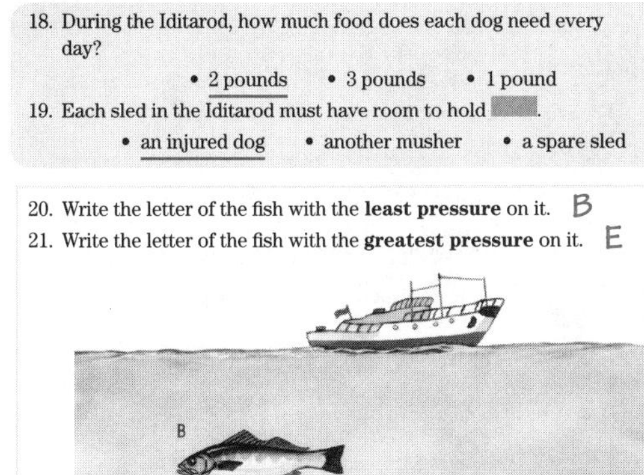

TEXTBOOK

18. During the Iditarod, how much food does each dog need every day?
    - 2 pounds
    - 3 pounds
    - 1 pound
19. Each sled in the Iditarod must have room to hold ▬.
    - an injured dog
    - another musher
    - a spare sled

20. Write the letter of the fish with the **least pressure** on it. *B*
21. Write the letter of the fish with the **greatest pressure** on it. *E*

WORKBOOK

118

Name ____________________

A Story Items

1. Is our sun a **huge** star? *no*
2. Al and Angela went to a huge star. Name the planets that would be inside that star if it was in the center of our solar system.
   Mercury, Venus, Earth, Mars, Jupiter
3. How long would it take light to travel from one side of that star to the other side? *(over) 45 minutes*
4. Name the galaxy that Al and Angela saw.
   Milky Way
5. How many stars are in that galaxy?
   100 billion
6. How long does it take light to travel from one side of that galaxy to the other side?
   - 100 thousand years
   - 180 thousand years
   - 40 years
7. One star in the galaxy started flashing. What's special about that star?
   Idea: It's our sun.

WORKBOOK

B Skill Items

temperature	pressure	giant	blue	squid	killer
thousand	hundred	skeletons	shells	coral	plants
two	ten	selected	exclaimed	tentacles	

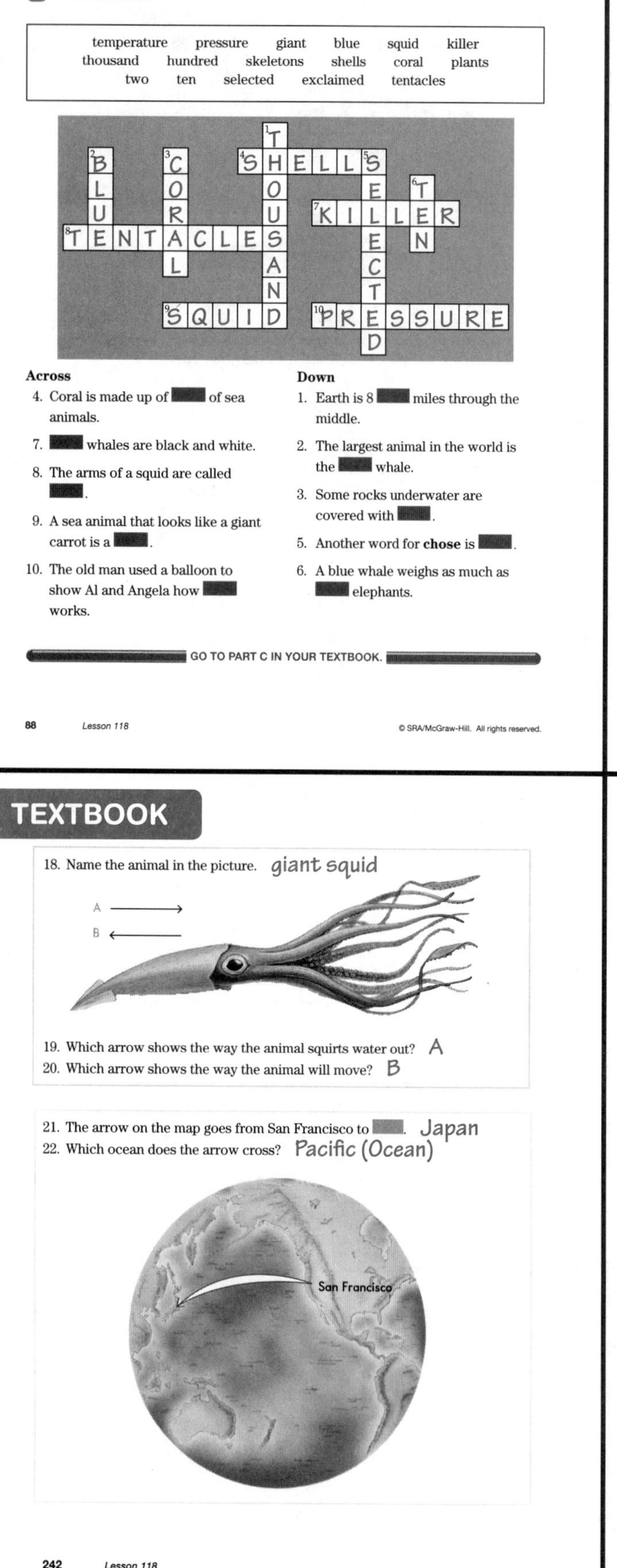

Across

4. Coral is made up of ___ of sea animals.
7. ___ whales are black and white.
8. The arms of a squid are called ___.
9. A sea animal that looks like a giant carrot is a ___.
10. The old man used a balloon to show Al and Angela how ___ works.

Down

1. Earth is 8 ___ miles through the middle.
2. The largest animal in the world is the ___ whale.
3. Some rocks underwater are covered with ___.
5. Another word for **chose** is ___.
6. A blue whale weighs as much as ___ elephants.

GO TO PART C IN YOUR TEXTBOOK.

TEXTBOOK

C Number your paper from 1 through 22.

Skill Items

Write the word from the box that means the same thing as the underlined part of each sentence.

receive	survive	whether	trembled
injured	appeared	erupt	selected

1. Most plants cannot live without sunshine. survive
2. She chose a very long book to read. selected
3. She was hurt when she fell. injured

Review Items

4. Which has **more** gravity, Jupiter or Io? Jupiter
5. Which is **smaller** than Earth? Io
6. Where can you jump 8 feet high? Io
7. How many miles does light travel in one second? 186 thousand (miles)
8. What else travels as fast as light? Idea: nothing
9. How long does it take light to travel from the sun to Earth? 8 minutes
10. How can you change a solid form of matter into a liquid? Idea: Heat it.
11. To change a liquid form of matter into a gas, you make the liquid ___. hotter
12. In which form of matter are molecules farthest apart? gas
13. In which form of matter are molecules closest together? solid
14. Earth is ___ through the middle.
    - 8 miles
    - 8 thousand miles
    - 8 hundred miles
15. Where would a balloon be bigger—at 100 feet below the surface of the ocean or at 200 feet below the surface? 100 feet below
16. How many mushers start the Iditarod at the same time? 1
17. How much time passes before the next musher starts? 2 minutes

TEXTBOOK

18. Name the animal in the picture. giant squid

A →
B ←

19. Which arrow shows the way the animal squirts water out? A
20. Which arrow shows the way the animal will move? B

21. The arrow on the map goes from San Francisco to ___. Japan
22. Which ocean does the arrow cross? Pacific (Ocean)

San Francisco

WORKBOOK

Name ______________________

A Story Items

1. The teacher told the class that in two days they would have a test on the human body.
2. Was Al excited about the test? no
3. Did Al want to learn about the human body? no
4. As the man's arm pushed the weight overhead, the muscle on the back of the arm got ___.
   - shorter and thicker
   - longer and thicker
   - longer and thinner
5. Why were the store windows decorated? Idea: It was almost Christmas.
6. Why did Al feel sad when he looked inside those windows? Idea: He didn't have money for presents.
7. What present did Al want to buy for his mother? a toaster
8. Who decided where to go on the next trip? the old man
9. At the end of the story, what did the old man do to one of the muscles? Idea: cut it
10. Name the muscle on the **front** of the upper arm. biceps
11. Name the muscle on the **back** of the upper arm. triceps
12. How many jobs does each muscle have? 1

13. Name the arm muscle that gets shorter when you straighten your arm.
the triceps

14. Name the arm muscle that gets shorter when you bend you arm.
the biceps

15. When you bend your arm, one of the muscles gets longer as the other one gets shorter. Name the muscle that gets longer. the triceps

16. Which letter shows the triceps? W

17. Which letter shows the biceps? R

18. Which letter shows the muscle that bends the arm? R

19. Which letter shows the muscle that straightens the arm? W

R
W

GO TO PART C IN YOUR TEXTBOOK.

"Wow!" Angela exclaimed. "I never knew there were so many muscles in the body."

"Yes," the old man said. "And every muscle has one job. Every muscle helps the man move one part of his body one way. Watch the man move. See if you can figure out which muscle is working."

The man's leg started to bend back. Angela pointed to the muscle on the back of the upper leg. "There's a muscle getting shorter and thicker."

The old man said, "That's right. The only muscle that can bend the man's leg is the muscle on the back of the upper leg. It pulls and gets shorter to bend the leg back."

Now the man's head started to move back and Al could see that the muscles at the back of the neck were getting shorter and thicker. He pointed to them and told the old man that they were the muscles that moved the head back.

As the man's head started to move forward, Al could see the muscles in the front of the neck getting shorter and thicker. They were moving the head forward.

Angela observed, "The muscles work in pairs. One muscle moves a part of the body one way. The muscle on the other side of the part moves that part the other way."

"Correct," the old man replied. "And if one of those muscles is cut, the part cannot move. Watch what happens when the muscle in the back of the upper leg is cut." The man's leg started to bend back. Suddenly, it stopped and came forward. The old man explained, "The muscle in the back of the upper leg is cut now, so the man cannot bend the leg back. There is only one muscle that can do that job, and that muscle is not working."

"That's amazing," Angela said.

C Number your paper from 1 through 21.

Story Items

1. The only muscle that can move your head **forward** is the muscle on the ▬ of your neck.
   - front (underlined)
   - back
2. The only muscle that can move your head **backward** is the muscle on the ▬ of your neck.
   - front
   - back (underlined)

Skill Items

Write the word or words from the box that mean the same thing as the underlined part of each sentence.

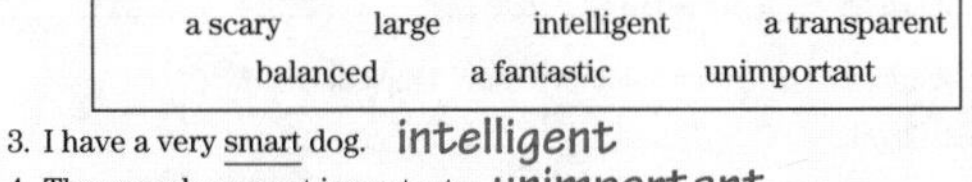

a scary	large	intelligent	a transparent
balanced	a fantastic	unimportant	

3. I have a very smart dog. intelligent
4. The speech was not important. unimportant
5. She told an amazing story. a fantastic

The triceps muscle is bigger than the biceps muscle.

6. What word names the muscle on the front of the upper arm? biceps
7. What word names the muscle on the back and side of the upper arm? triceps
8. What do we call a part of your body that is attached to bones and moves bones? muscle

Review Items

9. The sun is matter in the ▬ form. gas
10. What form of matter is the air around you? gas
11. Name the largest animal in the world. blue whale
12. That animal weighs more than ▬ elephants. 10
13. What's the name of a smaller whale that is black and white? killer whale
14. Al and Angela went to a huge star. Name the planets that would be inside that star if it was in the center of our solar system. Mercury, Venus, Earth, Mars, Jupiter
15. Name the galaxy that Al and Angela saw. Milky Way

Here's how big a balloon is at 50 meters below the surface of the ocean.

Here's the same balloon when it is **deeper** or **not as deep.**

16. Write the letter of each balloon that is deeper than balloon **J.** Q, R, S, T
17. Write the letter of the balloon that is closest to the surface. U
18. Write the letter of the balloon that is deepest. R

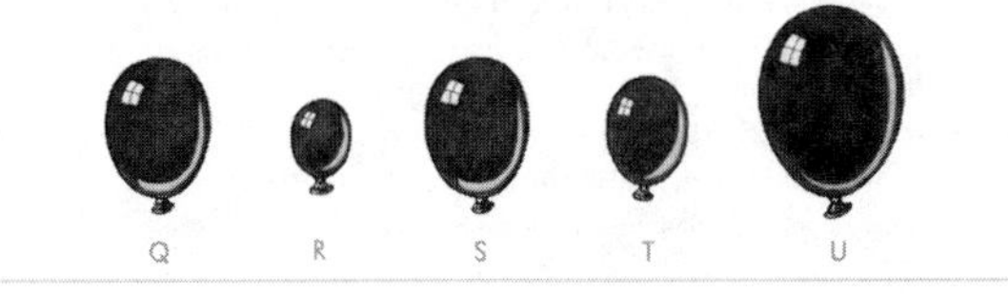

19. The rules for the Iditarod require each musher to have certain things. Write the letters of those things. a, b, e, h, i
    a. booties
    b. snowshoes
    c. extra dogs
    d. firewood
    e. a good sleeping bag
    f. extra shoes
    g. enough food for a week
    h. enough food for a day
    i. an ax
    j. a tent
20. When Iditarod mushers are on the trail, how much help can they get from someone else? none
21. Why can't you see molecules when you look at an object?
    Idea: They are too small.

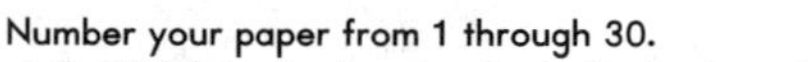

TEXTBOOK

TEST 12 | 120

Number your paper from 1 through 30.

1. In which form of matter are molecules lined up in rows? solid
2. In which form of matter do molecules move slowest? solid
3. In which form of matter do molecules move fastest? gas
4. In which form of matter are molecules closest together? solid
5. In which form of matter are molecules farthest apart? gas
6. Are whales fish? no
7. Are whales **warm-blooded** or **cold-blooded?** warm-blooded
8. What is animal A? giant squid
9. What is animal B? killer whale
10. What is animal C? blue whale

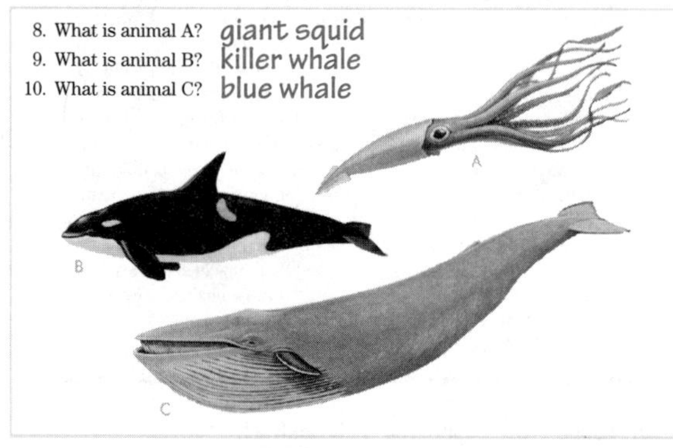

11. Name the galaxy that we live in. Milky Way
12. Name the muscle on the **back** of the upper arm. triceps
13. Name the muscle on the **front** of the upper arm. biceps
14. How many jobs does each muscle have? 1
15. Name the arm muscle that gets shorter when you bend your arm. biceps
16. Name the arm muscle that gets shorter when you straighten your arm. triceps

TEXTBOOK

17. When you straighten your arm, one of the muscles gets longer as the other one gets shorter. Name the muscle that gets longer. biceps

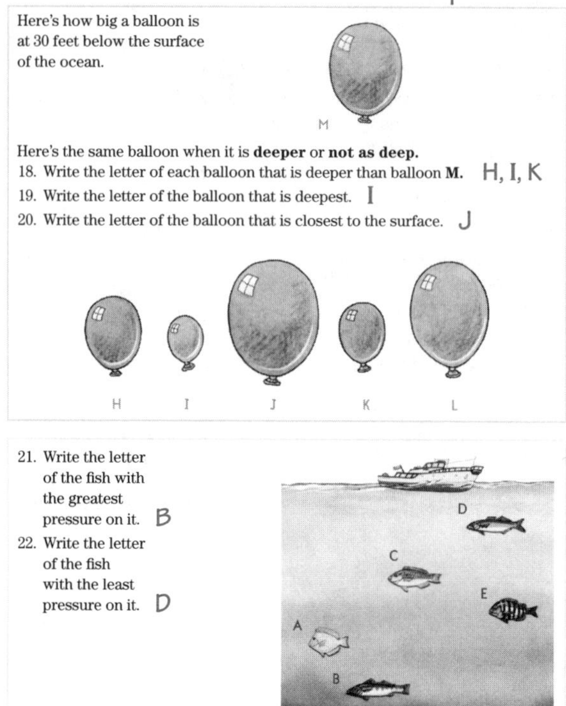

Here's how big a balloon is at 30 feet below the surface of the ocean.

Here's the same balloon when it is **deeper** or **not as deep.**

18. Write the letter of each balloon that is deeper than balloon **M.** H, I, K
19. Write the letter of the balloon that is deepest. I
20. Write the letter of the balloon that is closest to the surface. J

21. Write the letter of the fish with the greatest pressure on it. B
22. Write the letter of the fish with the least pressure on it. D

TEXTBOOK

Skill Items

For each item, write the underlined word or words from the sentences in the box.

> The poem they created was nonsense.
> The squid wriggled its tentacles.
> The triceps muscle is bigger than the biceps muscle.

23. What underlining refers to arms that are like huge snakes? tentacles
24. What underlining refers to a part of your body that is attached to bones and that moves bones? muscle
25. What underlining means **squirmed around in all directions?** wriggled
26. What underlining names the muscle on the front of the upper arm? biceps
27. What underlining means **made?** created
28. What underlining means **no sense at all?** nonsense
29. What underlining names the muscle on the back and side of the upper arm? triceps
30. What underlining names a sea animal? squid

END OF TEST 12

WORKBOOK

121

Name ____________________

A Story Items

1. Most muscles are attached to bones.
2. What happened when the old man removed the bones from the model's legs? Idea: The model fell over.
3. What is the skeleton of the human body made of?
   - bones
   - skin
   - muscles
4. How many bones are in the human body? 206
5. **Underline** the 2 things that bones do.
   - protect body parts
   - make the body move
   - get shorter and thicker
   - make the body strong
6. Did Angela like how the skeleton looked? no
7. Name the bone on the top of the head. skull
8. What does that bone protect? brain
9. What would happen if something hit the **back** of your brain? Idea: You'd go blind.
10. What would happen if something hit the **lower part** of your brain? Ideas: You couldn't breathe; you'd die.
11. What **2** body parts do the ribs protect? heart and lungs
12. Your heart is about as big as your fist.

WORKBOOK

13. What might happen if something hurt your lungs?
Ideas: You couldn't breathe; you'd die.

14. Does Al want to learn more about the body? yes

15. Had Al wanted to learn about the body before this trip started?
no

16. At the end of the story, Al and Angela were inside a large tube that was filled with liquid (Accept blood).

B Review Items

17. Name the largest planet in the solar system. Jupiter

18. How long does it take Jupiter to spin around one time?
10 hours

19. How long does it take light to travel from the sun to Earth?
8 minutes

20. Where would a balloon be bigger—at 40 feet below the surface of the ocean or at 80 feet below the surface?
40 feet below (the surface)

21. Are whales fish? no

22. Are whales **warm-blooded** or **cold-blooded?**
warm-blooded

GO TO PART C IN YOUR TEXTBOOK.

TEXTBOOK

11. Idea: don't give the animal a reward

C Number your paper from 1 through 18.

Skill Items 12. (Any 2:) a bone; a dog treat; a pat on the head; etc.

Use the words in the box to write complete sentences.

balanced	muscle	wriggled	biceps	presented
tentacles	elbow	triceps	fantastic	

1. The squid ___ its ___. wriggled, tentacles
2. The ___ ___ is bigger than the ___ muscle. triceps, muscle, biceps

Review Items

3. Name the muscle on the **front** of the upper arm. biceps
4. Name the muscle on the **back** of the upper arm. triceps
5. Name the muscle that works when you **straighten** your arm. triceps
6. Name the muscle that works when you **bend** your arm. biceps
7. How many jobs does each muscle have? 1
8. Name the arm muscle that gets shorter when you bend your arm. biceps
9. Name the arm muscle that gets shorter when you straighten your arm. triceps
10. When you're training an animal, what do you do each time the animal does the trick? Idea: give the animal a reward
11. What do you do if the animal does not do the trick?
12. Name **2** things you could give a dog to reward it.
13. When you straighten your arm, one muscle gets longer as another muscle gets shorter. Name the muscle that gets longer. biceps
14. Are killer whales fish? no
15. Tell if killer whales are **warm-blooded** or **cold-blooded.** warm-blooded
16. Name **3** animals that are warm-blooded. (Any 3:) bears; humans; dogs; etc.
17. Name **3** animals that are cold-blooded. (Any 3:) fish; sharks; reptiles; etc.
18. The ___s are the coldest places on the earth and the ___ is the hottest place on the earth. pole/equator

WORKBOOK

122

Name ________________

A Story Items

1. At the beginning of the story, Al and Angela were floating in a tube. What is that tube called? blood vessel
2. Name the liquid that was in the tube. blood
3. What color was that liquid? black
4. What was making the great pounding sound that Al and Angela heard?
the heart
5. Why was the pounding sound getting louder? Idea: They were getting closer to the heart.
6. What happens to the blood when the heart pounds?
Idea: It moves.
7. The old man told Al and Angela what the heart does. He told them that the heart pumps blood through the body.
8. What are the doors in the heart made of? muscle(s)
9. Which chamber of the heart was bigger, the first one or the second one?
the second one
10. How many doors were in the second chamber? 2
11. You can hear two sounds in the heart. The blood makes the little sound when it leaves the little chamber.
12. When does it make the big sound?
Idea: when it leaves the chamber

WORKBOOK

13. When Al and Angela left the heart, they were in another blood vessel. What was different about how the blood moved in that blood vessel?
   - Things kept starting and stopping.
   - Things moved at the same speed.
   - Things moved very slowly.
14. Where was that blood vessel going?
   - from the body
   - to the heart
   - to the lungs
15. What does blood get in the lungs?
   - water
   - oxygen
   - food
16. Things can't burn without oxygen.
17. In the lungs, the color of the blood changed from black to (bright) red.
18. What color is blood that does not have oxygen? black
19. What color is blood that has fresh oxygen? red

GO TO PART C IN YOUR TEXTBOOK.

TEXTBOOK

"This is amazing," he shouted to Angela.

The old man said, "The red blood is now full of oxygen. It picked up the oxygen from the lungs. Could you tell when the oxygen entered the blood?"

Al said, "When the oxygen entered the blood, the blood became bright red."

"Correct," the old man said.

C Number your paper from 1 through 20.

Skill Items

Here are 3 events that happened in the story. Write **beginning, middle** or **end** for each event.

1. When they were directly in front of the door, Al noticed that he and the others were in a small chamber. middle
2. "Blood is very important to your body," the old man said. beginning
3. The walls of the blood vessel were getting very thin and transparent. end

Review Items

4. Most muscles are attached to ▬. bones
5. What **2** body parts do the ribs protect? heart and lungs
6. How many bones are in the human body? 206
7. How many miles does light travel in one second? 186 thousand (miles)
8. Write the **2** things that bones do.
   - make the body move
   - make the body strong
   - protect body parts
   - get short and thicker
9. Name the bone on the top of the head. skull
10. What does that bone protect? brain
11. What would happen if someone hit the **back** of your brain?
12. What would happen if someone hit the **lower part** of your brain? Ideas: You'd stop breathing; you'd die.
13. Your heart is about as big as your ▬. fist
14. What might happen if something hurt your lungs? Ideas: you couldn't breathe; you'd die

11. Idea: You'd go blind.

TEXTBOOK

15. The only muscle that can move your head **backward** is the muscle on the ▬ of your neck. back
16. The only muscle that can move your head **forward** is the muscle on the ▬ of your neck. front
17. Which letter shows the biceps? F
18. Which letter shows the triceps? G
19. Which letter shows the muscle that straightens the arm? G
20. Which letter shows the muscle that bends the arm? F

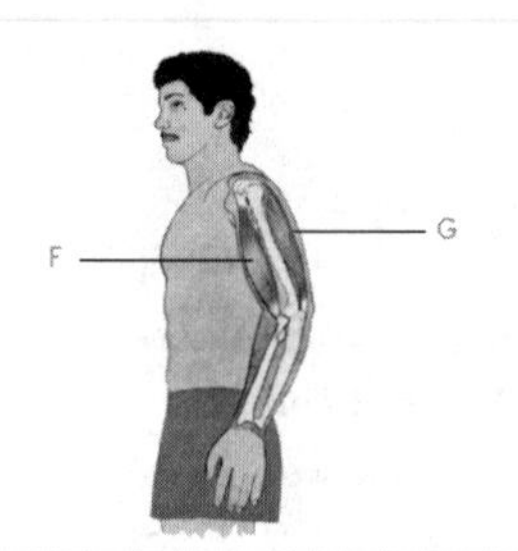

WORKBOOK

123

Name ____________________

A Story Items

1. When Angela and Al left the lungs, they were in a blood vessel. Where was the blood vessel going?
   Idea: to the heart
2. What color was the blood around them when they left the lungs?
   red
3. Why was the blood that color? Idea: It had oxygen in it.
4. How many chambers does the heart have? 4
5. How many chambers did Al and Angela go through **before** they went to the lungs? 2
6. How many chambers did they go through **after** they went to the lungs?
   2
7. Where does black blood go after it leaves the heart?
   to the lungs
8. Then the blood goes back to the heart
9. Then the blood goes to the Idea: body
10. Why does oxygen blood have to go back to the heart after it leaves the lungs? Idea: so the heart can pump it all over the body

WORKBOOK

11. Muscles are made up of tiny (muscle) cells.
12. When the oxygen left the blood, the color of the blood changed from red to black.
13. Muscle cells need oxygen to work.

Use these words to answer the questions below:
- blood vessels that lead from the heart
- blood vessels that lead to the heart

14. Which blood vessels pound every time the heart beats?
    blood vessels that lead from the heart
15. Which blood vessels do not pound?
    blood vessels that lead to the heart
16. Which blood vessels are blue?
    blood vessels that lead to the heart
17. Blood vessels that are blue are filled with black/dark blood.
18. Did Angela want to take the trip around the body again? no
19. Tell why. Idea: She didn't want to go through the heart again.

GO TO PART C IN YOUR TEXTBOOK.

TEXTBOOK

"No," Angela said. "I remember how it works. I don't want to go through the heart again."

"All right," the old man said, "Let's stay in the man's hand and look at another part of the body."

In an instant, Al and the others were no longer inside a blood vessel. They were floating next to something that looked like a huge white rope that stretched as far as Al could see. The rope had many branches coming from it.

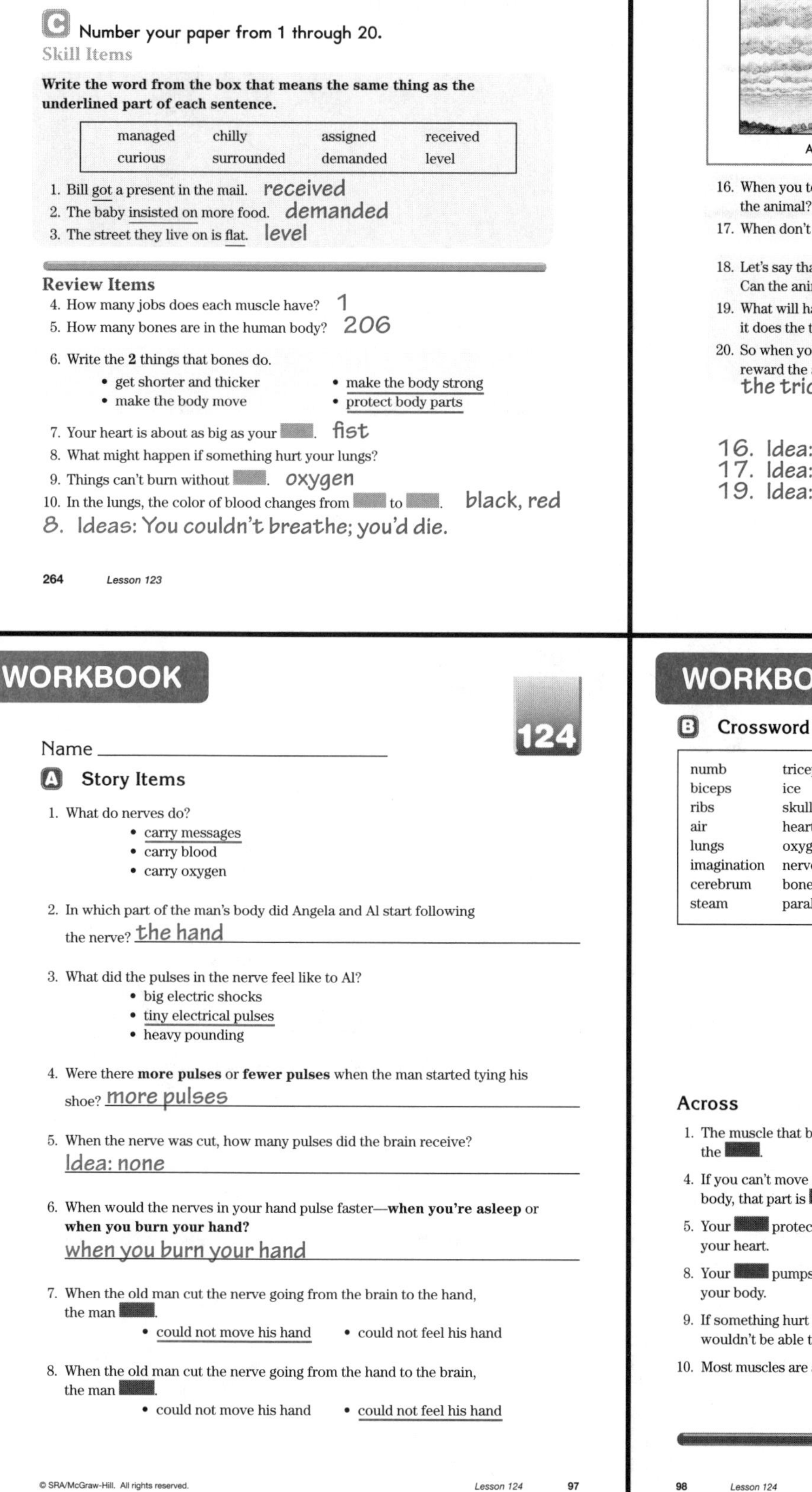

C Number your paper from 1 through 20.

Skill Items

Write the word from the box that means the same thing as the underlined part of each sentence.

managed	chilly	assigned	received
curious	surrounded	demanded	level

1. Bill got a present in the mail. received
2. The baby insisted on more food. demanded
3. The street they live on is flat. level

Review Items

4. How many jobs does each muscle have? 1
5. How many bones are in the human body? 206
6. Write the **2** things that bones do.
   - get shorter and thicker
   - make the body move
   - make the body strong
   - protect body parts
7. Your heart is about as big as your ▬. fist
8. What might happen if something hurt your lungs?
9. Things can't burn without ▬. oxygen
10. In the lungs, the color of blood changes from ▬ to ▬. black, red

8. Ideas: You couldn't breathe; you'd die.

TEXTBOOK

11. What color is blood that does not have oxygen? black
12. What color is blood that has fresh oxygen? red
13. Write the letter of the storm clouds. B
14. Write the letter of the clouds that have frozen drops of water. C
15. Write the letter of the clouds that may stay in the sky for days at a time. A

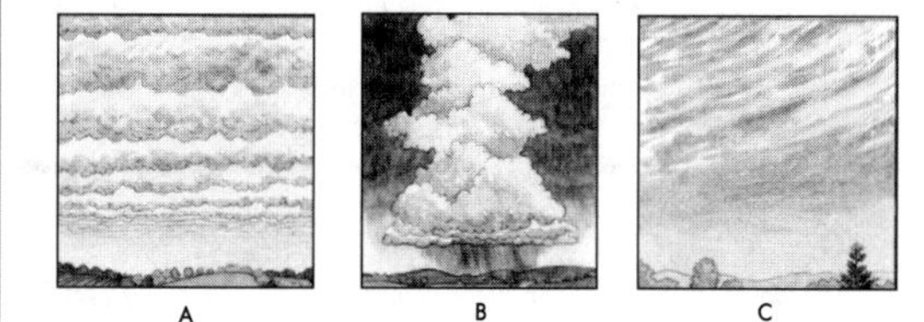

16. When you teach an animal a simple trick, when do you reward the animal?
17. When don't you reward the animal?
18. Let's say that you want to teach an animal a very hard trick. Can the animal do the trick at first? no
19. What will happen if the animal doesn't receive any rewards until it does the trick?
20. So when you're teaching the animal a hard trick, what do you reward the animal for doing? Idea: for trying to do the trick

16. Idea: when it does the trick
17. Idea: when it doesn't do the trick
19. Idea: It will stop trying to do the trick.

WORKBOOK

124

Name ____________________

A Story Items

1. What do nerves do?
   - carry messages
   - carry blood
   - carry oxygen
2. In which part of the man's body did Angela and Al start following the nerve? the hand
3. What did the pulses in the nerve feel like to Al?
   - big electric shocks
   - tiny electrical pulses
   - heavy pounding
4. Were there **more pulses** or **fewer pulses** when the man started tying his shoe? more pulses
5. When the nerve was cut, how many pulses did the brain receive? Idea: none
6. When would the nerves in your hand pulse faster—**when you're asleep** or **when you burn your hand?** when you burn your hand
7. When the old man cut the nerve going from the brain to the hand, the man ▬.
   - could not move his hand
   - could not feel his hand
8. When the old man cut the nerve going from the hand to the brain, the man ▬.
   - could not move his hand
   - could not feel his hand

WORKBOOK

B Crossword Puzzle

numb	triceps
biceps	ice
ribs	skull
air	heart
lungs	oxygen
imagination	nerves
cerebrum	bones
steam	paralyzed

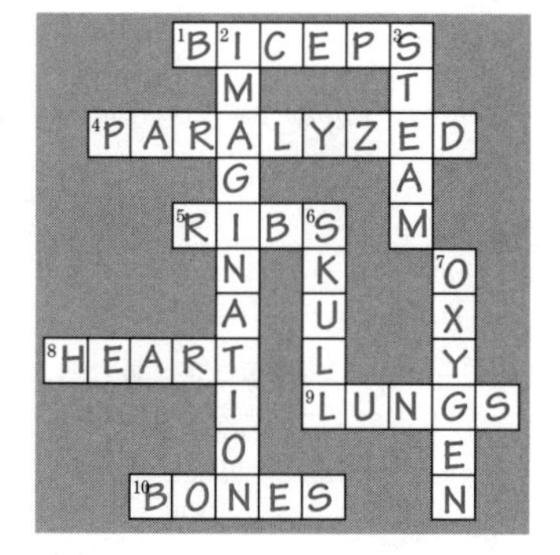

Across

1. The muscle that bends the arm is the ▬.
4. If you can't move a part of your body, that part is ▬.
5. Your ▬ protect your lungs and your heart.
8. Your ▬ pumps blood through your body.
9. If something hurt your ▬, you wouldn't be able to breathe.
10. Most muscles are attached to ▬.

Down

2. The part of your mind that can think of things that might happen is your ▬.
3. The gas form of water is ▬.
6. Your ▬ protects your brain.
7. Things can't burn without ▬.

GO TO PART C IN YOUR TEXTBOOK.

TEXTBOOK

C Number your paper from 1 through 20.

Story Items

1. The nerves that tell the brain what the hand feels go from the ▬ to the ▬. hand, brain
2. The nerves that tell the hand how to move go from the ▬ to the ▬. brain, hand
3. The nerves that tell the foot how to move go from the ▬ to the ▬. brain, foot
4. The nerves that tell the brain what the foot feels go from the ▬ to the ▬. foot, brain

Skill Items

The injury to his spinal cord paralyzed him.

5. What word means that a part of the body can't move? paralyzed
6. What word means **a serious hurt?** injury
7. What **2** words name the bundle of nerves inside the backbone? spinal cord

Review Items

8. Things can't burn without ▬. oxygen
9. In the lungs, the color of blood changes from ▬ to ▬. black, red
10. How many chambers does the heart have? 4
11. How many chambers did Al and Angela go through **before** they went to the lungs? 2
12. How many chambers did they go through **after** they went to the lungs? 2
13. Where does black blood go after it leaves the heart? to the lungs
14. Then the blood goes back to the ▬. heart
15. Then the blood goes to the ▬. Idea: body
16. Why does oxygen blood have to go back to the heart after it leaves the lungs? Idea: to get pumped through the body
17. When oxygen leaves the blood, the color of the blood changes from ▬ to ▬. red, black

TEXTBOOK

Here's how big a balloon is at 20 meters below the surface of the ocean.

X

Here's the same balloon when it is **deeper** or **not as deep.**

18. Write the letter of each balloon that is not as deep as balloon **X.** D, E
19. Write the letter of the balloon that is closest to the surface. D
20. Write the letter of the balloon that is deepest. A

A B C D E

WORKBOOK

125

Name ____________

A

1. What happens to light when it goes through a magnifying glass?
   - It goes straight.
   - It goes faster.
   - It bends.
2. If you make a picture of a tree using a magnifying glass, the top of the tree will be at the bottom of the picture.
3. The eye is like a magnifying glass.
4. Where does light enter the eyeball?
   - front
   - side
   - back
5. Where does the picture form?
   - front
   - side
   - back

B Story Items

6. What do nerves that lead from the brain to the hand tell the hand? Ideas: what to do; how to move
7. What do nerves that lead from the hand to the brain tell the brain? Idea: what the part feels
8. What is your backbone made of? little (hollow) bones
9. Name the bundle of nerves that goes up and down through the middle of your backbone. spinal cord
10. What's strange about the bones in the backbone?
    - They are hollow.
    - They are solid.
    - They are soft.

WORKBOOK

11. When Al and Angela left the spinal cord, they entered the brain.
12. What does your cerebrum do? Idea: thinking
13. When Al and Angela first entered the brain, they were in a part that controls some things the body does. Name 2 of those things. (Any 2:) sweating; breathing; heart pumping; etc.
14. When Al and Angela moved up through the brain, they came to another part. Did that part have **more nerves** or **fewer nerves?** more nerves
15. Name that part of the brain. cerebrum
16. Which part of your **brain** works when you think about what you are seeing? cerebrum

GO TO PART D IN YOUR TEXTBOOK.

TEXTBOOK

of the brain that is working. When you think about something that you see, this is the part that does the thinking. When you think about what somebody says to you, you are using this part."

Angela asked, "What did you say this part of the brain is called?"

Al told her.

"Correct," the old man said. "The thinking part of the brain is the cerebrum."

Angela and Al looked at the nerves that tangled this way and that way through the cerebrum. "Wow!" Angela exclaimed.

D Number your paper from 1 through 24.

Skill Items

Write the word from the box that means the same thing as the underlined part of each sentence.

applauded	concluded	warm	selecting	comfortable
chilly	observing	incredible	appearing	

1. They were watching the baby birds. observing
2. Her hands were sort of cold. chilly
3. The parents clapped at the end of the play. applauded

Use the words in the box to write complete sentences.

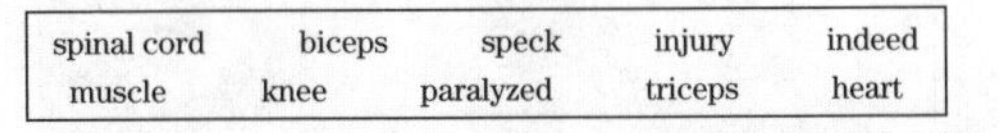

spinal cord	biceps	speck	injury	indeed
muscle	knee	paralyzed	triceps	heart

4. The ___ ___ is bigger than the ___ muscle. triceps, muscle, biceps
5. The ___ to his ___ ___ him. injury, spinal cord, paralyzed

Review Items

6. Which has **more** gravity, Jupiter or Io? Jupiter
7. Which is **smaller** than Earth? Io
8. Where can you jump 8 feet high? Io

TEXTBOOK

9. How long does it take light to travel from the sun to Earth? 8 minutes
10. Muscles are made up of tiny ___. (muscle) cells
11. Blood vessels that are blue are filled with ___.
    - red blood
    - dark blood
12. Muscle cells need ___ to work. oxygen
13. The nerves that tell the brain what the foot feels go from the ___ to the ___. foot, brain
14. The nerves that tell the foot how to move go from the ___ to the ___. brain, foot
15. If you cut the nerve going from your brain to your arm, you could not ___ your arm. move
16. If you cut the nerve going from your arm to your brain, you could not ___ your arm. feel
17. Write the letter of the blood vessels that pound every time the heart beats. a
18. Write the letter of the blood vessels that do not pound. b
19. Write the letter of the blood vessels that are blue. b
    a. blood vessels that lead from the heart
    b. blood vessels that lead to the heart
20. Which letter on the map shows Alaska? T
21. Which letter shows Canada? D
22. Which letter shows the main part of the United States? S
23. Which **2** letters show where Eskimos live? T, D

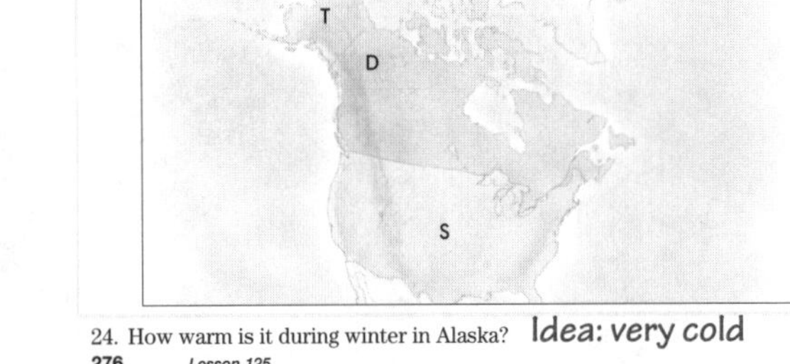

24. How warm is it during winter in Alaska? Idea: very cold

WORKBOOK

126

Name ____________________

A

1. Draw lines to show where the paths of light will go when they go through the lens.

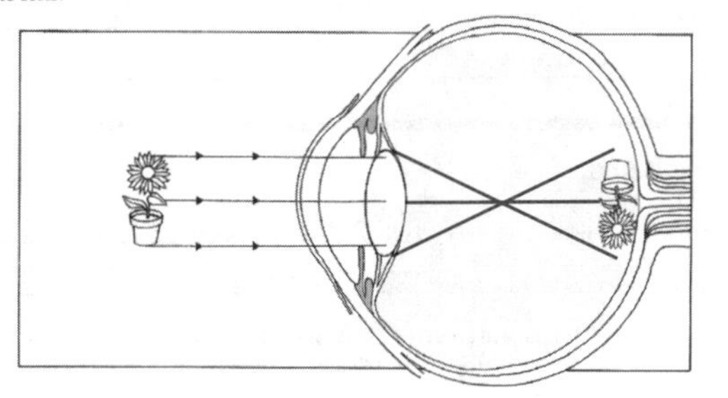

B Story Items

2. What did the old man do to scare the man?
   Idea: put a lion in the room
3. What happened to the nerves in the man's brain?
   - They pulsed more rapidly.
   - They pulsed more slowly.
   - They became cooler.
4. What did the nerves do after the lion disappeared?
   - They pulsed more rapidly.
   - They pulsed more slowly.
   - They became cooler.

WORKBOOK

5. The nerves from the eye go to the ___ of the brain.
   - front
   - side
   - back
6. After Al and Angela left the brain, they went inside a great round chamber. What was that chamber?
   - the heart
   - the eye
   - the lungs
7. What is the name of the round window in the chamber?
   pupil
8. On which part of the man's eye could Al and Angela see an image of what the man was looking at?
   - pupil
   - retina
   - lens
9. What was strange about the image they saw?
   Idea: It was upside down.
10. While Al and Angela were looking at the image, the man's shoes got bigger. Tell why. Idea: He was bending down (toward his shoes).

Review Items

11. Name the bundle of nerves that goes up and down through the middle of your backbone. spinal cord
12. What's strange about the bones in the backbone?
    - They are square.
    - They are hollow.
    - They are soft.
13. When you think, what part of your brain are you using?
    cerebrum

GO TO PART D IN YOUR TEXTBOOK.

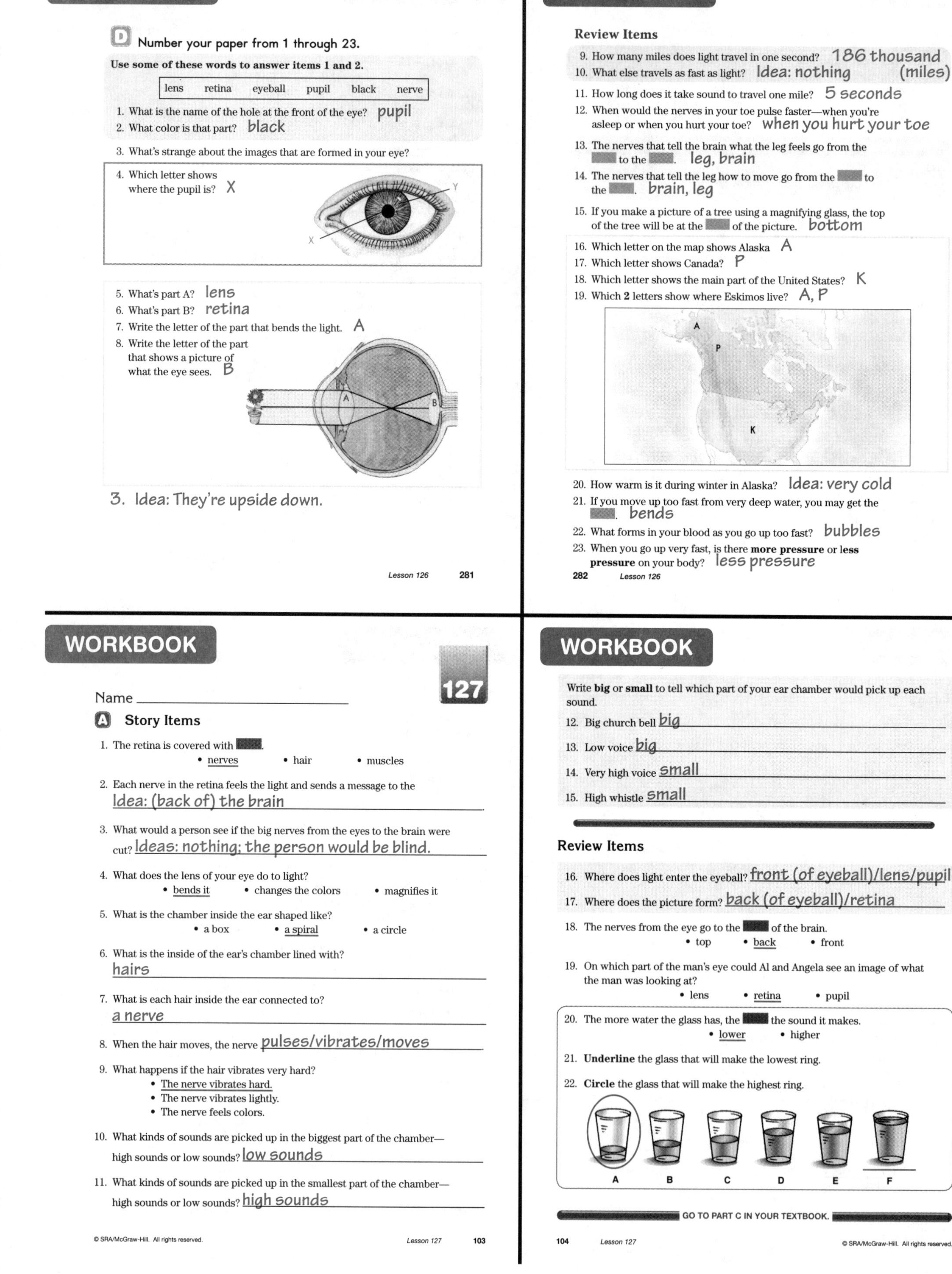

TEXTBOOK

D Number your paper from 1 through 23.

Use some of these words to answer items 1 and 2.

lens	retina	eyeball	pupil	black	nerve

1. What is the name of the hole at the front of the eye? pupil
2. What color is that part? black
3. What's strange about the images that are formed in your eye?
4. Which letter shows where the pupil is? X

5. What's part A? lens
6. What's part B? retina
7. Write the letter of the part that bends the light. A
8. Write the letter of the part that shows a picture of what the eye sees. B

3. Idea: They're upside down.

TEXTBOOK

Review Items

9. How many miles does light travel in one second? 186 thousand (miles)
10. What else travels as fast as light? Idea: nothing
11. How long does it take sound to travel one mile? 5 seconds
12. When would the nerves in your toe pulse faster—when you're asleep or when you hurt your toe? when you hurt your toe
13. The nerves that tell the brain what the leg feels go from the ▬ to the ▬. leg, brain
14. The nerves that tell the leg how to move go from the ▬ to the ▬. brain, leg
15. If you make a picture of a tree using a magnifying glass, the top of the tree will be at the ▬ of the picture. bottom
16. Which letter on the map shows Alaska A
17. Which letter shows Canada? P
18. Which letter shows the main part of the United States? K
19. Which **2** letters show where Eskimos live? A, P

20. How warm is it during winter in Alaska? Idea: very cold
21. If you move up too fast from very deep water, you may get the ▬. bends
22. What forms in your blood as you go up too fast? bubbles
23. When you go up very fast, is there **more pressure** or **less pressure** on your body? less pressure

WORKBOOK

127

Name ____________________

A Story Items

1. The retina is covered with ▬.
   - <u>nerves</u>
   - hair
   - muscles
2. Each nerve in the retina feels the light and sends a message to the Idea: (back of) the brain.
3. What would a person see if the big nerves from the eyes to the brain were cut? Ideas: nothing; the person would be blind.
4. What does the lens of your eye do to light?
   - <u>bends it</u>
   - changes the colors
   - magnifies it
5. What is the chamber inside the ear shaped like?
   - a box
   - <u>a spiral</u>
   - a circle
6. What is the inside of the ear's chamber lined with? hairs
7. What is each hair inside the ear connected to? a nerve
8. When the hair moves, the nerve pulses/vibrates/moves.
9. What happens if the hair vibrates very hard?
   - <u>The nerve vibrates hard.</u>
   - The nerve vibrates lightly.
   - The nerve feels colors.
10. What kinds of sounds are picked up in the biggest part of the chamber—high sounds or low sounds? low sounds
11. What kinds of sounds are picked up in the smallest part of the chamber—high sounds or low sounds? high sounds

WORKBOOK

Write **big** or **small** to tell which part of your ear chamber would pick up each sound.

12. Big church bell big
13. Low voice big
14. Very high voice small
15. High whistle small

Review Items

16. Where does light enter the eyeball? front (of eyeball)/lens/pupil
17. Where does the picture form? back (of eyeball)/retina
18. The nerves from the eye go to the ▬ of the brain.
    - top
    - <u>back</u>
    - front
19. On which part of the man's eye could Al and Angela see an image of what the man was looking at?
    - lens
    - <u>retina</u>
    - pupil
20. The more water the glass has, the ▬ the sound it makes.
    - <u>lower</u>
    - higher
21. **Underline** the glass that will make the lowest ring.
22. **Circle** the glass that will make the highest ring.

GO TO PART C IN YOUR TEXTBOOK.

TEXTBOOK

hairs will move in that part of the ear."

The old man clapped his hands, smiled, and then he put his arms around Al and Angela. "You are both smart and I am proud of you."

Al smiled. Angela smiled. The old man smiled. Then, "tweeeeet." The hairs near the small end of the chamber started to vibrate. The old man said, "That's all there is to the inner ear. High sounds are picked up at the small end of the chamber. Lower sounds are picked up in the middle of the chamber. And the lowest sounds are picked up where the chamber is the largest."

Al looked at the hairs inside the ear. He didn't say anything. He just observed them and thought.

C Number your paper from 1 through 19.

Skill Items

Here are 3 events that happened in the story. Write **beginning, middle** or **end** for each event.

1. Then "tweeeeet." The hairs near the small end of the chamber started to vibrate. end
2. Here's what somebody said: "The more the hair vibrates, the harder the nerve pulses." middle
3. By looking at the image on the retina, they could see a picture of everything the man saw. beginning

Review Items

4. What do nerves that lead from the brain to the foot tell the foot?
5. What do nerves that lead from the foot to the brain tell the brain? Idea: what the foot feels
6. Which part of your **brain** works when you **think** about what you are hearing? cerebrum
7. What is the name of the hole at the front of the eye? pupil
8. What color is that part? black
9. What part of the eye is just behind the hole? lens

4. Idea: how to move

TEXTBOOK

10. Which picture shows where the paths of light will go after they go through the lens? A

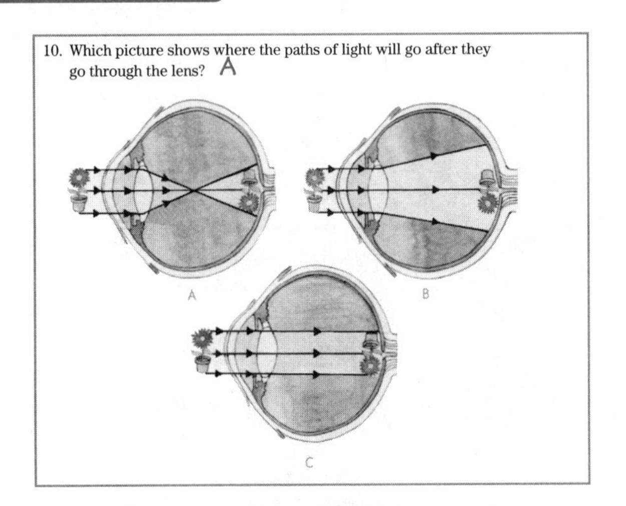

11. When you dive down 33 feet, you have ▇ times the pressure on you that you have at the surface. 2
12. When you dive down 66 feet, you have ▇ times the pressure on you that you have at the surface. 3
13. In what country are the states of Colorado and Utah? United States
14. Name the mountains you drive over to get from Colorado to Utah. Rocky Mountains
15. In which direction do you go to get from Colorado to Utah? west
16. Name **2** cities in Colorado. Denver; Greeley
17. Name one city in Utah. Salt Lake City

TEXTBOOK

18. Which letter shows Colorado? H
19. Which letter shows Utah? I

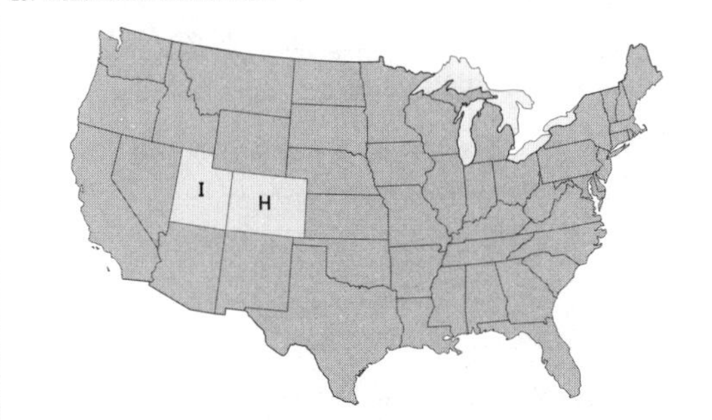

WORKBOOK

128

Name ______________________

A Story Items

1. After the trip, the old man gave Al and Angela a book. What was the title of the book?
   The Human Body
2. Why did he give the book to them? Idea: so they could study for the test
3. Did the old man want the book back? no
4. When will the old man give Al and Angela their test on the human body?
   Monday
5. Was there snow on the ground when Al and Angela left the old man's store?
   yes
6. About how much snow was on the ground the next morning?
   Idea: (almost) a yard
7. What did Al's mother ask him to do the next morning?
   Idea: shovel (snow off) the sidewalk
8. Who worked with Al? Angela

WORKBOOK

B Crossword Puzzle

spiral	numb	nerve	curved	blind
backbone	pupil	vessel	retina	hairs
paralyzed	four	cerebrum	red	black

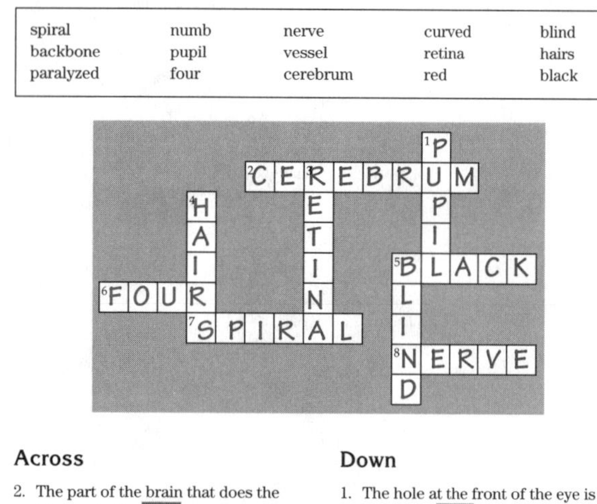

Across

2. The part of the brain that does the thinking is the ___.
5. Blood that does not have fresh oxygen is ___.
6. The heart has ___ chambers.
7. The chamber inside the ear is shaped like a ___.
8. Something in your body that carries messages is a ___.

Down

1. The hole at the front of the eye is called the ___.
3. The part of the eye where pictures are formed is called the ___.
4. The ear's chamber is lined with ___.
5. A person who cannot see is ___.

GO TO PART C IN YOUR TEXTBOOK.

TEXTBOOK

that said, "Bones do two things," Al said, "I know what those things are." He explained them.

For over four hours, Angela and Al went through the book and talked about the things they read. They discussed the heart and the blood. They talked about the two kinds of nerves that are in the body. They discussed the brain, the eye and the ear. When they were finished with the book, it was getting dark in the room.

"Hey, Mom," Al called. "What time is it?"

"Four o'clock," she called from the other room.

Al said, "I've had enough studying for a while. Let's go outside and I'll give you a lesson in throwing snowballs."

Angela said, "How can you give lessons in something you don't know how to do?"

They went outside, where the snow was still falling. The walk that they had shoveled earlier was covered with about three inches of snow. Al ran behind a tree, made a large wet snowball, stood up and said, "Here's how to . . ." Splat. Right in his chest.

C Number your paper from 1 through 22.

Story Items 1. Idea: It was almost Christmas.

1. Why were people out shopping for presents?
2. Why did Al feel sad about Christmas?
3. How long did Al and Angela study the book the old man gave them? (over) 4 hours
4. What did they do outside after they finished studying? Idea: had a snowball fight

Review Items

5. In what form of matter is air on Pluto? solid
6. In what form of matter is air on Earth? gas
7. In what form of matter is air on Saturn? liquid
8. When things are hard, what form of matter are they? solid
9. When hard matter gets hotter, which form does it change into? liquid
10. When matter gets still hotter, which form does it change into? gas

2. Idea: He didn't have any money for presents.

TEXTBOOK

11. If you make a picture of a tree using a magnifying glass, the bottom of the tree will be at the ___ of the picture. top
12. Where would a balloon be bigger—at 80 feet below the surface of the ocean or at 20 feet below the surface? 20 feet below

Write **big** or **small** to tell in which part of your ear chamber you would pick up each sound.

13. very high voice small
14. low voice big
15. high whistle small
16. big church bell big
17. Name the bundle of nerves that goes up and down through the middle of your backbone. spinal cord
18. What's strange about the bones in the backbone?
19. What's strange about the images that are formed in your eye?
20. The retina is covered with ___.
    - hair
    - nerves
    - blood
21. Coral is made up of the ___ of tiny ___. skeletons, animals
22. An underwater hill that is covered with coral is called a coral ___. reef

18. Idea: They're hollow.
19. Idea: They're upside down.

WORKBOOK

129

Name ___________________

A

1. Look at the picture below. Is the side of the earth that's closest to the sun **in daylight** or **in darkness?** in daylight
2. Is the North Pole tilting **toward the sun** or **away from the sun?** away from the sun
3. So does this picture show our **summer** or our **winter?** winter
4. As the earth turns around, which person is in darkness all the time? A
5. Which person is in daylight all the time? D
6. Write the letters of all the persons who are in daylight some of the time and darkness some of the time. B, C, D, E

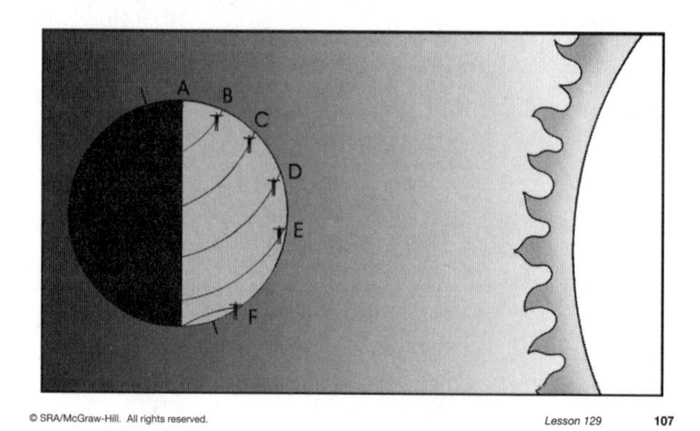

WORKBOOK

B Story Items

7. Who made fun of Al in school? Homer
8. How many questions were on the test that Al took in school? 40
9. What were most of the questions about?
   Idea: the human body
10. Who did better on the test, Homer or Al? Al
11. What grade did Al get on the test? A plus
12. How many questions did Angela miss?
    Idea: none
13. Why didn't the old man give a test to Al and Angela?
    Idea: because (he knew) they had both (taken and) passed the test.

Review Items

Write the missing numbers in the blanks.

0 feet	surface pressure
14. 33 feet	2 times surface pressure
15. 66 feet	3 times surface pressure
16. 100 feet	4 times surface pressure

GO TO PART D IN YOUR TEXTBOOK.

TEXTBOOK

As they went into the store, the bell went ding, ding. Inside, they waited.

Suddenly the old man was standing in front of them. He said, "There will be no test for you today."

Al looked at Angela. Then he looked back at the old man. Al asked, "But we're ready for the test. Why can't we take it now?"

The old man smiled. He said, "You can't take it because you have already taken it. I happen to know that both of you correctly answered all the questions on a science test. So why should I waste time giving you another test? Simply tell me where you want to go and what you want to see and we will go on another trip together."

D Number your paper from 1 through 24.

Skill Items

A single star was near the horizon.

1. What word names the line between the earth and the sky? horizon
2. What word means **one?** single

Review Items

3. What is the hottest form of any matter? gas
4. What is the next-hottest form of any matter? liquid
5. What is the coldest form of any matter? solid
6. Do all things turn into a gas at the same temperature? no
7. What are tiny parts of matter called? molecules
8. When sand molecules are as cold as they can get, how much do they move? Idea: not at all
9. Do they move **more** or **less** at room temperature? more

TEXTBOOK

10. Which letter in the picture shows the wheel dogs? N
11. Which letter shows the lead dogs? T
12. Which letter shows the swing dogs? L
13. Which letter shows where the musher is most of the time? Q
14. Which letter shows the tug lines? A
15. Which letter shows the gang line? W

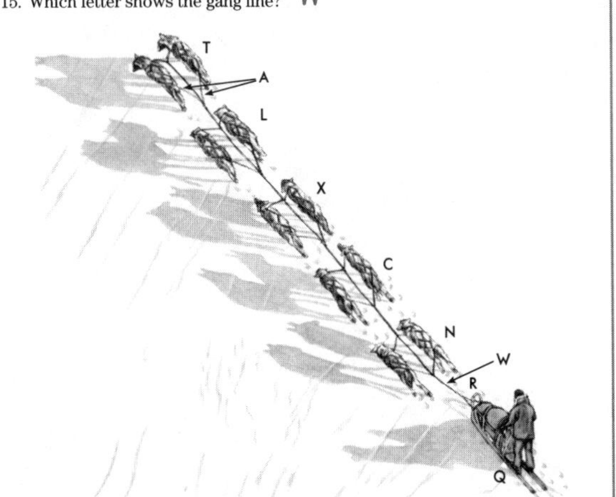

TEXTBOOK

16. In which form of matter are molecules farthest apart? gas
17. In which form of matter are molecules closest together? solid
18. What would a person see if the big nerves from the eyes to the brain were cut?
19. What is each hair inside the ear connected to? a nerve
20. What kinds of sounds are picked up in the smallest part of the ear chamber—high sounds or low sounds? high sounds
21. When you open a bottle of soda pop, what happens to the pressure inside the bottle? Idea: It goes down.
22. What forms in the soda pop? bubbles
23. Most sled-dog teams have an ▬▬ number of dogs.
    - even
    - odd
24. For the Iditarod, a sled-dog team can't have more than dogs. 16

18. Ideas: nothing; the person would be blind.

TEXTBOOK

TEST 13 | 130

2. Idea: make the body strong and protect body parts

Number your paper from 1 through 28.

1. How many bones are in the human body? 206
2. Name the **2** things that bones do.
3. Things can't burn without ▇▇. oxygen
4. In the lungs, the color of blood changes from ▇▇ to ▇▇. black, red
5. What color is blood that has fresh oxygen? red
6. What color is blood that does not have oxygen? black
7. How many chambers does the heart have? 4
8. How many chambers did Al and Angela go through **before** they went to the lungs? 2
9. How many chambers did they go through **after** they went to the lungs? 2
10. Where does black blood go after it leaves the heart? to the lungs
11. Then the blood goes back to the ▇▇. heart
12. Then the blood goes to the ▇▇. Idea: body
13. If you cut the nerve going from your brain to your hand, you could not ▇▇ your hand. move
14. If you cut the nerve going from your hand to your brain, you could not ▇▇ your hand. feel
15. Name the bundle of nerves that goes up and down through the middle of your backbone. spinal cord
16. What's strange about the bones in the backbone? They're hollow.
17. Which part of your **brain** works when you **think** about what you are seeing? cerebrum
18. What's strange about the images that are formed in your eye? They're upside down.

Write **big** or **small** to tell in which part of your ear chamber you would pick up each sound.

19. big church bell big
20. high whistle small
21. low voice big
22. very high voice small

TEXTBOOK

23. Which picture shows where the paths of light will go after they go through the lens? R

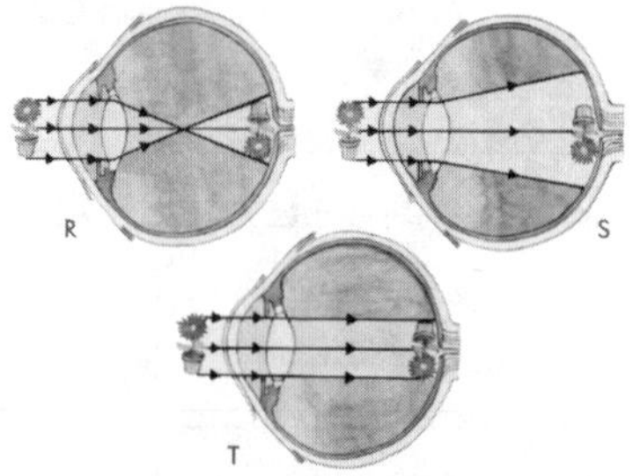

R S T

Skill Items

For each item, write the underlined word or words from the sentences in the box.

> The injury to his spinal cord paralyzed him.
> A single star was near the horizon.

24. What underlining names the bundle of nerves inside the backbone? spinal cord
25. What underlining means **one?** single
26. What underlining means **a serious hurt?** injury
27. What underlining names the line between the earth and the sky? horizon
28. What underlining means that a part of the body can't move? paralyzed

END OF TEST 13

WORKBOOK

131

Name ______________________

A Story Items

1. Who decided where to go on the next trip? the old man
2. Where did they go? North Pole
3. Why was it dark there?
   - It was winter. (underlined)
   - It was summer.
4. Why did Al's eyes start to burn? Idea: It was so cold.
5. What was the temperature at the North Pole? 60 degrees below zero
6. What would that cold air do if you breathed too hard? Idea: freeze your lungs
7. How much daylight is there during winter at the North Pole? Idea: none
8. How much nighttime is there during the summer at the North Pole? Idea: none
9. What season do we have when the North Pole tilts **toward** the sun? summer
10. What season do we have when the North Pole tilts **away from** the sun? winter

WORKBOOK

The old man made three tiny forms appear at the North Pole of the model Earth. Fill in the blanks with **dark** or **light.**

11. When it was **summer,** those forms stayed on the light half of the earth.
12. When it was **winter,** those forms stayed on the dark half of the earth.

Review Items

13. Muscles are made up of tiny (muscle) cells.
14. Blood vessels that are blue are filled with ▇▇.
    - dark blood (underlined)
    - red blood
15. Muscle cells need oxygen to work.

Use these words to answer the questions:
- blood vessels that lead from the heart
- blood vessels that lead to the heart

16. Which blood vessels are blue? blood vessels that lead to the heart
17. Which blood vessels pound every time the heart beats? blood vessels that lead from the heart
18. Which blood vessels do not pound? blood vessels that lead to the heart

GO TO PART C IN YOUR TEXTBOOK.

TEXTBOOK

Al watched the earth spin around one time, two times, three times. Then he pointed to the little people who were at the North Pole. He said, "Now the North Pole is always on the half of the earth that is lit up by the sun. The earth turns around and around but the North Pole is always in the sun."

The old man added, "That means the sun shines all the time during summer at the North Pole. There is no time when the sun sets. You can see the sun all day and all night."

The old man snapped his fingers and the models of the sun and the earth disappeared. It was now so dark that Al couldn't see anything except spots in front of his eyes. He rubbed his eyes as he listened to what Angela was saying. "So it is dark at the North Pole throughout the whole winter," she said. "The sun never shines because the North Pole tilts away from the sun and is on the half of the earth that is always dark."

"That is absolutely right," the old man responded.

Then the old man said, "I want you to feel winter at the North Pole for a few minutes. Think about what it would be like to live here."

The wind howled and Al felt it blowing snow in swirls around him. He could feel how cold it was. He wondered how anything could grow here or live here. What would they eat? How would they stay warm? How would they keep from going crazy even if they could stay alive? The strongest feeling that Al had was that he wanted to get out of this terrible place.

C Number your paper from 1 through 22.

Skill Items

Use the words in the box to write complete sentences.

paralyzed	difference	horizon	injury	blood vessel
chamber	single	lungs	spinal cord	

1. The ▇▇ to his ▇▇ ▇▇ him. injury, spinal cord, paralyzed
2. A ▇▇ star was near the ▇▇. single, horizon

TEXTBOOK

Review Items

3. The nerves that tell the brain what the hand feels go from the ▇▇ to the ▇▇. hand, brain
4. The nerves that tell the hand how to move go from the ▇▇ to the ▇▇. brain, hand

Write **big** or **small** to tell in which part of your ear chamber you would pick up each sound.

5. high whistle small
6. very high voice small
7. big church bell big
8. low voice big

9. Which letter shows the part of the earth where it is night? G
10. Which letter shows the part of the earth where it is daytime? H

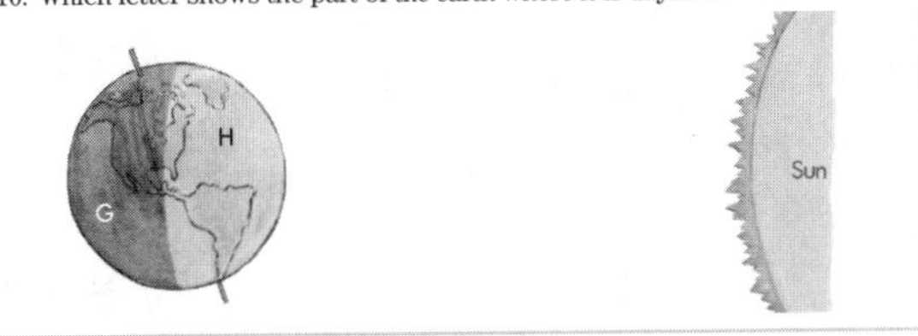

11. Which pole is at the top of the earth? North Pole
12. Which pole is at the bottom of the earth? South Pole
13. How many miles does light travel in one second? 186 thousand (miles)
14. What else travels as fast as light? Idea: nothing
15. How many suns are in the solar system? 1
16. How many planets are in the solar system? 9
17. Name the bundle of nerves that goes up and down through the middle of your backbone. spinal cord
18. What's strange about the bones in the backbone? Idea: They're hollow.

TEXTBOOK

Write which season each Earth shows.

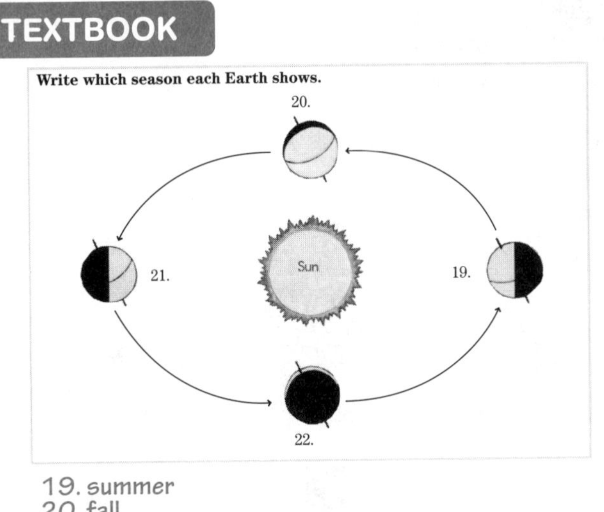

19. summer
20. fall
21. winter
22. spring

WORKBOOK

132

Name ____________________

A Story Items

1. Do any two snowflakes look **exactly** alike? no
2. How are all snowflakes the same? Idea: They have (6) spokes.
3. The old man made each snowflake as big as a basketball
4. About how deep is the snow at the North Pole? Idea: (over) 70 feet
5. What is under the snow at the North Pole? water; ocean
6. Which would be harder, snow that is **30 feet below** the top of a pile or snow that is **45 feet below** the top of the pile? 45 feet below
7. How much land is under the North Pole? Idea: none
8. How many states in the United States are as big as the North Pole? Idea: none

WORKBOOK

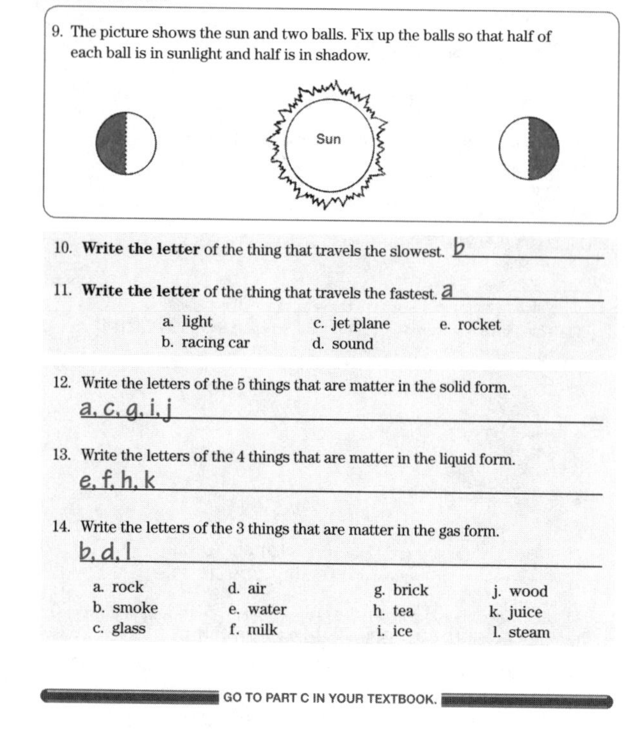

Review Items

9. The picture shows the sun and two balls. Fix up the balls so that half of each ball is in sunlight and half is in shadow.

10. **Write the letter** of the thing that travels the slowest. b
11. **Write the letter** of the thing that travels the fastest. a

a. light
b. racing car
c. jet plane
d. sound
e. rocket

12. Write the letters of the 5 things that are matter in the solid form.
a, c, g, i, j
13. Write the letters of the 4 things that are matter in the liquid form.
e, f, h, k
14. Write the letters of the 3 things that are matter in the gas form.
b, d, l

a. rock
b. smoke
c. glass
d. air
e. water
f. milk
g. brick
h. tea
i. ice
j. wood
k. juice
l. steam

GO TO PART C IN YOUR TEXTBOOK.

TEXTBOOK

pressure that it packs the snow together. That's why the snow down here is almost like ice."

"Correct," the old man said. "Let's go down to the bottom."

The hole got deeper. Angela, Al and the old man went down another 10 feet and stopped. They did the same thing again and again. Still, they had not reached the bottom of the snow.

"We are now 70 feet below the surface of the snow," the old man said. "Get ready for a surprise. We are going to see what is at the bottom of the snow."

The hole got a little deeper. Suddenly Angela, Al and the old man were no longer in the snow and ice. They were underwater.

The old man said, "There is no land at the North Pole. There is just snow and ice. The snow and ice float in water."

"No land?" Angela asked.

"That's right," the old man replied. "The North Pole is bigger than any state in the United States. But it is nothing but ice and snow floating in the ocean."

"Wow!" Angela exclaimed.

"Wow!" Al exclaimed.

C Number your paper from 1 through 26.

Review Items

1. Where does black blood go after it leaves the heart? to the lungs
2. Then the blood goes back to the ▬. heart
3. Then the blood goes to the ▬. Idea: body
4. When you think, what part of your brain are you using? cerebrum
5. The retina is covered with ▬.
   - blood
   - bones
   - nerves
6. What would a person see if the big nerves from the eyes to the brain were cut?
7. During what season is it dark at the North Pole? winter
8. How cold does it often get during that season?
   - 200 degrees below zero
   - 60 degrees below zero
   - 90 degrees below zero

6. Ideas: nothing; the person would be blind.

TEXTBOOK

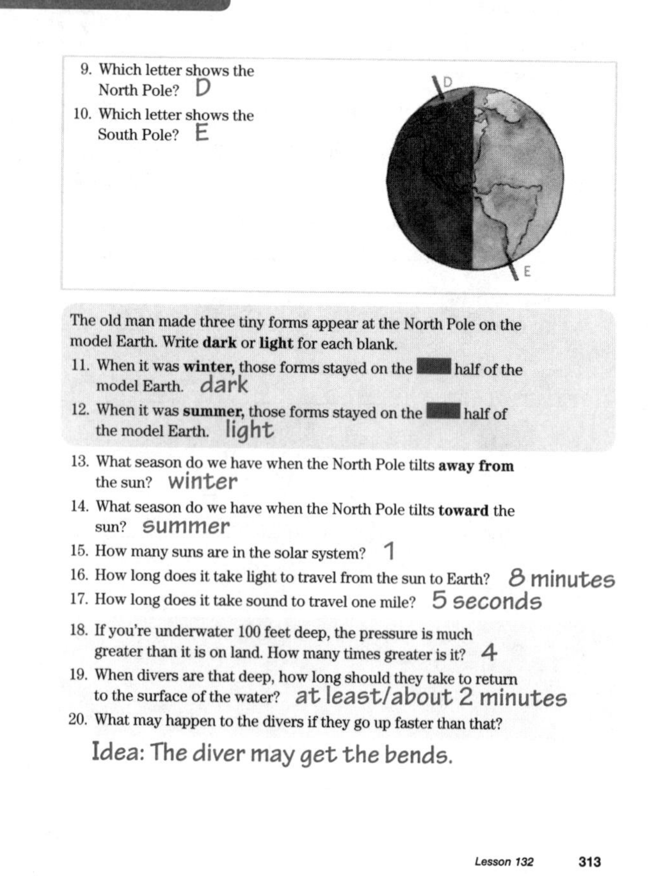

9. Which letter shows the North Pole? D
10. Which letter shows the South Pole? E

The old man made three tiny forms appear at the North Pole on the model Earth. Write **dark** or **light** for each blank.

11. When it was **winter,** those forms stayed on the ▬ half of the model Earth. dark
12. When it was **summer,** those forms stayed on the ▬ half of the model Earth. light
13. What season do we have when the North Pole tilts **away from** the sun? winter
14. What season do we have when the North Pole tilts **toward** the sun? summer
15. How many suns are in the solar system? 1
16. How long does it take light to travel from the sun to Earth? 8 minutes
17. How long does it take sound to travel one mile? 5 seconds
18. If you're underwater 100 feet deep, the pressure is much greater than it is on land. How many times greater is it? 4
19. When divers are that deep, how long should they take to return to the surface of the water? at least/about 2 minutes
20. What may happen to the divers if they go up faster than that?

Idea: The diver may get the bends.

TEXTBOOK

22. Idea: They are too small.

21. Name the two poles. North Pole, South Pole
22. Why can't you see molecules when you look at an object?

Write which season each Earth shows.

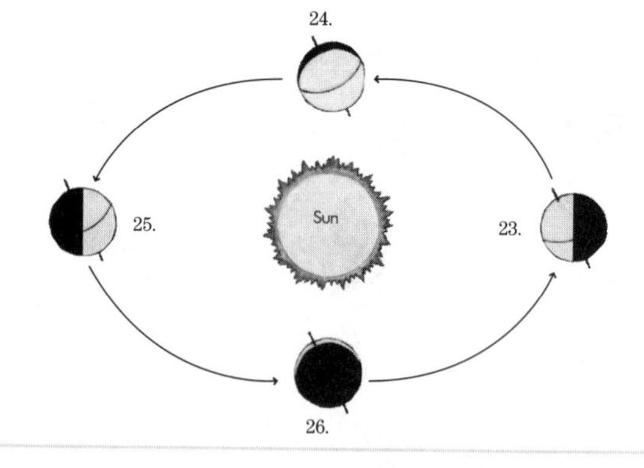

23. summer
24. fall
25. winter
26. spring

WORKBOOK

133

Name ____________________

A

1. Draw lines to show where the paths of light will go after they go through the lens.
2. Make an **F** in the box that shows where the film is.
3. Make an **L** in the box that shows where the lens is.
4. Make an **I** in the box that shows where the iris is.

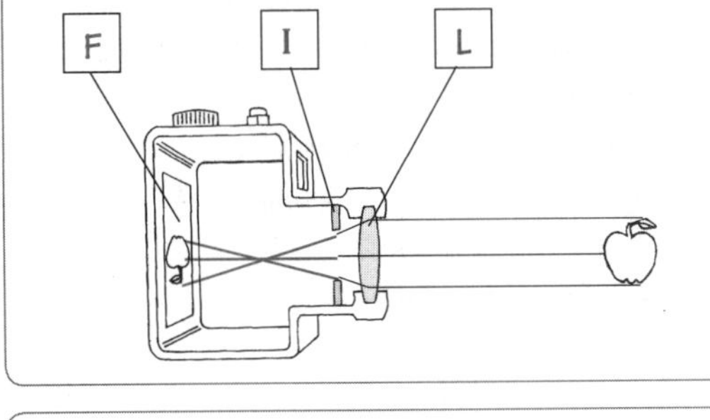

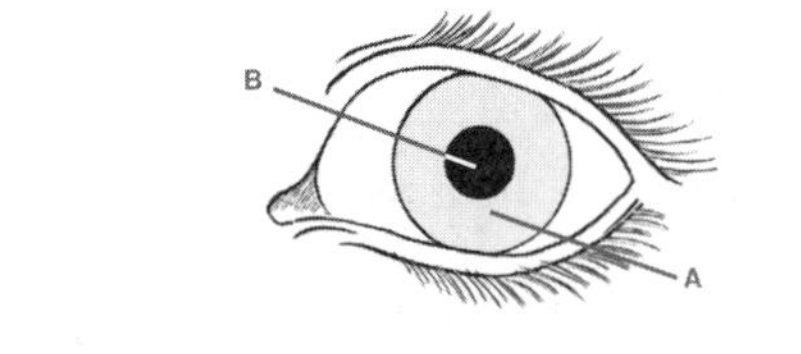

5. What is part A? iris
6. What is part B? pupil (Do not accept lens.)

WORKBOOK

B Story Items

7. Fill in the blanks with **toward** or **away from.**

   During our winter, the North Pole tilts away from the sun, and the South Pole tilts toward the sun.

8. Fill in the blanks with **dark** or **light.**

   During our winter, the North Pole is always dark and the South Pole is always light.

9. How many hours does it take the sun to make a full circle at the poles?

   24

10. What's under all the snow at the North Pole?

    water; ocean

11. What's under the snow at the South Pole?

    land; rock

12. How many square miles is the land under the South Pole?
    - 1 million
    - 5 hundred
    - <u>5 million</u>

13. About how deep is the snow at the South Pole?

    Idea: (over) a mile

14. Where is the snow deeper, at the North Pole or at the South Pole?

    South Pole

GO TO PART D IN YOUR TEXTBOOK.

TEXTBOOK

D Number your paper from 1 through 24.

1. Name the part of the eye where pictures are formed. retina
2. Name what's inside the camera where pictures are formed. film
3. What part of a camera bends the light that goes through it? lens
4. What part of an eye is like the lens of a camera? lens
5. What part of a camera lets just enough light into the camera? iris
6. What part of an eye is like the iris of a camera? iris
7. A camera lens bends light that goes through it because the lens is ▬.
   - straight
   - big
   - <u>curved</u>
8. If you're taking a picture where it's very bright, you would set the iris of a camera so the hole is ▬.
   - large
   - <u>small</u>
9. If you're taking a picture where there is very little light, you would set the iris so the hole is ▬. <u>large</u>
10. Which iris is right for taking a picture in a bright place? B
11. Which iris sees well in a bright place? A

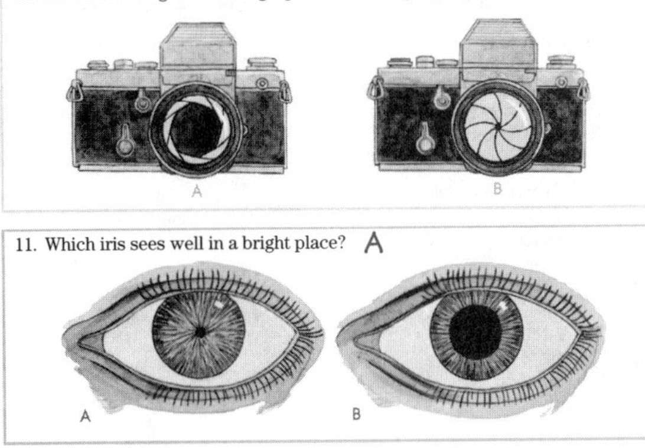

TEXTBOOK

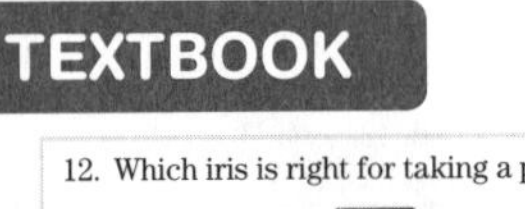

12. Which iris is right for taking a picture in a dark place? A

13. Which iris sees well in a dark place? B

A B

Skill Items

Write the word from the box that means the same thing as the underlined part of each sentence.

decorated	noon	permitted	chamber
protected	midnight	relaxed	window

14. The bell rang at <u>12 o'clock at night.</u> midnight
15. They <u>took it easy</u> at the beach. relaxed
16. The TV was in a <u>special room.</u> chamber

TEXTBOOK

Review Items

17. What is the chamber inside the ear shaped like? spiral
18. What is the inside of the ear's chamber lined with? hairs
19. Do any two snowflakes look **exactly** alike? no
20. All snowflakes are the same because they all have ▬ spokes. 6

21. About how deep is the snow at the North Pole? 70 feet
22. What is under the snow at the North Pole? water; ocean
23. How much land is under the snow at the North Pole? Idea: none

24. Which would be harder, snow that is **40 feet below** the top of a pile or snow that is **20 feet below** the top of the pile? 40 feet below

WORKBOOK

Name ______________________

A Story Items

1. A man gave Al and Angela each 5 dollars. Tell why.
   Idea: They had pushed his car out of the snow.
2. Why was the man in a hurry to get home? Idea: It was his wife's birthday.
3. Why did Al want to get some more money? Idea: so he could buy presents
4. About how deep was the snow in front of Al and Angela's house?
   2 feet
5. Why were the schools going to be closed the next day?
   Idea: because of the deep snow
6. How had Al felt about school before the old man's trips?
   Idea: He didn't like it.
7. How does Al feel about school now?
   Idea: He likes it.
8. Why does he feel that way about school now?
   - He's a poor student.
   - He's a good student.
   - He doesn't like school.
9. What is Angela and Al's last name? Johnson

WORKBOOK

10. What was the title of the book Al and Angela got in this story?
    The Poles
11. Who sent the book to them? the old man
12. The ship named *Endurance* was stuck in ice at the
    South Pole.
13. How many men on that ship died? Idea: none
14. What happened to Scott and the men with him?
    Idea: They all died.
15. What was strange about the food in Scott's camp when people found it fifty years later?
    Idea: It was still good.

Review Items

16. What is each hair inside the ear connected to? a nerve
17. What kinds of sounds are picked up in the biggest part of the ear chamber—high sounds or low sounds?
    low sounds
18. What part of a camera bends the light that goes through it?
    lens
19. What part of a camera lets just enough light into the camera?
    iris

GO TO PART C IN YOUR TEXTBOOK.

TEXTBOOK

C Number your paper from 1 through 18.

Skill Items

Here are 3 events that happened in the story. Write **beginning, middle** or **end** for each event.

1. The adventure of Robert Scott and four other men did not have a happy ending. end
2. Now the car started moving faster and faster as it got into the tracks that other cars had made. middle
3. Suddenly, everything started to grow dark, and Al realized that he was back in the store on Anywhere Street. beginning

Troops of baboons moved across the veld.

4. What word refers to **groups** of baboons? troops
5. What word names a large member of the monkey family? baboons
6. What word refers to a large field in Africa? veld

Review Items

Write **toward** or **away from** for each blank.
During our winter, the North Pole tilts **7.** the sun and the South Pole tilts **8.** the sun.

Write **dark** or **light** for each blank.
During our winter, the North Pole is always **9.** and the South Pole is always **10.** .

7. away from
8. toward
9. dark
10. light

TEXTBOOK

11. Which picture shows where the paths of light will go after they go through the lens? C
12. Which letter shows the film? J
13. Which letter shows the lens? L
14. Which letter shows the iris? K

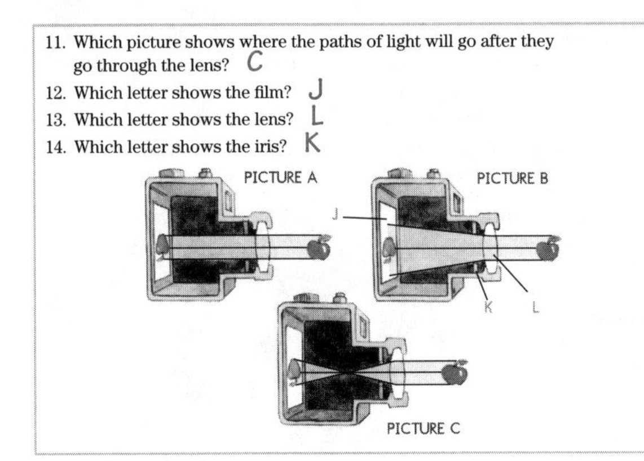

15. How many hours does it take the sun to make a full circle around a person at the North Pole? 24
16. What's under the snow at the North Pole? water; ocean
17. How deep is the snow at the South Pole? (over) a mile
18. Where is the snow deeper, at the North Pole or at the South Pole? at the South Pole

WORKBOOK

135

Name

A

1. What are groups of baboons called? troops
2. Name an animal that looks something like a baboon but is much bigger. gorilla
3. Name an animal in the cat family that is the size of a big dog. leopard
4. Name an animal in the whale family that some people think is the smartest. porpoise
5. Is that animal **warm-blooded** or **cold-blooded?** warm-blooded
6. How long ago did saber-toothed tigers disappear from the earth? 25 thousand years ago
7. It is called a **saber-toothed tiger** because it had teeth like sabers.

B Story Items

8. What did Al want to read about at the library? Idea: the poles
9. Was the library open? no

WORKBOOK

10. Why were most of the stores closed? Ideas: because there was so much snow; because of the snowstorm
11. Where did Al and Angela go after breakfast? Idea: to the old man's store
12. What did the old man want Al and Angela to do when they first got to his store? Idea: shovel his walk
13. What did the old man give each of them for doing that? 2 dollars
14. Did Al and Angela go to the store next door at the same time? no
15. What was the store next door filled with when Al went there? Idea: wallets and toasters
16. What was the store filled with when Angela went there? Idea: books and (women's) sweaters
17. What did Al buy for his mother? a toaster
18. What did Al buy for Angela? a wallet
19. How much did **each present** cost? 1 dollar
20. What did Angela buy for Al? a book
21. What did Angela buy for her mother? a sweater

GO TO PART D IN YOUR TEXTBOOK.

TEXTBOOK

After Al came back to the old man's store, Angela went to the store next door. While she was gone, Al talked to the old man. When she came back, she said, "That's the strangest store I have ever seen. It had nothing but books and women's sweaters." Al had a pretty good idea of what he was going to get from Angela for Christmas.

D Number your paper from 1 through 20.

Skill Items

Use the words in the box to write complete sentences.

message	veld	baboons	control	troops
horizon	pulse	hollow	bedroom	single

1. A ▬ star was near the ▬. single, horizon
2. ▬ of ▬ moved across the ▬. troops, baboons, veld

TEXTBOOK

3. What is animal A?
4. What is animal B?
5. What is animal C?
6. What is animal D?
7. What is animal E?

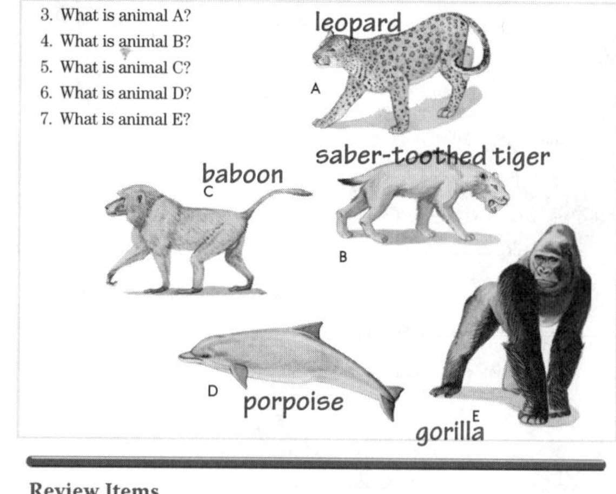

Review Items

8. How many hours does it take the sun to make a full circle around a person at the North Pole? 24
9. The ship named *Endurance* was stuck in ice at the ▬. South Pole
10. What happened to Scott and the men with him? Idea: They all died.
11. What season do we have when the North Pole tilts **toward** the sun? summer
12. What season do we have when the North Pole tilts **away from** the sun? winter
13. During what season is it dark at the North Pole? winter
14. How cold does it often get during that season?
    - 200 degrees below zero
    - 100 degrees below zero
    - 60 degrees below zero

TEXTBOOK

15. If you're taking a picture where it's very bright, you would set the iris of the camera so the hole is ▬.
    - big
    - small
16. If you're taking a picture where there is very little light, you would set the iris of the camera so the hole is ▬. big
17. What's part A? retina
18. What's part B? lens
19. Write the letter of the part that shows a picture of what the eye sees. A
20. Write the letter of the part that bends the light. B

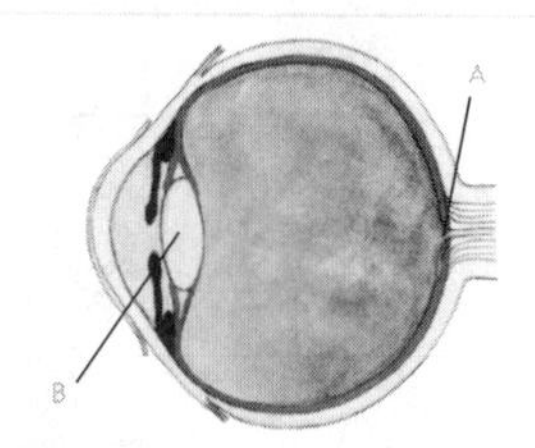

WORKBOOK

136

Name ____________

A Story Items Ideas: He needed to learn about the

1. Why did Al need the old man's trips when he first went to the store?
   world; he needed to learn that learning is fun; he needed to see things.
2. Why doesn't Al need the trips anymore? Idea: He has learned how to take a trip by reading a book.
3. Who decided where to go on this trip?
   the old man
4. Where did they go? to a library
5. About how many books were in the library?
   - 30 million
   - 2 million
   - 3 million
6. About how many of those books were about animals?
   - 3 thousand
   - 3 hundred
   - 3 million
7. What did Angela want to read about? animals
8. What was the brain of the library? computers
9. Did the old man order **one book** or **more than one?**
   more than one
10. What was the title of the first book the old man picked up from the table?
    Animals in Africa
11. Who will start reading from that book? Al

WORKBOOK

Review Items

12. What is animal A? porpoise
13. What is animal B? saber-toothed tiger
14. What is animal C? baboon
15. What is animal D? gorilla
16. What is animal E? leopard

A C B D E

GO TO PART C IN YOUR TEXTBOOK.

TEXTBOOK

Some facts appeared on the computer screen. The old man said, "The computer tells us that there are over three thousand books on animals. If you wish, the computer will list all the titles. Or you can give the computer more information about the kinds of animals you are interested in."

Angela said, "Well, I don't really care that much. I like all . . ."

Before she could finish her sentence, the old man said, "I will select some titles for you."

The old man quickly pressed some keys on the computer keyboard. Then he said, "Our books will be here in a moment."

The old man stood up and walked over to a small door in the wall. Suddenly a light over the door went on. The old man opened the door and there was a pile of books inside.

The old man picked them up and carried them over to a table. He picked up a book titled *Animals in Africa* and handed it to Al. The old man said, "Start reading for us and we'll go on a new kind of trip."

Al picked up the book and started to read.

C Number your paper from 1 through 23.

Review Items

1. Which iris is right for taking a picture in a dark place? D

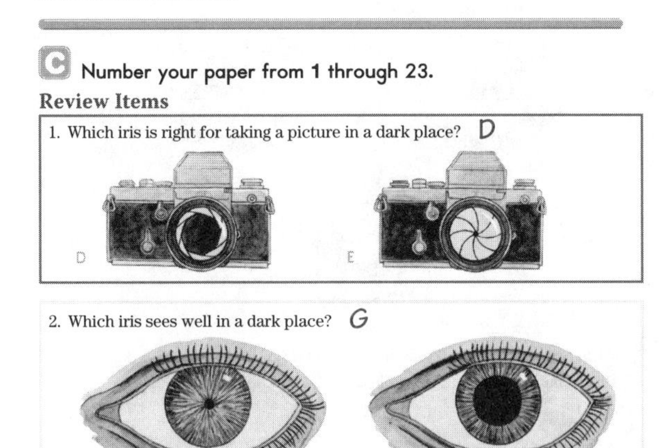

2. Which iris sees well in a dark place? G

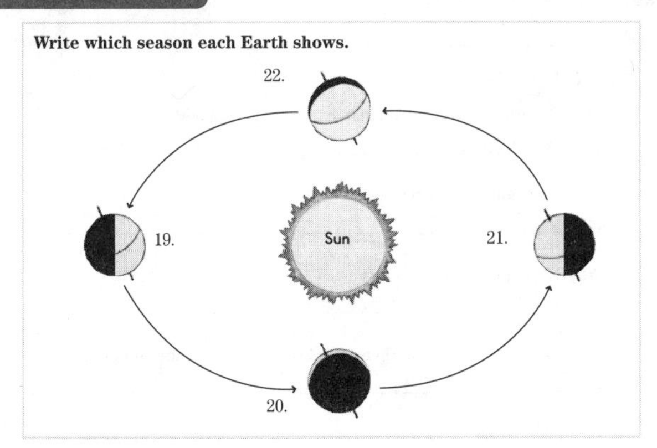

TEXTBOOK

3. What is part A? pupil
4. What is part B? iris

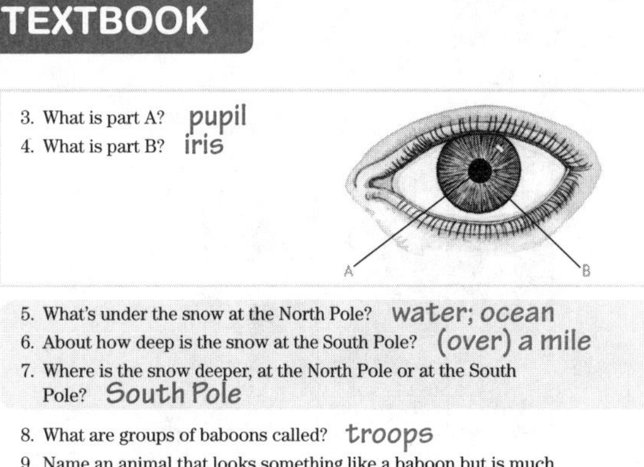

5. What's under the snow at the North Pole? water; ocean
6. About how deep is the snow at the South Pole? (over) a mile
7. Where is the snow deeper, at the North Pole or at the South Pole? South Pole
8. What are groups of baboons called? troops
9. Name an animal that looks something like a baboon but is much bigger. gorilla
10. Name an animal in the cat family that is the size of a big dog. leopard
11. Name an animal in the whale family that many people think is the smartest. porpoise (Accept dolphin)
12. About how long ago did saber-toothed tigers disappear from the earth? 25 thousand years (ago)
13. Which pole is at the top of the earth? North Pole
14. Which pole is at the bottom of the earth? South Pole
15. How many miles does light travel in one second? 186 thousand(miles)
16. What else travels as fast as light? Idea: nothing
17. Which letter shows the part of the earth where it is night? X
18. Which letter shows the part of the earth where it is daytime? Y

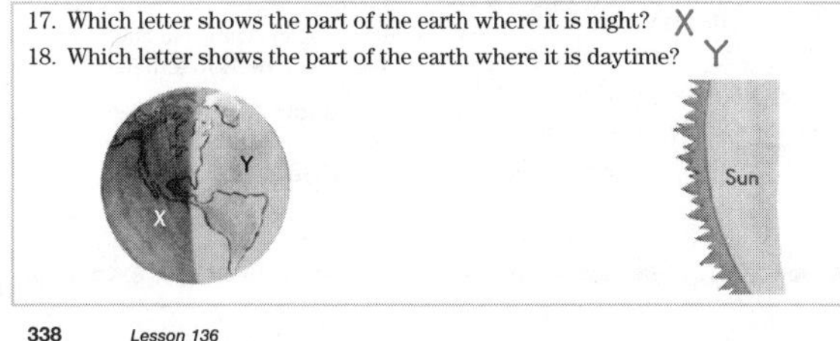

TEXTBOOK

Write which season each Earth shows.

22.

19. Sun 21.

20.

23. How much daylight is there during winter at the North Pole?
Idea: none

19. winter
20. spring
21. summer
22. fall

WORKBOOK

137

Name ____________

A Story Items

1. What are the 2 kinds of seasons that Africa has?
(2 ideas:) wet (season) and dry (season)
2. What is the veld of Africa?
Idea: a great field of grass
3. Name 3 kinds of animals that live on the veld in Africa.
(Any 3:) baboons; giraffes; lions; leopards; monkeys
4. Every day during the dry season, African animals go to a place where they don't usually fight. Name that place.
water hole
5. Did Al and Angela get to read the whole book about *Animals in Africa*?
no
6. What did the old man say they should do if they wanted to read more of the book? Idea: come back to the library (sometime and read it)
7. Al and Angela read part of a book titled *How Animals Learn.* Which animal did that book say is next-smartest after humans?
baboons
8. Why do troops of baboons need lookouts? Ideas: to look out for enemies/danger; to warn troop of danger

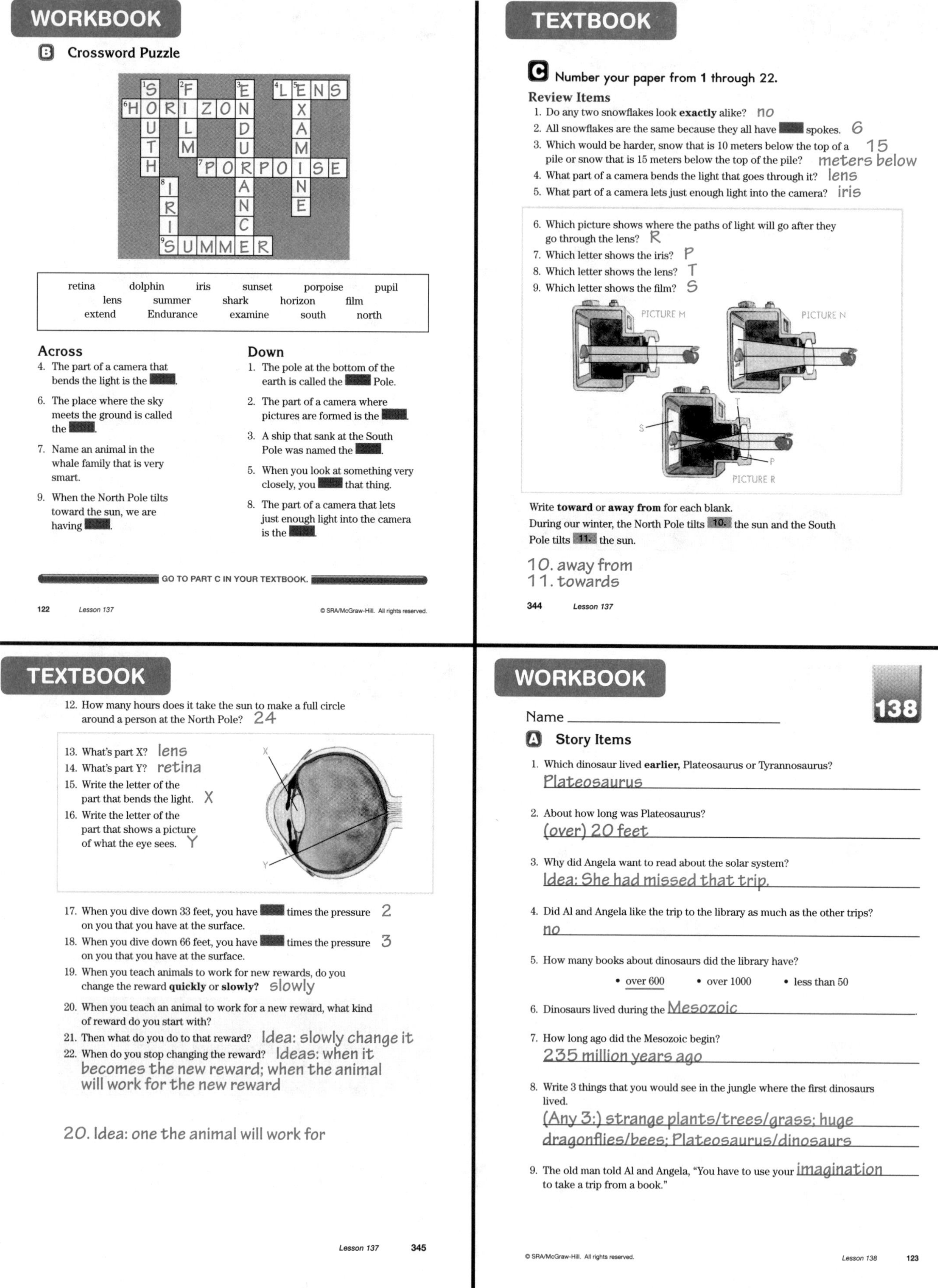

WORKBOOK

B Crossword Puzzle

Across: 4. LENS 6. HORIZON 7. PORPOISE 9. SUMMER
Down: 1. SOUTH 2. FILM 3. ENDURANCE 5. EXAMINE 8. IRIS

retina	dolphin	iris	sunset
porpoise	pupil	lens	summer
shark	horizon	film	extend
Endurance	examine	south	north

Across

4. The part of a camera that bends the light is the ▬.
6. The place where the sky meets the ground is called the ▬.
7. Name an animal in the whale family that is very smart.
9. When the North Pole tilts toward the sun, we are having ▬.

Down

1. The pole at the bottom of the earth is called the ▬ Pole.
2. The part of a camera where pictures are formed is the ▬.
3. A ship that sank at the South Pole was named the ▬.
5. When you look at something very closely, you ▬ that thing.
8. The part of a camera that lets just enough light into the camera is the ▬.

GO TO PART C IN YOUR TEXTBOOK.

TEXTBOOK

C Number your paper from 1 through 22.

Review Items

1. Do any two snowflakes look **exactly** alike? no
2. All snowflakes are the same because they all have ▬ spokes. 6
3. Which would be harder, snow that is 10 meters below the top of a pile or snow that is 15 meters below the top of the pile? 15 meters below
4. What part of a camera bends the light that goes through it? lens
5. What part of a camera lets just enough light into the camera? iris
6. Which picture shows where the paths of light will go after they go through the lens? R
7. Which letter shows the iris? P
8. Which letter shows the lens? T
9. Which letter shows the film? S

PICTURE M
PICTURE N
PICTURE R
S T P

Write **toward** or **away from** for each blank.

During our winter, the North Pole tilts **10.** the sun and the South Pole tilts **11.** the sun.

10. away from
11. towards

TEXTBOOK

12. How many hours does it take the sun to make a full circle around a person at the North Pole? 24
13. What's part X? lens
14. What's part Y? retina
15. Write the letter of the part that bends the light. X
16. Write the letter of the part that shows a picture of what the eye sees. Y

X
Y

17. When you dive down 33 feet, you have ▬ times the pressure on you that you have at the surface. 2
18. When you dive down 66 feet, you have ▬ times the pressure on you that you have at the surface. 3
19. When you teach animals to work for new rewards, do you change the reward **quickly** or **slowly?** slowly
20. When you teach an animal to work for a new reward, what kind of reward do you start with?
21. Then what do you do to that reward? Idea: slowly change it
22. When do you stop changing the reward? Ideas: when it becomes the new reward; when the animal will work for the new reward

20. Idea: one the animal will work for

WORKBOOK

138

Name ____________

A Story Items

1. Which dinosaur lived **earlier,** Plateosaurus or Tyrannosaurus? Plateosaurus
2. About how long was Plateosaurus? (over) 20 feet
3. Why did Angela want to read about the solar system? Idea: She had missed that trip.
4. Did Al and Angela like the trip to the library as much as the other trips? no
5. How many books about dinosaurs did the library have?
   - over 600
   - over 1000
   - less than 50
6. Dinosaurs lived during the Mesozoic.
7. How long ago did the Mesozoic begin? 235 million years ago
8. Write 3 things that you would see in the jungle where the first dinosaurs lived. (Any 3:) strange plants/trees/grass; huge dragonflies/bees; Plateosaurus/dinosaurs
9. The old man told Al and Angela, "You have to use your imagination to take a trip from a book."

WORKBOOK

10. Name 2 things that were different when Al and Angela left the old man's store.
    Ideas: The bell did not ding; the sign was gone.

11. What did Al do after dinner?
    Idea: wrapped presents

12. What was special about the next day?
    Idea: It was Christmas.

Review Items

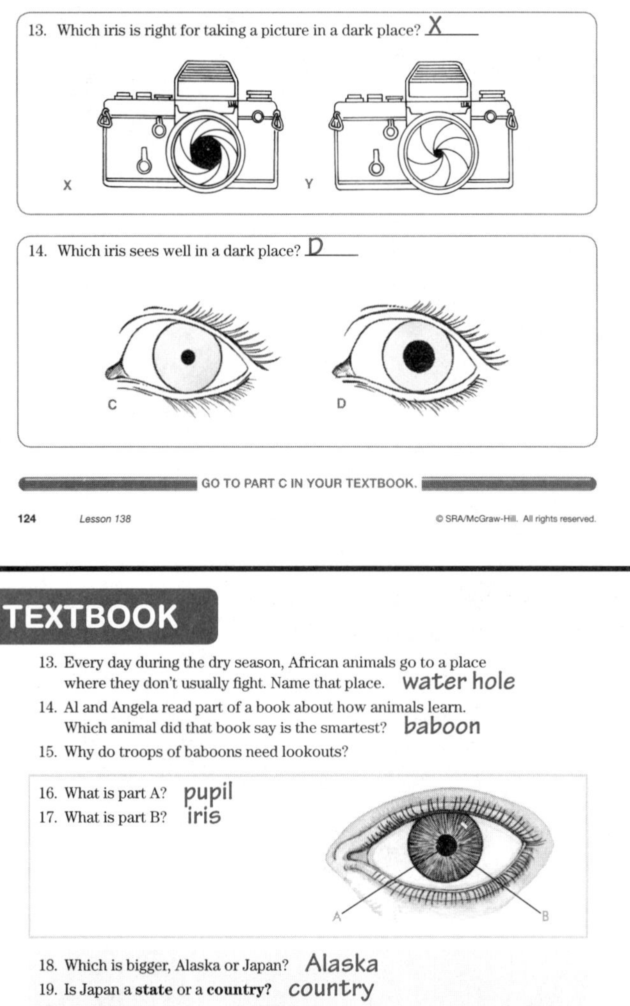

13. Which iris is right for taking a picture in a dark place? X

X Y

14. Which iris sees well in a dark place? D

C D

GO TO PART C IN YOUR TEXTBOOK.

TEXTBOOK

Al didn't say anything at dinner. After dinner he wrapped the presents that he had bought at the strange store. Imagine buying a beautiful toaster for only a dollar. It didn't make sense. Nothing made sense to Al on the night before Christmas.

C Number your paper from 1 through 26.

Skill Items

Write the word from the box that means the same thing as the underlined part of each sentence.

leopard	porpoise	bought	dinosaurs
history	sabers	transparent	created

1. The museum had a display of swords. sabers
2. She made a beautiful painting. created
3. We watched the dolphin do tricks. porpoise

Review Items 4. dark; 5. light

Write **dark** or **light** for each blank.
During our winter, the North Pole is 4. all the time and the South Pole is 5. all the time.

6. What's under the snow at the North Pole? water; ocean
7. About how deep is the snow at the South Pole? (over) a mile
8. Where is the snow deeper, at the North Pole or at the South Pole? South Pole
9. The ship named *Endurance* was stuck in the ice at the ___. South Pole
10. What happened to Scott and the men with him?
11. What are the two kinds of seasons that Africa has?
12. What is the veld of Africa? Idea: a huge field (of grass)

10. Idea: They all died.
11. wet (season) and dry (season)

TEXTBOOK

13. Every day during the dry season, African animals go to a place where they don't usually fight. Name that place. water hole
14. Al and Angela read part of a book about how animals learn. Which animal did that book say is the smartest? baboon
15. Why do troops of baboons need lookouts?

16. What is part A? pupil
17. What is part B? iris

A B

18. Which is bigger, Alaska or Japan? Alaska
19. Is Japan a **state** or a **country?** country
20. How many people live in Japan?
    • 127 • 127 million • 127 thousand

21. About how deep is the snow at the North Pole? 70 feet
22. How much land is under the snow at the North Pole? Idea: none

23. Which letter shows the South Pole? K
24. Which letter shows the North Pole? L

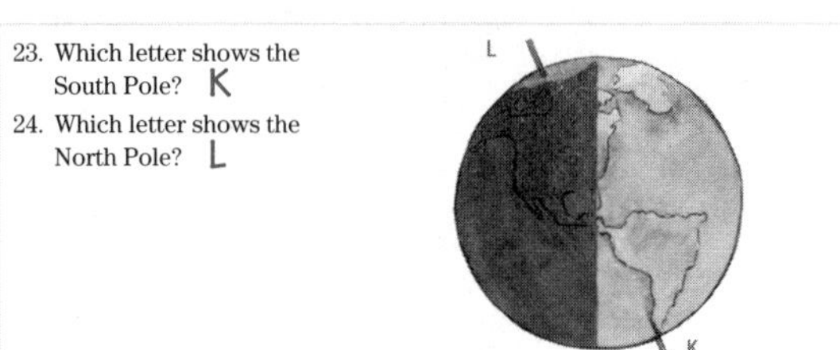

15. Idea: to watch for (and warn the troop of) danger/enemies

TEXTBOOK

25. The arrow on the map goes from San Francisco to ___. Japan
26. Which ocean does the arrow cross? Pacific (Ocean)

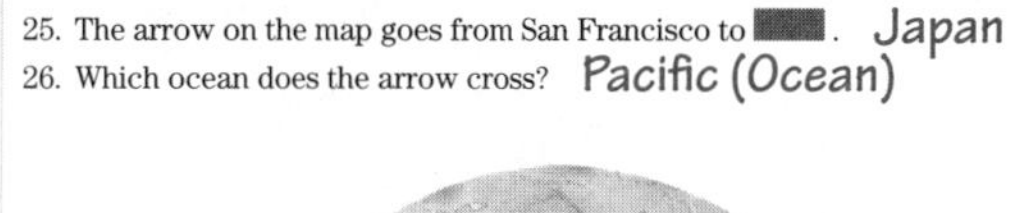

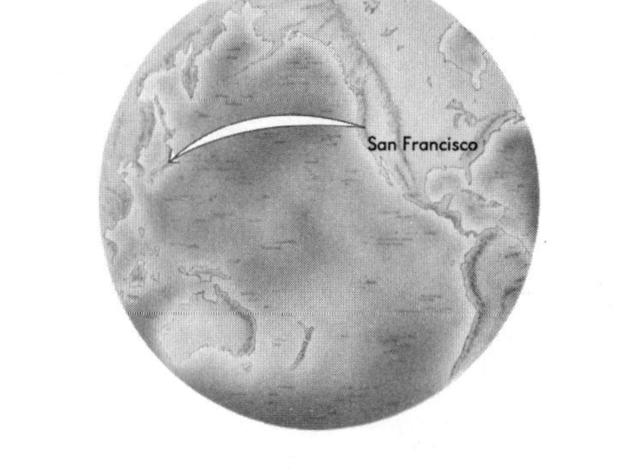

WORKBOOK

139

Name ______________________

A **Story Items**

1. What did Al's mother give Al for Christmas?
   Idea: a book (on animals in Africa)
2. What did Al's family do after breakfast?
   Idea: went for a walk
3. Did Al's mother think there was an Anywhere Street? no
4. Was Al's mother right? yes
5. What was the **real** name of the street?
   Anderson Street
6. What kind of store did the old man have?
   bookstore
7. What kind of book did the old man give Al's mother?
   cookbook
8. What was the title of the book the old man gave Al and Angela?
   Go Anywhere. See Anything.

Review Items

9. The dinosaurs lived in the Mesozoic.
10. Which dinosaur lived earlier, Plateosaurus or Tyrannosaurus?
    Plateosaurus

WORKBOOK

11. About how long was Plateosaurus?
    (over) 20 feet
12. Write 3 things that you would see in the jungle where the first dinosaurs lived.
    (Any 3:) strange plants; huge dragonflies/bees; Plateosaurus/dinosaurs
13. What is animal A? porpoise (Accept dolphin.)
14. What is animal B? gorilla
15. What is animal C? saber-toothed tiger
16. What is animal D? baboon
17. What is animal E? leopard

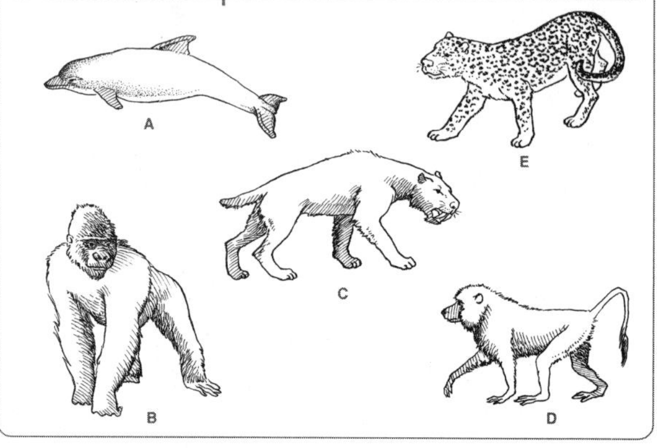

GO TO PART C IN YOUR TEXTBOOK.

TEXTBOOK

the human brain. It will take you anywhere."

"Wow!" Al said.

"Thanks a lot," Angela said.

The old man talked to Al and the others for a while. Then Al's mother said, "We'd better get going. I have to cook a big Christmas dinner."

When Angela opened the door, the bell went ding, ding. The old man followed them outside. "Have a merry Christmas," he said.

Al said, "This is the best Christmas I ever had." Al felt very happy and very sad at the same time.

The old man said, "And come back and see me sometime. I have a lot of good books. Come in and read them. You don't have to buy them. Come in anytime."

"We will," Angela said.

Then they all started walking back down Anderson Street. They walked past the gift shop to the corner.

When they reached the corner, Angela turned to Al. "Did this really happen? Did we really go on all those trips? Or was it just some kind of dream?"

"I don't know," Al said. "But it sure was great. It was really great."

Later that day Al's mother fixed the best Christmas dinner Al ever had. And after dinner Angela and Al read from the book *Go Anywhere. See Anything.* It was the best book that Al had ever read. And Al had the best Christmas ever.

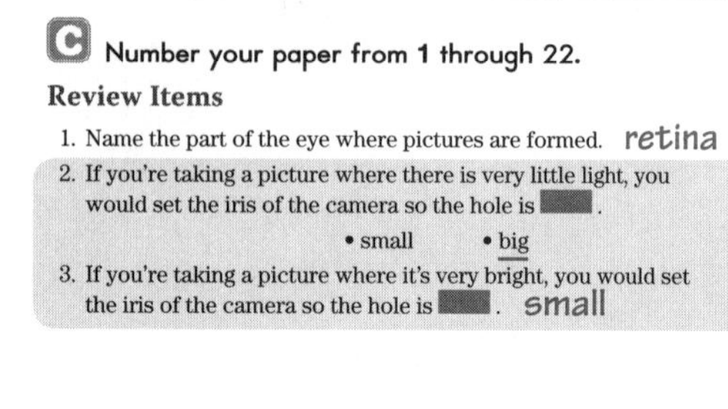

C **Number your paper from 1 through 22.**

Review Items

1. Name the part of the eye where pictures are formed. retina
2. If you're taking a picture where there is very little light, you would set the iris of the camera so the hole is ▬.
   - small
   - big
3. If you're taking a picture where it's very bright, you would set the iris of the camera so the hole is ▬. small

TEXTBOOK

4. Which iris sees well in a bright place? S

Write which season each Earth shows.

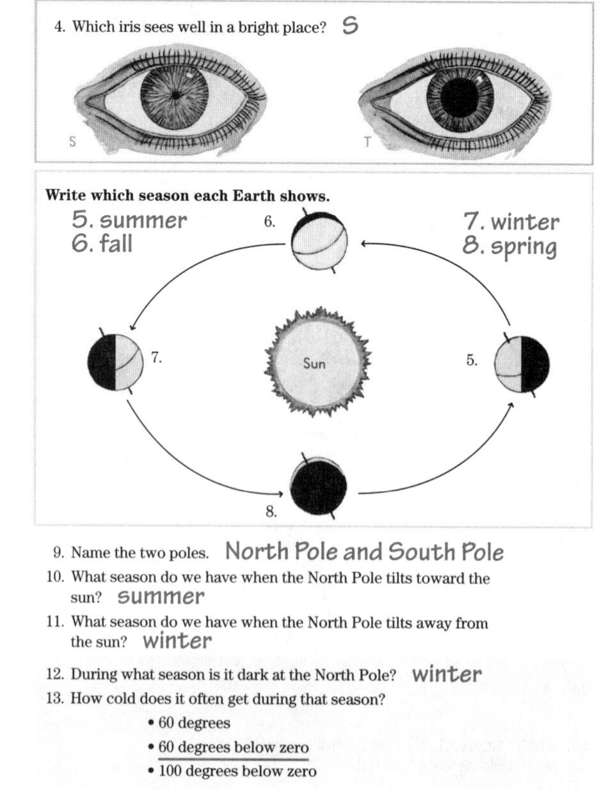

9. Name the two poles. North Pole and South Pole
10. What season do we have when the North Pole tilts toward the sun? summer
11. What season do we have when the North Pole tilts away from the sun? winter
12. During what season is it dark at the North Pole? winter
13. How cold does it often get during that season?
    - 60 degrees
    - 60 degrees below zero
    - 100 degrees below zero

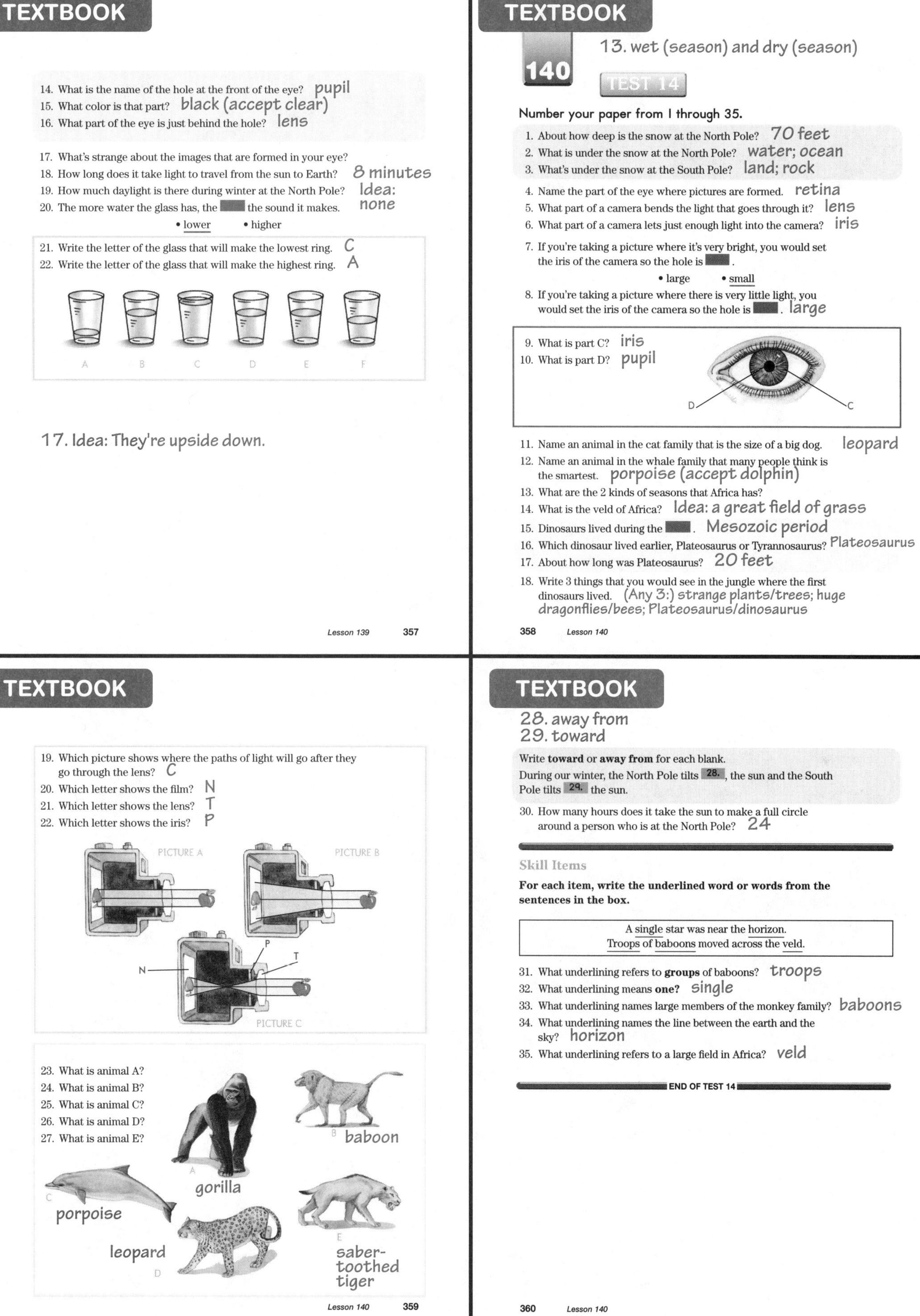

TEXTBOOK

14. What is the name of the hole at the front of the eye? pupil
15. What color is that part? black (accept clear)
16. What part of the eye is just behind the hole? lens

17. What's strange about the images that are formed in your eye?
18. How long does it take light to travel from the sun to Earth? 8 minutes
19. How much daylight is there during winter at the North Pole? Idea: none
20. The more water the glass has, the ▬ the sound it makes.
 • lower • higher

21. Write the letter of the glass that will make the lowest ring. C
22. Write the letter of the glass that will make the highest ring. A

17. Idea: They're upside down.

TEXTBOOK

140

13. wet (season) and dry (season)

TEST 14

Number your paper from 1 through 35.

1. About how deep is the snow at the North Pole? 70 feet
2. What is under the snow at the North Pole? water; ocean
3. What's under the snow at the South Pole? land; rock

4. Name the part of the eye where pictures are formed. retina
5. What part of a camera bends the light that goes through it? lens
6. What part of a camera lets just enough light into the camera? iris
7. If you're taking a picture where it's very bright, you would set the iris of the camera so the hole is ▬.
 • large • small
8. If you're taking a picture where there is very little light, you would set the iris of the camera so the hole is ▬. large

9. What is part C? iris
10. What is part D? pupil

11. Name an animal in the cat family that is the size of a big dog. leopard
12. Name an animal in the whale family that many people think is the smartest. porpoise (accept dolphin)
13. What are the 2 kinds of seasons that Africa has?
14. What is the veld of Africa? Idea: a great field of grass
15. Dinosaurs lived during the ▬. Mesozoic period
16. Which dinosaur lived earlier, Plateosaurus or Tyrannosaurus? Plateosaurus
17. About how long was Plateosaurus? 20 feet
18. Write 3 things that you would see in the jungle where the first dinosaurs lived. (Any 3:) strange plants/trees; huge dragonflies/bees; Plateosaurus/dinosaurus

TEXTBOOK

19. Which picture shows where the paths of light will go after they go through the lens? C
20. Which letter shows the film? N
21. Which letter shows the lens? T
22. Which letter shows the iris? P

23. What is animal A?
24. What is animal B?
25. What is animal C?
26. What is animal D?
27. What is animal E?

TEXTBOOK

28. away from
29. toward

Write **toward** or **away from** for each blank.

During our winter, the North Pole tilts 28., the sun and the South Pole tilts 29. the sun.

30. How many hours does it take the sun to make a full circle around a person who is at the North Pole? 24

Skill Items

For each item, write the underlined word or words from the sentences in the box.

A single star was near the horizon.
Troops of baboons moved across the veld.

31. What underlining refers to **groups** of baboons? troops
32. What underlining means **one?** single
33. What underlining names large members of the monkey family? baboons
34. What underlining names the line between the earth and the sky? horizon
35. What underlining refers to a large field in Africa? veld

END OF TEST 14